pauline

SAN FRANCISCO

spend less see more

1st Edition

by Jason Cochran

Series Editor: Pauline Frommer

WILEY

Wiley Publishing, Inc.

Published by:

Wiley Publishing, Inc.

111 River St.
Hoboken, NJ 07030-5774

ISBN 978-0-470-30873-8

Editor: William Travis
Production Editor: M. Faunette Johnston
Cartographer: Elizabeth Puhl
Photo Editor: Richard Fox
Interior Design: Lissa Auciello-Brogan
Production by Wiley Indianapolis Composition Services

For information on our other products and services or to obtain technical support,
please contact our Customer Care Department within the U.S. at 800/762-2974,
outside the U.S. at 317/572-3993 or fax 317/572-4002.

Wiley also publishes its books in a variety of electronic formats. Some content that
appears in print may not be available in electronic formats.

Manufactured in the United States of America

5   4   3   2   1

Contents

List of Maps

About the Author

Jason Cochran also wrote *Pauline Frommer's London* (awarded Guide Book of the Year by the North American Travel Journalists Association) and *Pauline Frommer's Walt Disney World & Orlando.* He has written for publications including *Budget Travel* (as senior editor); *Entertainment Weekly;* the *New York Post, Daily News,* and *Times; Travel + Leisure* and *T+L Family; Newsweek; City;* AOL's travel blog; Frommers.com; the South Florida *Sun-Sentinel; Arena* (U.K.); *Who* (Australia); *Scanorama* and *Seasons* (Sweden). He has been an arts columnist for

Photo: Maia Rosenfeld

both Inside.com (late night TV) and Sidewalk.com (theater). His writing has also been awarded the Golden Pen by the Croatian government and was selected to appear in a permanent exhibit in the National Museum of Australia. He also devised questions for the first American season of *Who Wants to Be a Millionaire* (ABC) and before that, spent nearly two years backpacking solo around the world. As a commentator, he has appeared on CNN, CNN Headline News, CNNfn, Australia.com, WOR, Outdoor Life Network, and MSNBC.com. He is an alumnus of Northwestern University's Medill School of Journalism and New York University's Graduate Music Theatre Writing Program.

Acknowledgments

Many thanks to all the people who have helped make this guide book different from all the others, including Tim Zahner at the Sonoma County Tourism Bureau, Mark Ellwood, David Lytle, Susan Wilson, Tanya Houseman at the San Francisco CVB, Tyffani Peters of the Culinary Institute of America, Judy Cronkhite, Molly Blaisdell, and all the people in the Bay Area who helped me toward my goal. A deep bow of gratitude also goes, of course, to those travel mavericks Arthur Frommer and Pauline Frommer, whose guidance was always backed up with true support. A special thanks goes to my family for pulling me through the tough spots.

An Invitation to the Reader

In researching this book, we discovered many wonderful places—hotels, restaurants, shops, and more. We're sure you'll find others. Please tell us about them, so we can share the information with your fellow travelers in upcoming editions. If you were disappointed with a recommendation, we'd love to know that, too. Please write to:

Pauline Frommer's San Francisco, 1st Edition
Wiley Publishing, Inc. • 111 River St. • Hoboken, NJ 07030-5774

An Additional Note

Please be advised that travel information is subject to change at any time—and this is especially true of prices. We therefore suggest that you write or call ahead for confirmation when making your travel plans. The authors, editors, and publisher cannot be held responsible for the experiences of readers while traveling. Your safety is important to us, however, so we encourage you to stay alert and be aware of your surroundings. Keep a close eye on cameras, purses, and wallets, all favorite targets of thieves and pickpockets.

Star Ratings, Icons & Abbreviations

Every restaurant, hotel, and attraction is rated with stars ★, indicating our opinion of that facility's desirability; this relates not to price, but to the value you receive for the price you pay. The stars mean:

No stars: Good
★ Very good
★★ Great
★★★ Outstanding! A must!

Accommodations within each neighborhood are listed in ascending order of cost, starting with the cheapest and increasing to the occasional "splurge." Each hotel review is preceded by one, two, three, or four dollar signs, indicating the price range per double room. Restaurants work on a similar system, with dollar signs indicating the price range per three-course meal.

Accommodations		Dining	
$	Under $95/night	$	Under $8
$$	$96 to $125	$$	$9 to $12
$$$	$126 to $189	$$$	$13 to $17
$$$$	$190 and up/night	$$$$	$18 and up

In addition, we've included a kids icon 😊 to denote attractions, restaurants, and lodgings that are particularly child friendly.

Frommers.com

Now that you have this guidebook to help you plan a great trip, visit our website at **www.frommers.com** for additional travel information on more than 4,000 destinations. We update features regularly to give you instant access to the most current trip-planning information available. At Frommers.com, you'll find scoops on the best airfares, lodging rates, and car rental bargains. You can even book your travel online through our reliable travel booking partners. Other popular features include:

- Online updates of our most popular guidebooks
- Vacation sweepstakes and contest giveaways
- Newsletters highlighting the hottest travel trends
- Podcasts, interactive maps, and up-to-the-minute events listings
- Opinionated blog entries by Arthur Frommer himself
- Online travel message boards with featured travel discussions

a note from pauline frommer

I started traveling with my guidebook-writing parents, Arthur Frommer and Hope Arthur, when I was just 4 months old. To avoid lugging around a crib, they would simply swaddle me and stick me in an open drawer for the night. For half of my childhood, my home was a succession of hotels and B&Bs throughout Europe, as we dashed around every year to update *Europe on $5 a Day* (and then $10 a day, and then $20 . . .).

We always traveled on a budget, staying at the mom-and-pop joints Dad featured in the guide, getting around by public transportation, eating where the locals ate. And that's still the way I travel today, because I learned—from the master—that these types of vacations not only save money but offer a richer, deeper experience of the culture. You spend time in local neighborhoods, meeting and talking with the people who live there. For me, making friends and having meaningful exchanges is always the highlight of my journeys—and the main reason I decided to become a travel writer and editor as well.

I've conceived these books as budget guides for a new generation. They have all the outspoken commentary and detailed pricing information of the Frommer's guides, but they take bargain hunting into the 21st century, with more information on using the Internet and air/hotel packages to save money. Most important, we stress "alternative accommodations"—apartment rentals, private B&Bs, religious retreat houses, and more—not simply to save you money, but to give you a more authentic experience in the places you visit.

A highlight of each guide is the chapter that deals with the "other" side of the destinations, the one visitors rarely see. These sections will actively immerse you in the life that residents enjoy. The result, I hope, is a valuable new addition to the world of guidebooks. Please let us know how we've done! E-mail me at editor@frommers.com.

Happy traveling!

Pauline Frommer

Pauline Frommer

1 A Distinctly American City

FEW MODERN VISITORS REALIZE IT, BUT SAN FRANCISCO HAS ALREADY lived several lifetimes. The city today bears little resemblance to the place it was just 150 years ago. Back then, it was a rough-and-tumble, seaside shantytown that had been cobbled together by refugees—mostly men—who came from the East (both the East Coast and the Far East) to seek their quick fortunes. Much of it was literally built atop the ruins of ships that brought them there, and the city's brothels and saloons were notorious around the world. Gradually, the city gained esteem as the most important banking center west of the Rockies. As America's westward population exploded, San Francisco was poised to be its unofficial capital. The bust-to-boom trajectory took less than two generations, and it typified the wild success America enjoyed after Manifest Destiny and during the Gilded Age.

Then the quake and fire of 1906 struck. Overnight, it was over. The palatial mansions and hotels of the grand city, the fruit of years of accumulated wealth, were destroyed. An entire world—the one visited by and written about by Oscar Wilde, Mark Twain, and every other great name of the age—was lost. Also decimated was the city's reputation as a safe, solid place to invest. Nervous bankers—made even more nervous by the prospects of more insurance disasters—diversified their West Coast investments by sinking them into Seattle and Los Angeles, and San Francisco's stature dwindled somewhat into what it is today: a respected, second-tier city with a spectacular setting.

But its influence didn't end there. The city rebuilt, and, within 50 years, some of the most important social changes of the late 20th century came from there—the Beat writers in the 1950s and the hippie movement of the 1960s both came out of San Francisco's neighborhoods. Even as recently as the 1990s, when the dot-com boom launched, and then shipwrecked, the world economy, the city was an epicenter of events. That's quite a lot of influence for a city of only about 775,000.

Today's San Francisco presents a character unlike that of any other modern city in America. It's not just that it looks different—the Painted Ladies, the hills crowded with old wooden buildings and stately stone towers, the Bay views peeking from the end of streets—but the city truly is different. What some more conservative Americans bemoan as the city's permissive, anything-goes attitude is actually representative of America at its best. It's a true melting pot, with many different types of people living in one place, all more or less getting along. Very few cities work as hard as San Francisco to make themselves hospitable and equal to everyone who lives there, and San Franciscans are proud of how multicultural and inclusive their home is compared to many other places of similar size. But there are also nuances to the city that most visitors are never made aware of; in some ways, it's a clubby insiders' city that requires you to meet and talk to strangers in order to fully know. This guide endeavors to uncover some of its lesser-explored aspects.

San Francisco is an exploration waiting to happen. There are very few American cities in which you can simply wander streets, no cash necessary, and still soak up a full complement of the city's unique culture and vibe. Anyone who is curious and stimulated will find it a playland of food, art, and evocative architecture. The various cultures, the unique clang of the cable cars, the sensational vistas—they're all part of the place that, all these years later, continues to call people out West.

SIGHTS YOU'VE GOTTA SEE, THINGS YOU'VE GOTTA DO

Your visit to this city would be woefully incomplete if you didn't see or do at least a few requisite things. For example, what would you tell your friends if you went all the way to San Francisco without riding one of the famous **cable cars** at least once? Fortunately, a ride also affords you some excellent views of the city's most historic areas. Take the car's Powell-Hyde line to **Fisherman's Wharf** (p. 100), not to indulge in that touristy area's sights, but to walk to the water and glimpse the magisterial **Golden Gate Bridge** (p. 93) off in the distance. Then catch your ferry to **Alcatraz Island** (p. 89), a scrupulously preserved maximum-security prison that is now one of the great museums in America. If you have a little time, take a taxi ride down the zigzagging block-long portion of **Lombard Street** (p. 99), a classic tourist pleasure and one of the city's most distinctive sights.

UNCOMMON LODGINGS

San Francisco's affection for its past, its soft spot for eccentricity, and its reluctance to destroy antiques translate into a higher-than-normal number of irregular old buildings. Hotels can, at times, be as distinctive as something in old Europe. Think of an old-world guesthouse—narrow stairways, pull-chain toilets—and you've imagined North Beach's homey **San Remo Hotel** (p. 39), where rooms go for just $65 in a friendly, no-frills environment. Its secluded rooftop suite has views of everything around, and it's one of the most delightful rooms in the city. For a cozy, family-run experience near Union Square and the cable cars, the **Golden Gate Hotel** (p. 36) is the kind of place where the rooms are full of antiques and there's a happy dog wandering the premises. The **Hotel des Arts** (p. 32) has rooms that have been individually decorated by local artists, yet the price is right ($89).

Also affordable and clean are some of the little-known inner-city motels, where parking is usually free: The **Phoenix Hotel** (p. 45) or the **Hotel del Sol** (p. 44) are popular properties that promise more style than at the average motel.

For a splurge, San Francisco happens to be home to several top-notch boutique hotel chains, Joie de Vivre and Kimpton; check into Kimpton's **Hotel Triton** (p. 37) or **Hotel Monaco** (p. 37), or one of Joie de Vivre's funky motels or its **Galleria Park Hotel** (p. 38), where daily city walking tours are offered to guests for free.

If you're on a supremely tight budget, the **HI Fisherman's Wharf** (p. 49) hostel, though a touch out of the way on Fort Mason, is in an under-built park on the waterfront with an excellent view of the Golden Gate Bridge; it even offers a free morning yoga class. Only in San Francisco!

DINING FOR ALL TASTES

It's tough to find a chain restaurant or fast-food brand in this town—it's a place to try cuisine put out by independent kitchens, and some of the best food in town is ethnic in nature. To best get into the rhythm of life here, bring a good book and a laptop, and settle into one of the countless cafes, particularly the ones in North Beach such as **Caffé Roma** (p. 85), which roasts its own beans right in the front window, or **Caffe Trieste** (p. 85), a longtime institution where Francis Ford Coppola is said to have written *The Godfather* in between espressos.

When it comes to Chinese cuisine, there may be no better place to go beyond boring old General Tso's chicken and egg rolls than the long-running Chinatown, where eating like a local means grabbing bite-size dim sum off carts as they glide by. Chinatown is all about this feast of small plates, and **Dol Ho** (p. 66), a side-street dive, little-known to tourists, serves some of the best. Or queue up for one of the addictive *banh mi* sandwiches at **Saigon Sandwiches** (p. 81)—bet you can't eat just one. But you can't leave town without sampling one dish the city is most famous for: a huge, overstuffed burrito from the Mission's **La Cumbre** (p. 75) or **El Farolito** (p. 75). They're big enough for three meals—so large they ought to be served in bassinets.

San Francisco nurtures some of the brightest chefs in the country, who come here to revel in the bounty of the Bay Area. They have turned cooking into an art form, so no visit would be complete without a special-occasion meal prepared by someone who cares deeply about the origin of the ingredients and the nuance of the final flavors; options are many, but I recommend North Beach's **The House** (p. 59), an Asian-fusion delight, or the Castro's Tuscan-styled **Incanto** (p. 81).

At day's end, raise a beer at a local joint like North Beach's **Vesuvio Café** (p. 205), a longtime haunt of writers; at the tack-tastic South Seas pastiche at the **Tonga Room Restaurant and Hurricane Bar** (p. 207), where it "rains" every half-hour; or at the tony **Maxfield's Pied Piper Bar** (p. 208), beneath a $2.5-million mural in one of the city's swankiest and most storied hotels, the Palace.

THE BEST "OTHER" EXPERIENCES

One of the most appealing aspects of the city is that it hosts an ever-changing world, a vibrant subculture, that only those in the know are invited to share. For example, have you ever eaten at a *pirate restaurant*—an establishment that's only open for a single night, designed as a showcase for experimental chefs? Join the club at **Ghetto Gourmet** (p. 132) or **Radio Africa & Kitchen** (p. 134), and you can toast the party while you're here. San Francisco's many vital immigrant groups bring their own traditions to the table, too: You can experience the intricacies of the etiquette at a classic tea ceremony, whether Chinese (**Red Blossom Tea Company,** p. 134) or Japanese (the **Asian Art Museum,** p. 135). On Sundays, spend your morning at the distinctive and heartwarming **Glide Memorial Church** (p. 147), one of the most inclusive and merry churches anywhere in the country.

Or bow to the altar of intellectual stimulation: Once a month, you can attend a fascinating night during which anyone is invited to share anything they wish—using 20 slides displayed for 20 seconds each. Creative types can honor San Francisco's stature as an artsy enclave at the **Craft Gym** (p. 141), where visitors work it out with scissors and clay instead of barbells. Even history hides in plain sight here: As you walk the streets, that hum you'll hear beneath the road is the looping wire to which the city's storied cable cars hook onto in order to move. At the **San Francisco Cable Car Museum** (p. 139), you'll find out what propels the wires through the city streets—it's a technology that your own city probably once used, but which only San Francisco was sensible enough to preserve. By evening, pay a visit to *Beach Blanket Babylon* (p. 133), an outrageous, rambunctious revue, famous for its oversized bonnets, that's been a city tradition since 1974. Outside of town, the **Jelly Belly** (p. 140) jellybean factory is a paradise for sugar junkies, and its free tour is both informative and productive—everyone gets a free bag of sweets at the end. And in the Wine Country, take a wine appreciation class at **COPIA** (p. 259) the "theme park for food," so that you'll know what you're tasting and how it was blended when you set out to sample the vintages of the local wineries.

2 The Lay of the Land

There's only one San Francisco: The city's top neighborhoods and the best ways to get around

THERE ARE PRECIOUS FEW AMERICAN CITIES WHERE IT'S POSSIBLE TO SEE all the wonders it has to offer without sitting your butt in a single car. New Orleans, maybe. New York City, Washington, D.C., and, well, that's almost the whole list. Add to that San Francisco. Because of the services of Muni buses, BART trains, and a series of tram lines, you can literally roll off the airplane, take a train to your hotel, and hit the town without ever going belly-up to the rental desk at Hertz. It's a beautiful thing.

The city occupies the hilly tip of a peninsula that juts northward around the west side of the bay that bears the city's name. Like ancient Venice, San Francisco is a world unto itself; the borders of its county are also the borders of the city, a rarity in America. To the west of the city lies the Pacific Ocean, wild and huge and the source of the area's unpredictable weather. To the east, the enormous San Francisco Bay, which, along with the interconnected San Pablo Bay, spans some 1,500 square miles. North of the city is a feisty stretch of water known as the Golden Gate; the tidal volume of both bays rush through this narrow channel, making it one of the most dangerous bodies of water in America—a perfect location, in other words, for a prison such as Alcatraz. (But, contrary to urban legend, great white sharks do not live in the Bay—it's not salty enough for them.)

Most of the oldest stuff in the city, all of the skyscrapers, and most of the action are located on the northeast of the peninsula. As you head west, neighborhoods tend to be more recently built, so that by the time you reach Divisadero Street, the westward areas might be best described as bedroom communities, although a few quiet pockets of ethnic enclaves exist. Neighborhoods such as Sea Cliff (mansions for the rich, such as Robin Williams), Richmond (Clement Street is like a mini Chinatown, and not to be confused with the crime-ridden Richmond across the Bay), and Sunset (yuppies, a small-town feel) are at the Pacific Ocean end of things. They're only about 5 miles from the Ferry Building, but as there is little to attract a tourist aside from the odd cafe or restaurant, they aren't covered in depth in this guide. Locals will vigorously defend these parts of town, and as is the case with many neighborhoods, there is much to recommend them, but there's nothing there that's truly world-class.

San Francisco is connected to the northern headlands of the Golden Gate, which are located in Marin (Ma-*rin*) County, by the legendary Golden Gate Bridge (p. 93)—and by no other vehicular crossing. The roadway is part of I-101, which cuts a north-south line through the western fringe of the city via the Presidio, a longtime military enclave that has been preserved as a hilly, forest-sheathed park. To the east, the city links with the major city of Oakland and the lesser city of Berkeley via I-80 by the mammoth Bay Bridge (p. 112) and by the underwater tunnels of the BART train system. To the south, the city is connected by land.

GETTING AROUND SAN FRANCISCO

It's fairly easy as long as you're not afraid of public transport. The city—at least, the parts you're likely to visit—is not too rangy, so even a bus trip will only take 10 or 15 minutes. The trick is knowing which mode to take for your journey, because different rides head to different parts of town. Fortunately, the cost of public transportation is always a reasonable $1.50 per trip (unless you take a cable car), so getting around town won't break the bank.

CAR RENTAL

The one huge mistake a visitor can make is to bring a car downtown. Even locals aren't so foolish; the tight parking situation is lamentable and expensive. The only time you should have a car is when you're on your way out of town. If you do have a car, you'll pay through the nose to park it (about $30–$45 a day downtown) unless you've secured a motel room with a free parking space (see chapter 3).

If you do drive in the city, be very careful around the cable-car lines—those carriages are sometimes gravity-powered and are not good at stopping quickly. Also, be mindful of what your wheels do when you're parked: If you're pointed uphill, turn the wheel to the left; if you're pointed downhill, turn it to the right. This way, if your parking brake fails, your car won't roll into the street. This is not just a suggestion; you'll be ticketed if you don't do it.

BART

BART (Bay Area Rapid Transit; ☎ 415/989-2278; www.bart.gov), aside from looking like a setting for the perfect 1970s disaster movie, is quick and efficient. Trains come every 15 or 20 minutes, although that figure calculates the arrivals of the same type of train; in truth, there's a train every 5 or so minutes that will take you at least down Market Street and then down Mission. Unfortunately, it doesn't go a lot of other places where you need to go—that's about it unless you need to go farther afield, say to Berkeley or Oakland. BART operates Monday through Friday from 4am, Saturday from 6am, and Sunday and holidays from 8am, and it always shuts down around midnight. Kids ages 4 and under are always free. Seniors and students can secure discounted tickets, but it involves bringing ID to the Muni booth at the Powell Street station.

The ticketing system is a pain. You get a ticket by sticking cash into one of the ticket machines located before the entry gates at every station; the machines won't give more than $4.95 in change. The trick of buying BART tickets is not over-purchasing; you load up a magnetized ticket with however much you plan to spend, and each time you take BART, the proper fare is deducted from your card (so you always have to keep your ticket handy, because it gets you both in and out of the system). If you spend too much, you've lost the money. If you spend too little, you have to go through the hassle of topping off your card with a live person, who is certain to be cranky.

San Francisco

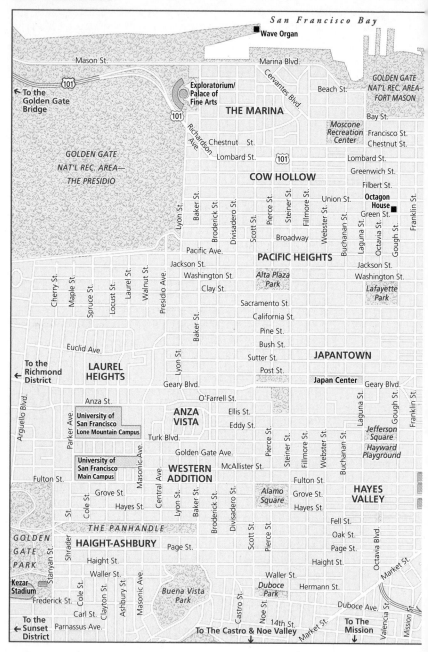

San Francisco Bay

Wave Organ

Mason St.

Marina Blvd.

Cervantes Blvd.

To the
Golden Gate
Bridge

Exploratorium/
Palace of
Fine Arts

THE MARINA

Beach St.

GOLDEN GATE
NAT'L REC. AREA—
FORT MASON

Bay St.

Moscone
Recreation
Center

Francisco St.

GOLDEN GATE
NAT'L REC. AREA—
THE PRESIDIO

Richardson Ave.

Chestnut St.

Lombard St.

Chestnut St.

Lombard St.

COW HOLLOW

Greenwich St.

Filbert St.

Baker St.
Broderick St.
Divisadero St.
Scott St.
Pierce St.
Steiner St.
Fillmore St.
Union St.
Webster St.

Octagon
House

Green St.

Buchanan St.
Laguna St.
Octavia St.
Gough St.
Franklin St.

Broadway

Lyon St.

Pacific Ave.

PACIFIC HEIGHTS

Jackson St.

Washington St.

Jackson St.

Cherry St.
Maple St.
Spruce St.
Locust St.
Laurel St.
Walnut St.
Presidio Ave.

Clay St.

Alta Plaza
Park

Washington St.

Lafayette
Park

Sacramento St.

California St.

Baker St.

Pine St.

Bush St.

Euclid Ave.

Sutter St.

JAPANTOWN

To the
Richmond
District

LAUREL
HEIGHTS

Lyon St.

Post St.

Japan Center

Laguna St.
Gough St.
Franklin St.

Geary Blvd.

Geary Blvd.

Arguello Blvd.

Anza St.

O'Farrell St.

University of
San Francisco
Lone Mountain Campus

ANZA
VISTA

Ellis St.

Jefferson
Square

Parker Ave.

Eddy St.

Turk Blvd.

Pierce St.
Steiner St.
Fillmore St.
Webster St.
Buchanan St.

Hayward
Playground

Golden Gate Ave.

Masonic Ave.

University of
San Francisco
Main Campus

WESTERN
ADDITION

McAllister St.

Fulton St.

Fulton St.

HAYES
VALLEY

Grove St.

Central Ave.

Cole St.
Lyon St.
Baker St.
Broderick St.
Divisadero St.
Scott St.
Pierce St.

Alamo
Square

Grove St.

Hayes St.

Hayes St.

Hayes St.

Fell St.

THE PANHANDLE

Oak St.

Octavia Blvd.

GOLDEN
GATE
PARK

HAIGHT-ASHBURY

Page St.

Page St.

Market St.

Shrader St.
Stanyan St.

Haight St.

Haight St.

Waller St.

Kezar
Stadium

Cole St.
Clayton St.
Ashbury St.
Masonic Ave.

Buena Vista
Park

Waller St.

Duboce
Park

Hermann St.

Castro St.
Noe St.

Valencia St.
Mission St.

Frederick St.

Duboce Ave.

Carl St.

To the
Sunset
District

Parnassus Ave.

14th St.

To The Castro & Noe Valley

Market St.

To The
Mission

8

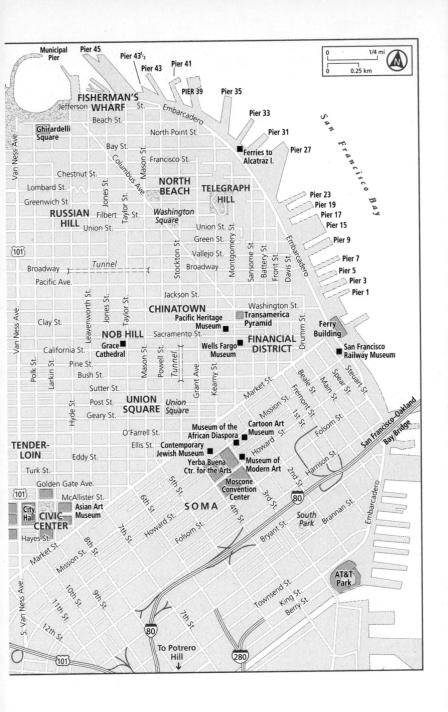

CITY BUSES

Buses go nearly everywhere in town, and they're fairly speedy as city buses go. Some are powered by overhead electrical lines, making them "clean" vehicles, while others are of the typical fume-spewing variety. Fares on buses are $1.50; exact change is required. Be sure to request a transfer when you pay, because that will get you a flimsy newsprint tag that entitles you to ride another bus for free within 90 minutes, which is often enough to see whatever you're headed to see and still have time for a free ride afterward. Given the transfer benefits, it's unlikely that the $11 daily visitor's passes will pay off unless you practically live on the buses—which some weird people do, so avoid riding late at night.

Locals are very peculiar about their bus etiquette. You must enter the vehicle by the front door and leave by the rear door. And to get the rear door to open, you have to physically step into the stairwell, where there are sensors. Neglect to do this and shout for the driver to open the door, and you run the risk of being on the receiving end of some sour stares.

Bus stops, when they're not obvious (such as where there are shelters), are typically denoted by yellow stripes painted around utility poles.

You'll often hear the buses referred to as **Muni** (Municipal Transportation Agency; ☎ 415/701-2323, or, within San Francisco, dial 311; www.sfmta.com), although in truth, Muni also runs the city's streetcars, trams, and even the cable car system. **Muni passes** (☎ 415/923-6050) are $15 for a week, valid Monday through Sunday (starting Monday and not on any other day), and if you have one, you're entitled to $1 fares on the cable cars. I am not a fan of the passes because their funky scheduling means that you could end up having to buy two passes if your trip spans a Monday. Figuring out if a weekly pass will work for you is easy: Will you take more than 10 bus rides before the pass expires on Sunday?

Useful Bus Lines

These bus lines hit a number of places where visitors like to go. Get your $1.50 ticket and a transfer, and ride away.

The 30: Goes through Chinatown from Union Square, veers through North Beach along iconic Columbus Avenue, goes a block within Fisherman's Wharf, and then heads west to Chestnut Street, the major shopping thoroughfare of the Marina. It turns around and heads back about a 10-minute walk east of the Exploratorium.

The 7 and 71: Both go down Market Street and wind up in the Haight-Ashbury, where Golden Gate Park is accessible.

The 2, 3, and 4: All go down Post Street to Japantown, somewhere trams and trains don't go.

The 39: It will do the climbing up to Coit Tower for you.

The 21: Heads down Market Street and then veers along Hayes Street, where the shopping is rich and the residents are richer. The route runs along the south of Alamo Square, home of one of the postcard-perfect views of the Painted Ladies.

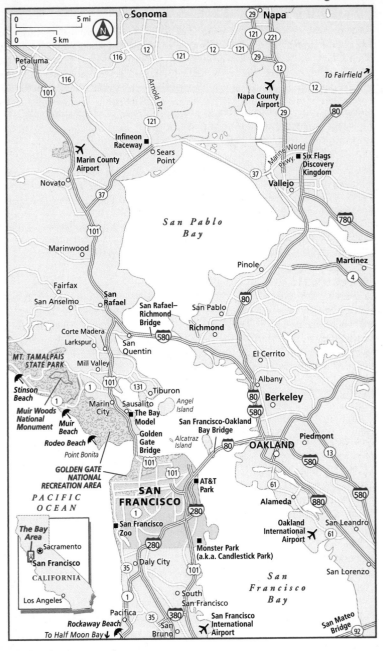

The Bay Area

If your answer is yes, a weekly pass may be economical, but otherwise, the $1.50-per-ride fare might work out to be cheaper. If the weekly pass's scheduling doesn't suit you, consider a Visitor Passport, which is good starting on whichever day you want it to start, but costs slightly more: 1-day passes are $11, 3 days are $18, and a week is $24. Here again, I find that simply paying $1.50 per ride works out cheaper considering the pace of most tourists. You can also secure an unlimited weeklong pass that starts whenever you want by buying a CityPass (p. 98), which you then simply wave at the bus driver (or cable-car conductor) for admission. (They rarely check the actual validity date.)

The most convenient places to buy Muni passes include the booth at Market and Powell streets (very crowded), as well as the Customer Service Center at 11 South Van Ness, at Market. There are also Muni booths at Hyde and Beach streets and Bay and Taylor streets, both around Fisherman's Wharf. You can also buy passes at the Muni information booths at the baggage claim areas at SFO (open 8am–8pm).

Between 1am and 5am, the regular bus service ceases and, instead, an intermittent and limited "Owl" service is run. Before starting any late night, know the schedule so that you don't end up stranded at a bus stop in the dark.

STREETCARS

Although San Francisco's street-level rail system dates to after the Civil War, most of the modern lines use stations and facilities that date only to the mid-1970s, as well as comfortable carriages built in the past few years. The streetcars are of limited usefulness to most visitors, because downtown, where tourists are most likely to be, all the lines follow the same route: Market Street. Five of the six streetcar lines stop underground in the same stations that BART does along Market Street, and BART's price between the same stations is the same as Muni's, which means that for short jaunts along Market (say, Civic Center to Embarcadero), it's irrelevant, price-wise, whether you choose Muni or BART. Streetcars, which run every few minutes, all cost the same per ride ($1.50); maps are available from the Muni site and info office (see the "City Buses" section, earlier).

West of the Civic Center stop, the streetcars fan out and travel different routes, coming up from underground, and head to various residential neighborhoods. Besides the F line, only the N line goes to places noted for tourist attractions; it's useful for reaching the southern reaches of Golden Gate Park and the San Francisco Zoo, as well as AT&T Park, south of the Bay Bridge landing.

There is one streetcar route, though, that you shouldn't miss: the F line. No, that's not something dirty; it's a fleet of streetcars from around the world, lovingly restored, that now run down Market Street to the Castro and around the Embarcadero to Fisherman's Wharf (p. 110). This successful transit experiment is also the only tram line to venture north of Market Street, which it does aboveground the entire way, ensuring views.

Most of the F-line carriages carry a sign that describes where the car originally ran, as well as its year of vintage. Some of them—such as the Italian ones, which have wooden benches—are incredibly noisy as they rumble along, so finish up your cellphone calls before boarding. If the whole concept of the refurbishment of this rolling stock interests you, don't miss the excellent mini-museum devoted to the project; it's located across the Embarcadero from the Ferry Building.

CABLE CARS

Don't make the mistake of calling these "streetcars," And for heaven's sake, don't utter the word *trolley.* These burgundy, wooden, single-carriage icons run by gripping onto a cable that runs continuously inside a metal slot in the road—hence, their only truly appropriate name. You can't miss them, and their miraculous survival into the 21st century makes this archaic form of transportation—once prevalent in nearly every American city—precious.

Unless you have a Muni pass, which makes a ride $1, a single one-way ride on the cable cars is a whopping $5. Seniors age 65 and up pay only $1, with ID, before 7am and after 9pm. Another way to get out of that is to have a CityPass (p. 98), in which case rides are free.

The cable car is so important to the fabric of the city that I've chosen to describe the system in the Attractions chapter (p. 97). The powerhouse of the whole system is also a museum; that's covered on p. 139.

TAXIS

Outside of the Financial District and Union Square, and outside of business hours, taxis aren't always that easy to find. Slipping a couple bucks to a hotel doorman might ease the search. Your fare will be $3.10 for the first fifth of a mile, and 45¢ per fifth of a mile thereafter or during each minute of waiting. If you think that's exorbitant, keep in mind that taxi drivers have to pay $91.50 per shift just to get on the road. They pay for their own gasoline and insurance, too. You should also tip at least 10 percent.

Given a choice between battling shinsplints on a steep hill at midnight and paying for a cab, I'd choose cab, but not until after making sure that there isn't a $1.50 bus that will do the job for me.

Here are a few established taxi companies:

+ **Arrow Cab Co.** (☎ 415/648-3181)
+ **Yellow Cab** (☎ 415/333-3333; www.yellowcabsf.com)
+ **Veteran's Cab Company** (☎ 415/552-1300)
+ **Luxor Cabs** (☎ 415/282-4141; www.luxorcab.com)

SF Green Cab (☎ 415/626-4733; www.sfgreencab.com) drives Prius vehicles that get 40 miles to the gallon in the city, but there are currently only two in the fleet, so you've got to call if you hope to ride in one.

SAN FRANCISCO'S LAYOUT

Neighborhoods change names in short order here—what's Chinatown on one block suddenly segues to North Beach on the next. Yet despite this fuzzy geography, locals are unusually possessive about what they call their neighborhoods. The practice gets rather obscure, with people parsing the names of their home turf into some ridiculously arcane sub-descriptions—adding an "Upper" to the front or contracting the whole name into a new coinage to, I guess, make it more attractive to real-estate agents.

The major 'hoods, though, the ones everyone seems to agree on, are described in this section. There are many more neighborhoods around, of course—particularly since locals keep renaming tiny slivers of older blocks—but the places listed here are the generally accepted major areas, and they're the areas you're most likely to visit as a tourist.

UNION SQUARE

Best for: Budget hotels, big-ticket shopping, transit links
What you won't find: Museums, quiet residential streets, views

Considered the de facto center of town, Union Square is also the city's main shopping district. Granted, pretty much every shop in this part of town is part of a national chain that probably also maintains a branch at your local mall, but there's a Saturday afternoon appeal in that kind of shopping, too. I particularly like the enormous Macy's that takes up the southern end of the park; it's so big that its men's section occupies its own building across Stockton Street. The Westfield mall lining Market Street between 4th and 5th streets is another popular destination. The area, which sadly lacks the wood-frame homes that typify so many other districts, is also rich with budget hotels, which is convenient considering the excellent transit links; the BART stops at Powell and Market, streetcars go down Market, and many of the city's most important bus lines make stops within a block. The cable car heads north from the turnaround located at Powell and Market streets, and because of the popularity of Union Square with out-of-town visitors, this location is often the one requiring the longest wait. The park in the square is a little weird—palm trees in San Francisco?—but its western end is where you'll find the half-price theater ticket booth that can save on your evening's entertainment.

NOB HILL & RUSSIAN HILL

Best for: Terrific views, handsome residential architecture, cafes
What you won't find: Museums, restaurants

North of Union Square, these mostly residential districts, each on its own hill, are called home by the wealthy, who generally inhabit stately stone apartment buildings. Not much has changed up here for decades; it's said the name Nob Hill came from the rich railroad-building nabobs who once had their mansions there. For its part, Russian Hill is less prestigious but still plenty expensive, and its many hidden alleys and back-of-building public stairwells make for an afternoon of intriguing exploration. There isn't all that much for a tourist to do in this part of town aside from gawk at the ritzy buildings and wish those people's lives were yours—then again, that can take a whole afternoon if you do it right. There are a few pleasing cafes, and the Powell-Hyde cable-car line rides the hills through both areas on its way to Fisherman's Wharf. The California cable-car line also climbs the hill. Grace Cathedral sits atop Nob Hill, and the "crookedest street," Lombard Street, zigzags down Russian Hill. Because it's closer to the water, Russian Hill has the better views, but the fancy hotels of Nob Hill are places where you'll want to linger.

NORTH BEACH & TELEGRAPH HILL

Best for: Family-run restaurants and shops, classic Italian cafes, unknown hotels, people-watching
What you won't find: Chain stores, large shops

North Beach's reputation as an Italian-American enclave is still deserved, although with time, the Italian aspects of town appear more and more touristy. North Beach is also where the Beat-generation writers held court, although modern-day writers are more likely to live in the Mission or farther out of town where rents are cheaper, and where experimental entertainment forms of the '60s were launched, although now the heady venues are spread more evenly around the city. North Beach is the kind of neighborhood that vigorously resists change of any kind; chain stores are banned, and landlords will let buildings stand empty for years rather than rent to a corporation. The result is a place where many of the businesses are mom-and-pop affairs that have been running for generations, and so this area is a delightful place to stroll and stop for house-roasted coffee—or for sexual aids: The drag of Broadway east of Columbus is full of adult stores. The area's other main drag, Columbus Avenue, cuts a diagonal from the Fisherman's Wharf area to the Financial District, and many of the area's primary places to eat line this street. The cable car's Powell-Mason line cuts through North Beach, and its terminus at Bay and Taylor streets is one of the least-crowded places to board for a complete one-way ride. Coit Tower stands atop Telegraph Hill, another fiercely protected residential enclave threaded with enchantingly secluded stairways.

FISHERMAN'S WHARF

Best for: Seafood, souvenir stands, maritime history, crowds of slow-moving tourists
What you won't find: Cheap food, peace and quiet

Every tourist makes at least one appearance here, although they shouldn't have to. The only sight of real historic value is the Hyde Street Pier, where a number of precious boats are docked as a living maritime museum. The ferry to Alcatraz Island boards at a wharf that's about a 10-minute walk east, and countless visitors combine their trips there with strolls around the shops here. Around the foot of Pier 45, at Taylor Street, a selection of restaurants serve up crab and other fresh seafood both indoors and at outdoor stalls; it's not hard to do a comparison of both fish quality and price on your own, although few of these restaurants are truly celebrated. Otherwise, the area is not very "San Francisco," but rather, typical of touristy districts anywhere: wax museums, souvenir shops, Häagen-Dazs. The F line historic streetcar boards at Jones and Beach streets, and it travels down the waterfront to the foot of Market Street, where it hangs a right and ends up in the Castro; quite a wide-ranging journey through town for just $1.50.

CHINATOWN

Best for: Cheap dim sum, silly knickknacks, unusual groceries
What you won't find: Cafes, Western cuisine

San Francisco's Chinatown, now one of the world's largest settlements of Chinese life outside of China, has been established for as long as the city itself, and a trip through here—mandatory, it would seem, for any first-time visitor—still reveals the echoes of a more tumultuous age. It has two main drags—Grant Avenue and Stockton Street from Sutter Street to Broadway—with two personalities. Grant Avenue is the touristy road, with tons of cheesy souvenir stores selling knockoff Buddha statues and other noisy knickknacks that children find hard to resist. Stockton, though, is more like the "real" China, with its butcher shops and its produce stalls selling fruit that most Western people have never heard of. The little side streets and alleys off these two streets host little dim sum places where you'll be the only outsider—unlike North Beach's elusive Italians, Chinese people really do come here on a daily basis. The cable car goes down Powell, a block west of Chinatown, although the neighborhood changes so abruptly that there's little sign of the area from the rails just one block away. Just as abruptly, Chinatown turns into North Beach around Pacific Street.

THE FINANCIAL DISTRICT

Best for: Impressive architecture, business-hours hubbub
What you won't find: Evening street life

The area at the eastern end of Market Street (sometimes known as Lower Market), where the substantial stone buildings dominate, is the Financial District, also called Downtown. Historically, this was the power center of town, and it's still where fine banking halls and classic stone skyscrapers rule. Interestingly, this part of the city has changed the most over the past generation; a horrible elevated highway used to run along the waterfront, separating it from town with a ribbon of asphalt and grime. The quake of 1989 took care of that, and now, the Ferry Building, a high-quality food mall at the foot of Market, is considered a model of urban renewal. Take a stroll through the streets of the Financial District, and, during business hours, duck into the banking halls—some of them are really spectacular specimens of 20th-century interior design and architecture.

SOUTH OF MARKET (SOMA)

Best for: Galleries, museums, sleaze bars
What you won't find: Parks, shopping

When people call SoMa "up and coming," which they frequently do these days, what they really mean is it's no longer a place you're likely to get shot. It'll be a long time before SoMa is considered a true part of the city equal to the north-of-Market blocks. For now, it's a place where old warehouses are slowly being converted to other uses. So it's mostly where you'll find big-ticket art museums that came about from massive redevelopment projects (the Yerba Buena Center for the Arts, the San Francisco Museum of Modern Art), as well as a variety of pubs, galleries, and the city's sleaziest gay leather bars. Walking more than a block or two off Market Street is not currently recommended, and that's doubly true for around 6th Street, which is the closest the city has to a pit of despair. However, the area of SoMa east of 3rd Street is the site of some of the city's biggest recent construction projects; it's only a matter of time before the rest of the neighborhood regains cachet as a place where you'll want to kick back.

THE TENDERLOIN

Best for: Inexpensive places to eat, nightclubs
What you won't find: High-quality hotels

SoMa's 6th Street is a dreadful mire of vagrants, and it connects to the north with Taylor Street, one of the worst drags in the Tenderloin. This is the high-crime part of town where the flophouses are located. As you walk through its streets, you'll find crowds of people standing idly in the streets, yelling obscenities at each other or at imaginary friends. Things don't get much better until you go north of Post

Street and start climbing the hard hill. The upside of the Tenderloin is its low rents, which attract hardy artists, nightclubs, immigrants—and liquor stores. It's surprising that such a squalid part of town could be located so close to the most prestigious parts of town, Union Square, Nob Hill, and the Financial District. The Tenderloin is best avoided after dark, particularly for single women; go north to Bush Street if you want to cross it and head west. Every time I'm in the Tenderloin, I get furious at San Francisco. How can a city so obsessed with fancy foods and wines, and with celebrating the good life, let its homeless problem get so out of hand? The Tenderloin, I think, isn't just San Francisco's shame—it's a national shame.

COW HOLLOW, PACIFIC HEIGHTS & THE MARINA
Best for: Upscale boutiques, sit-and-linger restaurants and pubs, a neighborhood feel
What you won't find: Attractions

Cow Hollow is the type of neighborhood with lots of shops selling designer clothes and useless imported silk pillows, but not many supermarkets. It's a terrific place to get an espresso or a pub burger, but when it comes to culture that you don't have to purchase to participate in, there's not much deeper beauty. Union Street between Laguna and Steiner is its principal shopping and dining thoroughfare—a few hours of window-shopping here can make you fall in love with the city. The Marina is even more about new money, much of it earned in a hurry during the dot-com boom and now being slowly spent at its upscale boutiques. Cow Hollow and Pacific Heights, both full of handsome old wooden homes that you and I can't afford, are built on solid ground, but the Marina is notorious for having been built, foolishly, on rubble from the 1906 quake, which means that in a really bad earthquake, the ground stands a very good chance of *liquefaction,* meaning it'll turn to pudding and everything on it will collapse in an instant. Yet the district is still popular with many of the city's newly wealthy, who build L.A.-style mansions in the blocks leading away from the Bay. I wouldn't live in the Marina; it just makes me nervous walking around there, no matter how nice its Apple Store is.

THE MISSION
Best for: Cool cafes and restaurants, cheap knockoff goods, people-watching
What you won't find: Museums, high-end shopping

Known principally as the down-at-heel district where Latin immigrants and young artists coexist in a past-its-prime urban landscape, the Mission is increasingly the sort-of-gentrifying place where you'll find some of the coolest cafes and places to eat—you'll find both yuppie chow rooms and down-and-dirty burrito joints. Mission, its main drag, has the air of an avenue that was probably a lovely neighborhood Main Street in the 1960s but is now a jumble of cheap clothing stores and loose street detritus. Some visitors find the atmosphere to be a little hairy, but really, the district's rough presentation is more a function of its residents' lower economic status, and not indicative of any predilection toward crime. Most of the restaurants and shops are on Mission and Valencia streets, so these places are perfectly safe. It's east of Mission where things get sketchier, so if that's where you're going, just get solid directions before setting out. BART connects to this part of town from Union Square. To the immediate east of the Mission, Potrero Hill is a post-industrial area where design shops and Whole Foods Markets have moved into old warehouses.

THE HAIGHT

Best for: Shops that dress you like you're still 19
What you won't find: Attractions

The Haight, also known as Haight-Ashbury after one of its intersections, used to be a place where cultural trends were called. Today, though, it's living as a shadow of its former self. You'll see far fewer groovy oddballs from the hippie area than you might expect. Even the collectors' art shops that sold concert posters from that long-ago era have moved on—but some of the old bohemianism remains in the form of a line of head shops and consignment stores. There are no real attractions to speak of here, save Golden Gate Park at its west, yet many tourists still come here, mostly on the back of the district's reputation from 1967. You're more likely to meet slumming rich kids from the suburbs who have discreetly parked their Beemers a few blocks away than you are to meet any actual hippies, who, sadly, burned themselves out chasing their psychedelic dreams years ago.

THE CASTRO

Best for: Gay bars and pubs, classic movie screenings
What you won't find: Big-ticket shopping

Although it's known as the gay part of town, it's actually one of several—but the Castro is, indeed, representative of a typical San Francisco neighborhood, full of local cafes, bars, and businesses that have been going for generations. When you're here, it's easy to imagine how nice life would be if you lived here, too—why is it that so many gay neighborhoods capture this lightning in a bottle? This area started as a typical working-class 'hood, but in the late 1960s and early 1970s, gay folks who were squeezed out of the Haight settled here, where it served as a flash point for the early gay rights movement. Again, there are not many attractions to speak of here, but that doesn't mean a stroll can't be rewarding (see the walking tour on p. 172). The biggest reason to come is probably the spectacular Castro Theatre, a popular revival film house and a glorious architectural specimen from the golden age of movies.

CIVIC CENTER & HAYES VALLEY

Best for: Giant attractions, expensive boutiques
What you won't find: Affordable shopping

The few blocks around City Hall are known as the Civic Center area. Its centerpiece is the City Hall building, a grandiose governmental palace worthy of an entire nation. Ringing City Hall is a fringe of monumental museums, performance halls, and libraries, making this district a magnet for the high arts. The streets are a little plain, and the hotels and restaurants a little nondescript, but the area morphs quickly into Hayes Valley to the west, where upscale restaurants and boutiques attract the cool kids.

BERNAL HEIGHTS & NOE VALLEY

Best for: Cafes, restaurants, up-and-coming boutiques
What you won't find: Attractions, street life

South of the Mission, and therefore out of range for most tourists, Bernal Heights is another mostly residential area where decent cafes and restaurants are springing up. Its neighbor Noe Valley is slightly more gentrified. Both areas are safe and pleasant to visit—24th Street around Castro Street is particularly rich with boutiques and eateries—although there isn't much of concerted touristic value in either one.

3 Accommodations, Both Standard & Not

In which we lead you to the most affordable options, from spare bedrooms in private apartments to trendy digs in boutique hotels

SAN FRANCISCO IS ONE OF THE MOST POPULAR DESTINATIONS IN AMERICA, but it's an expensive one. Even locals complain bitterly about the price of everyday items and the sometimes-oppressive cost of living. Real estate, especially, is at a premium because, like many of the other world's most expensive cities, there's only so much land to go around before the water and mountains take over. So it shouldn't surprise you that lodging is priced at a level that you'll probably consider to be higher than the norm.

What's more, when you finally check into your hotel, you may find that it's not as plush as what you think you ought to be getting for what you're paying. That's because a crucial thing to remember about San Francisco, when it comes to lodging, is that much of it was built a long time ago, and replacing those old buildings with something new is not usually smiled upon by the city stewards. So you're going to encounter a lot of buildings that meet a different standard than what we expect today. Different rooms in the same hotel might be wildly different sizes, or there won't be an elevator in smallish buildings, or the walls might be a touch thinner than you're used to. It's all part of hanging out in a historic city, and that old style is presumably one of the reasons you came to enjoy this place.

When conventions roll into town, which they often do, getting a room can turn into a challenge. So always book as far ahead as you can, and ask the booking clerk if there's a convention in town then—the folks at the hotel desk usually know—and if there is, be flexible enough to postpone or advance your trip to dates when more rooms are available and prices are better. An excellent starting point is the Convention & Visitors Bureau's Convention Calendar, posted in the "Meeting Planners" section of its website at www.sfcvb.org/convention/calendar.asp. Helpfully, each event is listed with an approximate number of hotel rooms that are going to be booked because of the event. Think of it this way: The city's total inventory is about 33,000 rooms; you're going to start seeing a rise in prices once about half that figure is reached. The booking website **San Francisco Reservations** (☎ 800/737-2060; www.hotelres.com) lists a few upcoming events for the next month or two on its home page.

And don't forget tax—it adds 14% to a nightly rate. Told you it's an expensive city.

Still, there are deals to be found. Skim through this chapter and you'll find techniques for shaving big bucks off your hotel bill, plus reviews for properties that give you excellent value. One big tip: Calling the hotels directly doesn't always get the best price; some properties offer online discounts that knock $40 to $60 off regular prices. The city is also plugged into the network of online sellers that slash prices—make sure you get prices out of Hotwire.com, Priceline.com (see the "Bidding Blind" box in this chapter), and Hotels.com before committing. Just make sure that if you do that, you also call the hotel itself to see if it can do even better on the quoted rate.

So what do all the dollar signs mean when they precede a listing? Simply the nightly price for two:

$	Under $95
$$	$96 to $125
$$$	$126 to $189
$$$$	$190 and up

RENTING A ROOM IN AN APARTMENT

It's a tradition in the Pauline Frommer's series to lead off with the most illuminating, most edifying, and most economical way to see any city in the world. Well, no, I'm not talking about staying with friends, although that's a really good idea, and if you can arrange that, you're way ahead of the game and can kindly skip this chapter.

But I'm talking about renting a room in the apartment of a local (I also cover renting a complete apartment a bit later in this chapter). If you've stayed in a hotel lately, you'll know why I have such a high opinion of private B&Bs. These days, when you check into even a middling hotel run by a well-known company, you start by paying a great deal for what amounts to a single smallish room. From then on, everything you do or say ends with a huge charge on your bill. Parking. Laundry. Lots of places even add "resort fees" for using the pool or the gym—the very perks that drew you to the hotel to begin with!

Renting a space inside the home of someone who has lived in San Francisco for a while affords you as much opportunity as you want to seize. Many of these owners, who meet people from around the world when they come to stay, are only too eager to share their favorite local haunts and insider's touring tips. Too often, expensive hotels are staffed by people who can't direct you further than the lobby cocktail bar.

You'll also be nickel-and-dimed much less and get a more personal experience when you go the private B&B route. And in San Francisco, that means working with the excellent **Bed & Breakfast San Francisco** ★★★ (☎ 415/899-0060; www.bbsf.com). Call it a cultural quirk, but there simply aren't many local brokers offering stays in hosted apartments or private-home B&Bs. The one exception is this agency, owned by Richard and Susan Kreibich, who started this service after falling in love with hosted stays during a tour of Europe. In 1978, they got their first booking—the commission was $7—and ever since then, they've been matching people's extra rooms and guest cottages with temporary visitors. Every property and host (teachers, lawyers, and other inquisitive types) has been vetted by the Kreibichs, a worldly couple—interestingly, Susan was once a showgirl for

Diana Ross. All its properties are required to be accessible to Downtown, and all must be private or semiprivate, never just simple, bare, spare rooms that someone wants to rent out—so you won't find the host trooping through your space on the way to work each morning. If you share a bathroom at all, it will be with no more than one other room. The Kreibichs are rigorous about the kind of friendly, homey experience they want guests to have, and that carries over to judicious screening of hosts. "If I'm asked, 'How much money will I make?' right away, that disqualifies them from being hosts," says Susan. "We want to hear, 'What can I do to make their stay really nice, and what more can I add?'"

Breakfast is always provided, although at some places, you'll be given the makings in a basket each night. They promise that the price you're quoted will be the final price; there are no extra charges. Not every place in its stable is an abject bargain, but deals do begin at a paltry $65 single/$75 double. That's for a cute room, hosted by a senior couple, in the Sunset district, which is about 20 minutes by city bus from Union Square. Some properties are little hideaways fresh out of *Tales in the City*—up this staircase, through this garden, until you reach a hidden door that leads to your studio. (The agency's Red Door Studio, $125 single/$135 double, is such a hideaway.) One property at Goldmine Hill, west of the Castro, is run by the very lawyer who, in the 1950s, fought on the same side as local heroine Friedel Klussmann to save the cable-car system from annihilation—and, to all of our benefit, won. Now elderly, he's retired and available to offer his own tales of the city ($75 single/$85 double). He's been working with the Kreibichs for nearly 30 years, and other hosts have been active for well over a decade. The Kreibichs also own and operate one of their 50 city properties themselves—a sweet cottage, built in 1909, that's a block from Dolores Park in a trendy part of town between the Mission and the Castro. Prices are more often in the low $100s, such as a "City Vista" B&B ($115) that boasts a redwood hot tub on its outdoor deck.

In addition to this local fave are some national organizations that deal in "hospitality" and offer a handful of places in the San Francisco area. **Educators Travel** (☎ 800/956-4822; www.educatorstravel.com), for teachers only, grants the right to stay for $40 a night in another teacher's private home. As I type this, Educators offers up 18 homes in San Francisco proper, plus another 18 in nearby Oakland and 17 in Berkeley; other bedroom communities surrounding San Francisco are also represented. Membership is $46 the first year, $36 for every year after, and covers two adults and two kids under 18, plus a $5 booking fee.

Those over 50 can join the **Evergreen Club** (☎ 815/456-3111; www.evergreen club.com; single membership $60/year, couples $75/year). Members, literally from all walks of life, from farmers to engineers, rent out their empty guest rooms to other members, give them advice about the area, and cook them breakfast in the morning. Half the intention is to give people a chance to meet each other—seniors on road trips use the service to cross the country and make friends as they go. There are only a handful of participants in San Francisco proper, but if you're wiling to expand your search to Oakland and to bedroom communities on the BART line, the menu widens. Room rates are just $10 for a single or $15 for two sharing a room.

And let's not forget free hospitality exchange programs: **CouchSurfing** (www. couchsurfing.com) was designed to be totally free. It's a rare organization designed to celebrate one of the original, but forgotten, benefits of travel—namely, getting to know people from all over the world. Members of this nonprofit site (mostly

Pauline Frommer Says:
Questions to Ask Your Potential B&B Host

Though most in-apartment B&B stays are fun, carefree holidays, some-times, well, things can go mighty wrong. It's extremely important to find out what sort of person you may be sharing your vacation with and what the apartment is like before you put down a deposit. Call your potential host or the agency to go over any concerns you may have before commit-ting to a hosted stay. You may want to ask the following questions:

1. **What is the host's schedule?**
   Some hosts will be in the apartment for most of the day, while oth-ers work outside the home, meaning that you'll have the apartment to yourself for large chunks of time. Find out before you leave.

2. **Where does the host sleep in relation to the room you'll be using?**
   Another privacy issue: Will your host be in the room right next door, eavesdropping (intentionally or not) on your every sigh or snore? Or will there be a room or two between your two bedrooms? In some extremely rare cases, cash-crunched hosts have been known to rent out their own bedrooms and take the living room couch for a week. If the listing is for a one-bedroom, you may want to find out if this is the case, as that can be an uncomfortable situation, especially if you have to walk through the living room to get to the bedroom or bathroom. (From what I understand, this is not a common scenario, but hey, it's better to ask.)

3. **Is the bathroom shared or private?**

4. **Are there pets in the house?**

5. **Are there any rules the host has for his or her guests?**
   Whether guests can smoke in the apartment is obviously a common issue, as is the guests' use of the shared space. (I once met a host who only allowed the guests she liked to venture into the living room.) Most hosts do not allow guests to cook, except to reheat pre-pared foods, so if this is an issue for you, discuss it before you book. And sometimes the rules can be even more unusual—I know of a kosher hostess who requires guests to separate the plates used for dairy products and meat products (not an easy task).

6. **What does the bedroom face?**
   Does the room get a lot of sun in the morning? Does it face a busy street or a quiet back courtyard? These questions may be key if you're a light sleeper.

under-40s) put up personal profiles that look a lot like Facebook pages and offer to meet, greet, and host strangers when they swing into town. In exchange, visi-tors might help with the chores, cook, or otherwise behave like good guests. This method of accommodation feels like a high-wire act for those who are unused to fraternizing with strangers, but many true travelers swear by the entree that knowing a local can bring. You can also spend as long as you like online in advance of your trip, vetting your prospective host (or guest). There are dozens of folks in the city—students, waitresses, and lots of artists—offering their space in this way.

Bed-and-breakfasts that operate more or less like hotels—that is to say, multi-unit properties where the owner doesn't also live—are listed with the hotels later in this chapter.

RENTING YOUR OWN APARTMENT

For those seeking more privacy, renting a complete apartment beats hotel stays on every front. And this form of lodging has many pluses—chief among them a kitchen! This is actually pretty transformative for a vacation, because Northern California is renowned for its wealth of fresh meats and vegetables. It's one of America's breadbaskets, and many of San Francisco's most charming spots happen to be ones where artisanal foods are made and sold, so putting yourself in the position to enjoy those foods by cooking them will bring you much closer to the essence of Bay Area life. (It'll also save you a small fortune on restaurants.) Second, many rental apartments have two or more bedrooms for the same price as a standard two-person hotel room. So for families and groups, they're a much smarter buy. Also, if you're traveling with more than two people, the close quarters of a hotel room may grate you, yet it's easy to find apartments that sleep up to eight people for as little as $200 a night, which split among eight would mean just $25 per person per night.

Another giant advantage is that the people who rent these places are usually proud to share their neighborhoods with you; and often, when you check into the place, you'll often find a helpful listing of all the local finds, such as which stores are run by friends, where to find the freshest bread, and so on. San Francisco is a city made up of dozens of cozy neighborhoods, and there's no better way to get to understand life in the city than to stay with the locals.

Now to the downside: Though apartments are a terrific option, they're difficult to book in San Francisco. Here, it's a rent-by-owner world. Unlike other world cities, no major rental offices handle short-term vacation rentals, meaning that there's no source acting as a middleman between the tourist and the owner, no third party to insure quality or step in when something goes wrong.

But there are services, some with nominal membership fees, that aim to help you find temporary homes inside real homes. Real estate is so expensive in San Francisco that most of the owners don't let their homes go for cheap, so it's unusual to find someone who advertises his place for less than $150 a night. That may be high for a double, but as I said before, groups can score on this type of lodging.

VACATION RENTALS BY OWNER

This is one of the most promising databases of apartments, because homeowners pay an annual fee to list their properties, so it's in their interest to give exhaustive information about them—and they usually do. And unlike craigslist (see below), **VRBO** (www.vrbo.com), HomeAway (see below), and Zonder (see below) will remove an owner if complaints arise about their property. Craigslist has no such policing capabilities. At any moment, you'll find more than 100 options, with lots

The Nitty-Gritty of Direct-to-Owner Rentals

Minimum stays: Two to four nights is standard.

Getting a deal: Worthwhile discounts (of 15% to 20%, usually) kick in if you volunteer to stay for at least a week, so use that as a bargaining chip.

Finding the right place: Most apartments are identified by the name of the neighborhood they're located in, so as you start your search, have a good map of the city handy. It's also smart to have a map of the city bus routes so that you'll know how easy your transportation connections will be; you can print one at www.sfmta.com.

Hidden fees: Keep a close eye on fees and security-deposit requirements; they change for every property and booking site.

Red flags: Walk away if an owner asks you to wire him the full amount before you get the key. This is an unsafe way to transfer money and gives you no way to get your money back should something go wrong. Instead, you should pay by credit card or PayPal. Also, if you're booking on a site such as craigslist, which doesn't police its advertisers, be wary of a renter who's unwilling to show you pictures of the property.

The "Renting Your Own Apartment" section in this chapter lists the best websites for San Francisco apartment rentals. *Remember:* Listings are ever-changing, and because these databases don't come out and inspect apartments themselves (members pay a fee to be listed), quality and selection changes by the day.

of photos. I've seen some excellent options here, including a one-bedroom flat in a Haight-Ashbury Victorian complete with computer, Internet access, washer and dryer, and a fireplace, for $135 a night or $900 a week. Again that's not drop-dead cheap, but if you can snag it for a week, you'll find it's a heck of a lot cheaper than pouring your money into a small hotel room. VRBO also represents the odd bed-and-breakfast, which are mixed in with the apartment options.

CRAIGSLIST

Craigslist (http://sfbay.craigslist.org) is probably the dominant website in town for casually finding an apartment for rent. This service functions pretty much like a newspaper's classifieds section, except it's free for landlords to place an ad. As I said above, the free setup also means that there's no one following up to check on the quality of what's being advertised, and photos are not included, so it's up to the you to do your own checking, get pictures, and hash out details with the other party. You may be renting a place that's usually occupied by owners who are going on vacation and want to make a little cash in their absence. You may also be renting one that's totally empty and just has a few sticks of furniture—there are as many potential arrangements as there are apartments in the city. So make sure you know, to the letter, what you're getting into, unless you want Judge Judy involved later on. Obviously, the options are always changing, and often they're only available for tight windows of time that may not agree with your own schedule, but I've seen some attractive offers, such as a place with a fireplace and a skylight on postcard-perfect Alamo Square for $120 a night. If you don't see something you like posted, go ahead and post a request of your own and include your trip dates—craigslist is popular in town and you never know what might come out of the woodwork.

HOMEAWAY

At any given moment, there are about 100 ideas on offer at **HomeAway** (www. homeaway.com), and the most affordable of them are in secondary areas of town that you'd actually want to stay in, such as Twin Peaks, Noe Valley, and the Castro. Prices for the best stuff are $155 to $200 per night, usually for places greater than 600 square feet; $900 for a week is a common rate. Many listings come with convenient calendars that mark off the dates for which the property in question is unavailable.

ZONDER

The deals at **Zonder** (☎ 866/613-3166; www.zonder.com) are, on average, no better than the ones offered by other sites, but now and then a real steal floats to the surface, such as a flat for two in Buena Vista Heights for just $92 a night, which is fairly unbeatable, even if you'll have to rely on public transportation to get to town. It also allows potential customers to call instead of using the Web, if they want (although I'd rather peruse the photos online first). Finally, Zonder is the only one of these sites that pledges it will move dissatisfied customers to new apartments or give them a full refund. That's an important distinction.

SERVICED APARTMENTS

In addition to privately owned apartments, there are companies offering buildings of apartments set up for itinerant types. Unfortunately, because San Francisco is heavy on banking and high-tech companies, they tend to demand top dollar and they get it. I've done what I can to weed out places that cater to down-and-outs, although clientele changes daily.

$–$$ The Halcyon Hotel ★ (649 Jones St., between Post and Geary; ☎ 800/627-2396 or 415/929-8033; www.halcyonsf.com), built in 1912, deals in efficiency-type units ($89 single, $99 double) 3 blocks west of Union Square. Its 25 rooms, mostly small but well kept with plain wooden furniture and private baths, are an exceptional value in a city that normally hits tourists for twice as much for similar amenities. You won't get a kitchen burner, but you'll have a toaster, fridge, and microwave and all the kitchenware you're likely to require. Local calls are free, so is Wi-Fi, and rooms have safes. Decor is hardly envelope-pushing, but at least it's not depressing. Some times of year (like, all winter), a 7-night minimum stay is required. The owners keep limited desk hours, but that's not because they don't care; in fact, they're a good source of information on doings in town. Guests tend to use this place when moving to the city or working in it for a few weeks; each room comes with its own doorbell in order to give a semblance of home life. Families might consider its largest room for $109, and standard rooms are rented by the week for $450.

$$$ Executive Suites (1388 Sutter St., Suite 904; ☎ 888/776-5151 or 415/
776-5151; www.executivesuites-sf.com) has about 75 units around town. It
focuses mostly on corporate rentals and stays of longer than a month, but two of
its properties—2000 Post (at Steiner, near Japantown) and Archstone South
Market (at 3rd and Folsom)—permit stays of as short as 3 days. The company has
controlled many of its apartments for upwards of 15 years, and it furnishes all of
them completely, down to pots, pans, toasters, coffeemakers, and ironing
boards—everything you'd need in a place, including weekly housekeeping. In
business since 1980, it now maintains about 75 hotel-decor units throughout
town. Per-night prices for studios (for two people only) start at $149, one-bed-
rooms (for three) at $189, and two-bedrooms (mandated for four, even if two of
them are kids) at $309, although you'll be able to negotiate deals for 30 days or
longer. All apartments have both queen-size beds and a queen-size sofa bed,
including studios, which means you can squeeze up to four people into a place at
the lowest price.

$$ It's got a range of sizes, but prices for studio apartments at the **Steinhart
Hotel ★** (952 Sutter St. between Leavenworth and Hyde; ☎ 415/928-0260; www.
personalityhotels.com; AE, DC, DISC, MC, V) go from $99 to $115 during most
periods. That includes a Murphy bed, fridge, sink, and—miracle of miracles—
two burners so that you can actually do some cooking and save cash, which is
something to talk about in this tourist-priced tangle of hotels west of Union
Square. Keep in mind that's for the smallest studio; larger studios are $150, and
all of the units require a minimum stay of 7 nights. This one is run by Personality
Hotels, so it's got a boutiquey vibe (but it's not too precious).

$ As long as you promise to stay at least a week, the value of **Gaylord Suites**
(620 Jones St. at Geary; ☎ 415/673-8445; www.gaylordsuites.com; AE, DISC, MC,
V) can save you a bundle. Your kitchen won't have a burner or an oven, but it will
have a fridge, microwave, sink, and utensils. There's Internet (it's free in common
areas), a 24-hour reception desk, free local calls, and weekly housekeeping. The
rooms are done in a simple black-and-white style that could be described as
"cheap chic." Unfortunately, the deposit situation is onerous, but it's designed to
keep out the riffraff, with $500 required, separate from rent, that remains on your
card for a week after you check out. The building is 12 stories tall, and prices rise
with the floors, from $550 a week for those on floor nine or below, and $650 for
the better views above.

$ Vantaggio Suites (www.vantaggiosuites.com) runs three properties in older
buildings around Union Square and the Civic Center, all of which are geared for
folks who need to stay for a few weeks, but all of which do rent by the night.
Expect a simple room, tired but clean, with a fridge and a microwave but nothing that can burn the place down—there's a community kitchen for that. A small
fitness room and weekly housekeeping round out the amenities. Nightly, that
costs $95 double, but stay at least a week and you'll pay $485 to $525 double
($460–$500 single), depending on the floor; upper floors, which are quieter, are
more expensive. Of its three properties, the lavender-hued one at 761 Post St., at
Leavenworth, (called "The Cosmo"; ☎ 415/614-2400; prices above) has the
best mix of amenities and location. Rooms are fairly small in all three. The Turk

location (835 Turk at Franklin; ☎ 415/922-0111) is in a nondescript area that requires you to trudge through the awful Tenderloin to get to Union Square, so it isn't worth the $80 you'll save over the Cosmo on a weekly rental. Because of its Tenderloin milieu, I wouldn't recommend **O'Farrell** (580 O'Farrell St.; ☎ 415/885-0111) to women traveling alone, despite the good weekly rate of $375 single and $400 double. If you really want to share cash, all three will pair you with a roommate in a shared room ($225/week). To quote a famous San Francisco flick, *Dirty Harry,* "Do you feel lucky, punk?"

$$$$ Castro Suites ★★ (☎ 415/437-1783; www.castrosuites.com) are colorful, charming, one-bedroom apartments—with fully equipped Technicolor kitchens—in an old wood-frame building at 927 14th St., at Noe, not far from a tram stop. Sam and Joel, a local couple, have filled the place, a one-time private home, with bright, cheerful fabrics, and Joel himself, an artist, painted many of the works on the walls. There's a minimum stay of two nights, and they'll knock off the usual discounts of around 15% for stays of a week or longer. Rates start at $200 a night for one or two guests and $220 for three or four—on the splurgey side, but the fact that this one has full kitchens, a big-time rarity around here, may make it worth it. Besides, it's adorable.

$$$ American Marketing Systems, Inc. (☎ 800/747-7784; www.amsires.com), sounds like a company that might install a computer system in your office, yet since 1970 it has dealt in both furnished and unfurnished apartments (with more of a focus on the latter, unfortunately). Frustratingly, it's tough to get a handle on its prices using its website; use it to see photos of places you might like, and then call to see which ones rent daily or weekly and obtain a verbal quote. (Apartments are brokered out by private owners, so the stable changes frequently.) Maid service comes once every 2 weeks. Paying $1,200 to $2,000 per week is standard for a small one-bedroom or studio in an older, wood-frame building, and prices tend to rise the newer the building is. It's generally possible to squeeze in a few kids, too, for that price, but if they're much over 16, you may get pressure to rent a larger place. You'll need to lay down a $400 deposit to start, plus a one-time cleaning of $175 for a studio or $275 for a one-bedroom. The company is in good standing with the Better Business Bureau.

Other companies are playing the game around town, too, but require minimum stays of at least 30 days, so I'll throw their names in quickly mostly as a resource for you: **Oakwood Worldwide** (☎ 415/658-0830; www.oakwood.com), **CitiSuites** (☎ 415/292-3904; www.citisuites.com), and **Marriott ExecuStay** (☎ 800/500-5110; www.execustay.com).

HOTELS

City hotels are completely unfriendly to smoking and they all charge 14% in taxes. Unless otherwise noted, expect a TV and a phone. Also, every one of them will float prices higher if they sense that availability is low, such as during major conventions (Macworld in January sees a spike, for example—you can find resources for learning when the conventions are held in the introduction to this section); the prices I supply are best-case scenario rates as quoted by the hotels themselves, so you'll know what the baseline is. But that doesn't mean you can't do better, particularly if you use hotel-booking websites (see below).

As I mentioned before, San Francisco isn't like most other cities. Its buildings are very old, having been built in a time when uniformity was not prized. In this way, its accommodations have more in common with Europe than with much of America. Many hotels on the affordable end of the spectrum date from the post-quake years, and by local values, tearing them down is out of the question. Consequently, you'll find creaky wood floors, inconvenient stairway placement, odd room configurations, rambling hallways, walls that are less than soundproof, and often, some rooms that are smaller than the modern chain-hotel standard. In a given hotel, rooms just a few doors down from each other may be drastically different in size and the amount of natural light. On the bright side, that usually comes with high ceilings. Be thankful for such idiosyncrasies, because it's what makes a room cost $100 in a $300 market. Unless the hotel is totally chock-ablock, most desk clerks will oblige you with a room change if you ask for one.

Calling the hotels directly doesn't always get the best price; some properties offer discounts on their own websites that knock $40 to $60 off regular prices. The city is also plugged into the network of online sellers that slash prices; make sure you get quotes out of Hotwire.com, Priceline.com, HotelsCombined.com and Hotels.com before committing, because it's very common to find discounts there—in some hotel listings, I note particularly good ones that I've found in the past. When you've a quote you like, call the hotel itself to see if it can do even better on the rate. Most of these online agencies work closely with the hotels, and at periods of loose occupancy, it's common to find rates there that are around 30% lower than what's quoted here.

Just make sure of a few things if you start your search on those sites. Have a map in hand, because not all computer-based sites screen adequately for location, and you wouldn't want to book a place too far from where you want to be; Momondo.com, an excellent site that culls quotes from a multitude of other sites and puts them on one page for you, recently offered me (from an Italian site called Venere.com) a hotel in Livermore, 44 miles away, in what was supposed to be a San Francisco search. Hotels near the airport that require the use of a car also frequently lurk among the results.

You're also likely to find spot sales advertised unexpectedly as hotels turn to the discounters to help build business when conventions aren't in town.

Some properties require 2-night minimums stays but aren't explicit about that fact on their online booking forms. Others may limit room occupancy to two people, so read the terms of your reservation very carefully.

For printable coupons good at highway motels outside of town (places I don't review here), consult the Hotel Savings Directory at www.hotelsavingsdirectory.com. Through that site, properties around the airport, for which you'll need a car, can cost $45 to $60.

UNION SQUARE & THE TENDERLOIN

I usually insist on staying around Union Square. First, it's accessible to nearly everything else without having to change buses or trains. Second, it's the historic heart of town. Third, many of the accommodations options are in older stone buildings with the accompanying antique vibe, which I love. There's also plenty

Bidding Blind

There are also good deals to be found at bidding sites such as Priceline.com, which allows a user to pitch city hotels with a price they'd be willing to pay, and if a hotel likes that number, it accepts, binding the user to a reservation. When you bid, you only know that you're bidding for a hotel in a certain neighborhood. The trick of the site is coming up with a bid that's neither too low to attract a room nor too high so that you pay more than you have to. The secret, instead of just pecking around and hoping that your bid is within the sweet spot, is to use third-party sites such as BiddingForTravel.com and/or BetterBidding.com, where people who have recently seen their bids accepted by the site spill the beans about what the rate was and which hotel took it. Through that, it's often possible to snare a four- or five-star room for under $100—even $50 for a small establishment. We studied the posts at BiddingForTravel.com over the last 12 months just to give you an idea of which major hotels are usually discounted. The patterns are striking; the biggest price cuts come from hotels with four or five stars. Here are some properties you might score:

- **Hilton San Francisco Union Square** (333 O'Farrell St. at Mason): The most likely "get" in San Francisco, especially if you bid for a four-star hotel in the Union Square West (USW) area, it's a truly massive place (which may be why it's discounting so often). The look is ultra-corporate, and hallways can be endless, but it has such nice amenities as room service (careful ordering, or you'll rapidly wipe out whatever savings you won in the first place!), health spa, pool, whirlpool, bar, and two restaurants. **Standard price (standard double room):** $180 to $450; **Priceline price:** $74 to $100, with the average accepted bid at $80.

- **Hilton San Francisco Financial District** (750 Kearny St. at Clay): Guess Hilton ain't doing too well here when there aren't conventions in town, as this is the second most-likely bid winner, listed as a four

of food at every price level. You won't find the old wooden Painted Ladies or Bay views, but the other conveniences make this district a logical home base.

Just west of Union Square, in the Tenderloin (or at least the northern fringes of it) you'll find affordable hotels in a higher concentration than anywhere else in the city, although the sketchy characters you'll also likely find in the streets might put you off the neighborhood.

$ Every lodging market needs a reliable place like the 76-room **Grant Hotel** (753 Bush St., between Mason and Powell; ☎ 800/522-0979 or 415/421-7540; www. granthotel.net; AE, MC, V), a simple, clean place at the bottom of the price spectrum. If you don't expect a view of more than a neighboring wall, and don't star in the Union Square East (USE) area. Converted in the last 2 years from a Holiday Inn, the 27-story hotel's rooms and gym are a bit smaller than most folks are used to at a Hilton. Still, it's freshly renovated with sleek decor, and many north-facing rooms have a sweeping view of Telegraph Hill. Restaurant, bar, room service, day spa, and iPod-docking alarm clocks round out the amenities. **Standard price (standard double room):** $209 to $370; **Priceline price:** $65 to $90 with the average accepted bid at $81.

- **Holiday Inn Fisherman's Wharf** (1300 Columbus Ave.): This is what Pauline Frommer got in San Francisco, the last time she bid on Priceline.com, and it's a common one for this company, particularly for those bidding three stars in the Fisherman's Wharf area. It's about a block from the frenetic energy of the wharf, quiet and cheery, in that bland chain-hotel way. On-site amenities include a pool and small fitness center. **Standard price (standard double room):** $200 to $255; **Priceline price:** $65 to $80, with average accepted bid at $73.

- **The Opal San Francisco** (1050 Van Ness Ave. at Geary): Ranked as a 2½-star choice, it comes up fairly frequently for the upper Civic Center area. An older property in a large stone building, it's a bit worn, but clean and with a small gym, and free continental breakfast. **Standard price (standard double room):** $99 to $169; **Priceline price (and average):** $65.

With the exception of the period around New Year's Eve, accepted bids on Priceline.com rarely ever jumped above $125 a night, and that also included such swank brands as Hyatt, Westin, and InterContinental. *One warning:* Make sure you use the location selector to ensure that the airport hotels are not included in your search; otherwise, you may get stuck with a place that requires a car. Often those who bid for "South San Francisco" also get an airport hotel, so leave that out of the search.

mistake it for something with more service standards than a clean crash pad, you'll find that it absolutely meets your expectations. Prices are sane ($72 for 2 in a smallish room on a full mattress including private bath and continental breakfast), though rooms vary greatly in terms of ambient light and size. For example, no. 111 is dark, on an airshaft, and eerie, while no. 115 is light and large with a newer bathroom. What you get appears to be luck of the draw, but hey, you can always ask to see another room if you're not happy upon check in.

$ If you don't plan to spend much time in your room, you could do worse than the seven-story **Dakota Hotel** (606 Post St., at Taylor; ☎ 415/931-7475; www. hotelsanfrancisco.com), where all the units have private baths but beyond that, aren't cushy or terribly up to date. This is a hotel with an antique cage elevator and one that laughably lists "blinds" as an amenity ("Hey, we've got ceilings, too!"), but it definitely is clean and respectable. Prices start at just $66 for a single and $70 for a double, although in very busy periods, prices are $80 to $100. The Adelaide hostel, around the corner, uses the Dakota for its private rooms—that should tell you something about the luxury level. Union Square is two blocks east; head west, as the Tenderloin can be a little dicey.

$ Everybody knows that accommodations at an American YMCA aren't going to be plush (although the one in Hong Kong is at the level of a brand-name chain hotel). So it won't surprise you to hear how plain the rooms are at the **Shuh Yu-Lang Central YMCA (220 Golden Gate Ave. at Leavenworth; ☎ 415/345-6700; www.ymcasf.org; MC, V).** But because it's a nonprofit, any corner-cutting is offset by other value, such as the right to use the on-premises fitness center with a 25m heated pool, weight training area, sauna and steam room, and rooftop garden. Its Tenderloin location is run-down, but happily, the management works to keep shiftless characters away; drugs and alcohol are rigorously banned. There's also a cafe serving free continental breakfast (cooked breakfasts are for sale for around $5). Rates start at $44 for one with a shared bath, $62 for two with a shared bath/$74 private. So for a week, single rates are $262 and doubles are $373. Be warned that bathrooms are dormitory style, so bring a robe.

$–$$ At the **Hotel des Arts** ✹✹✹ **(447 Bush St., at Grant; ☎ 800/956-4322 or 415/956-3232; www.sfhoteldesarts.com; AE, DC, MC, V),** each room has been painted by an artist, and I don't mean slapped with latex—the works in each Painted Room are distinct, detailed, intense, and surely worthy of future preservation. (But so are children's eyes from some of them—if you've got young ones, make sure your chosen room isn't, say, the punky pink one where "Lick It Up Bitch" is dramatically painted on the wall. The fairy-tale-like landscapes of painter Sam Flores might be better for a young 'un or a squeamish adult.) These works of art are set in a creaky old building, with narrow stairs and small rooms, but these things, instead of detracting from the place, make it feel like a homey harbor. I appreciate the unnecessary touches, such as the hallway art by graffiti artist Chor Boogie. And you can't beat the location: a few blocks east of Union Square, by the symbolic entrance to Chinatown. Shared-bath rooms go for $49 for an extremely teeny unit (which proprietors offer with apologies, despite the great price) to $89 for something more humane; there's also a choice of a $125 unit with a queen-size bed and a small private bathroom, although I'd say you could find better deals for that higher rate. During low season, the hotel often offers an "Explorer Package" (heralded on its website) that gets you a room for a week for $294. Wi-Fi and continental breakfast come with all deals.

$–$$ The 93-room **Adante Hotel** ✹ **(610 Geary St., ☎ 888/423-0083 or 415/ 673-9221; www.adantehotel.com; AE, MC, V)** is run by C-Two Hotels, an upstart company that's providing a low-cost alternative to self-important boutique-hotel puffery. There's no sense in pretending that the vibe here is anything less than weird, but it must also be said that the one-of-a-kind, but unquestionably odd, hand-painted murals, both in the hallways and the rooms, of European pastoral

Accommodations near Union Square

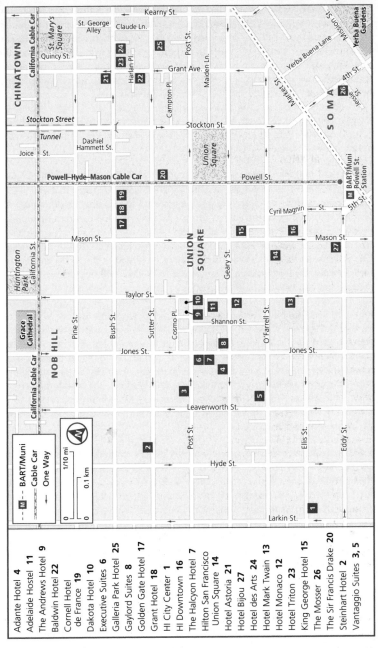

Adante Hotel **4**
Adelaide Hostel **11**
The Andrews Hotel **9**
Baldwin Hotel **22**
Cornell Hotel
de France **19**
Dakota Hotel **10**
Executive Suites **6**
Galleria Park Hotel **25**
Gaylord Suites **8**
Golden Gate Hotel **17**
Grant Hotel **18**
HI City Center **1**
HI Downtown **16**
The Halcyon Hotel **7**
Hilton San Francisco
Union Square **14**
Hotel Astoria **21**
Hotel Bijou **27**
Hotel des Arts **24**
Hotel Mark Twain **13**
Hotel Monaco **12**
Hotel Triton **23**
King George Hotel **15**
The Mosser **26**
The Sir Francis Drake **20**
Steinhart Hotel **2**
Vantaggio Suites **3, 5**

scenes lend the place a crude charm. Rates normally fall $89 to $99 for a room with two double beds, although when things are quiet, you can pull deals as low as $69 from its website, and that includes a light continental breakfast. Downstairs, there's an Internet cafe that doesn't see much action, possibly because in-room coffee is free, as are in-room Web access and in-room safes. The building is not new, but bathrooms (all private) are scrubbed clean. So why so cheap? Partly because it's basic and partly because if you head west out its front door, the neighborhood turns sketchy. East, though, to Union Square, you'll find all the cheap transit options you could want. I like the staff here, too—they're young and helpful and don't get into the transactional huff that plagues many other hotel workers of this price range.

$–$$ Each of the 65 rooms at **Hotel Bijou** ★★ (111 Mason St., at Eddy; ☎ 415/771-1200; www.hotelbijou.com; AE, MC, V) is named for a movie that was shot in San Francisco *(After the Thin Man, 48 Hours)*, and they're brightly decorated. The playful cinematic theme carries over into an off-lobby makeshift screening room, Le Petit Theatre Bijou, where DVDs are shown nightly to rows of antique cinema seats (not that most guests will want to sit around watching movies). Another cute touch: Current cinema timetables from around town are posted in the lobby, and if something's being shot on location in town, the front desk will help guests sign up as extras. Though the building is on the older side, it's not creaky, and all room doors are opened by modern key cards. Linens are on the worn side, and the hotel's location on the fringe of the Tenderloin is unappealing, but on the flip side of those negatives, it's very near the action of Union Square and many transportation options, which is what tips the scales in its favor. Rooms vary in size but do tend to have large closets, plenty of electrical outlets, and at least one soft lounging chair. A pastry breakfast is included. In sum, the place is invitingly gimmicky and a good value— $99 is a typical price, but $89 is possible with negotiation or during quieter periods. Earplugs are provided but hardly necessary; room numbers ending in 00 through 03 face Mason Street, which some may find noisy, while those facing the back tend toward the dark side.

$–$$ For the price, it's surprising to receive perks such as thick robes, iPod docking stations, a little exercise room, and flat-screen TVs the way you do at the **Hotel Mark Twain** ★ (345 Taylor St., at Ellis; ☎ 415/673-2332; www.hotelmarktwain. com; AE, MC, V). And what is the rate? About $109 usually for a standard queen room, although during downtimes it's possible to find one for $69, a fab deal— check Hotels.com, where you can also purchase a continental breakfast option for two for another $10. This 1928 building, solidly built but without air-conditioning, is eight stories tall, and the street it's on isn't very busy. The shady area of the Tenderloin kicks in just west, but that can't undermine the thoughtful things the management is doing to make a stay here a more refined experience.

$–$$ The acceptable **Baldwin Hotel** ★ (321 Grant Ave., between Bush and Sutter; ☎ 415/781-2220; www.baldwinhotel.com; MC, V) is simple and without an outgoing personality, but it's marvelously central and refreshingly well-run for a cheapie. Rooms have ceiling fans but not AC (not that you need AC in this town), closets (a rarity elsewhere), super-soft duvets, and spotless white tile bathrooms with very small tubs. Water pressure is iffy, but not disastrous, and the rooms facing Grant Avenue are nice and bright. The value is a little slim at $119, which it charges at busy periods, but it's a great deal at the more typical $89.

$$ The kind of no-frills hotel that I might pick if I were coming into town for the night to catch a concert or a comedy show, **Hotel Astoria** (510 Bush St., at Grant; ☎ 800/666-6696 or 415/434-8883; www.hotelastoria-sf.com; AE, MC, V) succeeds mostly on its prime location; some of its 80 rooms have a view of the top of the Chinatown gate on Grant Avenue. But what you get is nothing special, and wouldn't be even if it were 1985, with tube TV sets, a lack of alarm clocks, pink textured walls, clinical tile lobby, retrofit wiring, and room numbering derived from stick-on hardware-store numbers. However, here's the rub: Everything, including bathrooms, is remarkably clean, which distinguishes a junky hotel from someplace worth talking about. And the rates are downright cheerful: $85 to $100 a night including a feeble continental breakfast, although a phenomenal $69 rate can often be secured via the hotel website. It's tough to find rates that low in this part of town, and I for one am willing to sacrifice charm in exchange.

$$ Another popular little place of just 48 rooms, the **Andrews Hotel** (624 Post St., at Taylor; ☎ 800/926-3739 or 415/563-6877; www.andrewshotel.com; AE, MC, V) charges good prices for its smallish "cozy double," "corner king" and "comfy queen" rooms ($99–$139, usually with a shower stall, not a tub, and postage-stamp-tiny bathrooms). But beyond that, the value fades at $150 or more per room, not because of any issues of quality (things are clean, staff is attentive) but simply because of price. A small continental breakfast is served on every floor each morning, a free glass of afternoon wine is offered daily at the Italian restaurant off the lobby, and each room has a DVD player; free movies are available at the front desk. I actually covet the chunky black side chairs in every room—they're '80s chic—and you may appreciate the fully draped windows and the shaded reading lights above each place in the beds, which is a feature lots of places overlook but which makes couples' travels easier. Some of its front rooms have wide bay windows—ask for a room on an upper floor if street noise irks you (most urbanites won't even notice).

$$ Another good-quality, family-run hotel in an old building with odd-size rooms, the five-story **Cornell Hotel de France** ★ (715 Bush St., at Powell; ☎ 800/232-9698 or 415/421-3154; www.cornellhotel.com; AE, MC, V) comes with a full cooked breakfast, not just a continental one. Although the lobby is a curious mix of bric-a-brac, from heraldic crests to Latin bird pottery, the rooms upstairs are far plainer and less adventurous, which may be a relief to some. The most affordable ones (usually around $100) have showers but not tubs; spend more on a medium-size room ($115) and you'll get a claw-footed tub/shower combo. The little touches are generous, such as the use of real glasses instead of plastic cups, and the fact that breakfast includes cooked items like French toast and eggs, not just continental-style breads. The hotel offers a smart weekly rate of $725 for one and $1,050 for couples, and that includes both breakfast every day and dinner at the downstairs restaurant Jeanne d'Arc (French cuisine, of course) from Tuesday through Friday. That place is too pricey to be handy for a la carte

Boutique Bedders

There's something gratifying about patronizing a hotel group that's distinctly San Francisco, as the following small, high-quality boutique chains are. I've sprinkled a few of their best values throughout this chapter, but have a look at these websites to see if you can snag deals at the pricier properties not listed in this book (it happens). And you'll likely see the name of these places popping up among the deals at the discount sites.

Joie de Vivre (www.jdvhotels.com)

Praise be to Joie de Vivre, which takes worn-out old properties and transforms them into something cheerful but still affordable. The local paint stores must be out of teal and canary-yellow paints because of the appreciated efforts of this chain to refresh old properties into sunny affairs. I absolutely love this company not just for that, and for eschewing rip-off luxury pricing, but also because it actually endeavors to share the best of the city with guests. It has created the Golden Gate Greeters, a program that pairs any interested guest with a like-minded local willing to share the best of the city over a walking tour—for free.

Personality (www.personalityhotels.com)

I used to count this chain as one of the best fallbacks for budget travelers. Its holdings are all well-located and mostly interesting: The Hotel Vertigo (until recently the York) was where Hitchcock shot some of his famous film. Unfortunately, Personality has been renovating its properties one by one and reopening them with prices that are a little too high for this guide ($200/night). You might look around, though, and fish for deals, because the company is still testing the market on how much it can charge.

---

orders, but there are dozens more options in the neighborhood. The Powell Street cable car runs one building east, and National Car Rental and Alamo Rent A Car are directly across the street.

$$–$$$ The 25-room **Golden Gate Hotel** ★★★ (775 Bush St., at Powell; ☎ 800/835-1118 or 415/392-3702; www.goldengatehotel.com; AE, MC, V), built in 1913 as a working-class hotel, is the family-run B&B of my dreams come to life. Staying here seems to put guests in a good mood, because each morning, you'll find them meeting over the free continental breakfast (the fresh cinnamon croissants are addictive) and gabbing cheerfully with each other. Pip, the garrulous tailless tabby, roams the creaky halls trying to charm those who cross his path. Beds are supremely comfortable, paint jobs are fresh, and the rooms' furnishings are mostly antiques, lending a comfy, homey vibe. A fridge and a microwave are available for guest use, and to add to the charm, there's a cage elevator that owners are pretty sure is the oldest surviving one in town. Rooms facing Bush Street aren't terribly noisy (in fact, you can often hear the clang of the cable cars' bells at the end of the block, which I find wonderful), but if you want to save money with

Kimpton (www.kimptonhotels.com)

Kimpton is the plushest of the San Francisco boutique hotel brands, but, largely because its hotels are in older buildings with smaller rooms, it's still a step below luxury. This brand has expanded to open properties around North America, but San Francisco is still its base, and there are nine merry, fresh-faced, well-designed hotels in town (on discount sites often priced $150–$180) from which to choose. I especially enjoy the lavishly over-the-top, circus-like decor of **Hotel Monaco San Francisco** ★★★ (501 Geary St., at Taylor; ☎ 866/622-5284 or 415/292-0100; from $223), where doormen look like they've just jumped off the running boards of Capone's vehicle after a hit, and where rooms are decorated with oddities such as live goldfish and 7-foot circular mirrors. Also swell are the **Sir Francis Drake** ★★ (450 Powell St., between Post and Sutter; ☎ 800/795-7129 or 415/392-7755; from $167, which is darn good for a room with a view), a 1920s palace that towers over the north of Union Square; and the **Argonaut Hotel** ★ (495 Jefferson St., at Hyde; ☎ 866/415-0704 or 415/563-0800; from $174), which occupies a historic warehouse overlooking the Powell-Hyde cable-car turntable at Fisherman's Wharf—the most expensive rooms have dreamy bay views. The most reasonable of the Kimptons is the **Hotel Triton** ★ (342 Grant Ave., at Bush; ☎ 800/800-1299 or 415/394-0500), right at the gates to Chinatown, which prides itself on eco-friendly quarters (water-saving bathrooms, lots of recycling), for which it charges from $139—a lot less than the nearby Orchard Garden Hotel, a non-Kimpton hotel that sells itself as green, too. And that price *does* fit into this guide quite nicely.

a shared bathroom ($95, versus $150 for a private bath), you'll face the back. The owners, John and Renate Kenaston, clearly put love into their enterprise, and they get a lot of repeat business for their pains.

$$–$$$ The 166-room **Mosser Hotel** ★★ (54 4th St., at Market; ☎ 800/227-3804 or 415/986-4400; www.themosser.com; AE, MC, V), built in 1913 but renovated in lots of gray and graphite tones recently, has one of the best locations of any hotel in the city: right off Market Street and within a few steps of most of the major shopping, yet still in a neighborhood you wouldn't mind being in at night. Prices for a shared-bath room ($109) are a good deal, although $189 for a private-bath room is not competitive with other hotels of this level. Rooms have lots of high-design features (nice flat-screen TVs), but because human beings are still low-tech they might find some of them a bit annoying—the TV and Internet ($8/day) are unnecessarily complicated, the newfangled light switches don't always respond, and the flip-top garbage cans in each room look like tables and tend to swallow up little things when you forget and place them there. The showers, too, are weaker than I'd like. But these seem like small quibbles for such a handsome place, with its helpful staff, its double-paned windows (useful for screening out the whistle of the porter at the upscale hotel across the street), its self-serve washer/dryers, and all the free coffee and muffins they dole out in the mornings. And again, there's that unbeatable location. One final perk: There's a pub downstairs, which makes late meals easier than at rivals.

$$–$$$ The Union Jack flies above the three-star **King George Hotel** ★ (334 Mason St., at Geary; ☎ 800/288-6005 or 415/781-5050; www.kinggeorge.com; AE, MC, V), where you can often find rooms through Orbitz for around $100—a strong value. This cute place gives off good feelings—a step or two above crash pad but with saner prices than the big boys. It's well-maintained by an unusually attentive management, kept assiduously clean, and located in a terrific spot near Union Square and BART. Standard rooms, which are the smaller size typical for a building of this period, get you a queen-size bed and comfortable outfitting, although they aren't as plush as the hotel's boutique image might predict. Ask for one of the units on the north side of the building—they face open space and are consequently bright. Rates are more like $169 or $189 when things are busy— that's too high for even this quality, in my mind—which keeps this place from being at the top of my list. But the hotel's website often lists deals, such as a $109 rate throughout springtime.

THE FINANCIAL DISTRICT & THE EMBARCADERO

Because it's a business district, this area is quiet during weekends (so hotel prices go down then), but that's also one of the things that make life at these hotels a little more difficult, since finding meals isn't as easy in a sleepy district. Still, it's hooked up to the rest of the city in a fine way that most other 'hoods can't beat: BART, bus, cable car, and tram all zip through here.

$$$–$$$$ Count on some lovely plush features at **Galleria Park Hotel** ★★★ (191 Sutter St., near Kearny; ☎ 415/781-3060; www.jdvhotels.com), such as huge beds and shower curtains made of the same fuzzy terry cloth as the towels. Digs are of a luxury standard, which makes a room (not huge, though part of that is because of those copious beds) a tough place to leave in the morning, although the location (within a safe walk to Union Square and the Montgomery Street BART station—I just as easily could have slipped it into the Union Square section) is one of its brightest selling points. But better, and rarer, the hotel puts a premium on local culture, and not only does it offer a free architectural walking tour with an established expert (Rick Evans of My Favorite City tours) each day at 10am, but it also hooks up any interested guest with a program that matches them with local volunteers who are interested in sharing their city. There's even a hip, under-the-skin walking tour of Chinatown (located a few blocks away) posted in the elevators for guests to follow anytime they like. A potentially money-saving perk is the hotel's Galleria Park Suggests (GPS), which gives guests an inside line on discounted events tickets and backstage passes for big events, as well as hookups at festivals and at unusual off-the-mainstream sights (private winery tours, factory tours). I'd be hard pressed to find a hotel in any city that takes as much care to introduce guests to locals and their personal city experiences, and the fact it all comes with high standards in the rooms is a boon. Wine is served in the lobby every late afternoon. The building is shaped like a ring, with a courtyard in the middle; central rooms, the even-numbered ones, are slightly darker and less private than noisier street-facing rooms. Rates start around $179 for a weekend and bump as much as $50 when it's busy, although Priceline.com often brings things down to about $170, and Hotels.com has been known to slash down to $150.

$$$$ It's corporate through and through, of course, but there's no denying that the building housing the **Hyatt Regency San Francisco** (5 Embarcadero Center, at Market; ☎ 415/788-1234; http://sanfranciscoregency.hyatt.com; AE, DISC, MC, V) is a modern city landmark. This 802-room concrete behemoth at the foot of Market Street comes with a massive, zigzagging 17-story open atrium, designed by architect John Portman (also famous for Times Square's Marriott Marquis) in 1973, when atrium lobbies were a sign of the future. It's still impressive, and the Embarcadero of today is a much more appealing place than it was during the Nixon Administration, when an elevated highway (now gone) scarred the waterfront. The premises have a prime position right next to the Ferry Building and connected by heaps of ideal transit options, including Muni, BART, the California Street cable-car line (the terminus is right outside the hotel doors), and the F-line streetcar. Rooms are larger than the average, and many also have furnished balconies with views of the bay. On the downside, besides price ($159 is a starting point), is its size; walking back to your room from the elevator can take more than 2 minutes. It's overly popular with conventioneers, and it's the sort of hotel that considers it acceptable to charge guests for every little twitch. Because of its architectural importance to the city, and because some readers will want to know about at least one tried-and-true corporate hotel worth trying, I include it here, but not because it's the most affordable option for you. It also makes for a romantic splurge.

CHINATOWN & NORTH BEACH

Strangely, although these are two of the city's calling cards, tourism-wise, there aren't many newly built or large hotels here. Just about everything is small-scale. That's a big plus in my book (I guess that'd be the one you're holding), because I love a small hotel. Staying here, among the wooden houses and green parks, puts you close to plenty of entrenched and affordable cafes and bistros, within a 10-minute walk of Fisherman's Wharf, and gives you a sense for what it's like to be a resident of this city.

$ I adore the old-world charm of the **San Remo Hotel** ★★★ (2237 Mason St.; ☎ 800/352-7366 or 415/776-8688; www.sanremohotel.com; AE, DC, MC, V), a wood-frame warren of cozy rooms that was built in the months after the great earthquake and has changed little since then. This is boardinghouse-style stuff, very San Francisco, most with in-room sinks and shared bathrooms (bring slippers) outfitted with claw-foot tubs, brass fittings, and pull-chain tank toilets. The cheapest rooms ($65/night for 1 or 2 people, no in-room sink) might have windows facing the corridor and not the outside world—somehow, this setup isn't oppressive. Just because it all seems old doesn't mean it's decrepit; everything's in top repair because the owners, brothers Tom and Robert Field, are obsessed about

Accommodations Around Town

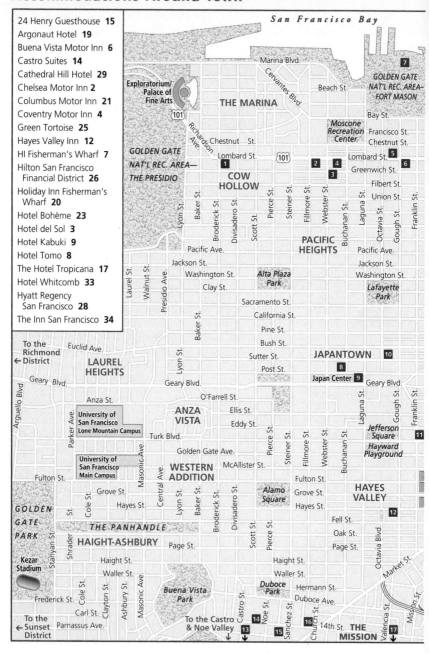

24 Henry Guesthouse **15**
Argonaut Hotel **19**
Buena Vista Motor Inn **6**
Castro Suites **14**
Cathedral Hill Hotel **29**
Chelsea Motor Inn **2**
Columbus Motor Inn **21**
Coventry Motor Inn **4**
Green Tortoise **25**
Hayes Valley Inn **12**
HI Fisherman's Wharf **7**
Hilton San Francisco
 Financial District **26**
Holiday Inn Fisherman's
 Wharf **20**
Hotel Bohème **23**
Hotel del Sol **3**
Hotel Kabuki **9**
Hotel Tomo **8**
The Hotel Tropicana **17**
Hotel Whitcomb **33**
Hyatt Regency
 San Francisco **28**
The Inn San Francisco **34**

San Francisco Bay

Marina Blvd.
Cervantes Blvd.
Exploratorium/
Palace of
Fine Arts
THE MARINA
Beach St.
GOLDEN GATE
NAT'L REC. AREA—
FORT MASON
Bay St.
Moscone
Recreation
Center
Francisco St.
Chestnut St.
Richardson Ave.
Chestnut St.
GOLDEN GATE
NAT'L REC. AREA—
THE PRESIDIO
Lombard St.
Lombard St.
Greenwich St.
Filbert St.
COW
HOLLOW
Union St.
Baker St.
Broderick St.
Divisadero St.
Scott St.
Pierce St.
Steiner St.
Fillmore St.
Webster St.
Buchanan St.
Laguna St.
Octavia St.
Gough St.
Franklin St.
PACIFIC
HEIGHTS
Pacific Ave.
Pacific Ave.
Laurel St.
Walnut St.
Presidio Ave.
Jackson St.
Washington St.
Clay St.
Alta Plaza
Park
Jackson St.
Washington St.
Lafayette
Park
Baker St.
Sacramento St.
California St.
Pine St.
Bush St.
Sutter St.
JAPANTOWN
Post St.
Japan Center
Geary Blvd.

To the
Richmond
← District
Euclid Ave.
LAUREL
HEIGHTS
Lyon St.
Arguello Blvd.
Geary Blvd.
Geary Blvd.
Anza St.
O'Farrell St.
Laguna St.
Gough St.
Franklin St.
University of
San Francisco
Lone Mountain Campus
Parker Ave.
ANZA
VISTA
Ellis St.
Eddy St.
Jefferson
Square
Turk Blvd.
Masonic Ave.
Golden Gate Ave.
Pierce St.
Steiner St.
Fillmore St.
Webster St.
Buchanan St.
Hayward
Playground
University of
San Francisco
Main Campus
WESTERN
ADDITION
McAllister St.
Fulton St.
Fulton St.
HAYES
VALLEY
GOLDEN
GATE
PARK
Cole St.
Grove St.
Hayes St.
Central Ave.
Lyon St.
Baker St.
Broderick St.
Divisadero St.
Alamo
Square
Grove St.
Hayes St.
Fell St.
Octavia Blvd.
Stanyan St.
Shrader St.
THE PANHANDLE
HAIGHT-ASHBURY
Page St.
Scott St.
Pierce St.
Oak St.
Page St.
Kezar
Stadium
Haight St.
Waller St.
Haight St.
Waller St.
Market St.
Cole St.
Clayton St.
Ashbury St.
Masonic Ave.
Frederick St.
Buena Vista
Park
Duboce
Park
Hermann St.
Duboce Ave.
To the
← Sunset
District
Carl St.
Parnassus Ave.
To the Castro
& Noe Valley
Castro St.
Noe St.
Sanchez St.
Church St.
14th St.
THE
MISSION
Valencia St.
Mission St.

40

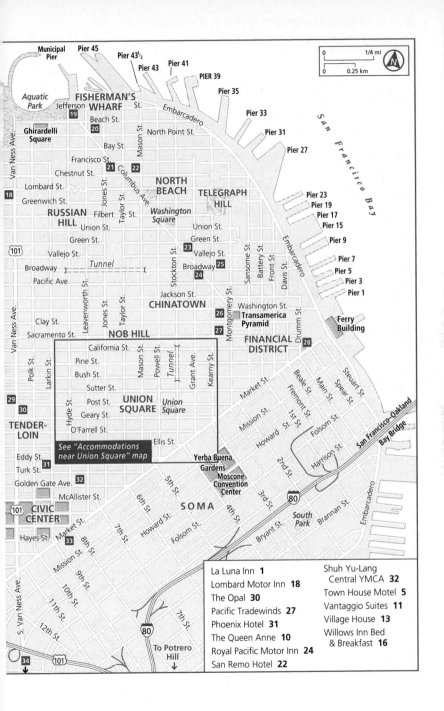

Municipal Pier
Pier 45
Pier 43½
Pier 43
Pier 41
PIER 39
Pier 35
Pier 33
Pier 31
Pier 27
Pier 23
Pier 19
Pier 17
Pier 15
Pier 9
Pier 7
Pier 5
Pier 3
Pier 1

Aquatic Park
Ghirardelli Square

FISHERMAN'S WHARF
Jefferson St.
Beach St.
North Point St.
Bay St.
Francisco St.
Chestnut St.
Lombard St.
Greenwich St.
Filbert St.
Union St.
Green St.
Vallejo St.
Broadway
Pacific Ave.

NORTH BEACH
Washington Square

TELEGRAPH HILL

RUSSIAN HILL

San Francisco Bay

Embarcadero

Jackson St.
CHINATOWN
Washington St.
Transamerica Pyramid
FINANCIAL DISTRICT
Ferry Building

Sansome St.
Battery St.
Front St.
Davis St.
Drumm St.

NOB HILL
California St.
Pine St.
Bush St.
Sutter St.
Post St.
Geary St.
O'Farrell St.
Ellis St.

UNION SQUARE
Union Square
Tunnel
Mason St.
Powell St.
Grant Ave.
Kearny St.

TENDER-LOIN

See "Accommodations near Union Square" map

Eddy St.
Turk St.
Golden Gate Ave.
McAllister St.

CIVIC CENTER
Hayes St.

SOMA

Yerba Buena Gardens
Moscone Convention Center

South Park

To Potrero Hill

Market St.
Mission St.
Howard St.
Folsom St.
Harrison St.
Bryant St.
Brannan St.

Beale St.
Fremont St.
Main St.
Spear St.
Steuart St.
1st St.
2nd St.
3rd St.
4th St.

San Francisco-Oakland Bay Bridge
Embarcadero

Van Ness Ave.
Polk St.
Larkin St.
Hyde St.
Leavenworth St.
Jones St.
Taylor St.
Mason St.
Stockton St.
Columbus Ave.

7th St.
8th St.
9th St.
10th St.
11th St.
12th St.
S. Van Ness Ave.

0   1/4 mi
0   0.25 km

La Luna Inn **1**	Shuh Yu-Lang Central YMCA **32**
Lombard Motor Inn **18**	Town House Motel **5**
The Opal **30**	Vantaggio Suites **11**
Pacific Tradewinds **27**	Village House **13**
Phoenix Hotel **31**	Willows Inn Bed & Breakfast **16**
The Queen Anne **10**	
Royal Pacific Motor Inn **24**	
San Remo Hotel **22**	

41

maintenance and cleanliness, and the desk staff is young and bushy-tailed. Rooms are tiny and don't have phones or TV (though there's a little lounge for that)—well, except for one: The sublime penthouse unit ($175 weekdays, $10 more on weekends) is a self-contained, private rooftop unit with its own outdoor terraces, a bathroom and TV, and some fabulous views of North Beach. Don't pack heavy, because there are stairs everywhere and no porters. There's no Internet access, but the front desk will give you a prepared leaflet directing you to several nearby cafes where you're welcome to linger and surf as long as you want. The seductive hotel, excellently located for North Beach cafe-going and dining, sometimes offers deals on its website (3rd-night rates of $40, for example), so check there. The terminus of the lesser-used Mason cable-car line is a block away, which connects the hotel nicely with Union Square, but remember that the fare is $5 a ride unless you've got a CityPass, in which case unlimited rides are free. Fisherman's Wharf is a 7-minute stroll north.

$$ Clean, basic, affordable, and with a defiantly 1950s exterior, **Royal Pacific Motor Inn** ★ (661 Broadway, at Grant; ☎ 800/545-5574 or 415/781-6661; www.royalpacificmotorinn.com; AE, MC, V) is special not for its rooms, which are predictable motel-style affairs, but for its location: balanced a few feet from Columbus Avenue between Chinatown and North Beach, and within walking distance of many of the great sights. The situation will make finding cheap dining easier than perhaps with any other hotel in town. Best of all, though, is the free parking, which is mostly unheard of in this part of town. An outdated but clean double room goes for $106. It won't change what you think about motels, but there's really not a thing to complain about.

$$$ You'll pay a tad more than you have to pay to stay at **Hotel Bohème** (444 Columbus Ave., at Vallejo; ☎ 415/433-9111; www.hotelboheme.com; AE, DC, DISC, MV, V), but there are precious few spots to stay in North Beach that don't ask you to pay even more. Its "cozy rooms," the smallest and often the darkest, go for $164, and larger rooms go for as much as $194 for a quad. The hotel, a low-slung post-earthquake building along busy and happening Columbus Avenue, right across from the famous City Lights bookstore, opened in 1995 but has decorated itself with antiques that give a sense of something older. You'll have to bus it or hoof it to get anywhere else in town, but there's no other neighborhood I'd rather immerse myself in than North Beach, with its cafes, restaurants, and parks for sitting back and observing the collection of eccentric locals.

FISHERMAN'S WHARF

Prices are higher here because many first-time visitors think, wrongly, that it's the best place to stay. Many of those who bunk here are on package tours, particularly ones purchased abroad. In fact, Fisherman's Wharf is closest mostly to Fisherman's Wharf, and to the bayward end of North Beach, but most of the city isn't all that easy to reach from it. The cable car heads to Union Square, but remember that's $5 a fare. There is the F line on the streetcar, which scoots down the waterfront from here and then up and down Market Street, but that method's hardly speedy.

$ The Columbus Motor Inn ★★ (1075 Columbus Ave., at Francisco; ☎ 415/885-1492; www.columbusmotorinn.com; AE, MC, V) is a drive-in motel that looks like it was taken from, say, outer Cleveland and plopped in among the homes at the northern end of North Beach. Other cities would have pulled it down for a posh apartment building years ago, but this city likes to cling to its mid-century identity. The place looks potentially scary from the outside, but it puts its efforts where it counts: the rooms, which happen to be larger than the average. It's sort of hard to go wrong with this deal: $83 to $93 for a basic motel-style room, none too flashy but clean and reliable, plus free covered parking, which is unheard of on this side of Russian Hill. I'd call this place an unqualified find and a strong value. Fisherman's Wharf is a 5-minute stroll north.

THE MARINA & COW HOLLOW

Cow Hollow, which abuts the yuppified Marina district, is actually one of the budget secrets of San Francisco—an entire neighborhood where you can find good-quality lodging for $75 to $100 a night. It's also where you stay if you've got a car and plan to zip out to Wine Country with it. Not only is the area relatively close to the Golden Gate, but there is also a smattering of '50s-style motor-court motels where parking is usually free—a rarity in this town. The downside to Cow Hollow lodging is that it's not terribly convenient to everything else, including the major sights, although that's nothing a 10-minute bus ride won't fix. (Second caveat: On weekends, buses usually arrive only once every half-hour.) Competition is pretty tight in this part of town—notice how most of the motels listed charge the same rate—so if you find a good price online, call your favorite property and see if it'll beat it to score your business.

$–$$ If you're a nature lover, particularly one with a car, **La Luna Inn** ✦ (2599 Lombard St.; ☎ 415/346-4664; http://lalunainn.com; AE, MC, V) may work for you, because it's one of the closest Marina/Cow Hollow motels to the Presidio. That means greenery and fresh air are about 2 blocks west, and the multi-million-dollar mansions of the Marina are just north, by the Palace of Fine Arts. Like the Del Sol, the Luna is a motel that's been given a smart but none-too-flashy once-over to capitalize on its mid-century style and to make it affordably hip. Expect a bright, colorful motel-style experience, with rods instead of closets but strong value otherwise. Also expect to pay $79 for a room with a (very comfortable) double bed, $89 for one with a king-size bed, and $99 for two beds; prices soar to $125 in busier times, which to my mind is a little steep for a place so far off the main paths. The included continental breakfast is nothing to get excited about, unless you dig white-bread toast.

$–$$ Another good value with free parking, the **Chelsea Motor Inn** (2095 Lombard St., at Fillmore; ☎ 415/563-5600; www.chelseamotorinn.com; AE, MC, V) is a three-story faux-Tudor job with a central courtyard. Rates for a room for two (king bed or 2 double beds) span $77 to $90 most nights and go to $135 when things are packed. The decor is ho-hum, motel-style, but perfectly acceptable, with the usual motel-style setup including a two-chair sitting area between the beds and the window. Rooms are on the large side. Parking is free, as is Internet access, and there are stretches of good shopping and dining on Chestnut, a few blocks north, and Union, a few blocks south.

$–$$ You'll find nearly an identical setting—same blah furnishings, same brilliant prices, and good maintenance—2 blocks east at **Coventry Motor Inn** (1901 Lombard St.; ☎ 415/567-1200; www.coventrymotorinn.com; AE, MC, V), which is managed by the same people. Just as at the Chelsea, windows are angled into a slight bay, which somehow makes the rooms feel ritzier than they really are. Rates may vary from the Chelsea by a few bucks here and there, depending on prior bookings. Third in the company's set of area motels with free parking is the **Lombard Motor Inn** (1475 Lombard St., at Van Ness; ☎ 415/441-6000; www.lombardmotorinn.com; AE, MC, V), which costs the same but is least preferable of the trio because it's located at the noisy intersection of Van Ness Avenue. On the positive side, you can walk to Fisherman's Wharf in about 10 minutes from it. Lombard Street can be a little harried in this part of town, so for all three of these motels, secure a room at the back if you notice the usual street noise.

$–$$ Rates are best during the week at the 50-room **Buena Vista Motor Inn** ★ (1599 Lombard St., at Gough; ☎ 800/835-4980; www.buenavistamotorinn.com; AE, MC, V), and they spike from around $80 to $110 or $120 on weekend nights. The look of the rooms is your standard, inoffensive mid-'90s design—it's not that it's personality-free, but just that it has the personality of a motel. Fortunately, the building was renovated a few years back. There is a small rooftop sundeck for guests' use. This is one of the few properties to offer smoking rooms. If you get a deal, take it, but overall, the above Marina properties are zestier.

$–$$ The way to get the best prices out of the 23-room **Town House Motel** (1650 Lombard St., at Octavia; ☎ 800/255-1516 or 415/885-5163; www.sftown housemotel.com; AE, MC, V) is to book online, where deals are around $75, as opposed to $90 to $120 by phone, for a king room. The facilities are boxy and very 1950s, with a similarly utilitarian continental breakfast thrown in. The building is L-shaped, a fact that doesn't provide the sound baffling from traffic that's available at the Del Sol or the Chelsea. Parking is free, but other hotels in the neighborhood have more style for the same price, to say nothing of more cheerful staff. I mention this one as a good second-choice option.

$$$ Popular with the keyboard-punchers who work at Lucasfilm's digital imaging complex in the nearby Presidio, the three-floor, 57-room **Hotel del Sol** ★ (3100 Webster St.; ☎ 415/921-5520; www.jdvhotels.com; AE, MC, V) may have started life as an also-ran motel, but the discerning Joie de Vivre hotel group has accentuated its California style while losing any lingering grottiness. Rooms, slightly larger than the city norm, feature contemporary art (sometimes, the works are for sale), fresh furniture, and bright colors (canary-yellow walls). At the center of it all, a heated pool oasis takes the sting off a rare sweltering day. Walls could stand to be thicker, and you have to remember to close your blinds because windows overlook the hotel's walkways, but in all, partly because its courtyard is completely enclosed, the del Sol is a good place to avoid the crushing sense of urbanism that crowds more-central properties, which is why it charges a little more than the other motels in the neighborhood. And those towering, holiday-lit palm trees in the courtyard are cheerful. Parking's free, too, which is a boon.

CIVIC CENTER

This part of town has a more banal personality than many others owing mostly to its heavily governmental presence. However, it's midway on the BART/Muni lines between the Castro/Haight zone and the Union Square/Tenderloin/Financial District one, which makes it well located if you don't plan on spending lots of time in your room. The trendy dining-and-shopping corridor of Hayes Valley is a short walk west.

$ A concrete bunker packed with 391 comfortable but careworn rooms, **Cathedral Hill Hotel** (1101 Van Ness Ave., at Post; ☎ 415/776-8200; www.cathedralhillhotel. com; AE, MC, V) is suspended in a busy no-man's-land between the Civic Center area, Nob Hill, and the Tenderloin, which means that at night, many patrons may feel more comfortable getting home in a taxi and not walking. With so many rooms, standards vary, and the small outdoor pool isn't alluring, but here, it's about price and not about a resort experience. A standard queen room, with one bed (a king or a queen), goes for around $89, and if you add $20, you can get two beds, sleeping four. Pay much more than that and you could have done better elsewhere, even considering the full buffet breakfast each morning. This hotel crops up a lot on Priceline.com.

$–$$ The building housing **Hotel Whitcomb** ★★ (1231 Market St., at Hyde; ☎ 415/626-8000; www.hotelwhitcomb.com; AE, MC, V) has a historic pedigree, having served as the city hall in the rebuilding years following the great earthquake, and it still retains some grand architectural flourishes in its lobby. So given that pedigree, and considering the grand introduction it presents to guests, it's a surprise to find prices from $79 to $99 for a modern, standard room many times of year. Perhaps the rates are kept low because there are 460 rooms to fill, and perhaps people are put off by the location on a patch of Market that's slowly (but perhaps not quickly enough) crawling out of hard times. Happily, buses and trams to just about everywhere else in town leave from right out the front door—a perk that's rarer than you'd think. Whatever the reason, digs meet a high standard for what you get; the hotel used to be the Ramada Plaza, and retains its corporate-level business travel amenities, including free in-room Internet. Bathrooms are only a few years old in general, and the management is attentive to rebuilding the property into being a strong contender in the affordable-hotel market. Unsurprisingly, it's growing in popularity among budgeters.

$$–$$$ This super-cool spot has just 44 rooms, and it's still a motel at heart, but the highly recommended **Phoenix Hotel** ★★★ (601 Eddy St., at Larkin; ☎ 800/248-9466 or 415/776-1380; www.jdvhotels.com/phoenix) has been going strong for more than 20 years and is one of Joie de Vivre Hotels' greatest treasures. The Bambuddha Lounge is popular beyond nightly guests, and the clientele of the hotel itself tends to the young side, so either enjoy a good party or be a heavy sleeper (walls are on the thin side). Rooms are festively colored but nothing more special than the typical motel—instead, it's the courtyard, with heated pool and piped-in music, that gets guests excited and returning for later visits. It's a quick hop from here to the dining scene at Hayes Street. Stay here and you can park for free, and you may sign up for a free city tour with Joie de Vivre's proprietary hospitality group, Golden Gate Greeters. For a motel with personality, social butterflies won't be disappointed. Rates go from $119 to $150 most times of year.

HAYES VALLEY & JAPANTOWN

These quieter neighborhoods require a bus to reach from the tourist-friendly parts of town. However, because they're located where locals tend to live, they're often near interesting eating and drinking areas, making evenings fun.

$–$$ The 28-room **Hayes Valley Inn** ★★★ (417 Gough St., at Hayes; ☎ 800/930-7999 or 415/431-9131; www.hayesvalleyinn.com; AE, MC, V) has small quarters, but it's priced well for what you get: $84 to $92 for two people on a double bed or $76 for a single, including continental breakfast. Like many San Francisco hotels of this price, it's privately owned and operated, except in this case, the owner's cocker spaniel may be seen roaming around the property. Each room is different, though they all share a rather dated look. Still, they're comfortable and each has an in room sink, TV, phone and shares a bath, European-style. Its prime room is the extra-bright Turret Room, which has a corner view through old-fashioned rounded-glass windows for $112. The neighborhood has much to recommend it, too; the trendy shopping and dining drag of Hayes Street is just a few blocks north, and the Civic Center's museum cluster is just east.

$$$ Sure, at heart, its size and motel-style amenities reveal it as the 1975-built Best Western it is, but in 2007, the 125-room **Hotel Tomo** ★★★ (1800 Sutter St., at Buchanan; ☎ 888/822-8666 or 415/921-4000; www.jdvhotels.com/tomo; AE, MC, V) was given a funky pop art re-imagining. The look is now hysterically bombastic, like something by Murakami, with enormous psychedelic wall paintings, glow-in-the-dark desk blotters, neon paint jobs, and Fatboy beanbag chairs for lounging in each room. West-facing rooms have the best view, but they're also situated over a schoolyard, which can make mornings noisy. Another downside is the general dearth of electrical outlets, which the Japanese themselves would never tolerate. The $159 rate is a touch higher than it ought to be for a Best Western–style deal, but overall, the bright colors and offbeat touches, as well as solid amenities (free Wi-Fi, a safe, and in-room tea and coffee), plus huge beds and iPod docks, put the joint into the mix and make a stay here a happy affair. On the second floor, the restaurant Mums jams in the evenings with its all-you-can-eat shabu-shabu (Japanese family-style hot pot). Japantown is slightly on the dull side, but a 15-minute bus ride brings you to Union Square, or you can walk 2 blocks west to the many pubs and boutiques of Fillmore Street.

$$$ Although the high-rise it's in was built in the late 1960s and served as a Westin for years, a fall 2007 renovation gave the 218-room **Hotel Kabuki** ★★ (1625 Post St., at Laguna; ☎ 800/533-4567 or 415/922-3200; www.jdvhotels.com/kabuki; AE, MC, V) an interesting, groovy Japanese personality suited to its location in the heart of Japantown. Just about everything it does strives to evoke Japanese culture by way of a comfortable Western hotel, starting with the free hot-tea service available at any time in every room and continuing with iPod docks in every room. The bathrooms are built more like wet rooms, with a bench in the tub area and a sheet explaining how to use the area to bathe Japanese-style, if you wish. Windows, which by virtue of the hotel's position on a hill, offer excellent views across the city, are concealed by sliding screens come bedtime. Even the carpets are designed to look like authentic tatami mats. Downstairs, there's a trendy cocktail bar and small-dish restaurant, O Izakaya Lounge. Every day there's a free sake tasting, and on Saturday mornings, a free origami class is conducted in the lobby overlooking a Zen garden. Guests may also sign up for a free tour with a Golden Gate Greeter, local volunteers organized by the hotel's owners (Joie de Vivre Hotels) to share the city with visitors on walking tours of 2 to 4 hours. Also choice is the location at the eastern end of a mini-mall of thoroughly authentic Japanese restaurants and shops. This is a case of a hotel with prices that are cheaper on weekdays than weekends. Weekday rates are about $129, and prices go up to $159 on weekends, when the place is popular with Fillmore Street clubgoers, and corner rooms are usually about $30 more. For a splurge, I like the Executive Sauna Suites, which have their own sitting areas and, yes, their own private Japanese sauna; those come in around $190.

$$$–$$$$ The building housing the atmospheric **The Queen Anne** ★★★ (1590 Sutter St., at Octavia; ☎ 800/227-3970 or 415/441-2828; www.queenanne.com; AE, MC, V) is so architecturally important that it's the first stop of the daily walking tour offered by the Victorian Home Walk (p. 129). Back in the day, it was a live-in finishing school for girls, and now it's a lovingly restored B&B with rich dark wainscoting, inlaid wood floors, and a remarkably wide stairway atrium that's open all the way up to a colored-glass skylight. Its ground-floor parlor is stuffed with antiques and upholstered sofas, drips with crimson draperies, and burns warmly with a gas fire—it feels like stepping into the past. Accommodations in the 48 rooms are also charming, if less ornate, and start at $140 in winter before jumping about 40% in summer. Beds are notably soft. Room 208 is used for wheelchair-using guests, which means the bathroom is enormous; ask if it's booked. A stay comes with a morning paper, continental breakfast, and afternoon sherry and cookies in the parlor.

THE MISSION & THE CASTRO

Not historically the favored locations for stays, these areas are gaining traction amongst those who want to sleep away from the briefcase crowd. Part of the rebirth is owed to the Mission, which over the last generation has become *the* place in town for hip cafes, clubs, eating, and shopping. The Castro, as always, attracts the Rainbow Flag crew, although in truth its westerly location on the map puts it far away from the major city attractions. Both areas, though, are suited to those who plan to have a nightlife in town.

$ Few large properties in the Mission have managed to crawl very far out of flophouse status, but it's gradually happening thanks to places such as 40-unit **The Hotel Tropicana** (603 Valencia St., between 17th and 18th; ☎ 415/701-7666; www.thehoteltropicana.com; MC, V), which charges an unheard-of $299 a week (no nightly rates) for shared-bath units with kitchenette (fridge/freezer, microwave, but no burners or ovens) and TV with cable. For your own bathroom, add $100 per week, which is still fantastic. Colors are bright and merry, with a bubbly tropical theme by way of IKEA, and the facilities are spotlessly taken care of—so much so that it looks brand-new. Even the guests seem more bushy-tailed than those typically attracted to places with weekly rates. I'd suggest you think twice about many blocks in the Mission, but this one is quickly gentrifying and plenty of cool, hipstery, and buzzed-about places to eat are within quick walking

Still Gay, Still Proud

San Francisco has long been known as a bastion of gay culture, so it only makes sense that there are a few guesthouses catering to a gay crowd. Not as many as there once were—society has changed and gay folks are welcomed at even the most mainstream hotels nowadays—but a few nonetheless.

$–$$ Although pretty much every hotel in town will support same-sex couples sharing a bed, some gay visitors will prefer gay-owned accommodations. One of the most affordable is the five-room **24 Henry Guesthouse** (24 Henry St.; ☎ 800/900-5686 or 415/864-5686; www.24henry.com; MC, V), where the majority of B&B rooms in the residential Castro District, which is well connected by several streetcar lines, cost from $75 to $95, plus $10 if you're only staying a single night. Naturally, each room was individually designed with pride by Walter, a man who liked staying here so much that he bought the whole building, a former residence that went up in the 1880s. The owners live in the same building, but on a different floor—you share the main entrance, but that's all. The same owners also have **Village House** (4080 18th St., at Castro; ☎ 800/900-5686 or 415/864-0994; www.24henry.com), which meets the same adorable standard but is priced about $10 more by virtue of being on the slightly more happening side of Market Street. At both, local calls are free, as is Wi-Fi; the Village House even has a piano you can play. They're both straight-friendly, although kids aren't invited.

$$–$$$ Slightly more expensive, and explicitly pitched to gay and lesbian clientele, is the 12-room, shared-bath **Willows Inn Bed & Breakfast** (710 14th St., at Church; ☎ 800/431-0277 or 415/431-4770; www.willows sf.com). All rooms, which have a mild pink-bamboo theme but are essentially classy, have a fridge, a sink, and kimono bathrobes (how *fabulous*) and rates start at $105 for two in a tiny room to $145 for two or $165 for four in the two-bedroom suite, which is a great deal. The location, which is perfectly safe, is divine—steps from the streetcar and a 10-minute walk down Market to Castro Street. Because it's so anything-goes, this is the place to stay if you plan to wear your leather panties in public.

distance. The nearest BART station is just 2 blocks away, which is hugely handy for reaching the sights. The family that runs things also lives on the premises (so the halls smell like South Asian meals during dinnertimes, which is frustrating when you can't have any), but don't expect stellar service just because of that fact. The owners must take a lot of grief from ne'er-do-well locals, because they seem to cast a suspicious eye on everyone. It's a very inexpensive crash pad, no matter how the chipper paint job may work to convince you to expect more.

$$$ There's good news and bad news concerning **The Inn San Francisco** (943 S. Van Ness Ave., near 21st; ☎ 415/641-0188; www.innsf.com; MC, V). On the bright side, it's charming, romantic, and full of antiques. Spending the night in a true Painted Lady is not as common as you'd think it would be in a city famous for them, but here, the privilege is yours. Given the antique construction, there are lots of stairs and rooms are tiny, but the homey sweetness of it all enables you to look past the shortcomings, and it's not too far from either the Castro (a 15-minute walk) or BART (10 minutes). Unfortunately, the dicey neighborhood (the Mission) is more of a problem; some guests will feel uneasy walking back to their hotel after sunset, even if only 4 blocks west some of the city's hippest restaurants are packing them in. The most affordable rooms are $145 with a private bath; subtract $25 if you're willing to share a bath with a minimum of other guests. For big rooms, the rate soars to $215, which would be more appropriate for a romantic weekend away. The included breakfast buffet is generous, and in the backyard, there's a sweet little wooden hot tub.

HOSTELS

San Francisco's long-running bohemian subculture, in combination with the fact that the city is on the "must-see" checklist of virtually every international back-packer, supports some excellent hostels. In fact, one of the choices may be considered the coolest independent hostels in the country, and its popularity spawned a line of popular backpacker bus tours around North America. Have your ID handy, because all local hostels require it in order to keep the riffraff from checking in and not checking out. Linens and towels will be included, but if you want to use a locker, it's smart to have your own lock. And, no, hostels don't require chores or enforce a curfew anymore.

$ The reliable, impersonal option is **HI Downtown** ✖ (213 Mason St., at Ellis; ☎ 415/788-5604; www.sfhostels.com; AE, DISC, MC, V), installed in a 1920s stone hotel a block west of Union Square. The desk staff is efficient but not terribly warm. Dorms cost $24 and come with one shared bath per room, and there are 39 private rooms, too, for $59 with a shared bath and $69 for a private one; prices rise about $10 on weekends and $20 when things are exceptionally busy. Guests who aren't already members of Hostelling International can still stay here—they just pay another $3. The hostel, which throws in a free continental breakfast and at least one free walking tour of the city each day, is among a thicket of car-rental companies, which may make it a smart option for people who plan to hop a car for the hills. As with most HI properties, there's a kitchen for guest use. There's a smaller HI near the **City Center** (685 Ellis St.; ☎ 415/474-5721; www.sfhostels.com), but this one is better located, so use the City Center one only as a fallback.

$ HI also runs an excellent, 142-bed hostel in a historic building within **HI Fisherman's Wharf** (Building 240, Fort Mason; enter Fort Mason at Bay and Franklin streets; ☎ 415/771-7277). This one's called the Fisherman's Wharf location, but it's really a good 15-minute walk west of there. If you stay there, you'll be able to wake up every morning and look out the window of the former military outpost at a million-dollar view of the beautiful Golden Gate Bridge in the sunrise. In fact, there's not a hotel in town, expensive or cheap, with a better view, and it's a treat to be able to sleep in one of the city's most historic maritime areas. You'll also get free parking (but don't leave anything valuable inside the car) and a free morning yoga class (how San Francisco!). However, that's the hostel's main draw; despite its quality, it's otherwise much too far away from most sights to be convenient, and not everyone will feel comfortable with how deserted Fort Mason is after dark.

$　Small and friendly, with none of the grotty party atmosphere that dominates other hostels (are you listening, Green Tortoise?), **Pacific Tradewinds** ★★★ (680 Sacramento St., at Kearny; ☎ 415/433-7970; www.sanfranciscohostel.org; AE, MC, V) has a truly helpful staff. Metal bunks are sturdy, linens are clean, and, praise be, so is the well-stocked kitchen. The hostel is the ideal size for friendly intimacy; not so big that you feel like a number, but not so small that you feel scrutinized. Beds are $26 in mixed-gender dorms. The neighborhood is slightly bland, but it's safe and it's close to North Beach and Chinatown, where things are more eclectic.

$　The choice for those who want to stay around Union Square in a place with some personality, the independent **Adelaide Hostel** (5 Isadora Duncan Lane, off Taylor between Geary and Post; ☎ 877/359-1915 or 415/359-1915; www.adelaidehostel.com; AE, DC, DISC, MC, V), tucked down a quiet side alley on the acceptable end of the Tenderloin, is attractive and cozy. There's a free continental breakfast, free Wi-Fi (why is it that even cheap hostels give free Wi-Fi, when the fancy hotels charge $15 a day?), and a giant homey lounge full of soft couches, antique lamps, and a thoughtful aura. Whereas some hostels encourage long-term dropouts to overstay their welcomes, this one never feels grotty or hopeless. Reception is 24 hours (manned by a flaky staff), and each night, a three-course dinner (soup, salad, and a main course) is cooked (in the equipped kitchen that all guests can use) for an incredible $5 a head, only for guests. Dorms (in 4-, 6-, and 10-bed flavors) start at $23, and private rooms (single or double; they're in the Dakota Hotel around the corner so they aren't part of the charm) go for $60. The hostel can also hook you up with $45 shuttle-bus rides to Los Angeles. This place books up quickly.

$　The location of the famous **Green Tortoise** ★★★ (494 Broadway, at Kearny; ☎ 800/867-8647 or 415/834-1000; www.greentortoise.com; AE, MC, V), in a well-loved old building and famous for spawning a celebrated backpackers' tour company, is both a blessing and a curse. Because it's in the middle of North Beach and on the fringe of Chinatown, two fascinating neighborhoods, you'll find lots of appealing things to eat and see. But it's not particularly near many rapid-transit lines, so you'll be walking and taking buses a lot. Also, its stretch of Broadway is full of strip joints, but don't let that worry you—it's unsavory but safe, and in free-spirited North Beach, titillation is permitted to exist for diversity's sake, not because the 'hood has gone to seed. Complete with wooden bunks and mural-slathered walls, it captures the anything-goes character of North Beach, down to frequent parties (which should inform you of the ideal clientele). For $25 to $29 a dorm bed (depending on the season), lots comes free, including breakfast, a cooked dinner three times a week, a sauna, and Internet. There's a fully equipped communal kitchen for cooking up all those North Beach grocery finds, and the hostel also offers private rooms (with TV/VCRs) for $60 to $72. If you want a quiet hostel, go with HI, but if you're in the mood to mingle, the Tortoise, endearingly shabby, is it. You must have an out-of-state ID to stay here, and you might be asked for proof of future travel bookings to prove that you don't plan to move in for months. The operators run regular summertime Hostel Hopper shuttles to Las Vegas ($59) and Los Angeles ($39).

4

Dining for All Tastes

This town knows food—and now you'll know some of its best value secrets

SAN FRANCISCO IS A FOODIE TOWN. THE PEOPLE HERE CARE ABOUT cooking styles, quality, provenance, and the nuances of flavors. Whereas experienced diners on America's East Coast might rave about the execution of the chef, diners in San Francisco are just as likely to praise the high quality of the ingredients themselves, many of which will come from the wealth of the farms in the region. The famous California Cuisine trend—local ingredients, prepared fusion-style with an elegant, artistic presentation—was started by chef Alice Waters across the Bay in Berkeley, and its careful blend of experimentation and exclusive provenance is now dominant across the entire dining scene. But it's never been known as a cheap style. Something about arty food seems to command yuppie prices.

You don't have to press against your credit limit, though, to partake in San Francisco's ongoing feast. The city is awash with a changing landscape of little come-and-go restaurants where young chefs try to make their names with assiduously selected and prepared dishes, and each neighborhood contains at least one hole in the wall that the glossy cooking magazine may ignore but about which locals are intensely possessive. In the Mission, the dish of choice is mighty, weighty burritos. In North Beach, you're more likely to come across Italian or fresh-baked goods. Fisherman's Wharf, of course, is where to find the day's catch. I'll introduce you to many of the smaller, local, often ethnic places where you can eat a full meal for less (often far less) than $20. And these places care deeply about their food—they just aren't all that precious about it. I've also dug up some ideas

Click & Chew

Bay Area residents love their food, but they also love the Internet, and there are a number of sites where locals regularly post reviews of pretty much every restaurant in town in an apparent effort to prove they know their stuff. The sheer volume of postings, high for any city, means that it's easy to make a judgment call about a prospective place based on the accumulation of opinions. Some establishments have been known to plant a few raves about themselves (and rivals plant pans), but if you take the average of the comments, you'll probably get a fair concept of the true quality of the place. Check out the restaurant news blog **Eater** (http://sf.eater.com) and the reader review site **Chowhound** (www.chowhound.com). The busiest of the bunch is **Yelp** (www.yelp.com).

Where Are the Arches?

If you're a grease addict, you might need help finding chain restaurants such as Wendy's and McDonald's, because there are almost none of them anywhere in town. In many neighborhoods, in fact, there are rules stating that if a store has more than a few locations anywhere in the country, it must go through a special permit process to open another here. It's a permit process that the stores almost always fail. But of course, even if it existed, I wouldn't be listing such industrial food, because you can get that at home. Interestingly, even the few fast-food counters that do exist try hard to fit in with the food snobbery that prevails in town; at one Burger King near the Civic Center, there's a sticker on the soda machine suggesting pairings for the soft drinks—apparently, Sprite goes best with Chicken Fries. Isn't that ridiculous?

for ordering styles that will win you entrée (pun intended) to some of those normally exorbitant gourmet palaces.

MAIN DISHES   I try to give you some sense of prices in each entry, but the dollar signs preceding each one give you a ballpark range for main dishes at dinner (lunch is usually a few bucks cheaper). Sure, some might be higher, some lower, but most of what each place serves falls into these ranges:

$	$8 and under
$$	$9 to $12
$$$	$13 to $17
$$$$	$18 and up

Yep, that's cheap! In fact, a few are locally adored but nationally anonymous hash-slingers under fluorescent lights—with amazing, affordable food. It's easy to find places in San Francisco where prices are $30 a plate and where folks with money to burn fall over themselves to get in. What you really need help with are locating the worthwhile no-name spots, the superlative greasy spoons, the beloved neighborhood purveyors of classic ethnic eats, and the deals on gourmet meals.

Unlike in many cities, it's relatively unusual to find a restaurant, particularly one dedicated to gourmet or fine dining, where you can sit down for a truly late meal. Many upscale places cringe at starting a service after 9pm or 10pm. If you plan to eat that late, call ahead to make sure your chosen establishment still serves full meals then. The same places that eschew late hours are also less likely to be open for lunch; for them, dinner is the great masterpiece that takes all day to prepare. Plenty of the more pedestrian kitchens gladly serve until the wee hours.

Important note: Don't be shocked or angered if your bill includes an extra charge labeled "healthcare" or something similar. The city recently mandated that restaurants must provide health benefits to all full-time employees, and some places choose to raise the extra expense that way instead of folding it into the cost of the meal.

UNION SQUARE

Because it's such a draw for tourists, Union Square is not the cheapest place to find food. Places gouge, cooking standards lag, and you're left with a lot of pricey tourist traps, pubs serving standard fare not worth our notice here, and corporate joints such as the Cheesecake Factory. It's not like you can't eat cheaply here—but it's not where the most worthwhile tables are. There are some exceptions, of course, and I've listed them below.

$ The ever-busy **King of Thai Noodle** ✪ (184 O'Farrell St., at Powell; ☎ 415/ 677-9991; daily 11am–1am; cash only) attracts a fair number of Asian shoppers not only for its affordable prices but for its authenticity. The look could be generously called "contemporary," if Home Depot–style fixtures are contemporary, but the cooking is solid and traditional, and prices are uniformly under $8—not so common. The pad Thai, always a test of a Thai place, automatically comes with shrimp (like the Thais themselves eat it), isn't too sweet, and has a nice twinge of spice to it. Trays of sauces are laid out on every table if you'd like your flavors even hotter or sweeter. If the tables fill up, there's a long counter at the side for more casual eating.

$–$$ Another good Thai option near Union Square, this one popular with families with kids, **Thai Stick** 🧒 (698 Post St., at Jones; ☎ 415/928-7730; www. thaisticksf.com; daily 11am–1am; MC, V) hits the spot (and without high prices— it's just $8–$10 for the standard Thai dishes). It's not common to find a Thai place that has *larb,* a spicy blend of ground chicken, lime, mint, and chilies, so take this chance to try some (but make sure you've got plenty of water on hand). It's also not too common to find a Thai place where kids are a prime customer, but each time here, I've seen several families eating happily. The pumpkin curry is another popular specialty.

$$–$$$ Major points are awarded to **Indonesia Restaurant** (678–680 Post St., at Jones; ☎ 415/474-4026; daily 11:30am–2:30pm and 5–10pm; MC, V) for the food, which hews closely to traditional recipes from its namesake country—rich, meaty, and big on the spice. Many dishes are served family-style (the better to sample more flavors). Carnivores will be pleased, since many of the options are thick stews or otherwise meat-based. Management puts on a show of service, so it wouldn't be a bad place to take your sweetie for something different, but don't expect flashiness—a low-rent slide show playing on a laptop in the window serves as the major advertisement to passersby and the space is cavernous and simple. I particularly enjoyed the *ayam kalasan* (fried, honey-marinated half-chicken). The lunch special is a strong value, buying portions of two entrees along with rice and steamed mixed vegetables with peanut sauce—all for just $8.50.

$$–$$$ A few doors away, **Borobudur** (700 Post St., at Jones; ☎ 415/775-1512; www.borobudursf.com; Mon–Thurs 11:30am–10pm, Fri–Sat 11:30am–11pm, Sun 1–10pm; MC, V) is another Indonesian place that eases up a bit on the spice, which

Dining in Union Square

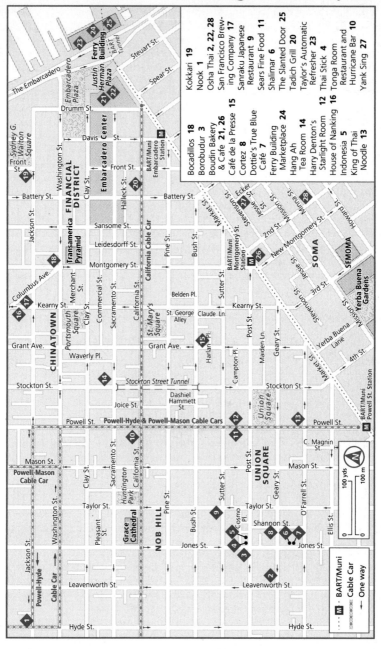

Bocadillos **18**
Borobudur **3**
Boudin Bakery & Cafe **21, 26**
Café de la Presse **15**
Cortez **8**
Dottie's True Blue Café **7**
Ferry Building Marketplace **24**
Hang Ah Tea Room **14**
Harry Denton's Starlight Room **12**
House of Nanking **16**
Indonesia **5**
King of Thai Noodle **13**
Kokkari **19**
Nook **1**
Osha Thai **2, 22, 28**
San Francisco Brewing Company **17**
Sanraku Japanese Restaurant **9**
Sears Fine Food **11**
Shalimar **6**
The Slanted Door **25**
Tadich Grill **20**
Taylor's Automatic Refresher **23**
Thai Stick **4**
Tonga Room Restaurant and Hurricane Bar **10**
Yank Sing **27**

may please those who have never tried the cuisine before. I could dine all day on the *roti prata*, which is stringy, pan-fried bread served with curry dipping sauce—a treat in Indonesia and Malaysia. That seems to be a theme here—food is not strictly Indonesian, but endemic to Muslim Southeast Asia in general. Don't make the mistake of tempting the chefs to hurt you by asking for dishes to be made hot—they will. For dessert, the black rice pudding stands astride sweet and salty—either you can't get enough of it or a single spoonful will do. Even among Indonesian-descended diners, there's an ongoing debate concerning which of these two restaurants do things best.

$$–$$$ A Union Square institution since 1938, **Sears Fine Food** ★★ (439 Powell St., at Sutter; ☎ 415/986-0700; www.searsfinefood.com; daily 6:30am–10pm; AE, MC, V) is famous for serving mini Swedish pancakes—18 delicious little ones per plate, to be exact, served only until 3pm for some odd reason ($8). You can order diner-style dishes such as burgers, pot roast, and sea bass, too ($14–$24), but the best value is in the breakfast foods. I've endured some horrific service train wrecks here, but I find it endurable when I'm not in a hurry because the scene—a crowded dining room that looks a little like a greasy spoon and a lot like an old saloon—is so old-fashioned and yet still energetic. Sit at the bar, for example, and you're as likely to be next to a wide-eyed tourist as you are beside a newspaper-reading matron who has her bowl of clam chowder here every day of the week. It makes some 77,000 pancakes a week, most of those on weekends when a line of brunch-goers stretches out the front door.

NORTH BEACH & TELEGRAPH HILL

North Beach is heavily touristed, so you'll find lots of spots that glide by on foot traffic despite higher-than-necessary prices and plainer-than-acceptable food. In general, this is not the area you go to for novel dishes, but it's where you head for classics, or with your mom on her birthday.

$ Greasy as you please, **Buster's** 🧒 (366 Columbus, at Vallejo; ☎ 415/392-2800; daily 11am–2am; cash only) is probably the best place in town to pick up a Philly-style cheese steak. Seating's at the counter, where you can observe the cook scatter and grill the meat. The bright-yellow walls could use a good sponge, but otherwise, the food is quick and manly, and everything's made to order. Choose from five types of cheese topping including, of course, Cheez Whiz, as every Philly fan would insist upon. From the fridge, pull out a bottled Mexican Coke, which are made with real sugar and not the industrial high-fructose corn syrup that makes American-made Coke so cheap. A small sandwich costs $5.50 and is more than enough food for most people.

$–$$ My favorite North Beach Italian restaurant, **L'Osteria del Forno** ★★★ (519 Columbus Ave., at Green; ☎ 415/982-1124; www.losteriadelforno.com; Wed–Mon, 11:30am–10pm, closed Tues; cash only) is everything a family-run restaurant ought to be—sensible prices, attentive service, a lovely central location, and a 12-table dining room, which has yellow walls that gently evoke Tuscany but is ultimately as unfussy as the food. Arrive early unless you want to wait because

Bocadillos **20**
Brandy Ho's **17**
Buster's **11**
Caffe Roma Coffee
  Roasting Co. **5**
Caffe Trieste **12**
Capp's Corner **8**
Da Flora **1**
Dol Ho **16**

Gold Mountain **14**
Hang Ah Tea Room **21**
Hing Lung Restaurant **15**
The House **13**
House of Nanking **18**
Italian French Baking
  Company **6**
Liguria Bakery **3**
L'Osteria del Forno **7**

Mama's **2**
Mario's Bohemian
  Cigar Store Cafe **4**
Molinari Delicatessen **10**
San Francisco Brewing
  Company **19**
Victoria Pastry Co. **9**

La Boulange
543 Columbus Ave.
415-399-0714

locals prize this place, run by two Italian women since 1990. At one point during a recent meal, I accidentally dropped a knife on the floor. Even though the waitress was across the room, she noticed, and I had a new one within 10 seconds without having to ask. Salads are $6 to $9, but the best dishes are the pizzas (just $5–$7) or the oven-baked dishes—try the *crespelle*, crepes filled with porcini mushrooms and topped with béchamel sauce ($12). One thing you won't find lots of is pasta; there are a few dishes, but the chef generally likes to come up with more adventurous oven-baked items such as pumpkin-filled ravioli and Cornish hen roasted in white wine.

$$ Here's what stinks about tiny **Mama's** ✹ (1701 Stockton St., at Filbert; ☎ 415/362-6421; Tues–Sun 8am–3pm; cash only): the lines. Especially on weekends, it can stretch around the block and take more than an hour to get through. The reason, of course, is that the breakfast food is delicious, and servings are generous. Like Dottie's near Union Square (p. 72), it's a beloved brunch institution that deals in comfort classics, but unlike Dottie's, which is in the Tenderloin, you won't feel uneasy waiting outside of Mama's, which is in the heart of homey North Beach. To stand a chance of getting in, arrive around 2pm, keep your party small, or come on a weekday. The signature dish is the Monte Cristo, served with homemade jam (there's a pot on every table), but the chocolate cinnamon toast, smothered in chocolate sauce, also has its believers. Dishes are mostly under $13.

$–$$ Up to seven house-made beers, none of them pasteurized or filtered (so they're packed with flavor) are served at **San Francisco Brewing Company** (155 Columbus Ave., at Pacific; ☎ 415/434-3344; www.sfbrewing.com; daily noon–1am; AE, MC, V) each day; they're $4.75 per bottle, if you prefer it that way, or $9.25 by the gallon, if you're crazy-thirsty. Your pint will be served warm, as is the British style. All are served at a fabulous mahogany bar, and both the tile floor and the ornate skylit ceiling date to the early days of the 20th century. Between 4pm and 6pm daily, most beers are just $1 a glass and $1.75 a pint. There's pub-level food, of course, along the lines of burgers, gumbo, and a sausage sandwich that's made on the premises ($7–$9). Mondays, Thursdays, and Saturdays after 8:30pm or 9pm, there's live entertainment—usually jazz. In good weather, the seating out front are a sublime place to watch the characters of Columbus Avenue glide by.

$$$–$$$$ A persistent stereotype of North Beach, no longer apt, is that it's a hotbed of old-fashioned red-sauce and meatball joints. That might have been so a generation ago, but most of those have long since disappeared. One exception is **Capp's Corner** ✹ (1600 Powell St.; ☎ 415/989-2589; www.cappscorner.com; daily 11:30am–2:30pm and 4:30–10:30pm; AE, DC, MC, V), which is the type of a sweet trattoria you've possibly been fantasizing about—family-run since forever, red-checked oilcloth covering the tables, walls hung with old San Francisco photos and memorabilia, and a waitress with a gentle smart mouth. It's the sort of place you wouldn't mind going to every afternoon with a newspaper when you're an old codger. Meals are served family-style, meaning they're shared, and come at two price levels: $17.50 or $20 per person ($13 for kids) for minestrone soup, salad, and a main (such as pasta, veal Milanese, or my favorite, veal tortellini in sun-dried tomato cream sauce). Food is excellent but homey, meatballs are moist, and service is quick enough to shuttle guests through in time for the curtain at *Beach Blanket Babylon* a few doors down.

$$$$ If you want to get lucky, take your date to snug, burgundy-red **Da Flora** ★★ (701 Columbus Ave., at Filbert; ☎ 415/981-4664; Tues–Sat 6–9:30pm; MC, V), a Venetian-Italian restaurant owned by a female (Flora, the Hungarian owner) and where a female chef is handling the pans—together, these ladies know how to unlock the romanticism. The handwritten menu changes often, especially seasonally, and the list of Italian wines (again, curated by Flora, who knows her stuff) is distinguished by unusual selections. Quiet, calm, and dim, it serves some excellent classics: sweet potato gnocchi is a standout, and the salty-fluffy focaccia is made daily. The pork chops are massive, but my favorite dish is a dessert: a lemon pistachio cake that mostly consists of actual crushed nuts. It's not a definite money-saver—a full meal could hit you for $50—but in North Beach, where truly tasty Italian is not that easy to find anymore, it's worth savoring, and it makes for a very "local" special-occasion selection. And after all, lots of folks come to San Francisco for romantic getaways, and this place is the tonic.

$$$–$$$$ Small, cramped, and absolutely requiring reservations, the Asian-fusion cuisine of **The House** ★★★ (1230 Grant Ave., at Broadway; ☎ 415/986-8612; www.thehse.com; Sun–Thurs 11am–2:30pm and 5:30–10pm, Fri–Sat 11am–2:30pm and 5:30–11pm; MC, V) takes a little advance planning to obtain, but The House is nonetheless a favorite place to eat for many locals, even if they can only afford to go on for celebrations or for lunch. I guess that's my tip here: Go for that meal, and you'll pay around $12 for what would cost twice that at twilight. If you really want to dine here after dark, expect to pay about $35 per person with drinks. The menu is just long enough to promise uniformly inventive dishes, all twists on Asian food, such as flank steak with wasabi noodles and pomegranate-currant pork chops—that sort of cleverness. The grilled sea bass is considered to be one of its signature dishes, but I can honestly say that I've never had anything here that wasn't delicious.

FISHERMAN'S WHARF

The base of Pier 45 hosts several competing seafood restaurants as well as fresh and fried fish and crab at booths out front. Just compare the day's catch and prices of Fisherman's Grotto 🦀 by walking along the short, steaming run of establishments—even most locals agree that because of the vagaries of the day's catch, and the fact that the stalls' deep-frying methods level the playing field, there's no one booth that you simply *must* visit. The major players include Tarantino's, Guardino's, Nick's Lighthouse, and Sabella & La Torre. Bring cash, and be very alert for the seagulls, which are aggressive . . . and incontinent. In the beginning of the year, when they're in season, the big score is Dungeness crab. Whole crabs go for about $10 a pound.

But be aware that if you sit down at the indoor dining rooms, you'll rest your feet but you'll also pay tourist prices.

Many locals feel that the better seafood in town is to be had a bus ride away at the Swan Oyster Depot (p. 84). Don't forget that the San Francisco map is crowded, so the restaurants of North Beach, listed a few pages back, are also a 10- to 15-minute walk southeast.

$ The producer of what's probably the most beloved fast-food burger in America, **In-N-Out Burger** ★★★ 🧒 (333 Jefferson St., at Leavenworth; no phone; www.in-n-out.com; MC, V; daily 10:30am–1am) occupies a near-mythic role in the Western American burger lover's palette—yet, their loss, most Midwesterners and Easterners have never even heard of it. The chain, which is 100% privately owned and serves no pre-frozen food, began in Los Angeles in the late 1940s and judicious expansion has restricted its fewer-than-100 precious locations to three states: California, Nevada, and Arizona. This is the only one in San Francisco. You'd never know it from the menu posted in the restaurant (which is led by the Double Double, a double cheeseburger), but there's a second, "secret" menu available—every In-N-Out fan knows the lingo. "Animal style," the most popular variant, means that mustard is fried into the meat patties and you get pickles, extra sauce, and extra grilled onions. "Protein style" is for Atkins slaves—it replaces a bun with lettuce leaves. "Extra toast" means your bun will be toasted and crispy. Clerks, who are paid substantially more than the state minimum wage laws decree and are consequently courteous and capable (the company is regularly praised for keeping some of the country's best business practices), will make any variety you can dream up, down to mixing chocolate, vanilla, and strawberry shakes into a Neapolitan, if that's what you choose. French fries are fresh-cut from whole potatoes and fried to order, and once you taste their natural crispness, you'll wonder why you put up with McDonald's for all these years. Many locals would never set foot in Fisherman's Wharf if not for this place. The line can be enormous here, but it moves quickly; if the dining room is full, which it usually is, there are more tables out the side door in the courtyard.

$$–$$$$ Homemade chowders, fresh fish dishes, and a cheerful, kid-friendly, warehouse-like atmosphere make **Blue Mermaid** 🧒 (471 Jefferson St., at Hyde; ☎ 415/771-2222; www.bluemermaidsf.com; Sun–Thurs 7am–9pm, Fri–Sat 7am–10pm; AE, DC, MC, V) a popular place to eat at the Wharf where you won't feel like you're interrupting a fish market. The lunch and dinner menus are nearly identical, including in price: sandwiches around $14, chowder by the bread bowl $10 ($8 in a standard bowl), or a plate of fresh daily fish for about $24. At lunch, though, there's a good deal for the Wharf: chowder or salad, a fish dish, and a choice of a drink including beer or wine, for $20.

$$$$ If you insist on having a sit-down meal at the Wharf, prices be damned, then **Scoma's** (Pier 47 on Al Scoma Way at Jones Street; ☎ 800/644-5842 or 415/771-4383; www.scomas.com; daily 11:30am–10:30pm; AE, MC, V) is a popular choice with a Bay view that serves some half-million customers a year. Whole Dungeness crab is about $27 here—that's about $10 more than what it would cost at a stall outside—and crab-cake sandwiches are $17. Pricey, but portions are generally enormous. I also appreciate the "lazy man's cioppino," in which the crab has been shelled for you (not the usual preparation). The restaurant is fairly old school, with waitresses who have been there since dirt was new. There's also a kid's menu.

Dining Around Fisherman's Wharf

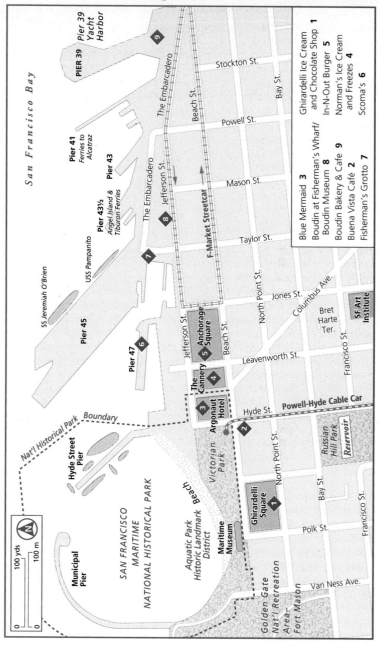

Ghirardelli Ice Cream and Chocolate Shop **1**
In-N-Out Burger **5**
Norman's Ice Cream and Freezes **4**
Scoma's **6**

Blue Mermaid **3**
Boudin at Fisherman's Wharf/Boudin Museum **8**
Boudin Bakery & Cafe **9**
Buena Vista Café **2**
Fisherman's Grotto **7**

Cuckoo for Cocoa

The line of tourists snaking into **Ghirardelli Ice Cream and Chocolate Shop** [kids] (900 North Point St.; ☎ 415/474-1414; www.ghirardelli.com; Sun–Thurs 9am–11pm, Fri–Sat 9am–midnight; AE, MC, V), at Fisherman's Wharf's west end near the cable-car turnaround, is testament more to the fame of the ice-cream shop/chocolatier than it is its superiority. I far prefer Norman's, which is a 3-minute walk away, and not just because Ghirardelli is otherwise available across the country, from Chicago to Orlando. However, there's no denying that Ghirardelli (*Gear*-ar-delli with a hard "g") is a San Francisco mainstay, and its success as a destination is a big reason Fisherman's Wharf has turned from blue-collar workers' area to a legit tourist attraction. Ghirardelli Square is where the chocolates were once manufactured, from 1895, but the company moved its operation across the Bay to San Leandro generations ago, leaving the one-time factory to be converted into a bricked terrace of very fancy shops and restaurants. Despite the fact that Ghirardelli is, in fact, made elsewhere, tourists are not strongly disabused of the belief that it's still made here in quantity and are tempted by the allure of chocolate to queue here. The brand maintains both a small "on-the-go" storefront (Mon–Sat 8:30am–5pm, Sun 9am–5pm) for chocolate sales only, where tastes are often doled out for free, and a full-fledged ice-cream parlor selling overpriced ($9) sundaes piled with rather bland ice cream and pleasingly rich chocolate; both get packed on weekends and holidays. If you just want chocolate, no sundaes or lines, skip to Ghirardelli's Union Square shop (42 Stockton St.; ☎ 415/397-3030) instead, where there's never a crowd. Then if your friends ask you if you went to Ghirardelli, you can say yes—just don't waste an hour of your precious vacation on it.

CHINATOWN

The food offerings in Chinatown are plenty—so numerous that if you ask 10 locals to name their favorite restaurants, you probably won't hear the same place named twice. Stroll Grant Avenue for the more Westernized of them, and then Stockton for the (usually less expensive) places where you may have to point at something to order it. South of California Street, the restaurant options thin out as you approach Union Square.

$ Hing Lung Restaurant ★ (674 Broadway, at Stockton; ☎ 415/398-8838; 8am–1am; cash only) is better than your average jook joint. What's that? A joint selling *jook*, a term for the rice porridge (also called *congee*), which many Chinese eat by the tankerful every morning, noon, and night. If you're going to be trying it for the first time, this is a great place to do it, because they make congee well— not too watery or thick with rice. The custom is to pile the stuff with whatever savory garnish appeals to you, be it duck, quail egg, pork, abalone, or any number of other authentic toppings. That costs about $4, and it also buys a cruller-like bread for sopping up whatever flavor is left over. Or just get a traditional rice-and-meat dish. Everything is cheap, including the decor, but people have a good time here. Another fave: the kung pau calamari ($5). Lots of dishes are $2.50 or under, but servings are generous and although the fowl in the window prove that Middle Americans are perhaps not the target clientele, non-Chinese patrons are not made to feel unwelcome.

$–$$ Most Chinatown restaurants don't actually serve the spicy variety of cuisine known as Hunan—they serve the blander Cantonese to suit the many immigrants from Hong Kong. Hunan cuisine, richly colored and powerfully flavored, is what distinguishes **Brandy Ho's Hunan Food** ★ (217 Columbus Ave., at Pacific; ☎ 415/788-7527; www.brandyhos.com; Sun–Thurs 11:30am–11pm, Fri–Sat 11:30am–midnight; AE, DC, MC, V) from the pack. Its location on North Beach's fringe, away from the main Chinatown hubbub, also separates it. The interior is bland, but the dishes aren't, and the chef is only too happy to pep up every dish with spice. The cook is also generous with ingredients—you never get the sense of corners being cut, despite the low prices ($8 for most entrees)—and the owner greets most guests at the door when they enter. The lunch special (soup, onion cake, spicy vegetables, and a main for $7) is a true value. There is a second location in the Castro (4068 18th St., near Castro; ☎ 415/252-8000).

$–$$ Normally I'm wary of any restaurant that needs to hire salesmen to drum up business, as **Hang Ah Tea Room** (1 Pagoda Place, off Sacramento btw. Grant and Stockholm; ☎ 415/982-5685; Sun–Thurs 10am–9pm, Fri–Sat 10am–11pm; MC, V) does on Grant Avenue, but there's a good reason for it. It's kind of tricky to find, as it's located in a little alley shooting north off Sacramento (it's beside the

A Word on Dim Sum

by Pauline Frommer

The classic Chinatown meal is the dim-sum brunch or lunch. Dim sum, for those who've never tried it, is a meal made up of many small dishes, primarily different sorts of dumplings and buns, a tradition that started in the teahouses that lined China's Silk Road many centuries ago (scholars believe the custom began shortly after A.D. 300, when the long-held notion that tea should not be accompanied by food fell out of favor). In China, as well as in Asian communities across the world, it remains a social occasion, a chance for family and friends to gather and talk. That may be why the words *dim sum* don't actually refer to food; they can be roughly translated as "a little bit of heart." Today, when you go for a dim-sum brunch, it's likely that you'll be seated at a large round table with other diners, so don't be shy; use that seating as an opportunity to meet the locals.

Dining Around Town

See "Dining Around The Castro & The Mission" map

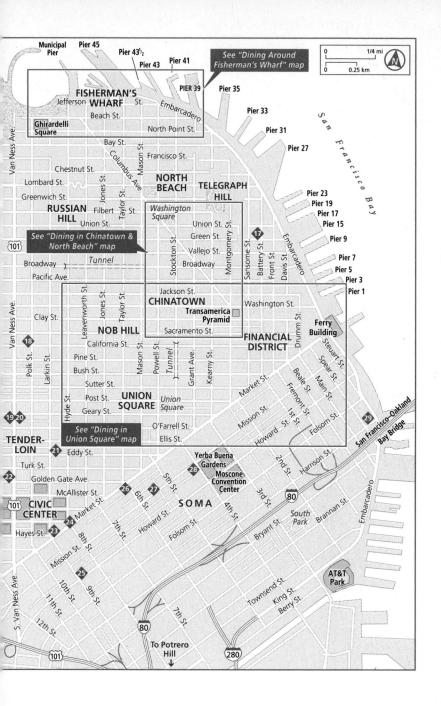

Pauline Frommer Recommends . . .

$–$$ House of Nanking ★★ (919 Kearney St., at Columbus; ☎ 415/421-1429; daily 11am–10pm; MC, V). As Jason said at the top, everyone has his favorite Chinatown haunt, and you're most likely to find me here, when I'm in town. Shanghai is the origin of the cuisine and my particular magnet on the menu is the exquisite peanut sauce, a not-at-all-gloopy, slightly fiery smear that elevates the dishes that feature it, like the crispy tofu ($7.95) and the fried shrimp cakes ($4.95) onto another gastronomic plane (no, really). In fact, when I'm alone, I'll stop by and make an entire meal out of that shrimp-cake appetizer and leave satisfied. When I'm with friends, I let owner Peter Fang do the ordering; he inevitably includes something with his famed peanut sauce, as well as whatever's freshest from the market.

$$–$$$ Sanraku Japanese Restaurant ★ (704 Sutter St., at Taylor St.; ☎ 415/771-0803; www.sanraku.com; Mon–Sat 11am–10pm, Sun 4–10pm; AE, DC, MC, V). Pairing the words *cheap* and *sushi* together in a sentence usually scares diners. But at this little haven of blond woods and hanging scrolls, the fish is super fresh, the rice well molded, and the prices surprisingly low; $4.50 to $6.50 for most regular rolls, up to $12 for glitzier specials; try the fab $9.50 lunch special of several courses. What I especially like about the sushi bar here is that it's a community gathering place and many of the diners hang out each day. Sit down alone and you're sure to be quickly swept up in a conversation as you dine.

Willie "Woo Woo" Wong Playground). The dim sum here, though, is excellent—shrimp dumplings, turnip cakes, pork buns, and so on, plus a selection of Americanized Chinese like sweet-and-sour chicken. The place bills itself as the oldest dim-sum house in town, which is tough to verify, but the kitchen has been in operation since 1920—the orange-and-lime dining area has obviously been attended to since then. You'll find it difficult to spend more than $12—most dishes are $5 and under. Dim-sum service halts at 9pm, but dessert goes on until after midnight.

$–$$ For a filling dim-sum feast, Chinese locals know to pop in at **Dol Ho ★** (808 Pacific Ave., at Stockton; ☎ 415/392-2828; Thurs–Tues 7am–5pm; cash only), a hole in the wall that's virtually unknown among outsiders. As the cart slides by, point to what you want, and indulge. Don't think you've seen all there is after the first cart, because different food types (fried vs. rice-based vs. steamed) are loaded onto different carts. The decor has all the charm of the lobby of a no-star hotel, with four sad chandeliers hanging dismally over the proceedings, but I can't complain I'm not getting my money's worth when I can come out of a place having slurped down eight shu mai and shrimp-and-vegetable dumplings, with a drink, for just $7. Seriously—as much as you think you're pigging out here, the dollar tally is still unlikely to break one digit. They make and sell their own hot sauce, too. Not all the staff speak good English, but good enough.

A second dim-sum option, and one that perhaps has a more aloof service staff, is the slightly more expensive **Gold Mountain Restaurant** (644 Broadway, at Stockton; ☎ 415/296-7733; AE, MC, V). If you can tolerate the slightly more non-touristy energy at Dol Ho, you'll find better food there.

THE FINANCIAL DISTRICT

The power players of the city dine here, among the skyscrapers and the oldest parts of town, so it's a better locale for finding a chic wallet-drainer than a bargain. But there are a few bright spots. Despite the businessy crowd, places remain open for evening dining.

$$–$$$ Bring your eyeglasses to **Gordon Biersch Brewery Restaurant** (1 Harrison St., at Embarcadero; ☎ 415/243-8246; www.gordonbiersch.com; Sun–Thurs 11:30am–midnight, Fri–Sat 11:30am–2am; AE, MC, V), because the view of the Bay Bridge is remarkable. In fact, it's the major reason why you'd want to kick back here for a while, nursing a homemade brew. The service can be lame, but I'd still pick this successful microbrewery chain as a nice spot to raise a beer, even if there is better food elsewhere. As there aren't many other places to eat in this part of town, and places with views are rare in general, this joint gets a nod. The grub consists of heightened versions of bar food, about $11 to $17. To fit in, order a beer served in a glass boot.

$$ **Taylor's Automatic Refresher** ★★★ 🧒 (One Ferry Building at Market and Embarcadero, Space 6; ☎ 866/328-3663; www.taylorsrefresher.com; daily 10:30am–10pm; AE, MC, V) has, since 1949, operated as a beloved drive-in burger joint in Napa County's St. Helena (p. 230). When the Ferry Building re-opened as a food destination focusing on local brands, it was invited to open a San Francisco version at the northern, city-facing end of the Marketplace. Diners sit on stools at long, communal tables, where the view is of the historic F-line trams trundling by. Ingredients are fresh and meals are made to order, but it still has the heart of a '50s-style drive-in, with a full slate of fat burgers (the Wisconsin Sourdough [$9] has mushrooms, bacon, barbecue sauce, cheddar, on grilled sourdough), excellent $5 shakes (using real malt, if you like), and plenty of options that won't weigh you down with grease (including seared ahi-tuna burgers [$14] and crunchy Chinese chicken salad [$9]). The spicy tomato soup ($6) is tasty (and so rich you could use it as a sauce) but served in impossible-to-finish portions. Wines are from Sonoma and Napa, but the scene is generally much more kid-friendly than the rarified gourmet environment in the rest of the Marketplace. Prices and menu here are exactly the same as in Napa, so don't hold off on a visit thinking you'll save in the sticks.

$$–$$$ High-design decor and affordable Thai food is the stock-in-trade of **Osha Thai Restaurant** ★★ (4 Embarcadero, behind the Hyatt; ☎ 415/788-6742; www.oshathai.com; 11am–11pm; AE, MC, V), a chic but approachable place where you're as likely to drink a specialty cocktail as you are to enjoy a pad Thai. Menu

The True San Francisco Treats

Forget Rice-a-Roni. No one here eats that stuff. (Did they ever?) The real San Francisco treats could more appropriately be considered to be these dishes, all of which are said to have had their origins here.

San Francisco sourdough: That lightly tangy taste of sourdough has become a city standard, not just because some varieties of yeast, such as Boudin's recipe, only thrive in the Bay Area microclimate. Hollowing out a bowl of it is a popular way to serve chowder, although you usually get more chowder in a standard bowl (and bread is usually served with it anyway).

Irish Coffee: It wasn't invented here, but it was popularized here by a travel writer who picked up the recipe at an airport in Ireland. The Buena Vista (p. 206) is now considered the place to drink one.

Cioppino (*chop*-peen-no): A variety of fish, crab, and shellfish, all simmered in tomatoes, garlic, and red wine—it was originally something easy that immigrant fisherman could whip up with whatever fish they caught that day. Now, it's a city signature that'll make *you* shell out.

The Fortune Cookie: The first ones, folded-over *sembei* tea crackers, were given as a kind of party favor in 1914 to people who showed up at Golden Gate Park's Japanese Tea Garden. They evolved into the platitude-stuffed sweets we know today. But did they absolutely originate here? Even Confucius can't say for sure.

Chop Suey: Pieces of meat stir-fried with celery, onion, sprouts, mushrooms, and other veggies, chop suey is said to have originated with Chinese laborers in town. San Francisco's Chinese population meant that the city was closely associated with the late 19th-century popularity of what was then considered an exotic dish.

Mai Tai: This potent rum-and-syrup cocktail was invented in wartime by Trader Vic's restaurant (now gone) and exported just as the Pacific Islands craze set in.

items rise beyond the traditional curry, although you can get that, too; I like the salmon cubes with red chili paste and garlic ($15), as well as the fresh mango salad served with shrimp and spicy lemongrass dressing ($10). In general, the sauces are rich and flavorful and make dining different. Other locations: Cow Hollow (2033 Union St., at Buchanan; ☎ 415/567-6742); Civic Center (696 Geary St., at Leavenworth; ☎ 415/673-2368); the Mission (819 Valencia St., at 19th); and SoMa (☎ 415/826-7738; 149 2nd St., at Natoma; ☎ 415/278-9991).

$$$–$$$$ After a few days of noshing on bread and chocolate, two of the city's more famous outputs, you may be grateful for the clean Mediterranean flavors that are lovingly cultivated at **Kokkari** (200 Jackson St., at Front; ☎ 415/981-0983; www.kokkari.com; Mon–Sat 11:30am–2:30pm and 5:30–10pm; AE, MC, V), where classics like grilled tuna, grilled whole fish, and some sizable salads hit in the mid-teen dollar range. Meats are roasted on spits by an enormous fireplace, the centerpiece of the establishment's architect-designed space.

$$$$ The word *iconic* is often bandied about to describe **Tadich Grill** ★★ (240 California St., near Battery; ☎ 415/391-1849; daily 11:30am–9:30pm; MC, V), which has been in business in one form or another since 1849—in this Financial District location only since 1967, although the tile floors and brass fittings give off a men's-club aura that comes across as much older. There's still a whiff of the gold rush here, and you won't get out of this dusky spot for cheap; mains are around $19 but hearty and manly, including oysters, ahi tuna filet, and that city standby, cioppino. Meats are cooked on a mesquite-fueled grill. Because even the lesser dishes' portions are more than enough for a meal, I am usually satisfied with the clam chowder ($7/bowl), which isn't skimpy with the meat, and I eat it at the 80-foot-long bar where, no doubt, many world-changing business deals have been casually closed. Every established local, from former mayors to titan bankers, knows Tadich, but reservations aren't accepted from any of them—they have to wait if there's a line, just as you do. Waiters wear white coats, tablecloths are crisp, and when you walk out of here, you really feel like you've eaten at a restaurant.

$$–$$$$ Perhaps the most celebrated restaurant in town of late is **Slanted Door** (1 Ferry Building; ☎ 415/861-8032; www.slanteddoor.com; daily 11am–2:30pm and 5:30–10pm; AE, MC, V), a high-end Vietnamese wonder where unlike flavors are blended to great acclaim by chef Charles Phan, whose family owns the place. The restaurant used to be in the Mission, but in 2004 it moved to the Ferry Building, where prices went up and availability became tough. Dinner is expensive, and the wait brutal, but come for lunch, and you can try the award-winning cuisine for much less. It's also possible to make a meal of the vegetarian options (which are delish, even for carnivores), for about a third as much as the meat and fish-based dishes. The caramelized tiger prawns ($15.50 at lunch) are a favorite, but the menu runs dozens of options long, and many of the items deliver new fusion twists on Vietnamese recipes. The *prix fixe* lunch (about $40) lets you try seven small-plate menu items from a list. The cheapest way of all to go is to visit Out the Door (☎ 415/321-3740), the restaurant's small sampling shop, located next door. Here, a few of the menu's favorites, like spring rolls and grapefruit and jicama salad, are served from a counter for about $8 a plate.

SOUTH OF MARKET

The blend of restaurants in SoMa reflects the fact that the district is leaping from borderline squalor to condos and office towers. The places to eat fall along a similar divide. You'll find lots of after-work drinkeries and capacious new-brew restaurants catering to the conventioneers around the Financial District end. In the tattier Mission area, there are more low-down, steamy kitchens catering to the frugal.

A Gourmet Food Mall

The Ferry Building is a true city landmark, having been one of the only structures to survive the quake and fire, and serving as a visual landmark at the foot of Market Street. It took the earthquake of 1989, though, to deliver the building unto popularity again. That's when the hideous elevated highway that ran in front of it and along the waterfront, cleaving the Bay from the city, was so seriously damaged by tremors that dismantling it became the most attractive option. That got the ball rolling, and by 2004, the Ferry Building reopened, beautiful as a modern-day cathedral (in fact, the main shopping area is called "the Nave") and as a hip minimall for fancy foods. Its gorgeous renovation has spurred the revitalization of the entire Embarcadero district.

The **Ferry Building Marketplace** (1 Ferry Building; ☎ 415/693-0996; www.ferrybuildingmarketplace.com; Mon–Fri 10am–6pm, Sat 9am–6pm, Sun 11am–5pm) sells artisanal wares that are almost uniformly delicious, but for many budget travelers a visit here is as much about window shopping (and getting ideas for recipes) as it is about shopping. Certainly, the sellers all have detailed explanations of their wares, and *pesticide* and *non-organic* are the equivalent of four-letter words. Here, a tomato isn't just a tomato; here, it has a story behind it. As you walk from stall to stall, browsing the fresh produce and wishing your last meal had been smaller, you'll learn quite a bit about how food is produced. Half the vendors were selected by a tough curation process that insisted on local provenance. Nothing is made or sold in bulk. Many of the offerings lend themselves to impulse buys (chocolates, nuts, cheeses) and are not true staples, which is convenient for visitors. You won't find many people doing honest-to-goodness daily grocery shopping here. Even most of the restaurants are high-end.

$ The newspaper clips in the window offer 20-year-old praise, but there's no need to update them because the steaming, aromatic **Tú Lan** ★★★ (8 6th St., at Market; ☎ 415/626-0927; Mon–Sat 11am–9:30pm; MC, V) has been a solid, unchanging value in Vietnamese food since 1977 that's packed for every meal, despite the fact it's on the "wrong" side of Market in a sagging neighborhood. Julia Child herself elected to eat here in 1985—she pigged out and ordered spring rolls, pork shish kebabs (pork is a specialty), lemon beef salad, fried fish in ginger, and a Tsingtao beer. She came for the food, not the service, which is workmanlike at best. Ask about the brilliantly priced specials, such as the Family Dinner for two or more, with soup, salad, and up to two main dishes, for $10.75 per person. And that's pricey for this place—you can get a heaping plate of food and a Vietnamese beer for $8.

$$–$$$ Here's the gimmick at **Asia SF** ★ (201 9th St., at Howard; ☎ 415/255-2742; www.asiasf.com; reservations required; daily 6pm–10pm; club until 2am; AE,

Among the good stuff for sale:

- **The Cowgirl Creamery** (☎ 415/362-9354) sells cheese from a rare breed of Holstein cows, and it doesn't ship well, so this is the only place to pick some up.
- **The Ferry Plaza Wine Merchant** (☎ 415/391-9400) sells a small section of $10 wines, but, in general, it's for folks with cash willing to sit at its wine bar and splash on $19 cheese tasting plates.
- **Lulu Petite** (☎ 415/362-7019) sells sauces and ritzy Fig Balsamic Vinegar, while **Miette** (☎ 415/837-0300) must spend untold hours making its unbearable adorable pastries and cookies.
- **Slanted Door** (p. 69; ☎ 415/861-8032) sells its deservedly celebrated Vietnamese food at a take-away window called **Out the Door** (☎ 415/321-3740; closed Sun) where dishes are simply not as elaborate but still excellent, and cost about $7.
- **Taylor's Automatic Refresher** (p. 230) is one of the only truly affordable places to get a seated meal on the premises.

This upscale showmanship is complemented on Tuesdays from 10am to 2pm and Saturdays from 8am to 2pm by a true **farmer's market** at which vendors are required to produce their own stuff. If you show up early, there will be few other customers there with you, and you can use the opportunity to chat with the sellers, who are more likely to dole out free samples then than they are when the tourist hordes show up and splinter their attention. A few of the vendors don't open on Monday, but otherwise, it's a week-round affair.

DC, MC, V): Waitresses are in fact lady-boy drag queens, and throughout the evening, they mount the bar and perform burlesque-like amusements. Nothing too dirty, mind you, but edgy enough (and skilled enough, to the consternation of more than one straight frat boy) to make this a favorite spot for birthday parties and office farewells. Food is pricey (appetizers are around $12, and mains $15–$20), but it's surprisingly tasty (miso-glazed king salmon, truffled soba noodles, sesame steak salad). It's lots of campy fun, and downstairs there's a subterranean dance floor for continuing the fun after dinner. Especially because this is the kind of place where you're likely to order a few cocktails (or like the group of howling secretaries at the next table over, more than a few), you'll spend more money than you predicted if you're not careful from the start, but because of the show, you really are getting more value for your buck. Consider this splurge a memorable example of "real" San Francisco.

Make a Date with Dining

In January and mid-June, dozens of fine restaurants around town try to drum up further appreciation and goodwill by participating in the weeklong mass price-cutting known as **Dine About Town** (www.onlyinsanfrancisco.com/dineabouttown), during which a three-course meal is marked down to $22 at lunch or $32 at dinner. Not stone-cold cheap, but less expensive than you'd usually pay, and at name-checked places you might not otherwise find affordable to visit. Reservations are essential, so plan ahead.

$$ One of the city's best-known and busiest houses for dim sum, **Yank Sing** (49 Stevenson St., at Ecker; ☎ 415/541-4949; www.yanksing.com; Mon–Fri 11am–3pm, Sat–Sun 10am–4pm; AE, MC, V) isn't located in Chinatown, but in SoMa. (The second of two locations is at the Rincon Center at Spear and Mission.) Busy since the late 1950s, this dining room has all the decor élan of a hotel dining room, but with some 100 items from which to choose—the menus call it "deem sum"—it's tough to leave hungry. There are much cheaper dim-sum places in town, but for an upscale lunch (and never dinner—it's closed by then), this is a safe choice.

THE TENDERLOIN

Located and priced for quick-casual bites before the theatre or during Union Square romps, the Tenderloin's personality leans toward ethnic foods ranging from low-down hash-slingers to mid-priced niche kitchens angling for young diners. It's one of the more affordable neighborhoods for dining within the tourist zone.

$ It's just one homey room with nine tables and a few seats at the counter, which accounts for why **Dottie's True Blue Café** ★★★ (522 Jones St., at Geary; ☎ 415/885-2767; Wed–Mon 7:30am–3pm; MC, V) is perennially busy. Lines can start forming as early as 7am, with people peering in the front window at the lucky diners inside. Most of the dishes are breakfast classics, supplemented by gorgeous, fresh home-baked breads (the jalapeño cornbread with chipotle jelly—divine!). For non-eggy types, it also does a few sandwiches and other dishes. Coffee is generously topped up as long as you're seated (and it's good coffee, too, not diner water), and the maple syrup is real, not some Aunt Jemima fake. Come on weekdays or at around 2pm if you don't want to wait an hour; otherwise, the queues can ruin an otherwise heavenly food experience.

$ The flavorful Pakistani-Indian place **Shalimar** ★ (532 Jones St., at O'Farrell; ☎ 415/928-0333; www.shalimarsf.com; daily noon–midnight; cash only) is a popular neighborhood hangout that most visitors pass by without noticing. On my most recent visit, I was the only non-Asian in attendance. "No substitutions to fit the local tastes" is one of the establishment's culinary vows, and the integrity of the food shows it. So is another vow: "No frills." You BYOB and order at the kitchen, which is demarked from the dining room by mobile counters, and then sit; food arrives literally steaming hot. It's hard to tell in which decade, or century, the fluorescent-light decor was first installed, but there's no doubt the food is fresh, and at $7 a plate, it's one of the best values in town. If you require matching plates, look elsewhere, but if you like good Indian, you won't be disappointed.

Secrets to Saving on Gourmet Meals

If you want to sample the fancy foods that get the national magazines buzzing, try these tactics at your chosen four-star joint:

- **Go at lunch.** Take the **Slanted Door** (p. 69), one of the city's most popular gourmet experiences. Compared to dinner, where the dollar rate for a meal will hit you for three digits, rates plummet to around $10 a plate at lunchtime. Unfortunately, some of the city's most newsworthy chefs don't open for lunch—they use the time to prepare to charge $100-plus for dinner—so make sure to call ahead to check.
- **Go vegetarian.** Especially when your restaurant is stocking Niman Ranch naturally raised beef or meat with a similarly upscale provenance, you'll find that cutting out the protein for a single meal will jack the price way down.
- **Go with small plates.** To your advantage, one of the recent trends in city cuisine is small-plate dining, in which great effort is put into creating inventive and sophisticated appetizer-size portions meant for sharing. Depending on your hunger, you might be satisfied with a selection of these tapas, which are served in smaller portions than full entrees but are also less expensive. Try chef Gerald Hirigoyen's ever-changing Basque dishes at **Piperade** (1015 Battery St., at Union; ☎ 415/391-2555; www.piperade.com; Mon–Sat 5:30pm–10pm; MC, V); the international flavors at the celeb-scene **Andalu** (3198 16th St., at Guerrero; ☎ 415/621-5844; www.andalusf.com; Mon–Fri 5:30pm–10:30pm, Sat–Sun 10:30am–2:30pm and 5:30pm–10:30pm; MC, V); the Spanish-styled ones at cozy **Bocadillos** (710 Montgomery St., at Washington; ☎ 415/982-2622; www.bocasf.com; Mon–Fri 7pm–10pm, Sat 5:30pm–10pm; MC, V) in the Financial District; the Spanish dishes at **Laïola** (p. 74); or the bold Mediterranean plates at **Cortez** (in the Hotel Adagio, 550 Geary St., at Jones; ☎ 415/292-6360; www.cortezrestaurant.com; reservations recommended; daily 5:30–10:30pm; MC, V). Just don't be tempted to order one of these places' spendy entrees—this savings tip will fall apart if you do.

COW HOLLOW, PACIFIC HEIGHTS
& THE MARINA

These mostly residential areas are stocked with cafes, pubs, and trendy bistros that come and go. If you're stuck for a place to eat, take a walk down Union Street, Fillmore Street, or, to a lesser extent, Chestnut Street, and peruse the menu boards, but be warned that the prices cater to the areas' wealthy residents more than to scrimping tourists.

$$–$$$ The kind of barn where you wouldn't feel embarrassed to spill a beer, **Left at Albuquerque** [kids] (2140 Union St.; ☎ 415/749-6700; www.leftatalb.com; daily 11am–11pm; AE, MC, V) does filling barbecue, enchiladas, fajitas, nachos, and the like, all under the soothing glare of TV screens quietly showing the latest sporting event. The corn chowder ($4.50/cup) is heartier than you'd expect for corn chowder, and the Chuck Wagon Baby Back Ribs ($15/half rack) and the salmon filet smeared with barbecue spices ($16) hit the spot for folks craving rib-sticking Southern food. Most main dishes cost around $12, so you won't be stressing out about how much you spent even as you kick up your heels with a brew.

$$–$$$ The clubby energy of the lively and moodily lit **Betelnut** ★★ (2030 Union St.; ☎ 415/929-8855; www.betelnutrestaurant.com; daily 11:30am–11pm; AE, MC, V) is highly theatrical, as are the dishes (and the waiters too, dressed in tunics!). Created by a Malaysian chef, it gives a survey of the best of South Asia, with lots of aromatic dumplings, noodle bowls, and fiery offerings that don't water down the spice in deference to wimps (many are powerfully flavorful). Satisfying yourself with just a single visit can be tricky, because the garlic and spice smells wafting off other diners' tables will make you wish you'd ordered *that*, too. Starters and entrees are all about the same price ($10–$12), probably because appetizers are portioned for sharing, although I find the main dishes (such as "little dragon" dumplings of pork and shrimp with ginger vinegar) filling enough by themselves. I also find the *laksa,* a coconutty and warm soup of seafood and noodles, hits the spot, and the edamame drenched in spices and garlic are a sticky-fingered addiction. The restaurant also homebrews its own beer, but it's served cold and it's not so rich that it overpowers the Asian flavors. Come weekend nights, when even families and groups swing in, you can't get a seat without a reservation, although there is a bar, beneath gently swinging Malaysian-style leaf fans, to tide any wait.

$$$$ Most entrees at **Laïola** (2031 Chestnut St., near Fillmore; ☎ 415/346-5641; www.laiola.com; reservations not accepted; daily 5:30–10:30pm; AE, MC, V)—pronounced *Lye* oh la—cost around $22, but that doesn't matter all that much—folks in the know come here to load up on the appetizers. Everything at this dim and woody restaurant, which is good for groups on a classy night out, honors genuine Spanish cuisine, even the wines, all of which on the lengthy list come from that country. Chef Mark Denham's ideas kick off some bold California-meets-Spain flavors, such as wrapping local peaches in La Quercia jamon and then warming them to blend sweet and salty; or frying almonds in olive oil and dusting them with cracked pepper as an amuse bouche. Most appetizers—think of them as tapas—are $10 each. That means you can save some money on dinner here only if everyone at the table consents to a price limit; those small-plate meals can add up if you're ravenous.

THE MISSION

When I'm undecided about what I want to eat or I'm with someone who wants to get to know the real San Francisco, I lead them here, where no-frills Latin joints hang loose with a string of bohemian cafés and relaxed restaurants. There's something for everyone, and little of it is overly fussy or exclusive.

$ The facilities at primo taqueria **El Farolito** ★★ (2779 Mission St., at 24th; ☎ 415/824-7877; Sun–Thurs 10am–3am, Fri–Sat 10am–4am; MC, V) are unprepossessing to say the least: chipped red and yellow diner tables and mirrored beer ads. It needed renovation a generation ago. The food, though, is incredibly fresh, and, for that, there's usually a line out the door and a 20-minute wait for some of the Mission's best Mexican. But the burritos! They're simply more massive than you'll be able to contemplate, let alone actually finish. Seriously—expect a true foot-long, 4-pounder for a mere $7.75, stuffed with your choice of meat (*carne asada* is popular; tongue or brains less so). Avocado is scooped right out of the fruit and onto your meal, and meats are constantly re-marinated even as they're being served, but be warned that burritos here have slightly more beans in them than some Mission rivals. Most orders come with free chips and salsa. Plan to eat here, because the juices in which the meats marinate can cause tortillas to go soggy after an hour or so; you won't finish, anyway. The homemade *agues frescas* (sugary fruit drinks) are a sweet midnight kick. It's open until the wee hours (last orders at 2:45am) every day.

$ The much-celebrated taqueria **La Cumbre** ★★★ (515 Valenica St., at 17th; ☎ 415/863-8205; daily 11am–9:30pm; MC, V), which began life in 1967 as a grocery before catching wise that custom-made, overstuffed burritos were its true bag. This place has fed the city since then, long before mega-chains like Chipotle and Qdoba stole its shtick. In the never-ending battle for the Mission's best burrito, La Cumbre's name is almost always at the top of the list. *BusinessWeek* reported that this original store and its brother in San Mateo together took in $2 million in 2004. Customers line up at the counter, order, and then register shock when they're handed burritos the size of fresh fire logs for $5.50 to $9. I can't seem to break myself away from a burrito habit here, but you might also try its homemade *caldo* soups, each made to order. If you don't know Mexican fast food, there may be no better place to become acquainted. There's little chance you'll be able to finish everything, so don't plan to make a taco crawl by combining with a trip to El Farolito. San Francisco residents take their burritos *very* seriously, so I'm actually worried that I'm going to take some flak for just mentioning these two. I think they're at the top of the heap, but for reviews of well over 500 establishments around town, delve into the burrito universe being explored at Burrito Eater (www.burritoeater.com). Its e-mail newsletter? *The Intestinal Apocalypse Monthly.*

$–$$ The fish dishes of **Weird Fish** (2193 Mission St., at 18th; ☎ 415/863-4744; www.weirdfishsf.com; daily 9am–10:30pm; AE, MC, V), while not weird in the traditional sense, are all comprised of swimmers that have been sustainably farmed, and they're incredibly well-priced—$8 each for selections such as blackened catfish with fruit salsa and sautéed tilapia (a mild fish) with carrots and leeks. Vegetarians aren't left out; in addition to fish and chips done with tilapia ($10), it does the dish with tofu, tempeh, or seitan. As you can imagine by the name, it's a self-mocking, arty scene: the storefront is denoted by a hanging sculpture of a horse with a curvy fishtail. In 2008, locals voted it their favorite seafood restaurant in *SF Weekly.*

$$ The owners of **Dosa** ★ (995 Valencia St., at 21st St; ☎ 415/642-3672; www.dosasf.com; Sun–Fri 5:30–10pm, Sat 11:30am–11pm; AE, MC, V) are aware that not everyone will have tried South Indian cuisine before, so they delight in walking guests through the experience when asked. The specialty here, in a simply decorated space, is the most theatrical dish: the *dosa* (most are $10.50), a huge cone of crepe-like bread stuffed with your choice of masala and chutney, along with spicy sambar soup for dipping. A meal here is lively and lots of fun. The dinner menu is fuller than the lunch one, with several additional meat dishes added for around $14 each. Try the saffron-flavored *kulfi* (ice cream).

$$ For real Spanish, not the Mexican and Central American that pervades the rest of the Mission, the joyous and busy **Esperpento** ★ (3295 22nd St., at Valencia; ☎ 415/282-8867; daily 11am–10pm; AE, DISC, MC, V), buzzing into the night, could fool you into believing you were hanging out in a neighborhood joint in Barcelona with a bunch of sangria-soaked friends. The menu is affordable tapas (take note of the grilled artichoke, a specialty) and given that the orders emerge from the kitchen in small portions, the flavors are permitted to pack a punch, including tons of garlic in nearly everything. Paellas go for a little less than $10 per person, as do combo platters of an entree and two sides, but the real appeal are the grilled mussels, clams, shrimp, and other seafood. On fine days, there are a few tables out front, but the big difference between this place and Barcelona is that it's easier to get a table late (after 8:30pm) than earlier.

$$$ The upscale **Medjool Restaurant/Lounge** (2522 Mission St., at 21st; ☎ 415/550-9055; www.medjoolsf.com; Sun–Thurs 5–10:30pm, Fri–Sat 5pm–1am; AE, MC, V) pretty much has it all. For before dinner, it has a wine bar. Then, its kitchen produced gourmet-level, authentic dishes from the Mediterranean and the Middle East (like sugar-crusted quail, grilled baby octopus, or sumac-dusted calamari)—the meats are particularly well done. It's reasonably priced (all dishes, served as small plates to share, are in the low teens). And late in the evening, it turns into a DJ bar, and that's when you head up to the rooftop "sky terrace" to enjoy the view of the city—one of the best enjoyed by any restaurant here. The terrace also has its own menu of skewers and other simple dishes for about $12 each.) Then you can dance and watch the people. So it's an excellent place to spend a complete evening.

$$–$$$ Social and festive, with an open kitchen and hung with chandeliers, the hipster-chic **Luna Park** ★ (694 Valencia St., at 18th; ☎ 415/553-8584; www. lunaparksf.com; Mon–Thurs 5:30–11:30pm, Sat 11:30am–11:30pm, Sun 11:30am–10pm; AE, MC, V) is one of a bunch of popular, groovy dining spots along Valencia

Dining Around the Castro/Mission

Bi-Rite Bakery & Creamery **7**

Brandy Ho's **2**

Chow **6**

Dosa **12**

El Farolito **16**

Esperpento **14**

Home **5**

Incanto **18**

La Cumbre **8**

Lime **4**

Luna Park **9**

Medjool Restaurant/ Lounge **13**

Osha Thai **11**

Philz Coffee **17**

Revolution Cafe **15**

Squat and Gobble **3**

Sumi **1**

Weird Fish **10**

How Sweet They Are

$ Few tourists know it's here, tucked behind Jack's Cannery in a dormant courtyard of Del Monte Square. Yet the closet-like **Norman's Ice Cream & Freezes** ★★★ 🄺 (2801 Leavenworth St.; ☎ 415/346-3046; cash only) serves some of the best ice cream I've ever tasted. Let the hordes stuff themselves indiscriminately with Ben & Jerry's and Cold Stone Creamery, both doing big business among the touristy shops of Beach Street. Here, lines are usually shamefully short, but my memories of fine dessert (oh, my goodness, the creamy caramel praline . . .) are long. The ice cream is made by Mitchell's, a local favorite since the 1950s, which runs a shop that's too far away for most tourists to visit (688 San Jose Ave., at 29th, in Noe Valley), so this is the place you should try it. And stay away from Häagen-Dazs, because you can get that at home.

$ **Victoria Pastry Co.** ★ (1362 Stockton St., at Vallejo; ☎ 415/781-2015; www.victoriapastry.com; Mon–Fri 7am–7pm, Sat 7am–9pm, Sun 8am–6pm; MC, V) makes one of the best cannoli ($3.80) I've ever had—the ricotta is cool, the shells crisp, and they're filled throughout, not just at the ends. If you don't see any in the case, ask, because they'll often prepare one fresh for you. Pair it with a coffee for just $1.25, sit in the window, and watch the northern fringe of Chinatown go by. They've been making them since 1914. Don't stop with the sweets, though, because downstairs, there's an enormous antique brick oven where all sorts of other baked goods are prepared.

in the Mission. The cuisine is hopped-up, well-made comfort food (country-fried trout, roast pork loin, burgers), priced higher than a diner ($12–$19) but not back-breaking. The wide-open room is configured to please both romantic date-goers (the sexy booths in the back) and blithe people-watchers (the tables in the front). Save room for the bananas Foster.

HAIGHT

With a few notable exceptions, the primary scene in the Haight is lunchy or pubby, with a concentration of fast-draw counter-service choices. That makes the area a good choice for combining with a casual day spent in nearby Golden Gate Park.

$–$$ Simple breakfast food all day in a simple atmosphere; that's the winning formula for the diner-like **Squat & Gobble** (3600 16th St., at Market; ☎ 415/552-2125; www.squatandgobble.com; AE, MC, V; daily 8am–10pm), which charges between $7 and $9 for most dishes, including both sweet and savory crepes, omelets, soups, salads, pasta, and stuffed sandwiches. Friends of mine come here just for the crab-cake Florentine ($8). S&G, with its beat-up, no-frills dining

$ Said to be the longest-running Japanese confectioner (since 1906) in a city where that heritage goes back a long way, **Benkyodo Co.** (1747 Buchanan St., at Sutter; ☎ 415/922-1244; www.benkyodocompany.com; Mon–Sat 8am–5pm; cash only) does an array of *mochi* (soft rice cakes) *manju* (mochi with sweet bean paste)—all handmade, under $1, and not easy to find outside of Japan. Naturally, it has a huge following, so show up earlier in the day to stand a chance of getting the most popular flavors, such as strawberry. It's cash only, and the lines can be unpleasant around the holidays and the New Year.

$ The Bi-Rite Grocery, a yuppie supermarket across the street, runs the equally adorable **Bi-Rite Creamery and Bakeshop** ★ (kids) (3682 18th St., at Dolores; ☎ 415/626-5600; www.biritecreamery.com; AE, MC, V; daily 11am–10pm), where homemade ice cream is scooped within sight of the sunbathers and Frisbee tossers of Dolores Park. Besides the high quality of the product, the Creamery is known for a few of its more adventurous flavors such as ricanela (a snickerdoodle-like concoction) and, my favorite, salted caramel. It does more conventional flavors, too (the rocky road is rich and addictive), but if you have the chance to try something like Sam's Sundae—a chocolate ice cream topped with Bergamot olive oil, sea salt, and whipped cream—shouldn't you seize the chance?

halls, is a good fallback for filling food. Other locations: Lower Haight (237 Fillmore St., at Haight; ☎ 415/487-0551), Upper Haight (1428 Haight St., at Masonic; ☎ 415/864-8484), and Marina (2263 Chestnut St., at Scott; ☎ 415/441-2200).

$$–$$$ After crawls through the Haight's secondhand stores, **Magnolia** (1398 Haight St.; ☎ 415/864-7468; www.magnoliapub.com; Mon–Fri noon–midnight, Sat–Sun 10am–1am; AE, DC, MC, V) makes a fitting and kicked-back finale. Here we have pub-style food (burgers, sandwiches, home-cut fries and onion rings) done with local and seasonal ingredients and served with a selection of wittily named homebrews (the Kalifornia Kolsch, the Cole Porter—many are made in the basement). Sodas are home-brewed in root beer, grape, and orange cream. Prices are sane (about $12 per entree) and the menu isn't overly long, although the psychedelic wall murals are wild enough.

$$$–$$$$ The baby of chef-owner Justine Miner, **RNM Restaurant** (598 Haight St., at Steiner; ☎ 415/551-7900; www.rnmrestaurant.com; Tues–Thurs 5:30–10pm, Fri–Sat 5:30–11pm; AE, MC, V) does surprisingly large "small plates" (about $10) by way of France and Italy. Like many young chefs, she uses the menu as a proving ground for whatever seasonal ingredients spark her imagination, but past dishes have included tuna tartare with waffle chips and a quail egg, and grilled hearts of romaine with Fuji apples and a champagne vinaigrette. Miner, who loves using her truffle oil, isn't above a little careful pandering, either, as proved by her slider burgers with onion and fries and her well-used cocktail menu. Despite a sleek, gray, upscale atmosphere that's completely at odds with the gritty Haight, there's not an attitude from the staff. And there's the usual early-bird (Tues–Sat 5:30–7pm) *prix fixe* that serves three courses for $28.

THE CASTRO

Most of the choices around the Castro lean toward all-American fare like burgers, pizza, comfort food, and beer. You're more likely to find an amiable hangout than an establishment where the waiters dash around with white linen over their arms.

$–$$ The high-energy **Lime** (2247 Market St., near 16th; ☎ 415/621-5256; www.lime-sf.com; Sun–Thurs 5pm–midnight, Fri–Sat 5pm–1am; AE, MC, V) is known for three things. One is its innovative/retro shared-plate dishes, mostly $5 to $10, such as mini-burgers, deviled eggs, and *Buddha's cups* (lovely finger-food blends of avocado, ginger, peanuts, shallots, and soy-miso dressing). Another is its Saturday and Sunday brunch, packed with trendy gay folk from the Castro and lubricated with all-you-can-drink mimosas ($7—yes, all you can drink). And third would be its prickly *Jetsons*-like decor, sure to impart a super-cool Eurotrash sense of self to even the most jaded visitor. Sit in the rear if you need a backing to your chair, otherwise, you'll be on a stool. If you show up late in the evening, when crowds arrive and the lights start twittering, you'll be forgiven if you confuse the place with a flashy nightclub.

$$ Popular for its soothing, satisfying seasonal menu, the casual and comfortable **Chow** ★★ 🅺 (215 Church St., at Market; ☎ 415/552-2469; www.chowfood bar.com; daily 8am–11pm; AE, MC, V) shoots to re-create home cooking, with a few modern Asian favorites thrown in for diversity. The changing daily sandwich comes with salad, fries, or soup for $10, there's a selection of wood-baked dishes ($10–$14; an oven sizzles away through an open wall in the kitchen), and for dessert, there's a cream pie of the day on offer, about $6. (Don't ya love it?) Thoughtfully (and unusually in town), there's a kids' menu, and what's more, just about everything is available in two or three varying portion sizes, making Chow a smart pick to satisfy the hunger of a varied group. All of this goes down within view of the intersection of Market and Church, and watching trams load and unload makes a meal worth lingering over. Happily, beer is served on tap.

$$$ Across the intersection, dinners-only **Home** ★ (2100 Market St., at Church; ☎ 415/503-0333; www.home-sf.com; daily 5pm–midnight; MC, V) is for those folks who find meatloaf sexy, because the down-home food is served in a dimly lit environment suited to date night. Portions are huge and free soda refills keep on flowing. Home doesn't have the alienating utilitarianism of a diner, although the dishes, which change regularly, are generally interpretations of familiar classics: meatloaf with brown-sugar carrots and potato puree ($14), duck spring rolls with hot chili sauce ($9), and banana bread pudding accented—and not over-whelmed—by a lovely thin bourbon sauce ($6.50). Reservations are suggested on weekend evenings. There's a full bar. It's busy for brunch, served on Saturdays and Sundays until 2pm.

$$$–$$$$ A neighborhood mainstay since the mid-1980s, **Sumi** ★★ (4243 18th St., near Collingwood; ☎ 415/626-7864; www.suminthecastro.com; daily 5:30–10pm; AE, MC, V) is one of the few places willing to serve up high-quality California cuisine (meaning fresh, local ingredients, usually with an Asian twist) at prices that the hoi polloi can swing. A major reason is its Castro location, far from the bankers and investors, and another is the devotion of its chef-owner, Sumi Hirose. Entrees off the regular menu cost in the upper teens, but I will steer you to the three-course *prixe fixe*, offered nightly from 5:30 to 7pm and costing $28. Menu items change, but they're always sassy in more ways than one—a recent menu entry was called "Check Out that Rack . . . of Lamb," although I'm even more taken with the inventive sides (truffled mashed potatoes, tamarind but-ternut squash soufflé) than I am with the well-cooked meat mains. As a sign of how justifiably confident of their work Hirose is, your bill will arrive with a com-ment book filled with the thoughts of previous customers.

$$–$$$$ Chef Chris Cosentino of the Tuscan-styled **Incanto** (1550 Church St., at Duncan; ☎ 415/641-4500; www.incanto.biz; Wed–Mon 5:30–9:30pm; AE, MC, V) does smart Italian-style dishes with fresh ingredients. Among the more inter-esting dishes of late are ramp and fiddlehead fern risotto; white wine and rose-mary smoked rabbit; and parsnip ravioli with pine nuts and sage brown butter. Meat dishes are about $20, which is a great price for solidly done *carne* in this town, and pasta dishes can be had as filling half-orders for about $11. Save room for dessert, because they're curious, too (flourless chocolate cake with pink pep-percorn ice cream). There's also a wine bar here, with more than 20 varieties avail-able by the glass.

CIVIC CENTER, HAYES VALLEY & JAPANTOWN

The places nearest the Civic Center veer toward unspectacular joints serving lunching city workers and salt-of-the-earth grub slingers. Within walking dis-tance, Hayes Valley has a more style-aware vibe, good for dinner dates and brunches, and attracts discerning young couples living off the proceeds of the dot-com boom (or preparing for the next one). Japantown, as the name implies, draws young Asian patrons with a semblance of authenticity.

$ There's always a bewilderingly disorganized, seemingly unmoving group of people snaking out the door for the *banh mi* at **Saigon Sandwiches** ★★★ (560 Larkin St., at Eddy; ☎ 415/474-5698; Mon–Sat 6am–6pm, Sun 7am–5pm; cash only); now and then, one of the women behind the counter takes the orders of about 10 customers at a time, many of whom, you'll notice, order huge bagfuls to take back to friends and co-workers. (You'll probably want to take yours away, too, since there are only two rickety wooden chairs crammed into this closet-like space.) These baguette sandwiches are well-stuffed but dirt cheap ($2.75–$3.25 each, depending on your choice of meat), and scrumptious. If you don't like spice, do be alert and order one without jalapeños; otherwise, you'll feel the burn when you bite into one. The blend of meat, carrots, onion, cilantro, and other greens elevate a sandwich into a meal. But I think the special sauce, which I'd say has a little honey it, makes them as addictive as they are. These babies may be the best food bargain in the city. Take a few back to your hotel—they're just as good 6 hours later.

$ Meatballs and spaghetti for $6.50. Salmon fillet with rice for $7.75. Buffalo-meat chili for $6. Welcome to ever-filling **Tommy's Joynt** ★★★ (1101 Geary Blvd., at Van Ness; ☎ 415/775-4216; www.tommysjoynt.com; 10am–1:45am; cash only), a scream from the past, lined on one wall with a busy steam table and on the other with a big, boozy bar with a huge list of imported beers and plenty of football memorabilia. Going strong since 1947 (check out its antique neon sign), Tommy's may be the last place on Earth to serve martinis for $3.50. Although this place has the outward personality of a beer hall, and its cuisine is appropriate to a *haufbrau* and nothing more swish, it's at its prime during lunch, when folks from all walks of life line up at the carvery. This is definitely a carnivore's paradise: huge chunks of meat are served fresh daily, with daily specials (Mon is oxtail), and some of the city's best pastrami. A particular value is Tommy's Big Sandwich ($5.50), with your choice of four meats piled much higher than you might think possible. I honestly don't know how they do it for the price. Amazingly, this value continues on until 1:45am daily.

$–$$ Soothing even when busy, which is often is, **Ananda Fuara** ★★ (1298 Market St., at 9th; ☎ 415/621-1994; www.anandafuara.com; Mon–Tues and Thurs–Sat 8am–8pm, Wed 8am–3pm; cash only) is a top value. Everything vegan is marked as such on the menu; otherwise, it's vegetarian and homemade. The soup of the day is usually something enticing (I like the Thai coconut), as is the Neatloaf (made of grains, eggs, ricotta, tofu, and spices). The staff, all followers of spiritual teacher Sri Chinmoy, a pan-religious, Hindu-inflected movement of celibacy and vegetarianism (they sell yoga and meditation books by the register) are helpful but on a different wavelength. Specials are more likely to be in stock during lunch, but servings are enormous no matter the time of day. It's ironic that a place dedicated to peace and non-consumerism should waste such a huge amount of food. I love its *lhassis* (yogurt drinks), and I particularly love the fact it sells baked potatoes—a rarity in this nouveau foodie town—for $4 to $7 with elaborate toppings.

$–$$ A modernized classic diner, **Mel's Drive-In** (kids) (801 Mission St., at 4th; ☎ 415/227-0793; www.melsdrive-in.com; Sun–Thurs 6am–1am, Fri–Sat 24 hrs; AE, MC, V) has been around for 60 years. Befitting its 1950s shtick, it serves an array of classic diner food, such as meatloaf sandwiches, patty melts, and burgers in the $8 zone. The steak-and-eggs plate is a huge deal: a 6-ounce hunk of meat, three eggs, grilled potatoes, and toast and jelly for $7.50. Late-night noshers should venture here, because the kitchen serves until 1am Sunday through Thursday and round-the-clock on weekends. This location isn't actually a drive-in—for that, there's a Mel's at 2165 Lombard St. that was used as a location in the movies *Guess Who's Coming to Dinner* and, most notably, *American Graffiti*.

Another Mel's is located near the Civic Center (3355 Geary Blvd., at Van Ness; ☎ 415/292-6358).

$$ Sushi restaurants are treacherous territory. If you're like me, you can easily turn an affordable meal into a blowout with the merest slips of willpower. That's why it's only with trepidation that I include **Isobune** ★ 🔟 (1737 Post St., at Buchanan; ☎ 415/563-1030; daily 11:30am–10pm; AE, MC, V), a rotary sushi restaurant in the ever-unordinary Japan Center where many dishes are $2 to $4. Many Americans may not be familiar with conveyor-belt sushi, in which customers sit along a bar and dishes cruise past them; if they want something, they grab it, and the value of the plates are calculated at the end of your meal. This place opened in 1982, when the notion was completely new to America. I personally love the style, because it's casual and it tempts me into trying more than the usual salmon and tuna—if I don't know something's name as it glides by looking appetizing, I'm more likely to try it. The twist here, one that kids will love, is that instead of a belt, the delivery method is little linked boats in a flowing stream. Like many of its forebears that feed salarymen in Tokyo or Nagoya, this restaurant is more of a joint—of average decor and not much space (so go in the late afternoon before there's a wait). My advice is to sit at the end of the long part of the bar where you can see the fish coming for a while, because, that way, you can think everything through and avoid the trap of making expensive snap decisions about what to grab.

$$ While you're in Japantown, see if you can squeeze into the contemporary all-you-can-eat shabu-shabu restaurant a block away at **Mums** 🔟 (1800 Sutter St., at Buchanan; ☎ 415/931-6986; www.mumssf.com; daily 7am–10pm; AE, MC, V) in the Hotel Tomo. Just $40 will get you limitless food, beer, and sake, and if you don't want the booze, $24, including dessert, is the magic number. And, boy, do people give the staff, which isn't stingy about seconds and thirds and fifths, a run for its money—crowds are thick on weekend nights, so have a reservation ready. *Shabu-shabu*, or family-style hot pot, is simply a lot of fun and ideal for spending a couple of hours as a family or a group of friends: Broth cooks in the middle of your table (kids, who pay $13, should be old enough to keep away) while you're served plates of thin-sliced meats and vegetables to dip in the soup yourself. It's a social dining style that's popular across East Asia, sharing space with the McDonald's and KFCs. Meats are a twitch fatty, but that gives them more flavor. A la carte mains are also served for about $14, and the place is even open for breakfast, when it serves the budget-mod Hotel Tomo (p. 46) upstairs.

$$ German classics in a rustic, jolly, beer-hall setting: That's **Suppenküche** (525 Laguna St., at Hayes; ☎ 415/252-9289; www.suppenkuche.com; daily 5–10pm; MC, V). You'd better like meat, because once you leave the realm of the appetizers (like a velvety potato soup [$5]), you'll be partaking of the kind of peasant food (priced in the mid-teens) that grannies everywhere have been cooking up for generations, including wiener schnitzel, bratwurst with sauerkraut, and good old sautéed trout. The place gets jammed, partly because a host of unusual European beers attract aficionados.

$–$$ For something different, try **On the Bridge** (1581 Webster St., Suite 205; ☎ 415/922-7765; daily 11:30am–10pm; MC, V), which presents a quirky mélange of American and Japanese food known as the Yo-Sho-Ku-Ya style. Yankee classics are given an Asian spin, including calamari and kimchee (Korean pickled vegetables) spaghetti ($10.25) and a selection of rice bowls piled with vegetables, béchamel sauce, and three types of cheese ($8.75 to $10.75). Sometimes it works, sometimes it's noble experiment—with mixes like these, it's a matter of taste—but you're sure to find something memorable. Perhaps most interesting of all is its location inside a narrow, arched bridge over Webster Street that connects two buildings of the Japan Center. If the food here doesn't interest you, have a stroll around the Japan Center, where a few other noodle houses and sushi bars (and an expensive Benihana grill) also fish for customers.

$$ A charming Italian spot that's well situated for Civic Center jaunts (crowds build before showtimes, so plan accordingly), the bistro **Stelline** ★ (330 Gough St., at Linden; ☎ 415/626-4292; Mon–Fri 11:30am–9:30pm, Sat 5–9:30pm, Sun 4–9:30pm; MC, V) is popular with locals. There's not much concerted drama in terms of decor—red-checked tablecloths, a crude painting of the Leaning Tower of Pisa—but the menu is solid across the board (the *osso bucco* [$12] and garlic bread, served free with many mains, have strong adherents) and prices are affordable, too, at around $10 a plate of pasta. Considering how pricey the rest of Hayes Valley can be, this place is a gem. And it's right across the street from the beloved Blue Bottle Coffee Kiosk (p. 86), so hold off on the post-meal espresso.

$$–$$$ A classic hole in the wall with just a few stools at a marble counter, **Swan Oyster Depot** ★★ (1517 Polk St., at California; ☎ 415/673-1101; Mon–Sat 8am–5:50pm; cash only), which opened in 1912, is revered in town for its fresh seafood and its salt-of-the-earth service staff. There's usually a line; an hour's wait isn't unusual at high mealtimes. The only problem is that it closes right around the time the rest of us are gearing up for dinner, but that's by virtue of the fact that seafood arrives freshest in the morning. The shellfish is absolutely, just-spent-the-morning-flipping-around-on-the-dock fresh (oysters, crab, lobster—most around $11). If you don't like any of that, Swan won't have much else for you, despite its perky hand-painted menu on the wall. While not dead cheap, it's still a better value than any of the tourist traps at Fisherman's Wharf, and when I'm in the market for seafood, I come here first.

$$–$$$ The service is frenzied but the food connects at **Max's Opera Café** 🧒 (601 Van Ness Ave., at Golden Gate Ave.; ☎ 415/771-7301; www.maxsworld.com; daily 11:30am–10pm; MC, V), a very busy deli-style bistro by the Civic Center slinging massive portions of piled-high salads, fat sandwiches (I like the bacon, lettuce, tomato, and avocado [$12]), the drippy Reuben ($14). You could share nearly everything. It's rare to have space in your stomach after the giant portions cross your table, so try to save room. As inspiration, have a look at the dessert-stuffed glass case that's by the entrance, which enshrines some insanely intense treats such as five-layer chocolate cake (around $7). This spot is popular with the California state workers from the government buildings across the street, so try to time your arrival out of lunch hour. And then there's that gimmick: aspiring-singer waiters who, in the evenings, sometimes break into song with a staff pianist. That'll bore most kids, but there is a kids' menu anyway.

CAFES

This city is packed with 'em. Sometimes it seems as if the people here have no occupation other than caffeine ingestion. Nearly every establishment offers free Wi-Fi, which may save you some money, and most of them also serve light meals that will save you the time and money of having to shell out for an elaborate sit-down meal. Here are some of the more notable ones, but I heartily encourage you to find your own favorites based on location and vibe. Some of these places also serve light meals, some focus on coffee.

$ Established in 1956, at the height of North Beach's artistic fortunes, **Caffe Trieste** ★★★ (601 Vallejo St., at Grant; ☎ 415/392-6739; www.caffetrieste. com; daily 7am–10pm; MC, V) has survived the generations to become what's probably the most beloved cafe in the neighborhood, if not the city. There may be no better place in San Francisco to kick back with an espresso and watch the city scene file by. Coffee nuts count it as serving some of the best brew in town, and the selection of pastry is homemade. Francis Ford Coppola is said to have written most of *The Godfather* at the same tables where, today, locals read poetry and surf the Web. Although it receives its share of tourists, the Trieste is really a friendly joint, where established customers are treated like gold by the otherwise harried staff and then spend hours sitting and reading the paper. For a real taste of North Beach eccentricity, running since 1971, stop by Saturdays from noon to 2pm, when Giotta family members and their friends pick up the accordion and entertain customers with live concerts of Italian opera songs, Dean Martin hits, and even show tunes—all for the price of a cup of coffee. Granted, you'll have to fight the line to get that.

$ On weekend afternoons, people hang out on the heated front porch of the Mission's **Revolution Café** (3248 22nd St., at Bartlett; ☎ 415/642-0474; daily 9am–1am; cash only) and listen to live music—usually, someone with a guitar, a harmonica, or both. A modest wood-floored place with only a dark banner to signify it's even there, the bohemian Revolution feels like the sort of hipster cafe that the Beat writers might have hung out. It serves salads and sandwiches for $6 and tomato soup for an unheard-of $2.50 a cup. Music becomes the focus, and seats scarce, nightly around 9pm. Try the ginger latte ($4).

$ The huge red Probat roaster in the window signifies what makes **Caffé Roma Coffee Roasting Co.** ★ (526 Columbus Ave., at Union; ☎ 415/296-7942; www. cafferoma.com; daily 6am–7pm; MC, V) superior to all the other coffee houses around. And it takes its coffee very seriously; although a cup of fresh-made espresso costs $2, if you're foolish enough to order it with a slice of lemon, you'll be charged $20—the owner, Anthony Azzollini, a third-generation roaster, insists that citrus masks the true flavor of his labors. Bags of coffee are also sold to go. This location is smack-dab in North Beach, and the family runs another location in SoMa (885 Bryant St., at 7th; ☎ 415/-296-7662).

$ No sign of a shop here—just an industrial-chic fold-up garage door and a gaggle of caffeinated hipsters gathered expectantly below. But **Blue Bottle Coffee** ★ (315 Linden St., at Gough; www.bluebottlecoffee.net; closes at 6pm daily ; cash only) in Hayes Valley is a revered coffee brewer in a city where tongues are discerning. The mandate here is to return to the flavor of the coffee bean, eschewing flavored drinks and pesticides. Beans are prepared in a roaster with a 6-pound capacity. Need I point out it's organic? And strong? You'll find it (but no seating or food) beside Dark Gardens, a custom corset maker (really). The beanery has also opened a small cafe with about a dozen seats south of Market near Union Square (66 Mint St.; ☎ 415/495-3394). There, check out its $20,000 Japanese cold-drip brewing machine with halogen flames and glass orbs—it's like something Captain Nemo would use.

$ Phil Jaber and his son Jacob have the elevated sensibility of winemakers, but they apply their sophisticated palates to five-star coffee blends instead, which they sell at the Mission's **Philz Coffee** (3101 24th St., at Folsom; ☎ 415/875-9370; www.philzcoffee.com; daily 6am–8:30pm; MC, V). Cups are brewed to order from a wide array of unusual blends (some two dozen; the Turkish Coffee is made with mint and cardamom), and couches are deep and soft. It operates a second location in the Castro (4023 18th Street, at Noe; ☎ 415/875-9656).

$ Smoking in restaurants is no longer legal in California, so North Beach's **Mario's Bohemian Cigar Store Café** (566 Columbus Ave., at Union; ☎ 415/362-0536; daily 10am–11pm; MC, V) won't live up to its name. What you will get, though, is a thoroughly local, long-running establishment situated on the south of Washington Square and popular with people-watchers but not so many tourists. There are plastic tables on the sidewalk, but inside, among the Italian art posters, is where it's at, as the servers plop down homemade Campari, intensely filling focaccia sandwiches ($8; try the meatball one), and a mean cappuccino, the house drink (although the homemade Campari is an acquired taste).

$ You'll find it at a perfect location for soaking up San Francisco atmosphere: on a corner along the Powell-Hyde cable-car line. That makes the quintessential cafe, **Nook** ★★ (1500 Hyde St., at Jackson; ☎ 415/447-4100; www.cafenook. com; Mon–Fri 7am–10:30pm, Sat–Sun 8am–9pm; AE, MC, V), a terrific place to sit at an outdoor table and soak up Nob Hill's distinct ambience—"So," you'll sigh to yourself as the car's bell clangs, "this is why I came to San Francisco." Menu selections are clean and basic (lots of small plates for $7–$8: artichoke bottoms with goat cheese; olive tapenade and hummus on ciabatta), and not only is the wine list long for a cafe, but it offers most choices by the glass (about $7). Salads ($5–$8) are good here in a way they almost never are at similar cafes. Now and then, the cafe books live music acts at night. The only downer is getting there; it's at the top of a hill. But if you need a simple, light meal with atmosphere, it's hard to do better.

$$–$$$$ A classy cafe that's close to Union Square (it's northeast of it), **Café de la Presse** (352 Grant Ave., at Bush; ☎ 415/398-2680; www.aqua-sf.com/cdlp; Mon–Sat 11:30am–2:30pm and 5:30–9:30pm, Sun 11:30am–4pm; MC, V) does the

Growth Markets

Besides the farmer's market at the upscale Ferry Building on Tuesdays and Saturdays (p. 71), there's another popular farmer's market in town, and this one, by dint of the fact that its overhead is lower, attracts more small-time vendors. Prices are also drastically lower than those charged at the tourist-destination Ferry Building. I'm talking about the Civic Center farmer's market, also known as the **Heart of the City market** (Market Street at 8th; Wed & Sun 8am–5pm). Get there early (before 10am) and try one of the sublime, sugar-dusted efforts from the Belgian waffle cart ($3 each). The owners say they're the only American seller to import their batter from Europe. Other booths sell fresh-pressed apple cider, affordable meats and vegetables, and cheeses, all at sensible prices.

Finally, on Thursdays from 11am to 3pm in the **Crocker Galleria** (50 Post St., at Montgomery; no phone; www.shopatgalleria.com; Mon–Fri 10am–6pm, Sat 10am–5pm), in the Financial District shopping mall, a small farmer's market deals in nuts, fruits, vegetables, cheese, and fish. Vendors only sell items they raise, catch, or grow themselves. Happily, this market is not only affordable but also covered, making it a pleasure in any weather.

cafe in the French style: with lots of reading material and an invitation to stick around for much longer than might be seemly anywhere else. It stocks dozens of international publications (some in English), all available to read for free. The location, right across the street from the Chinatown gate, is an excellent people-watching corner. The food, also very French, is not quite cheap despite the fact that it's light fare—onion soup is $8.50, and mains fall around $20. But you don't have to eat. You can just look at the pretty pictures in the Italian *Vogue* and have a pastry.

IT'S AN INTERESTING THING ABOUT SAN FRANCISCO. FOR SUCH A BELOVED tourist's city, there are surprisingly few world-class attractions such as museums and historic sights. Basically, there's not heaps to see, but there's tons to look at, if you know what I mean. Much of the lure of this town lies in things that are lovely to behold: the Golden Gate Bridge, for example, and the city's famous vertiginous streets where the lovely Painted Lady houses preen. A worthwhile visit to San Francisco could entail nothing more than strolling its pretty residential lanes, admiring its architecture, and sitting on the water; most of the city's appeal doesn't require a cent to enjoy. There's something to be said for a city that's memorable simply for what it is, without bells and whistles to muddy its charm.

That said, everything in this chapter is worth your time, even if I have critiques about some attractions. Only once or twice do I list something I consider to be a dud, which I only do because tourists are bombarded with entreaties to visit, and I want you to be warned. Generally speaking, it's hard to go wrong in San Francisco as long as you can see its architecture, taste its food, and soak up the clang of the cable-car bell. The entire city is an attraction, and one that people travel halfway around the world to absorb.

The chapter opens with the attractions that it would be a crying shame if you missed—Alcatraz Island, for one. Then I'll list the city's other best sights by where they're located so that when you find yourself in a certain part of town, you can look up what's worth checking out while you're there.

But these attractions are not the limit of things worth seeing and doing in town; not by a long shot. Make sure you look through chapter 6 (The "Other" San Francisco), which unearths lots of places and activities that most tourists never learn about.

Important note: Expect all the places in this chapter to be closed on Thanksgiving, Christmas Eve, and Christmas.

MAKING THE MOST OF YOUR TIME

IF YOU HAVE ONLY 1 DAY IN SAN FRANCISCO

Not a lot of time, but more has been done with less. If you know a few weeks in advance that you'll be coming, make a morning reservation for the ferry to **Alcatraz Island** (p. 89) and build your day around your visit there. The ferry ride will give you a decent view of the **Golden Gate Bridge** (p. 93) and of the city skyline. At **Fisherman's Wharf** (p. 100), have a peek at the resident **sea lions** and then drop into the bakery at **Boudin** (p. 137) and try some authentic sourdough—see whether the fuss is worth it (personally, I could eat it all day). Then take the **cable car** back to Union Square and either stroll through **Chinatown** (p. 125) or catch a historic F tram to the **Castro** (p. 172), where a stroll serves two purposes: an introduction to a typical local neighborhood and a walk through one of the world's most important centers for gay history. At night, head to **North Beach** (p. 109) for an Italian meal and for an after-dinner browse at the famous **City Lights** bookstore (p. 184), a First Amendment defender where the Beat-generation writers gathered.

IF YOU HAVE ONLY 2 DAYS IN SAN FRANCISCO

Think about starting your day with one of the city's excellent walking tours, such as the **Victorian Home Walk** (p. 129), on which you'll see dozens of colorful wooden antique homes, known here as "Painted Ladies." Then take the 1-day plan and spread it over 2 days, and throw in some museums. The **Asian Art Museum** (p. 114) offers a superlative collection, the **Museum of Modern Art**'s (p. 106) collection is no slouchy affair, or for those more into science, the **Exploratorium** (p. 121) and the **California Academy of Sciences** (p. 117) are two of the country's finest facilities devoted to learning about our world in high style. Also make a pass through the grand **City Hall** (p. 113), one of the most impressive civic buildings in the country—its cupola is larger than that of the nation's capitol.

IF YOU HAVE 3 OR 4 DAYS IN SAN FRANCISCO

Now you've got enough time to think about driving out to the Wine Country for a single day, although you'll only have time there for three or four visits to wineries. If that doesn't suit you, there are a number of interesting smaller museums worth adding into the list, including the **Cartoon Art Museum** (p. 106). Or take the BART across the bay and explore the college town of **Berkeley** (p. 104), long a cradle for brilliant minds and recalcitrant student movements.

IF YOU HAVE 5 OR MORE DAYS IN SAN FRANCISCO

Spend more time in the Eden of Wine Country, sipping a red that was made just feet away. If you're lucky enough to have this much time in the city, then by all means live a little more like the locals do: Head to a park or sweat a little. **Golden Gate Park** (p. 116), designed and sculpted by late 19th-century architects, is a particular bucolic pleasure, but the people watching is better at one of the city's smaller pocket parks, such as Washington Square Park, the heart of eccentric **North Beach** (p. 109). If you have the energy, rent a bike and take it over the Golden Gate Bridge—from its historic span—or, from May through September, take a ferry to the seaside settlement of **Sausalito** and from there, catch the shuttle to see the awe-inspiring redwood trees at **Muir Woods.**

ICONIC ATTRACTIONS

Probably the most famous prison in America, if not the world, **Alcatraz Island** ✹✹✹ (Pier 33, Embarcadero at Bay; no phone; www.nps.gov/alca; $25 ages 12–61, $23 seniors 62 and over, $15 kids 5–11; 9am–sunset, arrive at least 20 minutes before your reserved departure time) was where the worst of the worst

Major San Francisco Attractions

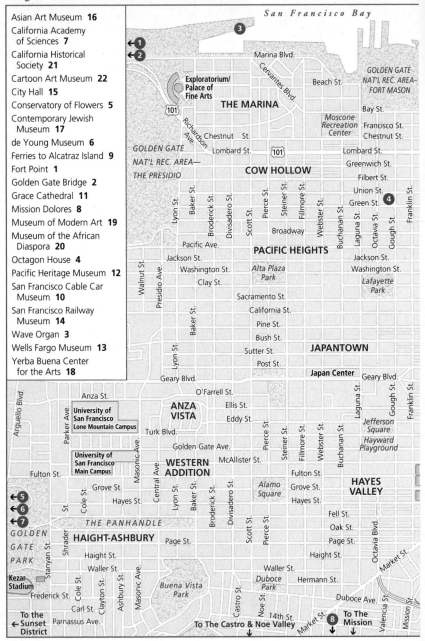

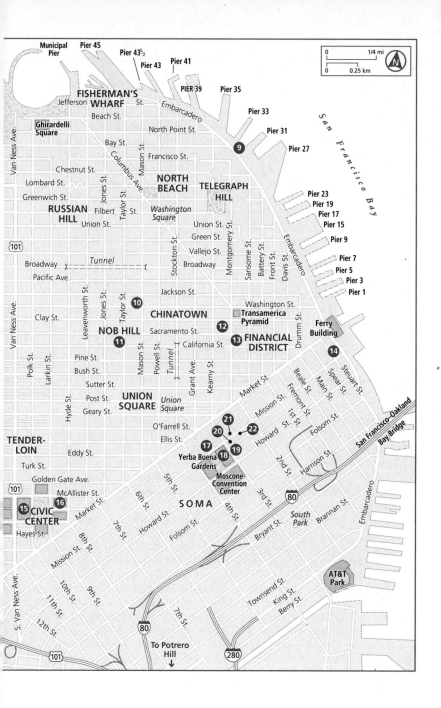

criminals were marooned to suffer and freeze in the Bay. Al Capone, the "Birdman"—if you've heard of a criminal who survived the gangster era without being gunned down, chances are they wound up here for a while. And to your amazement, you'll discover the building has barely changed at all from its days as a gray-bar hotel. It's like walking through the past.

From the middle 1800s to 1933, this National Historic Landmark was a military outpost protecting the harbor and then a military prison. But in 1934, it adopted its current reputation when the government converted it into a maximum-security pen for the nastiest crooks in the land—folks who deserved it, really. Inmates suffered psychologically and emotionally. The wind howled through the windows, the concrete was chilly and dank, and everything good and right in the world was perennially located at an unreachable distance. And that's still the case. Alcatraz Island, which is also known as "the Rock," was called at the time "Uncle Sam's answer to the gangster." A select few—1,500 prisoners—were ever guests of the government here, yet to this day, the place's name is still as notorious as its onetime inmates. A visit here isn't just morbidly fascinating; the prison is a rare case of a historic site being nearly perfectly preserved as it was in its heyday, and what's more, the view of the city skyline from here is sensational.

As a kid, I could never understand why the prisoners didn't just swim away, because the city is within sight across the water. But no documented person ever escaped and survived it. The cliffs are too tough, the Bay's water would cause rapid hypothermia, and there would be a strong likelihood of being swept under the Golden Gate and out to sea. In fact, the few that did escape either died or were immediately captured. The government finally shuttered the miserable cage in the early 1960s, citing maintenance issues that are still evident today. When the government closes a prison for being too uncomfortable, you know you've got a nasty place on your hands.

Today, it's owned and maintained (well, barely, given the meager budget) by the U.S. National Park Service, and it's surprising to see how untouched the place has been since the cons moved out. Look closely and you'll still see ancient urine stains around the old toilets, and in most cases, the doors of the 5×9×7-foot cells still function. A visit here can certainly make someone feel the winds of history chilling the napes of his neck, as the facility is so unchanged that the ghosts of the past aren't very far away.

Admission to the island includes a fascinating audio tour, *Doing Time: The Alcatraz Cellhouse Tour,* narrated by actual former convicts, who are less grizzled than you might guess; the main voice pronounces *escape* as "excape," as someone's adorable grandpa might. Don't be shy about pausing the recording with the Stop button; otherwise, it rushes you along a bit too quickly. And don't be afraid to break away after your first pass through Broadway (the main corridor) so that you can explore the recreation yard. If you don't want the tour (there are some signs, too, but the tour is richer), stop by the tiny gift shop across from the boat dock, and you'll get its cash equivalent, $8, back.

Before you climb the main hill to see the prison atop it, stop inside to see the fast-moving, intelligent Discovery Channel–style, 18-minute documentary that provides excellent background on the place. Also consider buying the $1 foldout map, which contains lots of facts and is a good value.

You'll then climb a paved slope to the prison building. It's the equivalent of 13 stories, which sounds worse than it is; if you can handle Powell Street north of Union Square, you can handle this, but do wear sensible shoes. (For those who need it, a tram runs intermittently.) Don't storm through the gift shop too quickly, because these souvenirs are among the most interesting in town, from tin cups ($10) to magnets that resemble the dummy human heads used in a famous escape attempt ($9). You can even buy a piece of the Rock, as they say.

If you come during winter, you'll be allowed to return down the hill using a path on the island's city-facing side, which is thick with agave plants and which boasts a terrific skyline view. But the other 8 months of the year, that area is closed to protect the nesting birds that have finally returned to the island after years of banishment.

GETTING THERE   There are two ways to get to the Rock, as it's known, and both of them involve a ferry operator called **Alcatraz Cruises** (☎ 415/981-7625; for prices, see above), which is contracted with the Park Service to bring folks to the island. Both require reservations as far ahead as you can make them, because this is one of the city's prime attractions and spaces do sell out. One method is to take the Day Tour. This tour allows you to book any available ferry—the ferries run more or less continuously, or at least half-hourly, from 9am to just before 4pm. Your ferry will go straight to the Rock's dock. Then, once you're satisfied, you can hop on any returning ferry. Alternatively, there's the Night Tour, which is offered once a day Thursday through Monday, around sunset. It goes once around the island, which the Day Tour boats don't do, and when you land, you'll get a guided tour that keeps you in its clutches. You may have some handsome views of the Bay in sunset, and you might find the evening light creepy and atmospheric, but you won't be able to explore on your own the way you can with the Day Tour. For that reason, I recommend the Day Tour. There's also an Early Bird tour, but there's nothing special about it other than the fact that it's first to depart. Even the price is the same. The departure point is Pier 33, which is about a 10-minute walk east of Fisherman's Wharf along the Embarcadero; any F-line streetcar will pass it.

Bank about 2½ hours to see everything that's open to visitors, and stretch that to 4 if you're the kind of person who asks questions of rangers. Eat before your appointment, because there's no restaurant on the Rock, and you're not allowed to picnic anywhere except on the boat dock, which is crowded with tourists most of the time.

Very few cities possess an icon that so distinctly pronounces, "I'm here." New York has the Statue of Liberty, Sydney has its Opera House, but nothing makes you sigh "San Francisco" like the elegant profile of the stupendous **Golden Gate Bridge** ★★★ (www.goldengatebridge.org), which links the city peninsula to the forests of Marin County. It's not just an emblem, it was also an epic engineering feat that, when it was completed in 1937, changed the city from a clunky, ferry-dependent one to one of the motor age. President Franklin Roosevelt, in Washington, pushed a button and opened it to traffic, and what was then the world's longest suspension bridge went into service, as it has been reliably ever

Little Known Facts About the Rock

♦ Although Burt Lancaster's film performance made the Birdman of Alcatraz famous as a gentle, nurturing soul, in reality, the guy was a psychotic maniac. What's more, he never had any birds at Alcatraz. Because prisoners here were refused special treatment, he was forced to give them up when he was transferred here.

♦ Al Capone was here, too, but not because he was bloodthirsty and unmanageable (although he did stab a fellow prisoner with some shears). Rather, the feds chose this prison because he was a celebrity crook whom they thought could be better protected here. He spent 4½ years on the Rock.

♦ The prison was closed for good in 1963. In 1969, a group of local Native American idealists peacefully seized the island, claiming an obscure law ceding unused federal land to its original Indian owners. It worked for a while: Some 100 people spent 19 months living in its cells—look for the old signs welcoming you to "Indian property." The island is full of other little mementos of this Utopian community as well, mostly in the form of graffiti, but also in the form of the charred remains of a fire that couldn't be fought because the government had cut the water supply. By the time the squatters started stripping the copper wiring from the buildings, public sentiment turned against them. Finally, the government won by pointing out that the lighthouse was in operation for the government and, therefore, the island belonged to Uncle Sam.

♦ On Sundays and Mondays, the gift shop (the one found at the tour's conclusion, and not the one by the dock) usually hosts Jolene Babyak, a woman who grew up on the Rock as a child of a warden, and who today is one of the world's foremost experts on everything to do with the island. She'll tell you stories about what it was like to be a kid on the island and take a ferry to school every day; surprisingly, she says it felt very normal, and she never saw any prisoners.

♦ Why haven't they turned some of the empty buildings into a historical resort? Mostly because the island is still operating on its antique sewer line, which is barely strong enough to support the guest restrooms and gift shop as it is. Any future restorations or development will probably require a new line, which has kept anyone from seriously trying. That didn't stop a group of activists from attempting to convince the government to convert the island from a museum into a "Peace Center," an idea that was soundly defeated in a 2008 referendum. Locals love their Rock as it is: harsh and creepy.

since (although now it's the second-longest in the country). It cost $26 million—less today than what it would cost to destroy it in an action movie, as so often happens. On the big day, cars paid 50¢, and pedestrians surrendered a nickel to thrill to the sight of the deadly swirl of rushing currents far below. In an era when strides in steel and engineering measured a country's worth, this was a potent symbol of power. And it still impresses; it's tough to look down from its span and watch the waters roil angrily without being a little thankful that the wonders of engineering have the ability to make modern life so comfortable.

The bridge also has a dark side; it's the site of a suicide every one or two weeks. (See the documentary *The Bridge* [2006] for a troubling look at some of them.)

The bridge is not named for its color—it's red, after all, not yellow—or even after the miners of old, but for the channel below, which was originally named by knowing sailors after the treacherous Golden Horn in Turkey. Depending on the weather or the time of day, the stately bridge presents a different personality. That mutable color, known to its 38 ever-busy painters as "international orange," can appear salmon in daylight or clay red as the sun goes down. (It was originally going to be gunmetal gray, like the Bay Bridge, but folks fell in love with the red hue of the primer coat.) Wisely, the architects worked wonders in figuring out how to integrate the bridge with the landscape and not obliterate everything that led up to it, as usually happened in the 1930s. Consequently, getting a good snap of the thing isn't as easy as you'd think. Don't assume that just because the weather's clear where you're standing means that it's also clear at the bridge. Meteorological conditions around the mouth of the Bay never seem to match the rest of the city, and even experienced tour guides have a hard time predicting what the bridge conditions will be without looking at it first, but you can preview the cloud cover by going to the Golden Gate Bridge website, where there's a live webcam. Just know that winds seem to be strongest in winter; all 3 days that the bridge has ever had to close due to high winds fell in December.

GETTING ONTO THE BRIDGE ITSELF   There's a pathway across the east side of the bridge for pedestrians (5am–9pm in summer, 5am–6pm in winter) that is on the best side for fantastic city views (the other side takes in the Pacific), but as you can imagine, it gets crowded on weekends. Cars must pay 10 times what they once did—a toll of $5 when they drive into the city on the bridge (driving out is free)—but these days, bicyclists and pedestrians pay nothing. Of the two, I'd pick wheels every time, because the bridge isn't easy to reach on foot, as its entry on the San Francisco side is tangled up among the confusing and unfriendly roadways of the Presidio. The six-lane bridge, built to 1937 proportions, isn't the easiest or safest place to take photographs from your car, although plenty of tourists snarl traffic in the effort. Instead, planners have also been intelligent enough to construct a viewing deck, complete with a restroom, at the bridge's northern end that is accessible no matter from which direction you're coming on the 101. I prefer using it on the way into town, because visitors from southbound traffic must use a walkway that goes underneath the bridge, giving them a unique second perspective of its structural underpinnings. Try to show up earlier in the day, when the sun is unlikely to ruin your shots. If you do go on the bridge, for an extra thrill, be in the middle when a boat goes underneath;

freighters are exhilarating when seen from above, and the regular tourist sightseeing boats bob helplessly for an amusing moment as they turn around in the teeming waters; sometimes, you can hear their passengers shout in alarm.

If you're visiting the bridge on Friday or over the weekend, you may be able to tour historic Fort Point beneath the southern anchor; see p. 122 for information on that.

One of the unmistakable symbols of San Francisco is, of course, the **cable cars** ★★★ 🎒, which climb Nob Hill and Russian Hill and traverse town from Fisherman's Wharf to Union Square. There's nothing like them in the world anymore. Although the cars really don't go many places in town, every tourist finds it necessary to ride these open-air cars at least once, and as well they should, because feeling the cool Bay Area on your face as you rumble along is one of the world's great travel experiences. One-way rides cost $5 and they come with a ticket stub that serves as a souvenir postcard.

Some people feel the cable cars are touristy, but I don't think anyone should confuse "popular with tourists" with "tourist trap." These vehicles are not tourist re-creations but are legit down to the last axle, and the fact they've been around as long as they have makes them more authentic, not less. The cars, which were able to climb hills that regular streetcars couldn't, have plied the streets since 1873, when the technology was fresh, and the last complete routes were built in 1889. In the 20th century, most of the existing lines were pulled out and converted to buses, and the lines that exist now were cobbled together from the few surviving stretches. Most American cities had their own systems at one point in time, but progress changed things, and today buses have replaced all of them.

There are two main lines, one of which splits into two branches. From Powell and Union Square, the Powell-Hyde cars roll through Nob Hill and Russian Hill, the Powell-Mason cars go a block west of Chinatown and then through North Beach, and the California line, which doesn't split, does a straight shot to Van Ness Avenue from just west of the Embarcadero. The Powell-line endpoints are

Pedal over the Metal

For getting an up-close look at the bridge, I recommend **Bike and Roll** (☎ 866/ 736-8224; www.bikeandroll.com; $7/hr. or $27/day) which rents cycles for the specific purpose of crossing the bridge. There's a location at 899 Columbus at Lombard between North Beach and Fisherman's Wharf. From there, you'll enjoy a mostly flat ride to the Golden Gate Bridge. You get helmets, of course, as well as locks, maps, and route suggestions, a rear rack and a handlebar bag, and bikes in excellent condition (the inventory is refreshed annually). The company often grants 10% discounts for booking ahead online. Of course, you don't actually have to get beside the bridge to admire it; it's viewable from nearly everywhere along the Marina and Fisherman's Wharf waterfronts, from Alcatraz, and even from many residential hilltops in Pacific Heights. But you have to admit that being able to say you've crossed it is a lot more special, and getting there purely on foot is too cumbersome for most people.

Cable-Car Tips

- The turnaround at Powell-Hyde, at Hyde and Beach streets, is almost always packed with tourists departing Fisherman's Wharf. Although the terminus is home base to an amusing singer-songwriter-comic ("Thank you for not overreacting," is a typical quip when his performances meet silence), it's busy, and you could wait an hour or more for a ride on that car. Head a few blocks east to Taylor and Bay, because that's where the Powell-Mason car loads with much smaller crowds in waiting. This line goes through North Beach and is just as scenic, and it winds up at Market and Powell, the same place as the Powell-Hyde line.

- Many guidebooks will tell you that you can grab a cable car anywhere along its route, but that's not always the case. By the time they leave the ends of the line, most cable cars have filled to the point where the only space they have is on the running boards. If you want a seat, you pretty much have to board at the start of the line.

- Riding on the runners takes arm strength—your shifting weight will be delivered to your arms. It also takes some dexterity, because you'll have to press yourself inward whenever you pass another cable car—they pass closer than you'd expect, so be alert. It also takes stamina, because on cold days, the fingers start to numb long before the job of holding on is done. Don't let kids or the elderly undertake this position lightly.

- If you want a ride without a wait, the California Street line almost never has a queue. Board right upstairs from the Embarcadero BART station, two stops east from the Powell station. This line doesn't have a turntable, or make any turns, either—it's a straight shot to Van Ness Avenue—so it's easier to ride on the running boards than it is on the twisty Powell lines.

- Cash fares on the cable cars aren't cheap: $5 each way, no transfers, no staying onboard for a round trip. But if you're toting a CityPass, all rides are included, as are all bus and tram rides. And seniors who ride before 7am or after 9pm pay just $1. Conductors are extremely laissez faire about collecting fares, so don't fret if you don't look like a senior but are.

- Don't call them "trolleys," "streetcars," or "trams." They are cable cars because, well, they're powered by cables, and locals will frown at you if you get it wrong. Besides, there are streetcars in this town, too, so you have to be specific. (And you already know to *never* call the city "Frisco," right? Just checking.)

The Big Passes

Several outfits in town will try to sell you a card that grants you discounts at a variety of attractions and restaurants. They really do grant what they promise, but there's a secondary problem with most of these cards: They usually include stuff you'd normally never want to see or have time to cram in. Visiting extra attractions in an effort to make a discount-card purchase pay off is a classic way to derail your vacation out of a sense of obligation. Never buy a discount card without first mapping out the plans you have for your visit's days, because you'll likely discover you'd spend more money obtaining the card that you'd make back in touring. Never buy a discount card, here or in any other city, on the spur of the moment.

There is an exception: If I were on my first trip to San Francisco, and I wanted to take in as much of the town as possible, I would spring for the **CityPass** (☎ 888/330-5008; www.citypass.com) for two reasons: It's got 9 days of validity, giving you plenty of time to make it pay off, (most other passes have much shorter validity periods), and it actually covers things you'd want to see and not the silly tourist traps you don't. Wait, three reasons: It comes with a 7-day unlimited Muni pass, which includes unlimited free rides on the normally $5-each-way cable cars; just flash the CityPass at the driver, and you're off. It's a real treat to be able to use the cable cars as a daily transit option. The pass ($64 adults, $44 kids) includes admission to the **San Francisco Museum of Modern Art, the Aquarium of the Bay, the California Academy of Natural Sciences,** a 1-hour cruise around the Bay on **Blue & Gold Fleet,** and either a trip to the **Exploratorium** or to the **De Young Museum** and the **Legion of Honor.** There's a little-publicized perk if you buy your CityPass through Alcatraz Cruises; that will entitle you to an Alcatraz Island ferry ride and tour instead of a Blue & Gold scenic boat ride that's normally part of the package. Because the Alcatraz shuttle is worth a few more bucks, it's the better option. You can purchase CityPass ahead of time online, or at the box offices of any of the above attractions.

---

interesting to see because they employ turntables; cars at the end of their runs are whirled around 180 degrees by workers and rolled back onto the track for their return journeys. This absorbing aspect of the cars' operation, though, comes with a price: The turntable locations are the busiest, and in summer, you can expect a wait of an hour or more to board. On the California line, cars are double-headed and can roll in either direction without having to be turned around, which means you can usually get right on without much of a wait.

Cable-car conductors pride themselves on their bell-ringing abilities. Each July, there's a competition held in Union Square to determine who can clang the

Something called the **Wharf Pass** (☎ 415/440-4474; www.wharfpass.com; $61 ages 12 and over, $38 kids 5–11) is also sold for Fisherman's Wharf attractions, but most of the places it gets you into are tourist-trap garbage like Ripley's Believe It or Not! Museum, the Wax Museum, and a simple carousel. Are you really coming all the way to San Francisco for a wax museum? The best attractions on the pass—the Aquarium of the Bay and a Blue & Gold cruise of the Bay—are on the CityPass, so there's no need to duplicate your purchase. One potential advantage of this pass is that it also includes a day on a hop-on, hop-off tour bus, but the problem I have with it is that there will simply be too much to do in one day for the pass to pay off. The pass also grants the right to secure nominal discounts on a few other tours around town, but chances are, you'll only have time to take advantage of one or two. The passes are valid for 3 days, but if you spend 3 days at Fisherman's Wharf, you'll be missing a lot elsewhere.

The **Go San Francisco card** (☎ 800/887-9103; www.gosanfranciscocard. com) is another option. It must be purchased in day increments, starting at $50 for a single day and climbing to $155 for a week (although there are sometimes discounts online for cards valid for longer than 2 days). It's highly unlikely (nay, downright impossible) that you'll be going to many of the 45 included attractions anyway, and you almost certainly won't be able to visit enough of them in your allotted time period to make your purchase pay off. If you're tempted, it's essential that you know which attractions you'd use the card for, and then do some math and some scheduling to make sure you'd actually be saving money and that you'd actually have time to see enough to make it all worthwhile. A list of its attractions is available online. The Go people also have something called the Explorer card, which allows customers to pick three or five attractions from a list, which is still fewer than what CityPass offers for around the same price. Do five minutes of math based on would-be box office prices before handing over your money.

bell in the most original and interesting fashion; cable news networks like CNN love being there for breaking news like this.

Known worldwide as the crookedest street, even if it's only for 1 block and there are ones more crooked, **Lombard Street** ★★ (between Hyde and Leavenworth) is one of those sights you've got to take in, even though there's nothing to actually do there. The eight switchback turns were created in 1922 to mitigate the block's steep grade, because most vehicles of the day couldn't handle it. Now it's a tourist attraction, and residents of the street vacillate between pride (they garden the in-between spaces) and grouchiness (they've debated forcing visitors to take shuttle buses down their street). Pedestrians use a staircase/sidewalk alongside the road, safe out of the path of cars; the view down the hill and across to Coit Tower is something drivers are too focused on the wheel to enjoy with you. On weekends, the queue of cars wishing to drive down the street can stretch west past Van Ness. It's better to walk it, and for that purpose, you can jump off the Powell-Hyde cable car right at the top of the crooked part and then head down toward North Beach on foot.

SIGHTS BY AREA

FISHERMAN'S WHARF

In the old days, before the Golden Gate eased the traffic situation, commuters would pour off the cable car at Fisherman's Wharf and head for **Hyde Street Pier** ★ (Jefferson and Hyde sts.; ☎ 415/447-5000; www.nps.gov/safr; free admission; late May–Sept 9:30am–7pm, Oct–late May 9:30am–5pm), where they'd catch a boat across the Bay. Nowadays, nothing leaves from the pier; since 1962, it has been lined instead with a one of the world's best collections of rare working boats maintained by the National Park Service's San Francisco Maritime National Historic Park. They include the Glasgow-built *Balclutha,* a gorgeous 1886 three-masted sailing ship that, most famously, appeared in the classic Clark Gable movie *Mutiny on the Bounty;* the *Eureka,* an 1890 paddle-wheel ferryboat that was once the largest of its kind on Earth; the *Hercules,* a 1907 tugboat that worked towing logs up the West Coast; and the lumber schooner *C. A. Thayer* from 1895. The *Alma,* built in 1891, was once one of many schooners that plied the many waterways of the Bay Area, but today, it's the only one left. Although you can admire the boats from the dock for free, $5 will get you onto the *Balclutha,* the *Eureka,* and the *Hercules* as much as you want for a week. (National Park Service passes get you on for free.) All the vessels are designated National Historic Landmarks.

On the way onto the pier, stop by the **information center** and **gift shop** to the left of the entrance; there, or on the stands outside, you can glean information about when to catch the **free daily tours** conducted by rangers. There's a general 1-hour walking tour that goes daily at 10:30am, and the rest of the day, especially on weekends, will be peppered with absorbing tours such as a 45-minute tour of the *Eureka*'s engine room. Although these tours are useful for some basic background information, I have to say that I found the expertise of the ranger who guided me most recently to be suspicious; he pronounced *Ghirardelli* with a "jeer" (instead of a "gear"), and any anyone who has lived in the city longer than 10 minutes knows not to do that, although I didn't question his passion for ships. There's a poorly publicized but well-assembled historical exhibit about the Hyde Street Pier and the Wharf in the lobby of the Argonaut Hotel across the street, which agrees to provide the space to the National Park Service in exchange for the right to run a hotel in a historic warehouse.

On the other side of the cable-car turnaround, but closed at press time for a 3-year renovation, the **Maritime Museum** (☎ 415/447-5000; www.nps.gov/safr) looks like a Streamline Moderne ship preparing to sail to sea from Aquatic Park. It began life as a *lido* (public pool) in the 1930s before being given over to a museum in 1952. It's famous for its superlative model-ship collection, which is

Fisherman's Wharf & Vicinity

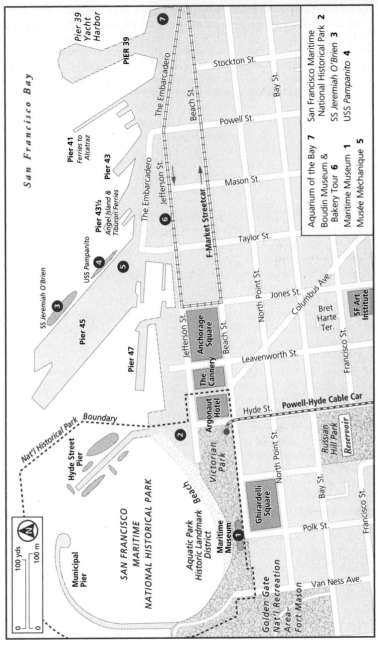

San Francisco Maritime National Historical Park **2**

SS Jeremiah O'Brien **3**

USS Pampanito **4**

Aquarium of the Bay **7**

Boudin Museum & Bakery Tour **6**

Maritime Museum **1**

Musée Méchanique **5**

expected to return, and for its Federal Arts Project murals, which will have been restored. The renovation is slated to end in 2009, when the museum is supposed to reopen.

There are two other interesting attractions in the area for boat and military nuts. A 10-minute walk farther east along Jefferson at Pier 45, on the water behind the Musée Méchanique, the submarine **USS *Pampanito*** ✦ (Pier 45 at Taylor; ☎ 415/561-6662; www.maritime.org; $9 adults, $5 seniors over 62, $5 students and kids 6–12, $20 families of 2 adults and 2 kids under 18; Sun–Thurs 9am–6pm and Fri–Sat 9am–8pm) sank six Japanese ships during four tours of the Pacific in World War II. The vessel, which is not for the claustrophobic or the infirm, has been painstakingly restored to its 1945 condition by admirers, who also run a smart, war-themed gift shop on the dock alongside it. Thanks to their efforts, she's still seaworthy, although, sadly, the last time she was taken out into the ocean was for the filming of the abysmal 1996 Kelsey Grammer film *Down Periscope*. How glory fades. . . .

Further down the pier, the **SS *Jeremiah O'Brien*** (Pier 45, at Taylor; ☎ 415/ 544-0100; www.ssjeremiahobrien.org; $8 ages 15–61, $5 seniors 62 and over, $4 kids 6–14, $20 families of 2 adults and 2 kids; 9am–4pm) is a Liberty-class ship from 1943 that served in D-Day; it sailed under its own power to the 1994 commemoration in France. Although the ladders can be challenging, it's easy to figure out where you are using the provided maps. The ship, as well as the *Pampanito,* is a National Historic Landmark.

Although it feeds off the overly touristy traffic of Fisherman's Wharf's Pier 39, the **Aquarium of the Bay** 🐟 (Pier 39, at Stockton; ☎ 800/732-3483 or 415/ 623-5300; www.aquariumofthebay.com; $15 ages 12–64, $8 seniors 65 and older and kids 3–11, $38 families of 2 adults and 2 kids; summers daily 9am–8pm, fall–spring Mon–Thurs 10am–6pm, Fri–Sun 10am–7pm) is actually principled, well-maintained, and informative. The admirable focus here is the aquatic life that thrives right outside in the Bay, which, because of its unique mix of water types and its steady flushing into the Pacific Ocean, is one of the world's best breeding grounds for oceangoing fish. The aquarium's highlights are two acrylic tunnels, totaling 300 feet, which pass directly along the bottom of two tanks. One highlights the kind of fish you'd find in the Bay (including rockfish and flounder—this section's the more varied of the two), and the other the kind of animals found right outside the Golden Gate (10-ft. sharks, 4-ft. lingcod). In between these two habitats, which you can see multiple times if you wish, you'll view a mesmerizing tank of jellyfish and get lots of printed lectures about conservation (preaching to the choir—you came to an aquarium, after all). The final attraction is called Touch the Bay, where you can lean over thigh-high rock-pool tanks and touch, with one finger and under regimented supervision, animals such as leopard sharks, skates, and starfish. Feeding times and story sessions happen roughly eight times daily from 12:30 to 4pm, so ask at the front desk what's upcoming. For another $6 you can join a "Behind the Scenes" tour (usually 2pm or thereabouts) that discloses some of the attraction's animal-husbandry secrets and allows you to peer at tourists in the tubes from a surface vantage point, but only the sincerest ichthyologist need apply. The aquarium's director, John Frawley, is a noted activist; recently, he's been famous for marking off lines across the city where the water level would be should the polar ice caps melt. Generally speaking, I'd visit this place if I had a pass that included admission to it, but unless you have a deep interest in the ecosystem of the Bay Area, you might not see it as anything but another aquarium.

At the end of the same pier, no. 39, don't neglect one of the city's unofficial attractions: a colony of **sea lions** ⭐ that took up residence here in 1990 for reasons unexplained that may have had to do with the major earthquake that happened the year before. Because the marina is protected, in winter the population can swell to a barking 900 lions. Most of them swim to the Channel Islands for the summer, but increasingly, a small population lingers behind, to the delight of restaurant owners on the pier. There's an information kiosk alongside the doglike creatures that's maintained by the **Marine Mammal Center** (☎ 415/289-7325; www.marinemamalcenter.org). They're one of the city's most delightful free attractions; find them near the end of the pier and to the left, in the marina at what's sometimes called the K-Dock.

Calling it a museum is stretching things, but **Musée Méchanique** ⭐ (Pier 45, at Taylor; ☎ 415/346-2000; www.museemechanique.org; free admission; Mon–Fri 10am–7pm, Sat–Sun 10am–8pm) is certainly fun, and the mechanical minded will find it fascinating. Straight out of the old school, this warehouse of dozens of antique coin-operated penny-arcade diversions, most of which you'll never encounter anywhere else, began entertaining people back in the 1930s, when a guy named George Whitney was his generation's leading impresario of cheap entertainment. Today, it's maintained by his descendent Daniel Zelinsky, an aficionado of such amusements, who stuck with a high-art name for his low-art attraction and showcases most of his 300-strong collection here. Because it's located among the pap of the Wharf, it's easy to confuse this one as a tourist trap, but the lack of an admission fee (you'll part only with whatever change you

---

Fishy Stuff at the Wharf

Be wary about spending too much time at Fisherman's Wharf. Most of the things to see and do at this carnival of ice-cream shops, crab stands, and tacky-souvenir stalls were created simply to capture tourist trade, full stop, and they offer scarce value to the visitor who wants to get to know the real San Francisco. There is very little of educational value to explore, although that doesn't stop tens of thousands of confused-looking tourists from making slow, dumbfounded walking circuits of Jefferson Street on weekends. Although the marina hosts some of the most-patronized seafood joints in town, by no means are they definitively the best. I'd give a visit to the area enough time so that I could walk from one end to the other, and maybe snap a few photos of the Bay. The places that I consider most worth your time and dollar, such as the ones operated by the National Park Service, include the **Hyde Street Pier** (p. 100), **Musée Méchanique** (see above), the **Aquarium of the Bay** (p. 102), the **Boudin bakery** (p. 137), the *Pampanito* (p. 102), and the **SS *Jeremiah O'Brien*** (p. 102).

Cal in an Afternoon: Berkeley, Breathlessly

Berkeley and Oakland, major American cities in their own right, are located right across the Bay, a 15-minute BART ride away. But I know that the vast majority of visitors to the area come to see San Francisco, not Oakland, where the sights are not as well known as they are in San Francisco.

Berkeley, for its part, has lots more going for it for a day's visit, particularly as a thriving college town. If you can take 4 or 5 hours out from your San Francisco sightseeing, a trip over is worth your time. That's because it's home to the legendary 178-acre university known simply as "Cal" for its claim of being the first University of California to be founded. That's the **University of California, Berkeley,** or even **UC Berkeley,** to the formal. While UC Davis is known for agricultural education, Cal is all about the sciences, and its students have been blowing the world's minds for more than 140 years. On weekdays, free tours of the main campus of 178 acres depart at 10am from the **Visitors Information Center** (101 University Hall, 2200 University Ave.; ☎ 510/642-5215). On weekends, meet at the base of the Sather Tower (the giant one—you can't miss it) at 10am Saturdays and 1pm Sundays. I strongly suggest taking one of these tours, because they sneak you into buildings where you otherwise couldn't go without a student ID.

The tours, which are led by trained students, are heavily used by prospective scholars, so in springtime your group may swell to 200 and your guide made dwell rather tediously on the school's rivalry with Stanford, but everyone is welcome, and you'll get heaps of fascinating historical information about the educational institution that fomented some of the strongest protests of the 1960s and 1970s.

Cal is responsible for tons of milestones, including the discovery of vitamins B, E, and K; plutonium; uranium 238; and the stumpy London plane tree, a hybrid that you'll see only here and in places in San Francisco. I consider the grounds, which are handsomely traversed by the quiet Strawberry Creek, one of America's quintessential college campuses: green, open, and interrupted by inhumanly blocky campus buildings you'd better pray you don't get lost in. You'll see Le Conte Hall, where the first atom splitters did their work. Keep your eyes peeled for parking signs that read, in total seriousness, "Reserved for NL"—meaning Nobel Laureate. (What kind of a car was in that space? I saw a Toyota Prius.) You know the parking situation is grim if you need a Nobel Prize to get a space. The Doe & Moffitt Library, mostly for undergraduates, doesn't allow public access to the 10 million books in its stacks, but its lobby areas, lined with glass cases filled with priceless manuscripts, is open to all. In a reading room upstairs, you'll also find Emanuel Leutze's 1854 *Washington Rallying the Troops at Monmouth,* which was intended to be a companion piece to his *Washington Crossing the Delaware* (now at New York's Met). Your tour will end with a discussion of the messy student protests for freedom of speech, in 1969, that resulted in the death of a student protester.

Although the university is renowned for the radicalism of its students, that label is mostly left over from the 1960s. It still operates under an uneasy alliance between conservative administration and liberal enrollees; a recent controversial development was British Petroleum's $500-million contract with the school for its programs to help develop alternative fuels that the company would, in turn, own.

To ascend the 307-foot-tall **Sather** (*Say*-ther) **Tower,** or the Campanile, pay $2. Like so many observation towers, its elevator stops short of the top, leaving the last 38 steps for you to navigate. Hours are funny: Monday through Friday 10am to 4pm, Saturday 10am to 5pm, and Sunday 10am to 1:30pm and 3 to 5pm. Its 61-bell carillon performs concerts daily at 7:50am, noon, and 6pm, and the week's longest concert is held Sunday at 2pm (https://music.berkeley.edu/carillon). The view from the pinnacle, on clear days, stretches all the way to the Golden Gate Bridge, lined up perfectly in the distance past the city skyline.

Also worth exploring is the clumsily named **University of California, Berkeley, Art Museum & Pacific Film Archive** (2626 Bancroft Way; ☎ 510/642-0808; www.bampfa.berkeley.edu; $9.50 ages 18–64; $6.50 seniors 65 and over, students, and kids 18 and under), where an exhaustive slate of screenings and exhibitions—often eight at a time, mostly dealing with contemporary art and politics—are scheduled. Something else that's cool: Visitors are allowed to audit Cal's undergraduate "Film 50" course, which screens at the archive across the street from the museum; book ahead online. The list of screenings is long and provocative; recent topics included the mainstream (Orson Welles) to the prickly (the riots of 1968), but as this is a film archive, titles are rarely something you'd find in a Netflix queue. It's free the first Thursday of each month.

It's no surprise that an institution so many mathies call home would produce several free podcasts and cellphone tours for visitors to use: Visit www.berkeley.edu/visitors/free_tours.html to download some of those.

As a public university, Cal has a surprising number of free sights and events ranging from concerts to brainy social and political discussions, to author readings—and not just any authors, but the cream of publishing; when I was there last, Pulitzer winner Michael Chabon *(The Amazing Adventures of Kavalier and Clay)* was booked. Pick the low-hanging fruit for yourself by hitting the school's jam-packed website (http://events.berkeley.edu), which also lists the various exhibitions that the school sponsors or hosts, either on campus or around town. When school is in session, you can also pick up a free copy of *The Daily Californian*, the student newspaper, where you can learn about more events, particularly student-organized ones.

deposit into the machines of your choice) proves that's not the case. Most of the machines require a few quarters to reveal their Coney Island–era thrills, and almost all the machines are representatives of a form of mechanical artistry rarely found in working condition anywhere. My favorite machines are the Opium Den, a morality tale in which a diorama of smoking layabouts comes alive with serpents and demons, and the Bimbo Box, in which seven monkey puppets respond to your loose change by playing the Tijuana Brass. The Guillotine is also macabre fun; its doors open to reveal the bloodless beheading of a tiny doll. But the stand-out machine is creepy old Laffing Sal, a funhouse figure that pretty much roars with laughter (and horrifies small children) upon the dropping of a coin. Kids who don't get it can head straight to the video games in the back. Every day except Tuesday, Zelinsky is on hand, repairing and polishing his beloved machines; he wears a badge reading "I work here."

SOUTH OF MARKET (SOMA)

The huge **Museum of Modern Art** ★★ (151 3rd St., at Mission; ☎ 415/357-4000; www.sfmoma.org; $13 adults, $8 seniors 62 and over, $7 students; open Thurs 11am–8:45pm, Fri–Tues 11am–5:45pm), or SFMOMA, is America's second-largest modern-art museum, and its breadth admirably provides something for most tastes. Regularly displayed works to look out for include Yves Klein's vibrant electric blue *Eponge*, which feels good on the eyes; two dark Diego Rivera paintings; and a passel of Paul Klee etchings and watercolors. The Anderson Collection focuses on modern and pop art, including Warhol, Rauschenberg, Lichtenstein, and a Jasper Johns flag. *Guardians of the Secret* is one of Jackson Pollack's more organized efforts. Just as popular as the permanent collection is the museum's steady program of big retrospectives and themed collections; on opening days, you may find a line around the block for a new show. The museum, housed in a cavernous 1995 building that is equally fun to explore as the works, is also notably inclusive, with plenty of representatives from the digital and filmed art worlds. Grab a $3 iPod walking tour when you enter, and check out the list of the day's free public tours by the staircase; they usually start at 11:30am with a general museum tour and wind up by around 3pm.

Right across the street at the **Yerba Buena Center for the Arts** ★ (701 Mission St., at 3rd; ☎ 415/978-2787; www.ybca.org; $7 adults; $5 seniors, students, and teachers; Tues–Wed and Fri–Sun noon–5pm, Thurs noon–8pm), or YBCA, the modern art on display is often slightly riskier—or even risqué—than it is at SFMOMA. You're far more likely to encounter an exhibition by a little-known artist or a maverick here than across the road. Many of the artists invited to show come from some kind of minority viewpoint, be it politically, racially, or through gender identity. When one of the galleries is in transition, the front desk will knock $2 off admission. I've always considered it a complementary space to SFMOMA, although, of course, it operates under its own power. As a testament to its quality, the museum also mounts traveling versions of shows for other museums, such as one examining the artist R. Crumb, once a local. The museum also curates a monthly series of video or film screenings that specializes in experimental film and documentaries, and you'll get in the galleries free with your ticket.

Major points go to **Cartoon Art Museum** ★★ (655 Mission St., near 3rd; ☎ 415/227-8666; www.cartoonart.org; $6 adults, $4 seniors and students, $2 kids 6–12; Tues–Sun 11am–5pm) for addressing what could be a tourist-trap topic with academic intelligence. In fact, it's probably not a place where young kids will have a good time unless they're steeped in pop art. Here, you'll tour several rooms of works by seminal and well-known comic artists, particularly ones whose efforts primarily appeared on newsprint. It began in 1987 with an endowment from Charles M. Schulz, the *Peanuts* creator (for an entire museum devoted to him, see p. 255), and since then, it's kept busy with up to seven changing exhibitions every year, and it has published 20 books (so far) on the neglected topic of cartoon history (the gift shop is excellent). I love anyplace that celebrates unsung Disney Imagineer Mary Blair, who created the distinctive look of "It's a Small World," as the museum did in a well-received exhibition in early 2008.

The **California Historical Society** (678 Mission St., at 3rd; ☎ 415/357-1848; www.calhist.org; $3; Wed–Sat noon–4:30pm), the state's official historical group, has a gleaming building near SFMOMA, and the ground floor hosts changing exhibitions about state history that have been put together with care. A recent one was "Past Tents," about the history of camping in California—a topic that nearly everyone in town has some experience in, but which usually gets no notice. Even if you're not interested in what's showing at the gallery, the small but well-inventoried gift shop is a strong source for books on state and local history.

The **Museum of the African Diaspora** (685 Mission St., near 3rd; ☎ 415/358-7200; www.moadsf.org; $10 adults, $5 seniors 65 and older, $5 students, kids 12 and under free; Weds–Sat 11am–6pm, Sun noon–5pmhttp://) is what I call a Spinach Museum—you go because it's good for you, or you go on a school field trip, but it's less than satisfying because there are almost no artifacts, only ideas. I smell lots of cash behind the enterprise, which is essentially designed to teach all the ways that people descended from Africa have enriched world culture. Undoubtedly true, that, but sitting in a darkened room while Maya Angelou's taped voice intones a few wordy narratives from slaves is not an electric way to bring that concept to life. Worse, the museum contradicts its own scholarship: Angelou reads that 20 million people were transported from Africa, and a sign outside the very same room gives the number as 10 million. There are occasional exhibitions worth catching, such as a recent cool photographic show depicting families around the world sitting amid piles of what they usually eat in a week, but in general, it's not worth the high price.

Opened in its latest home in June 2008, the **Contemporary Jewish Museum** (736 Mission St. between 3rd and 4th sts; ☎ 415/655-7800; $10 adults, $5 seniors over 64 and students, free for students under 19, $5 Thursdays after 5pm; Fri–Tues 11am–5:30pm, Thurs 1pm–8:30pm, closed Wednesday; www.thecjm.org) has won raves for its architecture, by Daniel Libeskind, who took a 1907 brick power substation and impaled its roof with powerful, geodesic outcroppings. (There is a free-with-admission architecture tour scheduled on most days.) Less celebrated is the museum itself. There isn't much on permanent display. Rather, it hosts various exhibitions, especially on art and photography, which change so regularly that deciding whether a visit warrants the ticket price depends entirely on what's showing right now. Whereas the Museum of the African Diaspora dwells on the ways black culture has enriched world culture, the Jewish Museum concertedly celebrates the reverse: the way the world has enriched assimilating Jews. Like the museum building itself, the collision of old and new ends up making a

Where the Views Are

Coit Tower? Sure. Looking back at the city from Alcatraz? Of course—it's gorgeous. But here are a few vantage points that you, as a tourist, may not have clued in on since they're off the main circuit.

Fort Point

Here's the classic panorama under the southern anchor of the Golden Gate Bridge—the one where Kim Novak drops into the sea before Jimmy Stewart's eyes in *Vertigo*. It's right above Crissy Field, a pasture-cum-beach with a picturesque bridge view that figures in countless other films and that is an ideal spot for picnics beside the bridge on nice days.

Alamo Square

Known to a generation of sitcom watchers as the picture-perfect exterior for *Too Close for Comfort* and *Full House,* the eastern end of Alamo Square is lined with seven gorgeous Painted Ladies (Victorian houses) framing a backdrop of the city's distinctive skyline. Bring a blanket, because the grass is often sodden and there are no benches in the area that has the best view. For a primo photo, line up the stone planter with the skyline and the Painted Ladies. Bus 21 from Union Square comes here, and you can walk to both Hayes Valley and the Haight from here. Afternoon light is best.

Tank Hill

Found north of Twin Peaks, this spot offers wide vistas of the Golden Gate Bridge, the Bay, and downtown from a distance. Go to the top of Stanyan Street, at Belgrave Park turn left, and then hike up the dirt path. The view at the top will wow you.

Grand View Park

If you'd like a water view of the Pacific Ocean and the Bay, this westerly park, scoured by cool sea winds, is not overly crowded. At 14th Avenue and Noriega Street, climb to the top of the steep stairs.

The Forbidden View

One place you *won't* be allowed to enjoy the view is from the 27th floor of the Transamerica Pyramid, the city's most recognizable skyscraper. After 9/11, its owners choked and closed the observation deck. Someone should probably tell them that metal detectors do wonders.

---

much stronger statement for modernity than for tradition. In fact, you won't find many antiques among the Judaica; the focus here is on current culture, so much so that the cafe isn't kosher and the museum remains open on the Sabbath.

I'd never given it much thought before, but it turns out that in America, you'll often find the largest concentrations of gay men in cities near the sea. Why? Because in the 1800s, being a sailor permitted homosexual men to live in all-male societies undetected, and the seaman's lifestyle enabled travel, free of unsupportive families. And the culture stuck through time. By World War II, the military embarked on a campaign to single out and decommission gay guys, and many of them were processed in San Francisco, where they simply stayed and made lives rather than go home in shame. This, and many other fascinating facts about a lesser-examined group of Americans, are scrutinized at the **GLBT Historical Society** ✦ (657 Mission St., Suite 300, at New Montgomery; ☎ 415/777-5455; www.glbt history.org; Tues–Sat 1–5pm). The facility is half a museum with changing exhibitions (a recent one was about gay members of the military) and half archive/reading room for use by folks interested in deeper research on the topic of what has largely been a shadow group throughout history. The holdings are unpredictable; every few years, a previously unknown collector of memorabilia will pass on and boxes of underground information, much of it concerning things thought to have gone undocumented, will show up on its doorstep. Anyone can visit; it's a gallery environment and not a meeting place, although some of the artworks on display are adult in theme. There are also intermittent events, such as reading series and lectures; these are announced online.

NOB HILL, NORTH BEACH & FINANCIAL DISTRICT

For a city monument that is so beloved, **Grace Cathedral** (1100 California St., at Taylor; ☎ 415/749-6348; www.gracecathedral.org; suggested donation $5 adults, $3 children; Sun–Fri 7am–6pm, Sat 8am–6pm), the third-largest Episcopal cathedral in America, is surprisingly imitative. Its face was designed to recall Paris's Notre Dame. The front doors are copies of Ghiberti's doors from the Baptistry in Florence. The cathedral is undoubtedly impressive and beautiful (check out the gorgeous stained-glass rose window), but in architectural terms, it lives in the mimicry of European originals. Where Grace really stands out is in the compassion of its congregation, in no finer display than in the Interfaith AIDS Memorial Chapel that's located to the right as you enter. Two weeks before his own death from the disease in 1990, pop artist Keith Haring completed a triptych altarpiece called *The Life of Christ.* The final 600-pound work in bronze and white gold patina sits in the chapel's place of honor. The church has been respecting and praying for AIDS victims ever since 1986, back when most people in our government were sitting on their hands even while this city was being devastated. A segment of the famous AIDS Memorial Quilt is displayed above the chapel; it's rotated on a regular basis with new pieces. The hand-bound book in the glass case seeks to record the name of everyone ever claimed by AIDS. Other objects worth checking out include the murals that retell stories of the church's history (including its destruction in the 1906 quake), as well as a chunky sculpture of St. Francis by Benny Bufano, who designed some of the city's most distinctive work. Toward the Chapel of Grace, toward the back and to the left, check out the life-size crucifix from 1200s Spain that reveals Christ in macabre suffering. Kids usually enjoy finding their way through the two labyrinths, one in front of the building and one just inside, which were once used in meditation. There are no walls—just lines in the ground—so there's no getting claustrophobic.

Next door at the associated **Diocesan House** (1055 Taylor St.), there's a small and pleasant sculpture garden as well as, inside, frequently a free exhibition of photography or art. Tour guides are generally on hand Monday through Friday 1 to 3pm, Saturday 11:30am to 1:30pm, and Sunday 12:30 to 2pm, although

History on the Move

New visitors might lay eyes multiple times on the rumbling streetcars on the F line, which goes on a round-trip journey from Fisherman's Wharf to the Ferry Building via the Embarcadero and then heads straight down Market Street to the Castro. But most of them don't register what they're seeing: streetcars from the early and mid-20th century. A hard-working nonprofit group helps Muni restore and maintain antique streetcars from around the world, and if you take the F, you'll board one of the fleet. A few hail originally from here in town, but most come from a wide variety of cities, from Blackpool, England, to Melbourne, Australia, to Brooklyn. There's usually a sign in the middle of the car that explains the particular pedigree of the one you've boarded. I'm not particularly a train spotter, but I find it thrilling to be able to experience an everyday commute that is pretty much exactly the way my forefathers did.

At the foot of Market Street, across from the Ferry Building and next to a streetcar stop (most tourists overlook it, too), the **San Francisco Railway Museum** ★ (77 Steuart St.; ☎ 415/975-1948; www.streetcar.org; free admission; Wed–Sun 10am–6pm) is a well-funded one-room history exhibition of the city's streetcars and cable cars. Don't neglect the video screens, where you can watch generously timed movies of streetcar rides down Market Street that were filmed just days before the '06 quake—it's a rare glimpse at what the city looked like in its true heyday.

docents are volunteers and sometimes don't show up. If the fact that the building is atop one of the city's highest points daunts you, remember that the California Street cable car goes right past it, so you can bypass an exhausting hike up its hill.

Visitors have a hard time keeping the city's various hills straight. Here's a helper: Telegraph Hill, east of North Beach, is signified by the 210-foot-tall **Coit Tower** ★★ ($4.50 13–64, $3.50 seniors 65 and over, $2 kids 6–12; cash only), opened in 1933. There are lots of apocryphal tales about the tower's design, but the only one that's certifiable is that it was created from a bequeath by a wealthy woman, Lillie Hitchcock Coit. Based on the suggestive design of the tower and on the fact that she hung out with firemen in her free time, her virtue has been questioned, but it's no surprise that locals have dirty minds. She was, in reality, probably just a liberated gal. Inside, you'll find one of the city's most charactered souvenir shops, a cramped clutter of ticky-tacky knickknacks. At a desk inside it, you can buy tickets for an elevator that takes you most of the way up to the top, where you'll climb another 37 steps to the open-air crown ringed with 24 person-wide observation windows (you may get rained on, but you won't feel like you can fall out). Part of the pleasure is watching other tourists laboring up the hill to get where you now are. You can technically enjoy much of what the tower has to offer without paying anything. There's still an excellent view from the base in what's called Pioneer Park, and a majority of the tower's most discussed aspects, its Social

Realist, New Deal lobby frescoes, can be admired for free; buy a brochure if you'd like a description of each artwork—the admission fee is only necessary for the elevator to the top. Probably the easiest way to reach the base, if you can call climbs of 115 steps easy, is to approach along Filbert Street from Washington Square in North Beach. Ultimately, it's just an observation deck, even if the view is of one of the prettiest cities in the world—both major bridges are in full view. For me, the real satisfaction is the effort it takes to ascend. While you're in the area (and up those grueling stairs), you might want to try your luck in spotting the Wild Parrots of Telegraph Hill (see below).

On paper, it sounds awfully dull, but in reality, the **Wells Fargo Museum** ✪ (420 Montgomery St., at California; ☎ 415/396-2619; free admission; Mon–Fri 9am–5pm) paints a vivid portrait of early California life by using the company's once-vital stagecoaches as a centerpiece. For generations, the Wells Fargo wagon was the West Coast's primary lifeline; if you didn't want to or couldn't afford to use it (a ticket from Omaha to Sacramento was $300), then you'd be forced to take a long boat trip around Cape Horn. The curators have done a good job bringing the past to life by including biographies of some of the grizzled drivers of the 1800s, posting plenty of old ads, allowing visitors to climb aboard a nine-seat wagon, furnishing a reproduction of a "mug book" of highway robbers from the 1870s, and even putting together a sort of *CSI: Stagecoach* re-created investigation revealing how they'd catch thieves after the fact. Wells Fargo has lost a lot of its cache in American culture; the Western theme fascinated kids in the 1950s but faded soon after. This well-assembled, two-story museum (budget about 45 min.) helps restore some of that imagination again. There's a free audio tour, too, although everything is so well-signed you won't need it.

If Asian art is an interest for you, the grandiosely named **Pacific Heritage Museum** (608 Commercial St., at Montgomery; ☎ 415/399-1124; www.ibank united.com/phm; free admission; Tues–Sat 10am–4pm) may have something modest to offer. Its several hushed rooms mount displays of artworks by Asian-descended

The Wild Parrots of Telegraph Hill

Like the sea lions of Fisherman's Wharf (p. 103), there's another group of animals nearby that nobody can account for. They're the **Wild Parrots of Telegraph Hill**, cherry-headed and blue-crowned conures that, despite being nonnative species, thrive in a feral flock. No one knows how the colony began, or exactly when, but if you're lucky enough to spot these bright green squawkers, consider yourself lucky. They seems to congregate most often on the northern slope of Telegraph Hill, and to glimpse them, you'll have to climb the steep steps around there. Those who don't want to break a sweat can try Washington Square Park, too, since they sometimes hang out there. They certainly require a little more luck and a lot more work than seeing the see lions does, mostly because they like to keep their distance from human hands.

A Double Crossing

The Golden Gate's impressive sister is the mighty Bay Bridge, which is not only much longer (8⅓ miles) but also older, having opened 6 months before, and busier, carrying more than twice the daily traffic. It was the largest and most expensive ($79.5 million) bridge for its time. But the Bay Bridge's clunky, gray, industrial look can't compete with the slender elegance of the blushing Golden Gate in the public imagination. While a suspension bridge worked well to span the deep water of the mouth of the bay, the muddy flats running for the 8 miles between San Francisco and Oakland demanded a different solution. The Bay Bridge is, in fact, two bridges (a cantilevered one and a multi-part suspension one) connected by a tunnel at Yerba Buena Island. It's also not so much of a thrill crossing it, particularly if you wind up on the lower deck, where views are obscured. None of this diminishes its triumph as a work of engineering or of the epic effort it took to raise it. Get a good look at its western span from behind the Ferry Building; its mammoth anchorage was, upon opening, the tallest structure in the city.

artists, both living and dead, but for me, the most interesting aspect of the place is the exhibit, in the basement, that uncovers the structure of the Subtreasury Building that stood in this spot from 1875 and was destroyed after the '06 quake. Of course, the palatial **Asian Art Museum** (p. 114) is the most elaborate repository in town for this type of art.

CIVIC CENTER & THE MISSION

The history of **Mission Dolores** ✪ (3321 16th St., at Dolores; ☎ 415/621-8203; www.missiondolores.org; Nov–Apr daily 9am–4pm, May–Oct daily 9am–4:30pm; suggested donation $5 adults, $3 seniors and students), more formally known as Misíon San Francisco de Asís, is the history of the early city, and there is no other surviving building that is more intrinsic to the early days of the town's formation. The tale goes back to the storied summer of 1776, when this site, then an uninhabited grove, was selected for a mission in a network that ran up and down the coast. Its first Mass was celebrated under a temporary shelter. The current building dates from 1791 and is the oldest in town. For such a rich representative of a city that has lost so much of its history, it offers a rare glimpse into the not-so-distant past and the troubled origins of California. This adobe-walled building, with its 4-foot-thick walls and rear garden, is hushed and transporting. It's also almost entirely original, having survived the 1906 quake by dint of good old-fashioned craftsmanship, and as you roam, you'll encounter gorgeous altars brought from Mexico during the days of the Founding Fathers. The trusses, lashed together with rawhide, are made of redwood, and, in 1916, they were reinforced with steel.

Following the chapel and the sanctuary, the tour's path visits a modest museum in the back before proceeding outside. In its heyday, the mission was home to some 4,000 people, but of course, most of that land was long ago sold

off; look for the diorama, built in 1939, for a clearer picture of how it was all laid out. The back garden contains the graves of California's first governor and the city's first mayor, as well as, shockingly, the bodies of at least 5,000 Indians who died "helping" (read: slaving for) the mission. Sad to say, while few people know about the mass extinction, the mission is famous for the one grave that isn't there: The headstone of Carlotta Valdes, which Kim Novak visits in *Vertigo* (1958) was a prop. Around the same time (1952), the compound was named a Basilica, an honorary Church of the Pope, and in 1987, Pope John Paul II swung by for a visit—naturally, the local Catholics are still buzzing about that. If you want to enjoy services in the Old Mission, you have to get up early, because they're offered Monday through Friday at 7am and 9:30am, outside of tourism hours, excepting a single one (a Vigil) on Saturdays at 5pm. Otherwise, you'll be worshiping in the generally ignored, modern Basilica (1918) out back.

San Francisco's Beaux Arts **City Hall** ★★ (1 Dr. Carlton B. Goodlett Place; ☎ 415/554-6139; www.sfgov.org; free admission; Mon–Fri 8am–5:30pm) was not built to be just another city hall. No, it was created with a measure of chutzpah that far outmeasured what the city was worth at the time. Having crumbled during the '06 quake, residents wanted to show the world that San Francisco was still an American powerhouse, so this current City Hall was designed (in 1915) to be as handsome, proud, and imposing as a government capital building. In fact, most visitors are shocked to learn that its mighty rotunda is *larger* than the one atop the U.S. Capitol in Washington, D.C. (Only four domes are bigger: the Vatican, Florence's Duomo, St. Paul's in London, and Les Invalides in Paris). If America ever moves its capital to San Francisco, its governmental home is taken care of. Should another horrible earthquake strike—make that *when* one strikes—a 1999 seismic retrofit saw to it that the structure can swing up to 27 inches in any direction; if you look closely at the stairs entering the building, you'll notice they don't actually touch the sidewalk because the entire building is on high-tech springs that had to be slipped, two by two, beneath a structure that already existed and was conducting daily business.

City Hall's most imposing attraction is indeed its fabulously ornate rotunda, a blend of marble (on the lower reaches) and painted plaster (high up), swept theatrically by a grand staircase where countless couples pose daily for their "just married" shots right after tying the knot (Fri is the busiest day for that). You've probably seen this staircase before. It featured in one of the final shots of *Raiders of the Lost Ark* (1981) as a stand-in for the U.S. Capitol. It was here, in 2004, that thousands of gay couples queued to sign up for their weddings; the first couple in line was an octogenarian lesbian couple that had been together for 51 years. Also, in 1954, Joe DiMaggio and Marilyn Monroe were married here and posed for photos on these steps. Not all the famous happenings at City Hall have been so hopeful. In 1978, the famous assassination of Mayor George Moscone and city Supervisor Harvey Milk occurred in two places on the second floor; the resulting trial, in which their killer got a light sentence because, as his lawyers said, he was high on junk food (the "Twinkie Defense") became a lynchpin of outrage for the gay-rights movement. In the rotunda, look up: Sculptures of Adam and Eve can be seen holding up the official seal of the city (so much for the old saw about San Francisco being godless).

Across the hall at the top of the grand staircase, the sumptuous Chamber of the Board of Supervisors is worth a peek if it's open; its walls of Manchurian oak, plaster ceiling created to mimic wood, and doors hand-carved by French and Italian craftsmen make this one of the most opulent rooms in the city. Sunshine laws dictate that it must be open to the public unless in a special session, so pop in for a gander. Better yet, drop in during one of its colorful meetings; see p. 136 for details of that.

Also, check out the Light Court off the main rotunda on the ground floor; there, you'll find the head of the Goddess of Progress statue; she was atop the prior City Hall, in fuller figure, but this is all that survives. The light-bulb sockets in her hair were later additions. Excellent 1-hour guided tours, which are not necessary to see the highlights, go at 10am, noon, and 2pm; sign up at the desk inside the Van Ness Avenue entrance (there's a security check, of course—one way in which Milk's death made a difference).

The three-level **Asian Art Museum** ✭ (200 Larkin St., at Fulton; ☎ 415/581-3500; www.asianart.org; $12 adults, $8 seniors 65 and older, $7 students and kids 13–17, $5 Thurs after 5pm; Tues–Wed and Fri–Sat 10am–5pm, Thurs 10am–9pm), located across from City Hall, is extremely well designed and stuffed with incredible artifacts spanning 6,000 years of culture, as befitting a city that has been home to some of the cream of Asian-descended people for more than 150 years. Jade,

Echoes of the Past: The Haight

Haight Ashbury, named for one of the neighborhood's intersections, was, for a time, one of the most influential neighborhoods in America. Seduced by cheap Victorian-era houses, early hippies moved in and forged a bohemian, freedom-first society. The late '60s counterculture movement, the one that was going to change the world forever, was centered right here. For a while, it was utopia. Young people hung out in the streets, invited each other to love-ins, and grooved to the emblematic music of the day; Janis Joplin and the Grateful Dead both played free concerts on the Panhandle, which is the park a few blocks north of Haight.

But eventually, the dream soured. Marijuana and LSD use turned to heroin, and the idealists of the Haight were lost in more than just a purple haze; they became junkies, infiltrated by revolutionary zealots such as Charles Manson (who lived at 636 Cole St.), and the neighborhood quickly slid into a poorly tended ghetto of lost souls living in the past.

Like Hollywood Boulevard in Los Angeles, though, the Haight retains at least a shimmer of its old reputation. Homeless kids and slumming suburbanites still come, hoping for a slice of that forgotten '60s dream, but all they really encounter are a string of cheap diners, head shops, and consignment stores (albeit some of the city's best; some are named in chapter 8). There's nothing really to see in the Haight unless you're a big fan of the Grateful Dead (the band lived at the pretty purple-gold-gray house at 710 Ashbury St., which isn't open to the public). That's the Haight in a nutshell: It's famous for what once happened there and for a time that's dead. Even the intersection of Haight and Ashbury is now as unremarkable as any other.

Still, it's worth a stroll down Haight Street to catch a whiff of the 1960s, faint and tawdry as it now is. If you're in the market for a pot pipe or a pair of used jeans or some Doc Martens, you'll find something to please you, and you may even glimpse a few elderly stragglers who never left after the Summer of Love. I suggest starting at Central Street (at Buena Vista Park) or Masonic Avenue and heading west; off Haight, it's residential, so there's not much need to veer off the street until you reach the edge of Golden Gate Park, 6 blocks west. One thing you won't find much of is chain stores; locals are still proud of the fact that a branch of the Gap failed to thrive at the famous corner (although there is a Ben & Jerry's there now).

daggers, altarpieces, drums, pots, ceremonial trappings, and 15,000 other priceless goodies and artworks are artfully lit and presented in a bright, multilevel space.

Simply because it means you'll be unlikely to miss anything, curators recommend you begin a visit on the third floor and work your way down, and by the time you reach the ground floor, you'll find a cafe ($8–$10, with food of all stripes). I think an even better course of action is to join one of the many regular tours that provide a useful breakdown of the Asian Art Museum's highlights (check at the information desk for schedules). Otherwise, you may find the welter of artifacts to be rather daunting. The Museum Masterpieces tour, usually held at 11am and 1:30pm, is a good start, but if you miss it, you can also grab a free audio-tour wand of the museum's highlights. About eight other free tours, focusing on China, storytelling, and the Himalayas, are usually scattered between 10:30am and 2:30pm. On Saturdays at 11:30am and 2:30pm, there are worthwhile tours of the museum that focus on the architectural triumph involved in converting it in 2003 from what was once the city's main library; Gae Aulenti, the same architect responsible for the conversion of Paris's Musée d'Orsay also handled this.

While its holdings are among the most impressive you'll ever see in Asian culture, I do have some tonal problems with the museum. This sign greets guests at the start of a tour: "Culturally, no 'Asia' exists, and the peoples who inhabit 'Asia' often have little in common with each other." It's a message I find insulting—embedded within is a potentially racist assumption that only the curators have a nuanced understanding of Asian cultures. Furthermore, it seems a disingenuous welcome message for a place called, duh, an Asian Art Museum, a name that by its own rules is faulty. All the same, the artifacts speak for themselves, and the elegant, well-designed gallery spaces are exemplary. If Asian art of any kind interests you, it's an absolute don't-miss. And even if you don't care about it, the architectural conversion is, in itself, a delight.

GOLDEN GATE PARK

Not just another city park, Golden Gate Park attracts some 13 million visitors a year (mostly locals), third in the U.S. only to Chicago's Lincoln Park and New York's Central Park, to which it's most often compared. As late as the 1870s, the park was mostly ocean dunes, but aggressive planting and design, which were indeed inspired by the Beaux Arts success of Central Park, have transformed the area into a wooded escape. Among the attractions embedded in the park are the **de Young museum** (p. 118), the **California Academy of Sciences** (p. 117), the **Conservatory of Flowers** (p. 120), and the **Japanese Tea Garden** (p. 116), all of which lie on the eastern, or city-side, end of the park and so are easy to visit on the same day. At the Pacific Ocean end, you'll find Ocean Beach, known not for sunshine and frolic but for summertime fog, mean currents, and surfers.

To tour the park itself, try the **San Francisco Parks Trust** (☎ 415/263-0991; www.sfpt.org), a free, volunteer-led system of tours, which carves out 14 different tours for this immense public space alone. Weekends are mostly for historical tours, while explorations of the Japanese Tea Garden, one of the park's most notable attractions, are Sunday and Wednesday ($4 to get into the garden). My favorite title is the Wild West Walk, which brings you to the paddock full of bison. Unexpectedly, the animals have called the park home since 1892. Among the other oddities on view in the park and covered by some tour or another: the Dutch Windmill, which has the world's largest wings; the Conservatory of Flowers, which is the oldest glass-and-wood Victorian greenhouse in the hemisphere; and the 7½-acre National AIDS Memorial Grove, a meditative walk where the names of 20,000 of the lost are engraved in stone; it's still the only national AIDS memorial in existence.

Free Days

The major museums offer free admission for 1 day once every 30 days or so. So if you want to save, the best time to hit San Francisco is the first week of the month.

California Academy of Sciences Free every first Wednesday of each month. Third Thursday of the month, $5, plus a cash bar. As the museum puts it, it's when "clownfish, coral, and cocktails converge."

de Young Free first Tuesday of each month.

Exploratorium Free first Wednesday of each month.

SFMOMA Free first Tuesday of each month; Half-Price Thursdays ($6.25 adults) 6–9pm.

Asian Art Museum Free first Sunday of every month; $5 Thursdays 5–9pm.

Yerba Buena Center for the Arts Free first Tuesday of each month.

Legion of Honor Free first Tuesday of each month.

San Francisco Zoo Free first Wednesday of each month.

Conservatory of Flowers Free first Tuesday of each month.

Cartoon Art Museum First Tuesday of each month "Pay What You Wish Day."

The Chinese Historical Society of America Museum and Learning Center Free first Thursday of each month.

San Francisco Cable Car Museum Always free.

Wells Fargo Museum Always free.

The **California Academy of Sciences** [kids] ★★★ (Golden Gate Park; www.cal academy.org; $10 adults; $6.50 seniors 65 and over, kids 12–17, and students; $2 kids 4–11), more than 150 years old, has moved its 38,000-odd animals and 20 million specimens to a lavish custom-built facility in Golden Gate Park, within sight of the equally impressive de Young museum. The $484-million, 410,000-square-foot museum was scheduled to open in September 2008, too late to be reviewed for this guide, but expect a top-flight celebration of all things natural in the West. That mandate spans animals, geology, and the aspect it's best known for, a 220,000-gallon Steinhart Aquarium complex with live fish, sea turtles, penguins, and one of America's largest tanks of live coral. This beautiful new home, which includes a rainforest with free-flying birds, is one of the largest "green" buildings in the world, in more ways than one; its roof is a gently undulating, 2½-acre planter that's lined with tiles made of coconut husks.

Golden Gate Park

The enrichment of children is a particular focus, so families comprise a good chunk of the patronage. There are lots of extracurricular kids' programs (as simple as temporary tattooing and as thrilling as snake encounters) and talks on the docket, too, so be sure to ask about special events.

Lectures, which go down several times a month for $19 a seat, are also well programmed, with plenty of famous authors (Michael Pollan and Bill McKibben both appeared in early 2008) and scientists bringing their findings in plainspoken English to the public. Inquire about feeding times, usually in the middle of the day, because that's when animals tend to be most active. The new opening hours had not been set at press time, but the prior incarnation was open 10am to 5pm daily, so expect something similar. If you're thinking of combining with a visit to the de Young and to the Haight, which are both within walking distance, don't come on a Monday, when the de Young is closed. Also, in the past, this museum was part of the CityPass booklet, so check to see if it's back on the roster.

The haughtiest museum in town, and more a showplace for San Francisco society than for the best in art, is probably the **de Young** ★ (Golden Gate Park, 50 Hagiwara Tea Garden Dr.; ☎ 415/750-3600; www.famsf.org; $10 adults, $7 seniors 65 and over, $6 kids 13–17, $6 college students, $2 less with a Muni transfer;

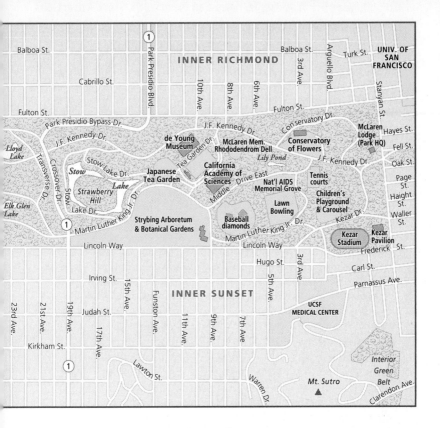

Tues–Sun 9:30am–5:15pm). While this 2005 building is architecturally striking—with its expansive, angular copper siding, designed to oxidize, and long interior ramps, it looks like a set piece from *Return of the Jedi*—the interior is not as crammed with works as the design might suggest. What you get is a hodgepodge of styles and eras as collected by wealthy patrons, from textiles (a major collection of Turkmen carpets) and ancient sub-Saharan African art to painted murals from Teotihuacan in Mexico and several upper-gallery rooms of lesser American artists such as Motherwell and Dine. There are a few marquee standouts, such as *The Last Moments of John Brown* by Thomas Hovenden (known more for its political echoes than its quality) and Edward Hicks's *The Peaceable Kingdom* (there are dozens of other versions, though, scattered around the planet). And there are frequent traveling shows of note, such as a retrospective of photographer Annie Leibovitz and a collection of British shock artists Gilbert & George—the choices tend to be thick with pop culture gravitas and aren't always suited to kids the way the permanent collection is. Also available, but not necessary for a complete visit, is an elevator ride up the building's 144-foot-tall tower for a view over the surrounding park; the tower closes at 4:30pm most days. A free daily introductory tour is offered at 10:30am, and there are usually other themed gallery tours on the

Get Back to Nature for $1.50

Not all tourists have cars, but there's a way to get a green fix without leaving the center of the city. Golden Gate Park (p. 116) is one of America's greatest urban expanses, packed with forests, grassy hills, and, at its western end, some vertiginous oceanfront cliffs. It's easy to reach and to handle. But San Franciscans would never be satisfied with just one urban getaway:

Waterfront Rambling

The experience: You won't need to pack many provisions for a walk along the 3½-mile Golden Gate Promenade (despite the name, not part of Golden Gate Park), which skirts the waterfront all the way from Fort Mason to the foot of a certain postcard-perfect bridge, which will be visible almost the whole time. Along the way, you'll see yachts, some jealous-making manses in the Marina District, and (for almost 2 miles of it) the light development of the Presidio. This is a good one for those with ADD, because it's usually pretty easy to jump off the paved path and back into town.

   The bus to take: Head west in the morning to keep the sun out of your eyes. Bus 30 lets you off about 4 blocks from the water. At the end, take number 28 home. Or reverse those if you take the trail east.

Old California

The experience: The 1,480-acres of the Presidio, located in the northwest part of town where the Golden Gate Bridge alights in the city, is the Bay Area as it used to be, with a mix of wooded hills, waterfront bluffs, and a few former military settlements that date back to the 19th century. There are some 11 miles of trails, too, almost all of which are under 3 miles. The facilities are well-tended; in 2008, it opened a new scenic viewpoint above Crissy Field that takes in the Bay, Alcatraz, and the city skyline. Free trail maps are available at the **Visitor Center** (in the former Officers' club, 50 Moraga Ave., ☎ 415/561-4323; daily 9am–5pm), but since that's best

hour until about 3pm. Conveniently, the museum is located within strolling distance from the California Academy of Sciences building, itself a newfangled architectural showpiece.

Within walking distance from the Haight and from the de Young, the **Conservatory of Flowers** (JFK Drive, Golden Gate Park; ☎ 415/666-7001; www. conservatoryofflowers.org; $5 adults; $3 seniors 65 and over, kids 12–17, and students; $1.50 kids 4 and under; Tues–Sun 9am–5pm, last entry 4:30pm) is beautiful both inside and out. Its Victorian wood-and-glass home, erected in 1878, is on the National Register of Historic Places, and mimics (but doesn't copy) Kew Gardens in London. It reopened in 2003 after a $25-million restoration. Inside, some 1,700 live plants enchant the horticulturally minded. Among the rare holdings are some 700 high-altitude orchids, which qualifies as one of the most complete collections in the world.

reached using a car, it's probably easier to download one ahead of time at www.presidio.gov. Most of the best natural areas around the city are federally managed together under the **Golden Gate National Recreation Area** (☎415/561-4700; www.nps.gov/goga).

The bus to take: I think the best trails pass near Fort Point, which also offers the best views of the Bridge; take Muni 28 or 29 to the bridge toll plaza and use the marked signs to descend to your trail.

Birding & Walking

The experience: With no cars and no mammalian predators, **Angel Island** (☎ 415/435-1915; www.parks.ca.gov; daily 8am–sunset), in the middle of San Francisco Bay near Alcatraz, makes for a fitting stopover for birds. It also makes for a fitting break from town for humans (Mar–Nov is the tourist season), and as a bonus, a visit here comes with a ferry ride with views of Alcatraz. Here, there's more to do than at a heavily regulated government park (think guided Segway tours, an intermittent tram tour, lots of biking and kayaking). The centerpiece is the 788 foot-tall Mount Livermore, ripe for a not-too-brutal hike, but the fire road that rings the island close to the water level is, of course, easier to tackle. The island was once the immigration checkpoint for people from Asia, and some of the old buildings remain, although the museum facilities are not extensive enough to warrant a trip on their own. (You can only see them by tour (☎ 415/262-4429; www.aiisf.org for the upcoming schedule.)

The bus to take: The F Tram goes right by the pier. One you're at the island, there's a visitor center at the Ayala Cove landing. Services usually leave from Pier 41 at Fisherman's Wharf (☎415/705-8200; www.blueand goldfleet.com; $15), although during winter you may be required to catch a ferry to Tiburon, across the Bay, before continuing on.

THE PRESIDIO & THE MARINA

You don't want to go alone to the **Exploratorium** 🧒 ★★★ (Palace of Fine Arts, 3601 Lyon St.; ☎ 415/561-0399; www.exploratorium.edu; $14 adults; $11 seniors 65 and over, kids 11–17, and students; $9 kids 4–12; Tues–Sun 10am–5pm), a kid-oriented, fully hands-on science museum on the edge of the Presidio. That's because many of the exhibits require a buddy to operate. Although you're familiar with the setup from your hometown science museum—press this button and create an electromagnetic field, shake this table and see where the balls roll— you've probably never enjoyed them on this warehouse scale (budget at least 3 or 4 hrs.—or even more—there's that much) or at this quality level. Unlike so many hands-on museums, nearly everything works. That's because there's an on-site workshop where the exhibits are designed, built, and maintained. In fact, you can watch the assortment of hot geeks and young engineers working on their latest creations. There are lots of unexpected bonuses, such as frequent demonstrations (the day I was there, someone was dissecting cow eyes for a gaggle of rapt kids, and a few feet away, a terrarium containing a dead rat was rotting away for the edification of decay science) and occasional evening talks for curious adults (such as on nanotechnology or string field theory; check the museum's online events calendar for advance word).

If you're weirded out by all those smeary kids touching all those exhibits before you do, tote some antibacterial wipes. Whatever your germ tolerance, you will not be bored here.

In the back, closed off within its own structure, the **Tactile Dome** ($17 with admission, ages 7 and up) is a strange enticement, on offer since 1971, making it a city museum institution. Visitors remove their shoes and then, one at a time and with plenty of space between them, crawl on hands and knees through a completely lightless obstacle course, using only their sense of touch to navigate the slopes, slides, and passageways. The adventure takes about 10 minutes, smells like feet, and if you're at all claustrophobic, forget it. But you can usually go more than once, if you're game.

One downside of the place is that you'll almost certainly have to take a bus to reach it (take no. 30 from Grant Ave.), and because its lunch counter seems geared to school groups and runs out of food by midafternoon, think about eating before you go.

The Exploratorium is situated next to the gorgeous **Palace of Fine Arts,** a colossal, sculpture-laden rotunda and colonnade left over from the Panama-Pacific Exposition of 1915. Although the name of the place suggests there's much more to see than there actually is, the neighboring pond is one of the locals' favorite spots for jogging, picnicking, and photography. It's most beautiful in the mornings, when it's bathed in eastern light.

Another nearby attraction that's maintained by the Exploratorium is the so-called **Wave Organ,** located on a jetty that protects the small boat harbor just north of the museum. It's a collection of 25 pipes made of PVC and concrete that are embedded in the jetty and submerged in the Bay so that, depending on the mood of the tides, a slow, eerie free-form music is generated. Sometimes, you won't hear a thing, but, at the very least, the jetty, which was partly created out of headstones from a disused cemetery across town, is a lovely place to soak in the view, including of the Golden Gate Bridge and of the ideal, full-on perspective of Alcatraz Island. To reach the Wave Organ, walk down Baker Street to the water, make your way to the end of the jetty by veering left around the boats, and walk right about 10 minutes along a sometimes-muddy path to the end of the promontory. The Exploratorium is part of the CityPass discount book (p. 98).

Beneath the Golden Gate Bridge's city-side anchor is **Fort Point** (www.nps.gov/fopo; free admission; Fri–Sun 10am–5pm), a National Park Service–maintained masonry fort that dates to the Civil War era; there's not a lot to do there beside learn a few things about how it once operated, and the hours are funky besides, but the rooftop views of the bridge are insanely spectacular. I want to thank the bridge's designers for bending over backward to avoid demolishing the fort for a southern anchor. From an era (the 1930s) when dams were laid and historic sights cleared in the name of progress, it's pretty rare to see the

Anatomy of a Painted Lady

So just what is a Painted Lady? Like art, it's tough to define, but you know one when you see one, and these lovingly restored homes constitute one of San Francisco's most distinct, and jealousy-inducing, sights. Loosely speaking, a Painted Lady is an old wood-frame home (usually redwood) built from the mid-1800s to about 1906, and it must be gussied up with three or more colors to qualify—otherwise it's just an old house. There are three general styles. The Italianate style has angled bay windows and often, a little rounded area above some windows; those usually date to around the Gold Rush. Then there's the stick style, in which bay windows are at right angles, like boxes; those were usually built around the 1880s. Finally, the Queen Anne style often has a rounded side that looks a little like a tower, and you'll often see a windowed gable atop it.

There's another type, too: The "smothered lady" has been gutted or otherwise marred by unthinking renovations; the city is full of ladies buried under cheap siding installed in the 1950s and 1960s, when living in a wooden house was considered low-rent and passé. Nowadays, of course, these ladies don't come cheap: $3 million is a standard asking price, and the yearly upkeep alone would break most people.

The greatest collection of Painted Ladies can be found west of Van Ness, where the fire line of 1906 stopped and homes were spared. Perhaps the most photographed ones, though, are at the east end of Alamo Square along Steiner Street. Those with a thirst for more information about and examples of the subject are encouraged to take the excellent **Victorian Home Walk tour,** held daily (p. 129).

evidence of such care. However, you'd probably never go here unless you were combining it with a trip across the bridge.

The **Art Institute of San Francisco** (800 Chestnut St., at Jones; ☎ 415/771-7020; www.sfai.edu; free admission) has a cool multilevel Diego Rivera mural, painted in 1931, that depicts the artist painting a mural (how meta!). Anyone is allowed to view it, as well as the student gallery in the same building. For information on touring the murals of the Mission District, see p. 129.

There were once something like 700 homes built in the style of the **Octagon House** (2645 Gough St., at Green; ☎ 415/441-7512; open 2nd Sun and 2nd and 4th Thurs of each month noon–3pm) throughout America. The rounded design was thought to be healthier for occupants; today, though, there are only two examples left in San Francisco, and this one's the only one you can visit. It houses lots of antique furniture, decorative arts from the Colonial and Federal periods, plus signatures of 54 of the 56 original signers of the Declaration of Independence. The house, which dates to 1861 but was moved to this location in 1951, is on the National Register of Historic Places. The hours are ridiculous, which makes visiting tricky, but admission is based on a pay-what-you-will policy.

WEST & EAST SAN FRANCISCO

It's too bad that the **Palace of the Legion of Honor** (Lincoln Park, 24th and Clement; ☎ 415/863-3330; www.thinker.org/legion; $10 adults, $7 seniors 65 and over, $6 kids 13–17; Tues–Sun 9:30am–5:15pm) is such darn trouble to reach: on the far west of town, in Lincoln Park on the Pacific Ocean. Its Beaux Arts home is beautiful, as are the views of the sea and of the Golden Gate Bridge. Its sculpture of August Rodin's *The Thinker* is a copy, but its presence in the museum's outdoor Court of Honor is theatrical. The museum is otherwise filled with nice but hardly seminal works, such as European paintings, 18th-century English and French porcelain, and plenty of decorative arts. A trip here is worth it if you're already in the neighborhood, which you'd probably only be if you were coming off the Golden Gate bridge in a car, or if you want an excuse to contemplate the ocean. Bus no. 1 reaches the edge of the park from Sacramento Street, but then you'll have to walk through the park for about 20 minutes. Your Muni transfer will get you $2 off. One bonus: Your ticket here will also get you into the de Young on the same day.

The 100-acre **San Francisco Zoo** 🎒 ★ (Sloat Blvd. at 47th; ☎ 415/753-7057; www.sfzoo.org; $11 adults, $8 seniors 65 and older and kids 12–17, $5 kids 3–11; daily 10am–5pm), a nonprofit zoological society also co-operated by the city, has sailed through some rocky waters lately; in late 2007, a tiger escaped from its enclosure and killed a young man before police moved in (although, in fairness, he was widely reported to have been part of a group of kids that was taunting the animal inside its enclosure). Still, the question of how the zoo managed to operate with a tiger barrier that was discovered to be shorter than the federal standard has given animal-rights activists new ammunition in trying to shut the place down. They're making it seem worse than it is. It's actually a very nice zoo, and one of the country's best, with nearly 1,000 animals of some 245 species, and its location near the sea makes for a good day out if you combine it with a stroll down Ocean Beach. Among the habitats are a grizzly bear "gulch," a 3-acre space devoted to some of the milder creatures of the African savanna (the giraffes are popular), and a lemur forest visible by an elevated pathway. You'll also find a children's zoo featuring lots of petable critters and inside that, an insect zoo. Consider renting a Zoo Ranger, a $7 handheld device that, when triggered by GPS, shows a movie clip that teaches how the zoo takes care of its residents, as well as background info about them. Feedings are generally in the morning and in the late afternoon, but there's usually something going on most of the day. Conveniently, the L Taraval streetcar line goes down Market Street right to it, and if you show your transfer, you'll get $1 off admission. Ultimately, it is a zoo, though, albeit a good one, so weigh for yourself if it's worth missing other, more "local" sights for a trip.

If California history gets you going, there's a large—7¾ acres on 4 city blocks—museum on the topic located across the bay in Oakland. The **Oakland Museum of California** (1000 Oak, at 10th, Oakland; ☎ 510/238-2200; www. museumca.org; $8 adults, $5 seniors 65 and older; Wed–Sat 10am–5pm, Sun noon–5pm; BART to Lake Merritt) is light on antiquities and heavy on artworks, photography, and generalized chatter about nature. There are quite a few artifacts of native people, and the facility has been around since 1969, giving it plenty of

Chinatown

Chinese immigrants first arrived in San Francisco way back in 1848, although no one can pretend they were treated with much equanimity. It seems like everything the government did was directed at trying to force them back to China. For years, Chinese immigrants survived by hook and by crook, doing the hard labor that no one else would do. Anti-Chinese laws were in effect for generations, and it wasn't until the mid-20th century that the government wised up and began protecting Asian émigrés. The 1906 quake was a blessing in disguise for many, because the loss of most public records enabled Chinese men to claim that they were always American citizens, something the government could not disprove, and then bring over family to live.

When you're part of a despised minority, you're more likely to live in an enclave with other people like you. Because of its proximity to the wharves in the mid-1800s, Chinatown became home to laborers and developed into its own ethnic universe. In recent generations, locals have cleverly dressed buildings with fake pagoda roofs and other visitor-friendly touches like the dragon street lamps, which had the intelligent effect of creating a tourist destination out of an area that was once avoided and feared. In 1970, the distinctive green-tiled gate at Grant and Bush was erected—but, it's interesting to note, as a gift from the government of Taiwan, not by the Chinese. Today, Chinatown is a top place to wander into little family-run stores and tea shops, absorbing another culture. But don't be deceived; it's still home ground for poor immigrants. The local newspaper recently estimated that 60% of the housing units in Chinatown still share kitchens and bathrooms.

First-time visitors to Chinatown should walk north on Grant Avenue, where the widest range of shops is located. The good stuff starts north of California Street. By Broadway, the neighborhood segues to the Italian bakeries and butcher shops of North Beach. The street parallel and to the west, Stockton Street, is where more local Chinese go, and its selection of Asian grocery stores sell some fascinating foods. Unlike many Chinatowns, the people here largely speak English, so don't be shy about asking questions about the foods or items that you see on the shelves.

For a more in-depth look at Chinatown, check out the walking tour that includes it. You'll find that on p. 162.

time to collect works, none of which will be interesting if you don't care about the subject. If you'd like to gauge whether the collections are for you before trekking across the water, the museum keeps about 7,000 images and documents online (http://collections.museumca.org).

BUS TOURS

To my mind, the high prices of the hop-on, hop-off buses don't match what you get. You can re-create their routes easily on a series of $1.50 city buses, armed only with a map and rubber-soled shoes. And in general, the information given is not as fluently presented or well-researched as on the walking and bus tours discussed below. But I know they have their devotees, so here's some information on each.

City Sightseeing San Francisco (☎ 866/641-8687 or 415/447-8442; www.citysightseeing.com) sends its open-top double-decker buses along two routes, both with a commentary. The Downtown loop ($27 adults, $21 kids; 90 min.) sticks to everything from Fisherman's Wharf and east (Financial District, Nob Hill, Union Square, North Beach, and Chinatown), while the Golden Gate loop ($22 adults, $17 kids; 75 min.) focuses on the Presidio, Marina, Palace of Fine Arts, and the Golden Gate Bridge. The first loop is useful for hitting the major tourist sights, while the second loop goes to fewer greatest hits, but the ones it does visit require wheels to reach. Both loops stop at Fisherman's Wharf and in North Beach, and both say they're good for 24 hours' use. (Be wary of that claim: You can hop on and off the buses, yes, but on slow days, there may be only two departures, which means if you're on the second one, you won't have an opportunity to hop on again until the next morning. Make sure you understand the day's schedule before buying your ticket.) The Night Loop bus, which runs weekend evenings at 6pm, is not a good value—it costs just as much as a day run but only lasts an hour. You can buy a 48-hour pass on all three loops for $65 adults, $35 kids, which is quite a lot of cash. This company is well-established and operates in dozens of cities, particularly in Europe.

With departures every 30 minutes, **Open Top Sightseeing** (☎ 877/332-8689; www.opentopsightseeing.com; $28 adults, $14 kids 4–15; 9am to final departure at 5pm daily), employing double-decker buses, is a bit more useful. Buying online saves $4 off the price above, but you don't need to make reservations. You can leap on and off at 14 stations around town; the entire loop, which is narrated, takes about 90 minutes if you don't get off. Tickets are valid for 2 days, but if you board after 3pm, you'll get a third day to make up for the time you missed.

GUIDED TOURS

You could honestly have a complete sightseeing experience of town based exclusively on tours run by qualified guides who love the city, and what's more, many of them are free. These are by no means all of them, but they're some of the best, and ones that get you up close to local life.

Don't forget to dress warmly on any walking tour. The weather can change rapidly here. Also, no heels. You never know when a steep incline is waiting just around the corner.

Note: Beyond the tours discussed below, I also recommend the excellent offerings of the San Francisco Parks Trust (p. 116).

Do not miss the opportunity to take one of the 89 absolutely free walking tours offered in rotation by **San Francisco City Guides** ✮✮✮ (☎ 415/557-4266; www.sfcityguides.org), a simply terrific volunteer organization that runs up to a dozen tours a day, from 10am to 2pm, all around town. You don't need to make a reservation; just show up at the place and time listed online on its home page, where the weekly schedule is kept up to date by the group's single paid employee. Tours are free, but at the end, your guide, who will be someone who loves and studies the city and wants to share that love, will pass around an envelope and hope for a few bucks. Some of the cooler tours include a walk through the historic Palace Hotel; City Scapes and Public Places, on which you'll discover hidden rooftop gardens and little-known financial museums downtown; a retelling of the history of the Mission Dolores neighborhood, one of the city's most historic; and Gold Rush City, which takes in the stomping grounds of the original 49ersers. Most of the city's great attractions, from Coit Tower to Fisherman's Wharf, will have a tour dedicated to their explication. Tours are probably the city's best bargain, and they're an inviting way to see some windswept places you may not want to go to alone, including along the walkway of the Golden Gate Bridge and the Fort Mason complex. Some 21,000 people a year take advantage of this terrific service, and frugal city buffs could easily fill their vacations with two or three a day.

My favorite paid walking tour in town is the never-boring **Local Tastes of the City** ★★★ (☎ 415/665-0480; www.localtastesofthecitytours.com; $59; reservations required; 3 hrs.), an extremely well organized adventure through artisanal food providers in a city famous for its quality foods. The principal guide, Tom Medin, also designed the tour. He has worked hard to befriend most of the vendors and shopkeepers in North Beach, and you, as a guest of this tour, get to enjoy the fruits of those years. When your tour drops into a store on the itinerary, he'll frequently vanish into the back and emerge a few minutes later laden with plates of fresh foods and baked goods produced by that place. Sometimes, you'll even be brought into the kitchens to learn more, including one bakery with brick ovens in continuous operation since the late 1800s. Among the stops: a focaccia bakery, a chocolatier, a coffee roaster, and the famous Caffe Trieste, plus lots of incidental historical sights around North Beach as you go. For an in-depth face-to-face with locals who have run their stores for years, usually following establishment by their own ancestors, this tour is an excellent example of local entree that gives access you'd never have on your own. Don't eat beforehand, because the price includes tons of food and you'll almost certainly come away stuffed. The company also does insider tours of Chinatown and 2-hour "Night Tours" (actually evening tours) combining Chinatown and North Beach.

A very close second for my favorite paid tour is the intelligently produced **San Francisco Movie Tours** ★★★ (☎ 877/258-2587 or 415/624-4949; www.sanfranciscomovietours.com; $47 adults, $37 seniors 65 and over, $37 kids 5–17; reservations required; 3 hrs.). Passengers board a comfortable rental-car-shuttle-type van equipped with a TV and DVD player, and they're taken all around town by a driver while a spunky movie-buff narrator cues up clips of movies—some 70 of them from 55 titles, all well-timed—that were shot exactly at the point you happen to be passing. It's astonishing to see just how many popular films have been shot here, and seeing the city this way is, far from being a cheesy gimmick, actually a great way to orient yourself to its geography in relation to your prior familiarity level with San Francisco. Lots of the sights are layered with an extra slice of city history, such as the spot in Alta Vista Park where director Peter

Bogdanovich allowed a car stunt to take a chunk out of an antique stone staircase and then left the disastrous moment in *What's Up Doc?*; ever since then, the city has been draconian about issuing permits. References run the gamut, from a 1922 Buster Keaton cable-car chase scene in North Beach, *Dirty Harry* and *American Graffiti* to *Vertigo, The Princess Diaries,* and half the movies in Robin Williams's cornball canon. Because we all go to the movies, the experience isn't dry. But it's not just about movies; you'll be shown other cultural highlights, too, such as the house where Alice Walker wrote *The Color Purple.* Tours on weekdays go into City Hall, while ones on the weekend trade that for the soaring bridge views at Fort Point, which is otherwise hard to reach without a car. Another benefit of a weekend tour is a pass by the exterior of Industrial Light & Magic's Letterman complex, where movie special effects are programmed; out front, there's a fountain of *The Empire Strikes Back*'s Yoda that tour guides jokingly call *The Incontinence of Yoda.* The tour picks up and drops off around Fisherman's Wharf.

The **Blue & Gold Fleet** ★★ (Pier 39, Embarcadero at Beach; ☎ 415/705-8200; www.blueandgoldfleet.com) is perhaps the best-known and most regular of the tourist ferry companies. Its most popular ride is the Bay Cruise Adventure ($21 adults, $13 kids) that goes around Alcatraz (but doesn't stop) and dips briefly into the roiling waters on the other side of the Golden Gate Bridge. Hold on tight and don't set your hot coffee down on the table in front of you, because the conflicting currents play havoc with the craft. The narration is prerecorded, and you won't hear what it's saying unless you're inside and not on the more pleasant outdoor decks. This cruise leaves pretty much hourly and is offered for free as part of CityPass (p. 98), but there are a few other options on the boards, including $18 adults/$10 kids for a round-trip journey from Fisherman's Wharf to the pretty town of Sausalito, across the water in Marin County. The company also provides transportation to Angel Island ($15 adults and $8.50 kids), behind Alcatraz from the city, for hiking and kayaking. The one thing it won't do is take you to the prison on Alcatraz Island; that service is provided by a company called Alcatraz Cruises (p. 93).

In 1989, one of the world's foremost experts on local gay and lesbian history, Trevor Hailey, began a walking tour of the primary gay district, the Castro, that she called **Cruisin' the Castro Tour** ★ (☎ 415/255-1821; www.cruisinthecastro. com; $35 ages 13 and over, $25 kids 3–12; Sat 10am–noon; reservations required). Hailey passed away in 2007, but her popular tour was assumed 2 years earlier by her protégé, Kathy Amendola, who sticks more or less to the same sights around eight of the neighborhood's 44 unofficial blocks, including Harvey Milk's camera shop, the Castro Theatre, and other spots connected with gay cultural and political history, including America's only park dedicated to the Nazis' countless gay victims. The winter schedule is sparse, and that time of year, Amendola might only conduct a tour if there's a group booked. The tour meets right outside a convenient Muni tram station.

Created with the cooperation of city authorities, the **Barbary Coast Trail** (☎ 415/454-2355; www.barbarycoasttrail.org) is a gold-rush-and-quake-themed tour that threads from Market Street all the way to Fisherman's Wharf, through what was once the rough-and-tumble area of the old city but is now home to corporate buccaneers. Although the trail is well marked by a multitude of brass markers and arrows embedded in the sidewalk, there are few informational signs along the way. That is remedied somewhat by the sale of a printed guide online ($9 for a 32-page booklet, $16 for a 275-page guide), providing downloadable audio tours ($10 each or $25 for all 3, plus a free downloadable map), and scheduling tours conducted by the trail's creator, Daniel Bacon ($22).

The city has put together a series of historic signs along the waterfront that it calls the **PortWalk** (☎ 415/274-0400; www.sfport.com; free admission). Because so much of the city's inception and early history had to do with the water, this trail traces lots of historic slips and dips into maritime history (there's a stop at a little church on the docks that has been used by sailors for years), and weaves into sections of marinas that you might never think to explore without the guidance. Unfortunately, as a city project, it was ineptly designed and advertised, and there's no way to easily tell your way among the signs. You'll probably find it easier to fend for yourself by finding the first signs at the Hyde Street Pier and then working your way east around the Inner Lagoon, to Pier 43½, and ending around the base of Pier 43.

Held every day with no reservations required, the **Victorian Home Walk** ★★ (☎ 415/252-9485; $20, cash only; 2½ hrs.) is cleverly planned so that you never have to hike up steep hills—merely a slope here and there. After meeting at the northwest corner of Union Square, groups take a public bus to Pacific Heights (bonus: the fare's included in the tour price, and you'll be done in time to use the free transfer to get back) and walk past some fabulous old wooden homes that make San Francisco so distinctive. Guides seem to know their stuff and aren't dry. Along the way, there are hilltop views of the Bay, some interesting facts (one: to be considered a "Painted Lady," your house must have at least three colors on it), and a swing by the homes used in *Mrs. Doubtfire* and *Party of Five*. The tour winds up a few blocks from the bistros of Cow Hollow.

Precita Eyes Mural Arts and Visitors Center (2981 24th St., at Harrison; ☎ 415/285-2287; www.precitaeyes.org/tours.html) was established in 1977 to sponsor and facilitate the painting of public-art murals around the Mission District by mostly poor local artists. It schedules a number of free weekly tours (times and locations change; $10–$12) that take in some of the Mission's 70-odd works, many of which are hidden in places where you'd be unlikely to find them on your own. It also helps to have an expert explain exactly what you're seeing on a given work so that you're not left to stand there and say something daft like, "Pretty colors." If you're determined to check out some of the works without benefit of a guide, two troves for the artworks are **Balmy Alley** (between Treat Ave. and Harrison St., off 24th; www.balmyalley.com), an ever-changing urban canvas packed with color, and the MaestraPeace mural, which coats the four-story **Women's Building** (3543 18th St., at Lapidge; www.womensbuilding.org), a headquarters for women's services.

Yes, the idea is touristy, but the theatrical enthusiasm of its founding guide, Jim Fassbinder, makes San Francisco **Ghost Hunt Walking Tour** ★ (☎ 415/922-5590; www.sfghosthunt.com; $20 adults, $10 kids under 16; 7pm daily except Tues; 2 hrs.) good fun. It comes with a surprising amount of history about Pacific Heights (its stamping ground, where many of the buildings predate the quake), even if most of that history has a supernatural or occult bent, so if you're a skeptic, you can still come away with lots of facts. The nervous type may feel scared, but generally, its campy and mild entertainment. It meets in the lobby of the Queen Anne Hotel at 1590 Sutter St.

Rental Car Respites

In other pars of America, calling someone a "granola" might be veiled a political dig, but here, it's a compliment—after all, granola can get you through a long hike. Few other American urban areas support such an outdoorsy population. That's because there are so many gorgeous and surprisingly varied nature reserves and parks within a few hours' drive of town. Northern California hoards some of California's most transporting wonders. Many are best accessed using a rental car; intermittent public transportation may be available at a low price—but at a high cost in terms of the time required to catch rides. Slip into some boots, grab the tick spray, and fill up a water bottle:

Muir Woods National Monument (☎ 415/388-2595; www.nps.gov/mywo; adults $5, children under 16 free; p. 252) is the dense redwood forest 12 miles from the northern anchor of the Golden Gate Bridge. This 560-acre park, which was protected from development more than 100 years ago, has a mere 6 miles of easy trails that swarm with people on weekends and during good weather. Despite its popularity, the park still presents a hushed, almost primordial personality. The park is clearly signposted on the 101.

About 30 miles north of the city along the sea, you'll find **Point Reyes National Seashore** (☎ 415/464-5100 ext. 2; www.nps.gov/pore; free entry and many free maps online), which has a more rugged, oceanside profile than the shady, woodsy Muir Woods just to its south. The some 150 miles of trails vary in intensity and topography (grasslands, steep overlooks of ocean breakers, something for everyone). The most popular for city folk is the very short Earthquake Trail, which takes you to a fence that

The most touristy of the bunch has to be **Gray Line** (☎ 888/428-6937; www.sanfranciscosightseeing.com; $44 adults, $42 seniors, $22 kids), which does 4-hour tours on air-conditioned coaches. To give you an idea of how inauthentic it is, you'll have the option of adding a trip to the local wax museum for another $18. Sometimes, too, the narration is taped and not live. I list it here so you'll know to avoid it—that is, if you want an authentic tour.

THEME PARKS (NEAR SAN FRANCISCO)

It can't compare to the lollapaloozas of Southern California, but **California's Great America** (4701 Great America Parkway, Santa Clara; ☎ 408/988-1776; www.cagreatamerica.com; $52 guests 48 in. and taller, $35 guests below 48 in. and seniors over 61; Apr–Oct, hours vary), for fans of amusement parks, offers the best thrill-ride experience in the region. The park's owner, Cedar Fair, also runs the esteemed roller-coaster mecca Cedar Point park in Ohio, and it's pouring cash into the facility here, including the addition of a new wooden coaster in 2009. From Memorial Day to Labor Day, the park also operates Boomerang Bay, a was dramatically broken apart by the '06 quake. That one leaves from the Bear Valley Visitor Center, just north of Olema. The San Andreas Fault, after all, separates the park from the mainland and account for the intrusion of Tomales Bay. For longer hikes, campsites can be rented at a fee.

Because it rises out of a virtually flat landscape, the 3,849 foot-tall **Mount Diablo** (☎ 925/837-2525; www.parks.ca.gov; daily 8am–sunset) offers some sensational views unmatched my many other peaks. Most of the peak is consecrated as a park, which means 19,000 acres of oak woodland, wildflowers, pine trees, and bizarre rock formations (oddly, the rocks get older as you climb, which is rare for any mountain). It's probably easier to reach the south entrance of the park from San Francisco. Find it through Danville off the 680; there's a visitor center (open daily 10am to 4pm) on the winding road entering the park. Although using a car is the easiest way to get close to the peak (there are lookouts), the mountain is also combed with trails suited to day hikes, which are easiest near the top.

The legendary **Redwood National Park,** in the area where the trees so big that cars can once drive through tunnels in them, is about 260 miles north, too far for a quick trip. But don't forget that the mighty **Yosemite National Park,** perhaps America's crown jewel of preserves, is about 180 miles (three hours' drive) east of the city, and the seaside drive south of San Francisco on **State Route 1** (also called Highway 1), is one of the most spectacular coastal scenic drives in the world. Some of the most famous segments occur around Big Sur, 113 winding miles south of the city, but the views commence almost as soon as you leave town.

standard water-slide park with a separate admission. The park is near the southern end of the Bay, not far from San Jose, so it's best to have a car if you want to see it.

The other major park, less elaborate but still worthwhile for fans, is **Six Flags Discovery Kingdom** (1001 Fairgrounds Dr., Vallejo; ☎ 707/643-6722; www.sixflags.com; $50 adults, $30 guests under 48 in. tall; Mar–Oct, hours vary), which was once known as Marine World. There's still a killer-whale act and questionable animal shows such as an elephant log pull, although the eight roller coasters seem to be a bigger draw. Skip paying the price listed above by booking ahead online, where tickets are often $15 cheaper. Fortunately, this park is linked to the city by high-speed catamaran from town, which leaves from Pier 41, includes park tickets, and links with a 20-minute shuttle ride. That service, which takes all day (10:30am–7pm) is operated by the **Blue & Gold Fleet** (☎ 415/705-8200). The park is also a half-hour drive from Napa, so it's more easily combinable with a visit to the Wine Country.

6 The "Other" San Francisco

You can mingle with the locals, if you know how

SAN FRANCISCO, FOR ITS REPUTATION AS A CITY OF SIN, IS ACTUALLY VERY much a cluster of thoughtful communities. It's a city whose residents enjoy feeling special, and who thrive on social occasions. The urge to belong to something important is behind the locals' fierce protection of their neighborhoods and the kind of stores permitted to open in them. Even in general terms, most residents feel lucky and proud to be a part of a city as storied as San Francisco. Wouldn't you be?

San Francisco is also a brainy city. Literacy, history, and discourse matter deeply to these people. It's not the sort of place with a sports bar on every corner; instead, it has cafes full of newspaper-reading folks curious to find out more about the world around them. It may not be setting the cultural trends anymore, but it is a place where the locals like to get together and learn more about the world around them, maybe get a drink or have dinner, and enjoy the good life.

Finally, San Francisco is a diverse city, albeit more in terms of ethnic makeup than in class. It's not hard to find pockets of immigrants still hewing to their families' traditions, and most of them are willing to allow visitors or guests into their world.

This chapter is about smuggling yourself into that world—really, the many worlds that actually make up San Francisco. Meeting locals, engaging in the heated discussions they're having, trying out their classes, joining their celebrations, seeing how they work. And because doing so involves some advance preparation, I encourage you to read this chapter well before you get to San Francisco so that you can comb through the websites to find the schedules of the activities listed below.

HOW LOCALS PLAY

We'll start with one of the best ways to meet locals, and that is by attending a local dinner party. **Ghetto Gourmet** (www.theghet.com) began by throwing what it calls a "pirate restaurant" at someone's apartment in Oakland. Today, much more popular, it calls itself a "wandering supperclub," which means that the chefs and locations change each time it goes on. These nomadic restaurants, which serve between 3 and 11 courses (really!) are a social trend that has been slowly growing in the Bay Area. This isn't some dinner party were strangers stare at each other and wait for the night to pass; all kinds of folks from all walks of life attend and spend hours socializing over some fine food that's begging to be appreciated and discussed. Pirate restaurants garner their members by putting the word out on the Internet, so you've got to belly up to the keyboard at home before filling your belly in SF. Their dedication to local ingredients and top methods make this a cool choice for genuine foodies. In fact, a club that started around the same time, Digs Bistro of Oakland, is now a real restaurant.

How Locals Look in Outrageous 15-Foot-Tall Hats

The longest-running musical revue in America and a fiercely protected theatrical institution is **Beach Blanket Babylon** (Club Fugazi, 678 Beach Blanket Babylon Blvd. [Green Street], near Columbus; ☎ 415/421-4222; www.beachblanketbabylon.com; $25–$78), a beloved cabaret-style show going since 1974 that everyone should see at least once—as recently, Prince Charles and Camilla did. The show's name doesn't describe what you'll see, except possibly the "Babylon" part; it's left over from its debut incarnation, when the theater was filled with sand and audience members had their hands slapped with Coppertone lotion. Some 12,000 performances and 4.8 million tickets later, the show's toothless political commentary and mild sexual innuendo hit just the right spot for an evening out in San Francisco. Everything about it is pleasingly silly, from the plot (something about Disney's Snow White searching San Francisco for a prince) to the songs (mostly radio standards in 1-min. bursts) and the impersonations (lots of people from the current headlines make appearances, usually emblazoned with their names so there'll be no mistaking their identities). A fake Kirstie Alley sings "Into Food" to the tune of Glenn Miller's "In the Mood," trash cans do a can-can, and Al Gore sings "Heat Wave"—you get the picture.

But the show's main claim to fame, besides its longevity, are the huge wigs and hats, which are as tall as the proscenium will allow. The climactic bonnet, an illuminated and mechanized city skyline, requires a hidden scaffolding to support. That piece of honor is worn by a campy and somewhat decrepit performer, Val Diamond, who has been endearingly belting out torch songs with the show since the late 1970s. Sophomoric? Absolutely. But few evening shows in America do it so cheerfully and so boisterously. The spectacle climaxes with a parade of insane hats while everyone sings along to "San Francisco," made famous (especially to locals) in the 1936 Clark Gable/Jeanette MacDonald movie of the same name. Lots of little shows have cropped up in an optimistic effort to become another institution, but no one has been able to steal BBB's outrageous crown. People under 21 are only allowed at matinees, and all guests at evening shows must bring their ID's. Tickets are cheaper in the rear balcony and for Wednesday and Thursday performances. Although drinks are served, you're not required to order any—although they help. Plan on several, because the pour isn't stiff.

Don't think you can just roll up and attend; these things book up weeks ahead of time, so it's essential that you stay on top of the website for new announcements.

Several other outfits do the same thing, but each has its own rules about membership, and they may balk if they hear you're not from the area. Still, it's worth a try: Check out the once-a-month **Sub Culture Dining Experience**

Three for Tea

Tea drinking is a culture unto itself. Given that the tea-drinking culture took hundreds of years to develop, the variety of leaves, brewing methods, and implements makes the tongue-tripping lingo that the baristas spout at Starbucks seem positively primitive. Because of its strong Asian-influenced culture, San Francisco is an ideal place to dip your toes in tea, so to speak, and two places in Chinatown are dying to steep neophytes in some tea talk.

I personally know next to nothing about tea. But that's not the fault of Peter and Alice at **Red Blossom Tea Company** (831 Grant Ave., at Clay; ☎ 415/395-0868; www.redblossomtea.com), who are happy to provide anyone who drops by with an education in a teacup, as it were, about the leaf and how it's best served. The best thing about Red Blossom is that even though it's been around for a generation, it's a hipper step above some of the tourist traps in Chinatown that also push tea. These guys know everything there is to know about what they sell, down to the altitude of the farm that grew it and what the weather is like there. Some of the other Chinatown tea shops just thrust a cup of hot tea at any visitor, but Red Blossom seems to understand that anyone who walks in is a potential tea convert. After all, some people spend hundreds or even thousands of dollars on tea, and they do it here, where the selection is wide.

A second choice is **Ten Ren Tea** (949 Grant Ave., at Jackson; ☎ 415/362-0656; www.tenren.com), which is actually part of a Taiwanese chain of tea shops with branches from here to New York City to Asia. That makes the experience less personal than at Red Blossom, but some people are

(www.thescdsf.com); **Radio Africa & Kitchen** (www.radioafricakitchen.com), started by an Ethiopian chef and dedicated to sustainable products ($20/main, $6/appetizer); and **Cook with James** (www.cookwithjames.com), masterminded by skilled chef James Stolich, who does mostly French and Italian cuisine, but only about every 2 months. If you want to gain invitations to any of these clubs, or any other one that might have sprung up after the publication of this book, let the organizers get a sense of your views about food, quality ingredients, and cooking—these groups are a bit snobby about their grub, but nothing opens their hearts like discovering they've run across a like mind.

San Francisco residents like to appear cool (well . . . who doesn't?). And one of the best ways to seem cool is to throw a party that not everyone knows about. They're called **"underground parties,"** which doesn't mean they're necessarily held in BART stations, but count on heavy dance music, a darkness that will put you in the mood to dance, and some interesting venues. They're always changing and promoters are constantly throwing one-offs, so it's impossible to say there is one place to get word of happenings. It's also impossible to say with any certainty what the vibe will be, since it changes with each gathering; ones held at Golden Gate Park during the day will have a different feeling and mood than ones held, say, in an old warehouse in more comfortable with the lowered intensity. When you go in, try to be enthusiastic about the teas and how they differ, because you'll find the service is better if you do. You can usually try most of the teas before you decide to purchase any of them, and be warned that the salespeople will work hard to push you toward buying the most expensive leafs. Ten Ren has installed a little dessert counter, too, with tapioca and bubble tea to round out the tourist experience, but this place is really about teas and not the food. The American HQ of Ten Ren is located in town, but it's an office without public tea service.

Another authentic place to go is the **Asian Art Museum** (p. 114), where there's a permanent Japanese Tearoom, complete with tatami mats; it was made in Kyoto and shipped here. The area is pretty impressive, with an electric well for water heating, an alcove for hanging scrolls, and other elements that have become parts of the ancient ceremony. The museum works with tea ceremonies of several styles; as it turns out, there are many different ways to perform a tea ceremony, including different implements, and the museum engages with experts in five of them. Attending these ceremonies, which happen at least bimonthly, costs $20 including the price of the tea. You must make reservations.

Finally, there's the **Japanese Tea Garden at Golden Gate Park** (☎ 415/752-1171; www.parks.sfgov.org; p. 116), which is mostly a pretty garden that has the cultural depth of a miniature-golf course. Tea is served, but in a touristy milieu (for instance, soft drinks cost more than $4). It's on the principal tourism circuit—the other three options are better.

SoMa. Some will have a barbecue going, and some will be no-nonsense for serious music-heads. Some parties are announced with only a few hours' notice, so having access to the Internet is pretty crucial to knowing where the shindigs are. Illegal? Not all of them, and even then, only technically, unless the venue tries selling alcohol.

If you see word of one of Pacific Sound's "Sunset Parties," jump at the chance—they're often relaxed and take place in interesting venues such as on a boat circling the Bay.

- **Hyperreal** (www.hyperreal.org) sends out a monthly e-mail calendar listing the upcoming events.
- **BayRaves** (www.bayraves.com) is a bulletin board where events are announced; sometimes it goes off-topic, but it's a good place for up-to-the-minute alerts of parties.
- **RaveLinks.com** links to a calendar of events.
- **SPRACI** (www.spraci.com) covers worldwide events, but its San Francisco offerings are well-maintained.
- **Nitewise** (www.nitewise.com) lists underground happenings as well as mainstream stuff, so it's a good place to check.

Literary Laundromats

If your clothes are dirty and your mind is open, head over to **BrainWash** (1122 Folsom St., at Rausch; ☎ 415/255-4866; no cover), a laundromat/cafe/evening performance space. Seven nights a week from 7 or 8pm, something's up, be it music, readings, or something more experimental. Thursday is Comedy Night, hosted by local name Tony Sparks. A good idea, right—to sit and enjoy a show while your duds are swishing around? Its website keeps current the list of upcoming acts, including links to the home pages of almost all of them.

Not quite stealing the same idea is **Soap Box at Bernal Bubbles** (397 Cortland Ave., at Bennington; ☎ 415/821-9530; www.bernalbubbles.com), which, on the first Saturday of the month at 10pm, invites 30-minute lectures by truly interesting or established names, which in the past have included Tiffany Shlain (founder of the Webby Awards) and Annie Sprinkle (porn star–cum–feminist performance artist). After the lecture, everyone adjourns to a gallery down the street to get to know each other better over drinks. And if you spill your red wine on yourself, you can just go back from whence you came.

CHESS WITH THE LOCALS

The Mechanics Institute (57 Post St., at Montgomery; ☎ 415/393-0101; www.mi library.org; $10 day pass, $35 weekly pass) is well-known for its chess club, the oldest in the United States (founded in 1854), which is a great place to get creamed quietly if you don't know what you're doing. It's open for casual play weekdays 11am to 9pm and weekends 11am to 5pm; on Saturdays at 10:30am, there's a lecture on chess technique followed by a play session. Absolute beginners are welcome then. Once here, you may check out the place (free tours are given Wed at noon). Founded in 1854 it's a priceless institution for the inquisitive, with some 140,000 items available for anyone to look at. In addition to the archives, the institute schedules frequent events and talks by world-class experts, and 9 months a year it programs its surprisingly intellectual CinemaLit film series (usually $10), in which movies both old and newish are shown and local film writers and critics weigh in.

HOW LOCALS WORK

True, you can't go to the offices and workshops where millions of San Francisco residents earn their daily bread, but there are a few places you can go to see them in action. I'll start with an opportunity to gape at politicos in action, go on to seven fascinating factory tours, and introduce you to the combination museum/engineering post that runs the city's famed cable cars.

The Board of Supervisors, the city's 11-member legislative branch, meets every Tuesday at 1 or 2pm in its opulent chambers at City Hall, and they keep snarking at each other, amusingly, until they're worn out. Debate is lively and can illuminate the often misunderstood, unusual, and liberal social goals of this city. Take for example the recent, envelope-pushing proposal to fine any restaurant or store selling food containing high-fructose corn syrup. And sometimes they're just dealing with the usual political shenanigans: One recent furor involved a supervisor who was lying about living in San Francisco; when the process server went to saddle him with legal papers regarding the lie, they found his address was false. Whatever the issue under discussion, goings-on here are usually nothing less than interesting. Check www.sfgov.org/bdsupvrs to see if there will be a meeting when you're in town, as well as to learn its start time. Anyone can sit in the audience for it and slip out again if they're bored, although during contentious debates, you may find yourself having to watch via closed-circuit TV from down the hall. (Local channel 26 also broadcasts the meetings, but your hotel is unlikely to carry that channel.)

FACTORY TOURS IN SAN FRANCISCO

Philadelphia has its Yuengling. New York has Brooklyn Lager. But San Francisco's hometown brew, the one folks fall back on when they're out with friends, is Anchor Steam. The name alone is steeped in history; experts think the "steam" harkens to a time when West Coast beers had to be brewed without East Coast perks such as ready ice. One of the most popular factory tours in town is the one that explores the **Anchor Brewing Company** (1705 Mariposa St., at DeHaro; ☎ 415/863-8350; www.anchorbrewing.com; free admission; reservations necessary); book as soon as you know you'll be coming to town, because these popular tours max out at 20 participants per day, and don't forget your ID, or you'll be denied the much-loved free tasting at the end. Although the company kicked off by buying an existing brewery in 1896, this facility, its sixth over time, dates to 1979. Its owner is none other than Fritz Maytag, of the famous cheese family, although this venture is all about creating a quality quaff. Tours last about 50 minutes, plus however long you'd like to spend having civilized tastes of about five of its eight typical and seasonal offerings in a woody, pub-like tasting room. Visitors can take the opportunity to purchase limited-edition drinking glasses and other souvenirs. One thing I love about this tour is the fact that the brewery hires dedicated staff whose only job is to know about beer, its manufacturing process, and then to convey that to the visitors; on my last visit, my guide was, the rest of the time, a trained actor who clearly knew his sudsy stuff. Photos aren't allowed on much of the tour, which includes the cacophonous, clattering bottling line where 15,000 drinks an hour are poured, but the most photogenic section—three 4,000-gallon copper tuns in a room with a million-dollar city skyline view—is photo-friendly. (When the manufacturing process got too noisy for my guide to be heard, he just held up signs that described what we were seeing.) The brewery also makes whiskey, but sadly, sharing hard spirits is not permitted. If you're also lucky enough to tour the Budweiser brewery in nearby Vallejo (p. 141), you'll really begin to understand the vast difference in brewing techniques. Here, the mandate is for a handmade, carefully mixed product that's made more or less how beer's been produced since the 19th century, and it tastes like it. There, beer-making is an industrial endeavor of scientific, alienating proportions.

When many people think of San Francisco sourdough bread, the main variety that comes to mind is produced by **Boudin Bakery** (160 Jefferson St., at Mason; ☎ 415/928-1849; www.boudin.com; $3; Wed–Sun noon–6pm). At great expense, the breadmaker recently built a fancy bakery-cum–tourist sight at Fisherman's Wharf. There are several places to get sidetracked at this facility, including a not-so-cheap bistro that catches a lot of business, but self-educators should climb the stairs to the self-guided museum that charges a few bucks to see. There, in a nifty bit of marketing, Boudin works hard to conflate its history with that of San Francisco, which isn't a stretch considering that the bread has been in production since 1849. You see, Boudin's sourdough relies on a blend of bacteria that, for reasons as yet unraveled by science, cannot survive outside of the Bay Area. Take some dough away, and the culture dies. That's what gives Boudin sourdough its distinctive flavor (although, if you're like me, you wouldn't be able to tell it from another maker's—you'll just know you like it), and why it's thought to taste pretty much exactly as it did in the gold-rush days.

After the San Francisco history primer comes the main event: You walk along catwalks over the main baking room, where large Kemper appliances shape loaves, roll them in metal blades shaped like enormous tulip petals, and then cook them. Check out the area known, deliciously, as the "Mother Dough Vault," where batter descended from the original recipe is stored so that the special bacteria won't be lost. As you can imagine, it smells divine, and at the end of your tour, you'll end up in a tasting room where you'll be offered free samples of several varieties including raisin, multigrain, chocolate, and a sourdough Asiago cheese. I still prefer the plain. You can buy bread on the premises, or head across the street into the courtyard in front of Pier 45, where a round rotunda-style cafe might have a shorter line. There's nowhere to buy cut-rate day-old bread, and sourdough isn't as nice if it's hard and dry, so just pony up the few bucks for the fresh stuff. There are a few other places to buy Boudin in town, including inside Macy's Union Square, but this is the most important location for learning about the process. If you want anything more than a loaf of bread, go to the location at Market and Montgomery—prices are lower there, including for my favorite: New England clam chowder in a sourdough bread bowl. Eat the chowder-soaked bread afterward—that's the best part.

Although a visit to the one-room **Golden Gate Fortune Cookies Co.** (56 Ross Alley, off Jackson near Grant; ☎ 415/781-3956) is worthwhile, you'll want to make it short. It's illuminating, from a personal standpoint, to see the workman environment that produces something so festive. The Asian woman sitting at the medieval-looking, gas-fired rotary griddle looks distant and possibly depressed. If you want to take her picture, she insists that you pony up 50¢, and to be honest, it looks like she could use it. The entire operation, in fact, isn't much more than a dingy room, painted a sickly green hue and lit by industrial fluorescents. Such is the no-nonsense environment people have cultivated at this outfit since 1962 to make you your favorite post-meal snack, the fortune cookie. They'll give you a free, unfolded wafer as an edible souvenir, but I'd buy a sackful of their sweetish wares for around $3.50, which countless do and then can't figure out how to pack to get it home without crushing them. Hours vary; go during a weekday for best results. There is some debate about when and where the cookie was invented, so I'll just say it has strong roots in San Francisco. Another interesting fact about them: Because they arrive with the check when customers are about to tip their server, they almost always only contain uplifting, positive slogans.

Keeping the Cable Cars Running

You can tell you're near the mesmerizing **San Francisco Cable Car Museum** (1201 Mason St., at Washington; ☎ 415/474-1887; www.cablecarmuseum. org; free admission; Apr–Sept 10am–6pm, Oct–Mar 10am–5pm), the ever-running powerhouse for the whole car system by the distinctive smell that, to me, proclaims San Francisco more than any of its famous food dishes. It's like the combined aroma of grease and electrical discharge that follows the famous cable cars wherever they roll. Here, in this warehouse that combines a museum experience with a real inside look at the inner machinations of the system, four mighty winding machines work the underground cables that propel the entire system, and if there's a cable break, this is where engineers splice it back together using some seriously medieval-looking implements. From decks overlooking the roaring machines, you'll see the cables shoot in from the streets, wind around huge wheels, and be sent back underground to carry more tourists up the city hills. You'll find out how the whole system works, including a look at the gripping mechanism that every car extends below the street level. I find it remarkable to think that nearly every American city of size once had systems just like this, but now only San Francisco maintains this antique (1873) but highly functional technology.

Alongside the spectacle, there's a museum telling the story of how, in 1954, some parking-garage builders persuaded citizens to somehow support the destruction of most of the cable-car network, leaving us with what you see here today. The museum also tells about Friedel Klussmann, a society member who made saving the system her cause and for whom the Powell-Hyde turnaround at Fisherman's Wharf is now named. There's also a terrific gift shop for all things cable car (books, souvenirs) that sells antique street signs ($50–$90) from all over town; since San Francisco's streets are mostly named and not numbered, you're likely to find a sign that rings a bell with you or your family. Also check out the Clay Street Hill Railroad's Car No. 8—from 1875, it's the oldest cable car in the world; can you imagine getting to work on that coal-cart-like contraption?

Whatever you do, don't miss the chance to go downstairs, under the entrance to the building, where, in the darkness, you can peer at the whirring 8-foot sheaves that hoist in the cables from their various journeys around the city. Now and then, a real cable car will stall as it attempts to navigate the intersection outside, where drivers have to let go of one cable and snag another, and a worker will have to drive out in a cart and give it a nudge. This may be my favorite museum in town, and there's no other museum around that is as distinctive to the city, but mysteriously, few tourists bother to go.

FACTORY TOURS IN NEARBY BERKELEY & FAIRFIELD

Since Ghirardelli doesn't offer factory tours in town, the best a tourist can hope for—and it's still pretty darn good, chocolate-wise—is a trip to **Scharffen Berger Chocolate Maker** (914 Heinz Ave., at 8th, Berkeley; ☎ 510/981-4066; www. scharffenberger.com; Mon–Sat 1–6pm, Sun 10am–5pm), just over the water in Berkeley. Although its manufacture is a complicated process involving lots of specialized equipment, you'll be impressed by how homegrown the outfit really looks, and the aromas just may drive you insane. The factory, essentially a few big rooms with personal-feeling redbrick walls, prides itself on making chocolate in the old style; in fact, one of its principal machines (the one that draws out the cocoa butter from the beans) is almost 100 years old and is nearly identical to one used as far back as the 1800s. If you're lucky, you'll get to witness the most mouth-watering part of the process: when the liquid chocolate is poured into the molds in a final step. Or perhaps you'll find the factory store to be the best moment, when you can load up on sweets. Don't show up at the factory without a reservation, and wear closed-toed shoes. The factory is about a 15-minute walk west of the Ashby BART station. Kids have to be 10 or older. If all this is too much effort (or temptation) for you, there is a simple sales shop available at the Ferry Building, which is at the foot of Market Street. The only other Scharffen Berger store is in New York City.

The **Jelly Belly** factory (1 Jelly Belly Lane, Fairfield; ☎ 707/428-2838; www. jellybelly.com; free admission; 9am–4pm) produces two things en masse: jelly beans and tours for visitors like you. Schoolchildren pour in by the busload, snack on jelly-bean-shaped pizza in the large cafeteria, and then load up on a sugar high that no amount of cajoling can assuage. If you can handle the intensity that a jelly bean factory whips up among the knee-highs, you'll surely find a visit fun. Tours, which require no reservations, go in batches every 15 minutes and follow a 40-minute route along enclosed, elevated walkways over the factory rooms. If you don't have your own hat to wear, you'll be given a cute paper souvenir one—and required to wear it. Below, you see the beans being shaped, batched, moved, and sorted, and all around, you'll smell the sugary goodness of the flavor in production (the last time I was there, I got lucky and the aroma of the day was the buttered-popcorn flavor, which is surprisingly delicious). Along the way, short videos that elucidate and illuminate the process, and give you further vantage points into it, are shown. Guides are usually just button-pushers/babysitters and can only answer the barest inquiries.

In San Francisco, Ronald Reagan is known for two things: looking the other way during the AIDS crisis and loving Jelly Belly beans (licorice was his favorite). This is the happier aspect to dwell on. There are lots of reminders of the bygone actor president, not least of which are portraits of him and Nancy in what are surely, by now, rotten beans, and a case full of memorabilia including letters and souvenirs from his inaugurals. You'll need the willpower of the pope to avoid taking home any of the little morsels; everyone who takes the tour receives a 2-ounce mixed packet of beans as a gift, and that just starts most people on a buying binge at the factory store, where every flavor from sour cherry or Dr. Pepper to pencil shavings or boogers (really—they make a line on a Harry Potter theme) is available. Prices are $2 for a quarter-pound—not cheap when you consider the mass manufacture you've just witnessed—but fortunately, this is the only store in which you'll also find "Belly Flops," which are misshapen beans that didn't make the commercial cut, for $8 per 2-pound bag. The free tour should be ample for most people, but the company does sell expensive ($45 adults, $30 kids) tours of the actual factory floor on a walk-in basis Monday through Friday, which it calls "Jelly Belly University"; you won't learn too much more than you'd learn on the free version, but you'll get a T-shirt. The factory is located in Fairfield, just a very short zip off the I-80 freeway (you won't get lost), about an hour north of San Francisco, far enough for a sugar crash to become a problem. If you'll be spending any time in Wine Country, it's about 30 minutes from Napa or Sonoma towns.

When you walk into the ginormous factory at **Anheuser-Busch Brewery Tours** (3101 Busch Dr.; ☎ 707/429-7595; www.budweisertours.com; June–Aug Mon–Sat 10am–4pm, Sept–May Tues–Sat 10am–4pm), you'd be excused for thinking that they're manufacturing passenger planes here and not 12-ounce bottles of beer. It's simply gargantuan. Although it seems, at first, as if a visitor might be disturbing the workflow at this industrial complex, the staff is, in fact, welcoming to the few visitors it receives (just 50,000 a year) relative to the bustling Jelly Belly factory across the street. (You should definitely combine them on a trip.) Here, you can just walk in anytime, and you'll be escorted above the factory floor to a gift shop–cum–tasting room, where you'll watch an overproduced video that cheerleads the Anheuser-Busch brands such as Budweiser and Michelob. Once the bald marketing bit is out of the way, though, you'll be taken on a walk-through of the mighty facility, from the deafening clatter of the machine that bottles 1,800 beers a minute (each bottle ends up spending 2½ hours on this daunting line) to the "cold room"—really more like a cold hangar—where 120 12-ft.-diameter, 72-ft.-long tanks are stacked up three stories high; they're filled with enough aging beer, 21 days at a time, to fill 60 million bottles. You wouldn't want to be under these full tanks in an earthquake. Impressively, this facility has gotten its waste down so low that only 0.9% of its refuse ends up in landfills—everything else is recycled or reused. Despite the truly staggering size of the facility, it's the second-smallest one in the Anheuser-Busch empire. All this effort to make such a disappointing beer! Kids under 21 are allowed, but, of course, they won't be permitted to indulge in the tasting.

HOW LOCALS LEARN

Here's a Left Coast idea: a **Craft Gym** (1452 Bush St., at Van Ness; ☎ 415/441-6223; www.craftgym.com). It's set up a lot like a gym where a person might work out, except everything is geared toward making crafts. The tools, reference materials, workspaces—all are waiting for anyone who wants to give their creativity a workout. Day passes cost $18, but the best way to go is probably to participate in one of its many workshops, which take 3 hours and happen during the day on Saturdays or during the evening on weekdays. They're led by local artists who work daily in that medium and usually cost about $65 including a $15 materials fee. Topics are nothing if not rangy—pewter casting, flip-book making, photo-frame-pendant making—and there's usually something planned every day except Wednesday. Some people use the Craft Gym as their own ateliers, so if you're crafty, you'll find it an interesting place to meet locals with like interests.

Most of the time, **Cheryl Burke Dance** (1830 17th St., at DeHaro; ☎ 415/252-9000; www.cherylburkedance.com; $12–$24 for 45–90 min.) keeps busy by programming four-week dance classes, but several times a week, it offers drop-in classes for those who'd like a one-time introduction to a variety of dance styles. Also popular are its parties, an informal atmosphere (as cheap as $5) where true neophytes won't feel singled out. You don't have to bring a partner because you'll be paired with another guest, which makes this activity a terrific way to meet and mingle with locals. It's also gay-friendly. Until the spring of 2008, the facility was known as Metronome Dance Center before the *Dancing with the Stars* two-time winner, a Bay Area native, saved it from financial ruin with the help of investors that included her mom. Have a look at its events calendar to see how the programming changes as Burke asserts her vision.

COOKING SCHOOLS

The excellent **Tante Marie's Cooking School** (☎ 415/788-6699; www.tantemarie.com) does cooking demonstrations of full menus on Tuesdays and Thursdays. Sometimes, the topic is simple but necessary to good cooking—"Purchasing Meat" was a good one—however, most of the time, courses are based around an ethnic food type (Malaysian, Chinese) or an international cooking method (Asian steaming, Asian stir-frying). Events are not cheap—$65 for most, $80 for dessert-based events—but they're well-received. Tante Marie does both participatory events, in which you do more than watch, and multi-day cooking courses that might fit into your vacation schedule, such as a 3-day Italian course and a 3-day run on herbs and spices. These, too, are not cheap ($575), but they take the full day and ingredients and tools are included. The full stable of 25-odd chefs who do the teaching are listed, with biographies, online; they're all established writers, professional restaurateurs, and educators.

Similar prices ($55 for a few hours; add $25 for wine pairings) are charged by **First Class Cooking** (www.emilydellas.com; emilyd@gmail.com), an outfit run out of its leader's Pacific Heights home. The focus is on quality ingredients and on meals with strong nutritional value. Lessons usually are in preparing a full meal, which participants—only 12 at a time, maximum, because there aren't individual cooking stations—then sit down and enjoy at Emily's dining room table together. It sounds slapped together but, in fact, Emily has been studying food for years, has a huge and accessible knowledge of food and technique, and has been doing this as a career since 2004. Past students praise her accessibility and breadth of knowledge. Bring your own wine—it's not as if a setup like this comes with its own liquor license.

Check to see if **The Chronicle Cooking School** (☎ 415/777-7759; www.sfgate.com/food/cookingschool), located at the Ferry Plaza and sponsored by the city's main newspaper (its writers are the prime teachers), is back up and running. This popular event shut down, probably temporarily, in early 2008, but its popularity means it's likely to make a reappearance. Events are usually $60 for several hours.

LECTURE SERIES

Responsible for more than 50 evenings a year, the superlative **City Arts & Lectures** (☎ 415/392-4400; www.cityarts.net; most tickets $19) books contemplative speaking appearances by some of the most brilliant minds in thought and in the arts, moderated by another well-respected figure (usually, a journalist).

These aren't appearances by F-listers eager to promote their latest tiny titles; in a several-month period in 2008, guests included Barbara Walters, Stephen Sondheim, Steve Martin, Salman Rushdie, Amy Sedaris, Roz Chast, Meredith Monk, and Ani DiFranco. These appearances often resurface later, in edited form, on the radio, but frustratingly, you can't hear them unless you're in the right market and podcasts aren't produced, so catching them here, at the Civic Center's Herbst Theatre, will likely be your one chance.

Attracting some 10,000 people and 350 authors over the course of its bimonthly season, **Litquake** (☎ 415/750-1497; www.litquake.org) is one of the city's most popular regular readings series. Writers are from every background imaginable— kids' books, fiction, nonfiction, and so on—and events range from readings of the writers' own work to hands-on workshops. In mid-October, Litquake goes crazy with its annual festival, and it schedules several events a day over a week.

This is a literate city, and unlike many others, it runs its **Main Library** (100 Larkin St., at Grove; www.sfpl.org; Mon 10am–6pm, Tues–Thurs 9am–8pm, Fri noon–6pm, Sat 10am–6pm, Sun noon–5pm) the way powerhouse museums are normally run. There's always something worth your time going on. On the events board in the lobby, you'll find a long list of free exhibitions and talks—and not silly things run by dilettantes, either: One recent exhibition concerned how Picasso painted *Guernica,* including some of his studies; another was a talk about the Black Panther Party, the radical group with roots in '60s Oakland, by several original members, now elderly. There are often as many as 10 events planned a day, particularly on weekends. You can get an advance list by clicking "Events" and "Main Library" on its website. On the Market Street side of the building, check out the glass cases full of little items that were discovered in the brick foundations of the old city hall, which stood on this site; they include pottery shards, a creepy doll's head, and a walrus tusk that a sailor no doubt brought back from some 19th-century sea voyage.

A PowerPoint "Slam"

Think of it as show and tell for grown-ups: **PechaKucha Night** (www. pechakucha-sf.com). Once a month, usually midweek, a group of volunteers bearing PowerPoint presentations come together to share anything they like. From architecture to design to dog spirituality, topics are wide, but participants are restricted to only 20 slides that may be displayed for 20 seconds each. Get in, get out, make it snappy. It sounds like a pretentious idea, and maybe it is, but in truth the concept weeds out all the long-winded self-indulgences that often derail seminars. The effect, which rarely bores, is much less poetry slam than it is a set of mini-documentaries you might hear on National Public Radio or see on the CBS *Sunday Morning* show. There are usually around a dozen presentations. The concept is an export from Tokyo, where the name (pronounced Peh-*chach*-ka) means "chatter." Presenter slots fill up quickly, but anyone can come and soak up the range of presentations. The venue changes often, so go to its website for the latest plans.

SF in SF (Science Fiction in San Francisco; www.sfinsf.org) convenes some of the smartest writers in the genre to talk about literature, politics, their work, and whatever else the audience of forward-thinking geeks wants to hear. Events are usually scheduled monthly, cost nothing (though there's a cash bar), and they're usually held Downtown.

It only goes down a few times a month, always on a Tuesday, but it's absorbing stuff: **Ask a Scientist** (www.askascientistsf.com) is exactly what it sounds like; at one of two local cafes, listen to a smartie such as a UC Berkeley prof talk about a topic he knows a lot about, be it "Tornado Research in the Field," "The Science of Baseball," "Individual Differences in Perception," or whatever else the organizers have been able to book. No need to feel daunted; the speakers know that their crowd is full of laymen. Kids are welcome.

POETRY READINGS & LITERARY OPEN MICS

Poetry slams and **readings** are traditions that go way back in this town, and they hit their heyday in the 1950s, when daring new writers would gather, usually at North Beach cafes, to share their latest work and to garner praise from their contemporaries. To this day, there are aging writers and idealists who gather weekly around the city to share their writing and their dreams. There's no use pretending that the Beat-generation writers, or their ethic, still has much of a foothold in town; today's best writers are moderns, sure, but they have an interest in solid writing and descriptions and aren't as obsessed with a boat-rocking social style the way the Beats were. Still, because they're about sharing original ideas, a night among them can feel, at times, like a night that might have fomented the peace movement. Expect lots of anti-Republican—or, more accurately, anti-social-conservative—works.

Some events feature only one or two authors, who decide for themselves whether to take questions or whether to simply let the writing speak for itself. Others try to squeeze multiple writers into the evening. Still others allow anyone to get up and offer their own work (these events are usually termed *open mic,* which means the microphone is available to all. To read yourself (something I wouldn't do unless you're dead sure the venue is the right one for what you write), show up about a half-hour early and put your name on the list. Most of these events are highly informal so be sure to call ahead to make sure the evening is still on the books. Because these evenings are dependant on what participants bring to them, it's nearly impossible to categorize each one and to guarantee the kinds of things you'll hear. If it's important to you, also be sure to ask whether kids are invited; sometimes, if a reader plans to present something ribald, they may be discouraged from coming. Another reliable place to check on current events is the *Guardian* or *SF Weekly,* where pubs list such nights. Both publications are distributed for free from boxes on curbs around town.

Sundays

San Francisco Brewing Co. (584 Pacific St., at Columbus; ☎ **415/905-8837;** 7–9pm): Appropriate for kids.

Mondays

Rassela's Jazz Club (1534 Fillmore St., at Geary; ☎ **415/346-8696;** www.rasselasjazzclub.com; 9pm): Adults only; singing and spoken word.

Notes from Underground (2399 Van Ness; ☎ 415/775-7638): Appropriate for kids.

Sweetie's Café and Bar (475 Francisco St., at Powell; ☎ 415/433-2343; 7:30pm): Adults only; featured poetry reading, then open mic.

Tuesdays

Java Source (343 Clement St., at 4th; ☎ 415/387-8025; 9:30–11:30pm)

Wednesdays

Sacred Grounds (2095 Hayes St.; ☎ 415/387-3859; www.sacredgrounds cafe.com; 7pm): Poetry-reading night that's been going since 1974.

Savoy Tivoli (1434 Grant Ave.; ☎ 415/362-7023; 7:30pm, except 3rd Wed): Reading followed by open mic.

Smack Dab at Magnet (4122 18th St.; ☎ 415/581-1600; www.magnetsf.org; 8pm every 3rd Wed): Participants must prepare 5-minute performances; discerning kids welcome.

Thursdays

Bird & Beckett Books (653 Chenery St., at Castro; ☎ 415/586-3733; 7pm 1st and 3rd Thurs)

FOR KIDS

826 Valencia (826 Valencia St., near 19th; ☎ 415/642-5905; www.826valencia.org) is a fabulous example of someone helping others simply by offering expertise and seeing what comes out of it. The writer Dave Eggers made millions writing *A Heartbreaking Work of Staggering Genius,* but instead of spending the cash on mansions and cars, he opened this storefront dedicated to encouraging an appreciation for reading and writing, particularly stuff school curricula ignore (comic writing, college-entry-essay writing) in the minds of kids ages 6 to 18. The staff is nearly completely volunteer. Although many of the programs require multiple weeks to participate in, there are opportunities for 1-day workshops such as "Sudden Fiction," an afternoon where kids are given stories as short as a single paragraph to as long as a page, and then turn around and write as many of their own as they can before the session ends. Sometimes, Eggers's colleagues from *McSweeney's* literary magazine, or Dave himself, are signed up for evening events for the grown-ups, too, and the outfit publishes a quarterly journal that presents kids' writing with all the respect and style of an adult journal.

The storefront idea, which has enlisted the support and time of the likes of Jon Stewart and David Byrne, is gradually being duplicated around the country. The venture is partly funded by a deadpan "pirate supply shop" (daily noon–6pm) at the front of the workspace, where all your eye patch and booty needs can be met—how endearing is that? Even if you have no intention of enrolling anyone in the programs, or if you're stocked up on peg legs, the front facade of the building is a work of art unto itself. Celebrated artist Chris Ware, author/illustrator of the wildly acclaimed graphic novel *Jimmy Corrigan, The Smartest Kid on Earth,*

Leafing Through History

San Francisco is a top-notch place to delve into a variety of topics important to the history of the United States. There are literally dozens of research libraries that, although by reservation, welcome visitors from all walks of life to plumb old papers, magazines, and other artifacts from the past. These unsung resources are broken down by subject matter; depending on what excites you, you'd be unlikely to go to more than one or two, but here are some of the options.

One of the world's great research oddities, **Prelinger Library** (301 8th St., Room 215, at Folsom; no phone; info@prelingerlibrary.org) is stuffed from floor to ceiling, and often in the middle of the aisles, with what the proprietors call "ephemera"—stuff that is either in the public domain or whose copyrights have expired but has some cultural value. A visit here is always surprising—you never know what you're going to stumble across in the stacks. These orphans of the research world include *Robert Merry's Museum*, a children's omnibus magazine from the Civil War era; the 1978 survey of 42nd Street that kicked off the Times Square revitalization; and a 1958 carnival of marketing stereotypes known as Wolff's *What Makes Women Buy*. The gray archive boxes are, for me, where it's at, since they contain a mixed bag of (often totally unrelated) items that haven't been bound in book form.

As its organizers (if that's the term) phrase it, "The freedom to browse serendipitously is becoming rarer. Now that many research libraries are economizing on space and converting print collections to microfilm and digital formats, it's becoming harder to wander and let the shelves themselves suggest new directions and ideas." Opening hours vary and you should e-mail ahead, but it's generally open Wednesdays from 1 to 8pm.

For those interested in the high seas, the **J. Porter Shaw Maritime Library** (Building E, Fort Mason; ☎ 415/561-7080; Mon–Fri and 1st Sat of each month) is a repository for timetables, scrapbooks, sailor's crafts, machinery, and other items that tell the rich story of West Coast maritime history.

was tapped to create it. The result is a complicated, whimsical flowchart of boxes and seemingly simple images that ingeniously tell a tale of the evolution of human communication. It's the kind of work that takes a while to fully decipher, and unfortunately, to do that properly in this case, you'll be standing in moving traffic on Valencia. Better to take some digital photos of it and inspect it safely later.

HOW LOCALS WORSHIP

People in other parts of America, particularly souls who have never been to San Francisco, like to mock the city as a bastion of godlessness. In fact, nothing could be farther from the truth. In part because of a long working-class tradition, San Francisco is an extremely churchy town; in particular, its Catholic and Episcopalian

The **California Historical Society** ✦ (678 Mission St., at 3rd; ☎ 415/357-1848; www.calhist.org; Wed–Sat noon–4:30pm; $3) maintains a collection of some half a million photographs, books, and paintings concerning the state's complicated history. There's also a well-respected library, the Kemble Collections, devoted to the history of printing; its star holding is the Taylor & Taylor Archive, one of the world's two most complete archives of a printing office. Obviously, it's for font nuts.

The famous Sierra Club, the century-plus-old society dedicated to the preservation of America's natural treasures, maintains a library of its archive material, the **William E. Colby Memorial Library** (85 2nd St., 2nd Floor; ☎ 415/977-5506; www.sierraclub.org/library). Probably the most interesting holdings are the 20,000 photographs—many were taken on trips in the early 1900s, and some are more modern masterpieces by Ansel Adams.

The **Museum of Performance and Design** (401 Van Ness Ave., 4th Floor, at McAllister; ☎ 415/255-4800; www.sfpalm.org; Tues–Sat noon–5pm) was being renovated at press time. But its previous incarnation had a top reputation as a repository for artifacts of theatrical history, and it booked several themed exhibitions a year. The library includes a 60,000-piece sheet-music collection and a 10,000-item musical-theater collection. Because so much of theatrical history dovetails with general American history, it's a fairly fascinating place to explore for 30 minutes or so.

The **Chinese Historical Society of America Museum and Learning Center** (965 Clay St., at Joice; ☎ 415/391-1188; www.chsa.org; Tues–Fri noon–5pm, Sat 11am–4pm; $3 adults, $2 seniors and students, $1 kids 6–17) takes a long look at the establishment of Chinese people in the Americas, starting in the 1600s and focusing on their contributions to recent national history and to recent struggles for equality.

See also the **Mechanics Institute** (p. 136).

populations are active and long-established. The churches in this city are also big on something that Jesus himself was big on: mercy, diversity, and non-judgmentalism, which makes visiting them not just easy, but also encouraged by the local congregations. Of course, there are lots of houses of worship where the congregation would be glad to welcome you, but these are among the most notable or unforgettable.

When you first walk into the sanctuary of **Glide Memorial Church** (330 Ellis St., at Taylor; ☎ 415/674-6000; www.glide.org), the first thing you'll notice—other than the fact that about three different people will have warmly welcomed you—is the big, blank white wall above the altar. That's because back in the 1960s, when the church's legendary pastor, Texas-born Cecil Williams, took over this 1931 church, he decided to remove the imposing cross that once hung there. It was all about trying to connect his congregation with God and the Spirit, no matter their background; indeed, at a service here, Jesus is never mentioned, although the clergy is certainly Christian. At the Sunday morning 90-minute "celebration" services, the congregation looks as if someone threw a net over whomever was passing by on the Tenderloin street outside: young, old, black, white—even, one recent morning, a little kid who wanted to wear his tiger costume to church. I've never seen anything like it, but I get the strong sense that it's what a Christian church is supposed to look like.

Williams, who retired the pastorship but is usually on hand anyway, is a little like a kindly high school principal, and his services are a little like a late-night TV talk show, accompanied by a skilled six-piece jazz band (Leonard Bernstein was a fan, and Quincy Jones still is), backed by a 100-plus-voice choir (the Glide Ensemble, and man they're good) and peppered with "Right on!" and "Shalom." He's a solid American institution, counting Oprah Winfrey, Maya Angelou, and Robin Williams among his fans, and having appeared by himself in the Will Smith movie *The Pursuit of Happyness*. His wife, Janice Mirikitani, a well-known city poet, has also been working at the church since 1969. Their message, repeated throughout, is one of diversity, compassion, ending racism, brotherhood, and acceptance, and it doesn't take long before the crowd is on its feet, clapping, swaying, and otherwise digging what I consider to be a real embodiment of Jesus's central New Testament message: Never once does anyone pretend that he knows which political party that God would vote with. Instead, the church operates 87 entities designed to help others in a city that desperately needs such outreach, from help with housing and healthcare to jobs training. Don't miss it; there's nothing else like it, and it's impossible to feel unwelcome. Services are at 9am and 11am; don't show up with less than 15 minutes to spare or you'll almost certainly have to participate by TV from a fellowship hall, and that would be a shame.

A similar worldview is espoused by the **Swedenborgian Church** (2107 Lyon St., at Washington; ☎ 415/346-6466) a place that cares less about the specific ideological aspects of Christianity as it has been lately interpreted and more about the spiritual and historical lessons in the Bible. The philosophy is based on the teachings of a guy named Emanuel Swedenborg, a Swedish scientist who lived in the early 1700s. Here, a worship service is, well, more Scandinavian, and less demonstrative than at Glide. Here, the Oprah-ready aspects of Swedenborg's spirituality—we are all in charge of our own destinies, and it's better to live truthfully than to beat the Bible and evangelize—are explored in an intelligent fashion, and Jesus is not left off the roster of invoked names. It's the denomination-free church for the brainy; Glide is for the singalong crowd. Bonus: The little brick Swedenborgian Church, built in 1895, is such an important and early example of the Arts and Crafts movement that it has been designated as a National Historic Landmark. Sunday worship is at 11am.

Old St. Mary's Church (660 California St., at Grant; ☎ 415/288-3809; www. oldstmarys.org) has an interesting background, having been built in 1854 as California's first cathedral and, miraculously, surviving from then to now. The interior isn't particularly beautiful, ornate, or old, but the parish's congregation, which has evolved into a blend of Chinese-born and English-speaking worshipers, would count as unusual almost anywhere in America. Mass is celebrated twice daily. At

12:30pm on Tuesdays, it offers its Noontime Concerts ($5 suggested donation), live performances of classical or sacred music by single artists or small ensembles.

The newer version of Old St. Mary's Church, the Roman Catholic **Cathedral of Saint Mary of the Assumption** (1111 Gough St., at Geary Expressway; ☎ 415/567-2020; www.stmarycathedralsf.org) isn't usually described with the esteem of its predecessor, although the reason for that is its progressive architecture. I would describe this blocky monument as swooping, concrete-heavy beehive layers with mesmerizing geometrics, but critics are more succinct, linking its profile to that of a washing machine (for sins?) by calling it "Our Lady of the Maytag." (Not really astute, since the real Mr. Maytag is making good beer across town—see p. 137). Either way, the style may have been cool in 1969, but in the '80s and '90s, it went through a period when it was out of favor, and only now is it becoming something considered hip again. The 4,842-pipe organ is balanced precariously on a relatively narrow pedestal. Docents, when they're on duty, are dressed in red jackets; the best times to find one is Saturday and Sunday from 9am to noon and Sunday following the 11am Mass (about noon). Open services are held Monday through Saturday at 12:10pm, and the best time to go on Sundays is 11am, when the full choir is in attendance.

On Sunday mornings from 9:30 to 10:30am, just before services, **Grace Cathedral** (1100 California St., at Taylor; ☎ 415/749-6348; www.gracecathedral.org) hosts its free, long-running Forum speaking series, which books experts in spirituality, politics, the arts, and activism. You really never know what kind of personality will be appearing, but expect an intellectual, not overtly emotional approach to spirituality. One day, it might be an author and expert on food safety in America, another week could bring Pico Iyer or theater director Carey Perloff, or you could even catch Father Guido Sarducci (comic Don Novello) himself. Such activities designed to edify the general public are not commonly undertaken by cathedrals anywhere. The cathedral doesn't stop there, though; it programs a fascinating slate of events all year, most of which you'd never peg for a holy place. One New Year's Eve, I was able to attend a $10 screening of a restored copy of the 1929 classic film *The Phantom of the Opera* that was accompanied by a live musician on the sanctuary's mighty organ. Check its website to see what's coming.

HOW LOCALS HELP

San Francisco, it must be said, is one of the more troubled cities in America. Its homeless problem is fearsome. Thus, there are heaps of opportunities for volunteering, many of them requiring commitments as short as a day. Needs change almost daily, so check the following websites to see what volunteering organizations require in the way of manpower.

The concept at **One Brick** (www.onebrick.org) combines volunteering with socializing. After events (which take 3–4 hrs.) are over, the collected volunteers are invited to go out for a beer or food together. The notion has taken flight in several American cities in addition to San Francisco. Because it enables you to insinuate yourself into the community on two levels, through volunteering and meeting people, this is the one I recommend—if it has something going on that you can do, which it may not always have. Other organizations that can hook you up with shorter volunteer opportunities of all kinds include **Hands On Bay Area** (www.hosf.org) and **The Volunteer Center** (www.thevolunteercenter.net).

Swap, Meet

"Free trade is a contradiction of terms." So goes a mantra of the **Really Really Free Market** (www.reallyreallyfree.org), which meets once a month in Dolores Park. Consider it a freegan fantasia—bring useful items, food, or skills and use them to share or trade for other people's useful items or services. It's that simple. Meet days have a breezy, hippy energy, with folks playing music, sitting in the sun, and generally being neighborly, although the wares tend heavily toward clothing. It's not the kind of event that you have to bring something to in order to feel part of things. It's as much about making friends as it is about making trades. The market is held on the last Saturday of each month; consult its website to find the hours.

Golden Gate National Parks Conservancy (Building 201, Fort Mason; ☎ 415/561-3000; www.parksconservancy.org) is a group that supports the major National Parks Service–maintained sights around town: Alcatraz, Fort Point, Golden Gate National Recreation Area, Muir Woods, and Presidio. Locals love their parks, and they're outdoorsy sorts, so several times a week, there's a program planned across the city. Sometimes it's volunteering to garden somewhere like Crissy Field or on Alcatraz, sometimes it's more for pleasure, such as a free afternoon of off-pier crabbing at Fort Point. It also puts together arresting arts exhibition, such as a recent display of optical-illusion art by Chris Hardman at the Presidio's Officers Club. Check the online calendar or pick up a *Park Adventures* booklet at any of the visitor centers of the above parks.

A STROLL THROUGH JAPANTOWN

San Francisco's Chinatown is famous. Everybody who visits town ends up dipping his toes, at least for a few minutes, in the shops of Grant Avenue and Stockton Street. Most tourists aren't told, though, that over the past generation, many Chinese residents have pulled up stakes and moved their homes to western districts of the city, Richmond and Sunset. Many of the Chinese people you'll see in so-called Chinatown are, in fact, visitors themselves, which is why the buses are so crowded in this part of town.

There's another enclave of Asian culture, though, plenty close to the central sights of town, that many tourists don't know about, despite the fact that it's right under their noses and all but served up on a platter. It's **Japantown** (www.sfjapantown.org), which for most of the 20th century has been a hub for Japanese life, food, and culture. A visit here is a lot less frenetic than one to Chinatown. What's more, there are only two other Japantowns of note in America: in Los Angeles and in nearby San Jose.

Although the city has hosted a Japanese population since around 1860, it wasn't until the 1906 quake, when many of them were forced from their homes by fire, that so many of them settled in this part of town, known as the Western Addition. By 1968, the city has cleared a 5-acre, 3-square-block parcel of land

and arranged for the construction of two mini-malls for the Japanese community, the Japan Center. Near the east end is its most definable feature, a five-level pagoda given as a gift from Japan. The west side is anchored by the AMC Kabuki, a standard multiplex, while the rest of the complex, which links over Webster Street via an enclosed skybridge, is a fascinating place to stroll and shop, indoors, and peruse authentic Japanese wares. I like to enter around Fillmore, its western boundary, and then walk along inside until I reach the pagoda; then, cross the cobblestoned plaza and check out the quieter Miyako Mall segment. On Saturdays and Sundays from 1 to 7pm, the fortune teller Maya Linda sets up in the mall and gives inexpensive readings of many origins (including tarot and the Japanese astrology of Kigaku).

Not everything at the Center is so tempting; can you see yourself buying car parts at Auto Freak? Maybe not, but the fabulous **Ichiban Kan** (p. 192), modeled on the great 100-yen stores of Japan, may trap you. Across the street, don't miss **Uoki K. Sakai Co.** (1656 Post St.), a grocery store that has been in business somewhere around town for decades; it sells Japanese crisps, oils, spices, and other hard-to-find ingredients for supermarket prices. You know a place is trustworthy when you see lots of little old ladies filling their baskets there. It started as a fishmonger on Geary Street, and it's still known for fish, but no sane tourist will be packing that, will they?

Across the street, the gallery at the **Japanese American Historical Society** (1684 Post St.; www.njahs.org; free admission; Mon–Fri noon–5pm and 1st Sat) sells some fresh local handcrafts, such as peace ornaments and soy candles, and it mounts the odd historical exhibition. There are also a library and archives, too, for those interested in the sometimes-painful topic of how Japanese Americans lived and were treated on the West Coast of America in the 20th century. This is also the place to obtain a walking map of the San Francisco **Japantown History Walk,** a series of 16 well-written signs that thread through the area; the first sign is by the pagoda across the street, by the entrance to Kintetsu Mall. Also at Buchanan and Sutter, check out **Benkyodo Co.** (p. 79), said to be the oldest Japanese confectioner in town, well-loved for its mochi and manju cakes.

Tuesday is a lousy day to go, because many of the shops at the Center will be closed, but otherwise, they're open from around 10:30am to 8pm. Much of the food at the Center, typically noodles, is perfectly good and, with the exception of the Benihana, affordable. The city's well-known boat-sushi place, **Isobune** (p. 83) is also here, as is the all-you-can-eat shabu-shabu family/party restaurant **Mums** (p. 83). Most places post pictures of the dishes in the window, making knowing what you want to eat easier, although all servers speak English.

7 Walkabouts

Step into San Francisco's story with a free, curbside view of the city's dramatic past

PAYING FOR A SIGHTSEEING BUS TOUR MAY SEEM SMART—AT FIRST. BUT 20 minutes in, as you zip by the 10th thing you would rather be exploring in depth, and the narrator's facts start jumbling together—was she talking about that building on the left, or the right?—you realize that a whirlwind tour is no way to get to know a place.

So be your own leader. With my self-guided walking tours, there's no "hurry up," and you can break away at any moment to chase whatever catches your interest. I supply commentary and point you toward adventure. The rest is up to you.

My walking tours cover three important areas in town—and I've been careful to select routes that won't drag you, breathless, up any brutal hills. The first tour, Market Street, trails through the historic heart of the city, where you'll learn about the frightful quake and fire of 1906. The second tour introduces you to two of the city's most colorful ethnic enclaves, Chinatown and North Beach, for a glimpse into the here and now of San Francisco life. And the third tour, of the Castro and the Mission, eases up on the heavy history lessons and gives you a strolling tour through two of the most famous neighborhoods in America, which also happen to be two of the most typical residential areas in San Francisco, one for the affluent and one for our newest Americans.

Walking Tour 1: The Embarcadero & Lower Market Street

Start: At the Gandhi statue behind the southern end of the Ferry Building, located at the northern end of Market Street (Embarcadero BART station, J, K, L, M, N, T Muni lines, or any F streetcar)

End: Union Square (Powell Street BART station, J, K, L, M, N, T Muni lines, or any F streetcar)

Time: Allow approximately 60 minutes, not including time spent in attractions or on tangents.

Best time: Start the tour hungry, because one of the first stops will be the food stalls of the Ferry Building Marketplace. The prime times there are Tuesday 10am to 2pm or Saturday 8am to 2pm, when regular opening hours are augmented by a farmer's market. Otherwise, streets are at their most lively during business hours.

Worst time: There's no bad time, but on weekends, the energy drains from the area.

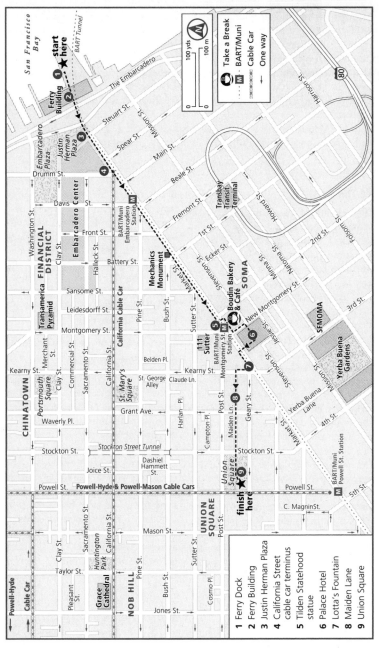

San Francisco Bay

start here

The Embarcadero

BART Tunnel

Ferry Building

Steuart St.

Mission St.

Spear St.

Main St.

Beale St.

Embarcadero Plaza

Justin Herman Plaza

Drumm St.

Embarcadero Center

Davis St.

Front St.

Halleck St.

Battery St.

Sansome St.

Leidesdorff St.

Montgomery St.

Washington St.

Clay St.

FINANCIAL DISTRICT

Transamerica Pyramid

California Cable Car

Pine St.

Bush St.

Sutter St.

Fremont St.

1st St.

Ecker St.

Market St.

Mechanics Monument

Transbay Transit Terminal

Howard St.

Natoma St.

Minna St.

New Montgomery St.

SOMA

Boudin Bakery & Café

SFMOMA

2nd St.

3rd St.

Yerba Buena Gardens

Harrison St.

80

2nd St.

Folsom St.

BART/Muni Embarcadero Station

111 Sutter

BART/Muni Montgomery St. Station

Jessie St.

Stevenson St.

Mission St.

Yerba Buena Lane

4th St.

CHINATOWN

Kearny St.

Merchant St.

Commercial St.

Sacramento St.

Portsmouth Square

Clay St.

California St.

St. Mary's Square

Belden Pl.

St. George Alley

Claude Ln.

Kearny St.

Grant Ave.

Waverly Pl.

Harlan Pl.

Campton Pl.

Post St.

Maiden Ln.

Geary St.

Stevenson St.

Market St.

Yerba Buena Lane

BART/Muni Powell St. Station

5th St.

Stockton St.

Stockton Street Tunnel

Joice St.

Dashiell Hammett St.

Stockton St.

Union Square

finish here

Powell St.

Powell-Hyde & Powell-Mason Cable Cars

Powell St.

C. Magnin St.

Powell-Hyde Cable Car

Sacramento St.

California St.

UNION SQUARE

Post St.

Mason St.

Huntington Park

Sutter St.

Grace Cathedral

NOB HILL

Pine St.

Bush St.

Cosmo Pl.

Pleasant St.

Clay St.

Taylor St.

Jones St.

Take a Break

BART/Muni

Cable Car

One way

100 yds

100 m

N

1 Ferry Dock
2 Ferry Building
3 Justin Herman Plaza
4 California Street cable car terminus
5 Tilden Statehood statue
6 Palace Hotel
7 Lotta's Fountain
8 Maiden Lane
9 Union Square

As long as anyone can remember, Market Street has been the spine of the city, and it remains its most important thoroughfare, cutting an oddball diagonal path through the traditional grid layout that rules the rest of Downtown. From the 1800s to today, it was the avenue by which the city moved and breathed, where its most important banks and hotels clustered, where the streetcars and ferries headed, and even today, where all the major political and social parades march. To walk down its span, twice as wide as most other streets around here, is to wander through the city's tumultuous history, from boomtown to shakedown to the classy Financial District that dominates it today. Illogical as it seems, the section of Market Street between the Bay and (roughly) Van Ness Avenue is often called "Lower" Market despite the fact that it appears higher up on maps than its other end, which threads through hills of Twin Peaks, southwest of the Castro.

❶ The Ferry Dock

If it's outside of rush hour, where you're standing right now may be virtually desolate. Today, just a few boats, including ones to Sausalito (near the northern landing of the Golden Gate) and to Oakland, leave from here.

The thing that will probably most catch your eye is the mighty San Francisco–Oakland Bay Bridge. From here, you'll get a panorama of its western spans. That massive stone support beneath the roadway between the two suspension towers (each 526 ft. tall) was, during construction, the tallest structure in town. The building of the bridge is described in the box on p. 112, but few people appreciate that it was completed just 6 months after the more famous Golden Gate—and at greater expense. You can't see it from here, but a new high-tech bridge for the eastern portion of the route—the one on the other side of Yerba Buena Island—is currently under construction until 2012 or 2013. The Bay Bridge lands nearly 5 blocks south, where it pours its 280,000 daily cars onto the 101, and where a new crop of skyscrapers is changing deep SoMa into something worth visiting again.

The statue of Mohandas Gandhi standing in the middle of the square didn't make it here without some controversy, which is not atypical of this town. First, people accused its donor of some shady dealings and said that the city shouldn't accept the gift. Then others objected to the work's placement behind the Ferry Building, which some considered undignified. Make amends for all the whining by enjoying the bronze sculpture now.

Enter the back of the Ferry Building.

❷ The Ferry Building

You're now entering the former baggage area for ferry passengers, now a 65,000-square-foot food marketplace. Although I deliver a thumbnail history and perspective of this place in the box on p. 70, happily, the boutique gourmet shops here are self-explanatory, and I encourage you to wander around, tasting things you've never tried before. Everything sold at stores here is from a Bay Area provider, so you're certain to eat something you probably can't get anywhere else in the world. If you can't get to the Wine Country, at least you can sample some of its bounty here. Much of what's on offer here consists of nibbles, but two affordable options, **Taylor's Automatic Refresher** (p. 67) and a lunch at the **Slanted Door** (p. 69), will furnish very different dining experiences.

For nearly a hundred years, from the Gold Rush to the Great Depression, the only way to get to San Francisco from the north and the east was by ferry—there were no bridges—and some 100,000 people a day poured through this building. This grand terminal was inspired by the craze for monumental, proto-Roman civic buildings inspired by Chicago's Columbian Exposition of 1893; it opened in 1898. For many years, this building symbolized San Francisco to the rest of the world. Then, it was as proud as a cathedral, with mosaic floors, ceramic and brick arches, and skylights. It managed to limp through the great quake of '06 by virtue of the firemen having just enough equipment to hose it down with Bay water. The Golden Gate Bridge, and the freedom it gave motorists, made the terminal obsolete, and its decline was swift. By the 1950s, this space had been brutalized by modern renovations and carved into office space. Some 90% of the floor under your feet was plastered with mastic or linoleum. For 50 years, this 660-foot-long space, called the Nave, was lost, but a celebrated renovation project, completed in 2003 and costing a reported $90 million, reintroduced it to some of its former glory.

Explore the Nave in its entirety, including the small exhibition about its renovation, which is located by the left-hand exit just past Ferry Plaza Wine Merchant and just before Kingdom of Herbs. That's the exit I want you to use when you're ready to move on.

❸ Justin Herman Plaza

You're now facing the city with the Ferry Building behind you, looking straight down Market Street as it heads southwest. Feel free to cross the few lanes of traffic and the streetcar tracks until you reach the bricky park on the right-hand corner as Market Street begins. Turn around and check out the neo-Roman facade of the Ferry Building, most notably its 230-foot-tall tower, and its 22-foot-wide clock. You'll notice that, although the tower is intended to be seen from all the way down Market Street, it's not aligned to face that avenue square on, but is instead angled slightly to follow the waterline. If you have the time, linger here until the next half-hour, when the bell inside rings the Westminster Quarters.

While you wait, imagine this place in the latter part of the 1800s. First, the shoreline was farther inland—pretty much wherever you see flat land, it was then water, and the gradual buildup of scuttled ships and landfill eventually created the present-day coast. The activity in those days was frenetic. San Francisco was the most important city in the West—Los Angeles was a nothing town; Seattle, too—and in both directions, the shore would've been clogged with masted vessels and teeming with sailors and longshoremen. The quays were a jumble of saloons and chandlers and off-color hotels. And in between them, industrial railway tracks threaded their way in and out of warehouses and along the waterfront.

Now put yourself into the mind of the cataclysmic events of April 1906. Imagine searing conflagrations pouring out of every window of every office building and smoke turning day into night. An entire city was ablaze. Thousands of people fled their homes and dragged a ludicrously impractical set of their best worldly possessions—jewelry boxes, desks, full armoires—down Market Street in the hopes of making it to the city of Oakland and beyond. Astonishingly, there were no riots, no ugly scenes of pandemonium, just dazed and determined faces; those of us who were in Lower Manhattan on

September 11, 2001, can grasp the surprisingly good behavior that people are capable of when circumstances get truly dire. When these now-homeless wanderers reached this place, they were told that they could only bring what they could carry in their arms. Countless people lost everything.

The nastiness didn't end with that chapter. When the era of waterfront trade died, so did the wharves. San Francisco's elders failed to prepare for container shipping, and Oakland poached much of its business while this city's docks became largely derelict. So as happened to so many waterfronts, locals simply wrote it off. In 1957, when Americans still believed the car was the talisman for a bright future, a two-level highway was plowed along the Embarcadero, darkening everything and cutting off the Ferry Building from the rest of the city. It took the so-called Lomo Prieta quake of 1989 to slap some sense into the town. The shaking damaged the highway so badly that it was dismantled, and the city's reconnection with its precious waterfront fostered a renaissance. (The lemons of major disasters have not always been turned so wisely into lemonade; check out the box on the 1906 quake, p. 160.) Pier 1, to the left of the Ferry Building as you face it (the even-numbered piers are right of it), is slated for a facelift of its own, with planned cafes and water-taxi facilities.

You may also cross paths with some antique-looking streetcars rolling through this intersection. Their history, and the story of their operation, is told at a free museum south across this plaza on Steuart Street; I talk about it on p. 110. It's a worthy detour, because inside you can see movies of Market Street, which you're about to walk down, that were taken just days before the great quake of 1906.

In the park around you, take a moment to notice the angular concrete tubes of the so-called *Vaillancourt Fountain* (1971), which was despised as hideous upon its opening and isn't much more popular today. Local support eroded when people learned the message of the piece was to support a free Quebec—hardly a Bay Area issue worthy of such a prominent location. The 710-ton tangle still routinely dodges efforts to demolish it, and the city pays $70,000 a year to pump water through it partly because, as one politician said in 2004, when it's dry, homeless people shelter there. Makes you wonder what kind of shelter $70,000 would buy.

Continue down Market Street.

❹ California Street

At California Street, you'll see the eastern terminus of the cable car's only true east-west line (1878), which trundles past the mansions of Nob Hill and winds up among the humbler residences around Van Ness Street. I love this line because there's rarely a big tourist queue and it's much more popular with commuters. That's probably because the route doesn't hit the major tourist sights: It goes past Grace Cathedral (p. 109) and then ends its journey at Van Ness Avenue. The line used to be about twice as long, but it got chopped in half in the 1950s—blame the American love affair with the car for that, too.

The concrete building towering above the terminus is the Hyatt (p. 39), which was also derided in its day but is now accepted as a landmark in brutalist architecture. Duck inside to the third-floor atrium lobby, which is 17 dizzying stories tall; it's one of the city's most dramatic indoor spaces next to Grace Cathedral.

Across Market Street from here is the San Francisco branch of the **Federal Reserve** (101 Market St.; ☎ 415/974-3252; http://frbsf.org), which runs intermittent tours and has an extensive collection of antique American currency. Arranging a visit would be a hassle except for anyone fascinated with finance, but there is a quick exhibition in the lobby's west end (how to spot a counterfeit, that sort of thing) that might be worth a few minutes' dabble.

Continue down Market Street, staying on the right-hand (northern) side.

❺ California to Montgomery streets

The going gets faster now. Three blocks on, where Market, Battery, and Bush streets converge, you'll find the Mechanics Monument, a tribute to laborers created in 1901 by sculptor Douglas Tilden, who happened to be both deaf and mute. Made of bronze, it somehow made it through the 1906 fire (there are some striking archival photos of this statue standing proudly amidst a field of rubble), but it's fun to imagine that the flames burned off all the clothes of the manly men depicted. Only in San Francisco would an ironworker let any of his bits dangle. (Guess what? Locals were scandalized by this artwork, too—they objected to the nudity.)

Just behind the intersection of Sutter and Sansome streets, the Romanesque, 22-floor tower at 111 Sutter St., built in 1927, was the location of detective Sam Spade's office in *The Maltese Falcon.* For years, the beautiful geometric painting of birds on the ceiling of its lobby was hidden by accumulated cigarette smoke and soot, but a recent renovation restored the architectural glories of this building, which was designed by the same men behind the Waldolf=Astoria in Manhattan.

Past the elevators, you'll find a small exhibition, assembled by an enthusiastic employee named Tony (ask if he's handy—he's often in the lobby) that includes background on the building and Sam Spade, plus an original finial that was removed from the parapet.

Just past Sansome back on Market, you'll see a sight that's very unusual for San Francisco: a McDonald's. Don't stop for a burger; I'm making a point here. The prevailing wisdom in town is that formula stores spell bad news for a thriving community, so companies that wish to open here usually face an obstacle course of permissions and permits, which they almost never obtain. And even when they do open, as a Gap did in Haight-Ashbury in the early 2000s, they're often rejected and soon close. But I'm sure you can't blame locals for feeling this way now that you've tasted the wonders of independent foods at the Ferry Building.

Proceed another block to Montgomery. Douglas Tilden, he of the naked ironworkers, also created this statue, unveiled in 1897 to commemorate Californian statehood, which came about in 1850. It originally stood where Mason reaches Market but was shifted here in 1977. Strangely, its western side has an octopus on it; I suspect it's a reference to the Southern Pacific Railroad, which at the time was often likened to the animal because of its many-tentacled reach and strangling death grip on anything that crossed its path. It would have been strange to include a jab at a major company on a public monument of this sort, but it would also be typical of San Francisco's habit of thumb-nosing the powerful. And I suppose it's no stranger than smelting something in your birthday suit.

Cross Market Street where you can, and continue down Market Street.

TAKE A BREAK

Opposite where Montgomery and Post come together at Market, you'll see a branch of the **Boudin Bakery & Café** (619 Market St.; ☎ 415/281-8200; closed Sun) sourdough bread bakery. The restaurant that previously occupied its building refused to sell to developers, so a dull office tower was simply built around it. The cafe inside makes for a good coffee (and bread) break, should you need one. Outside of the lunch rush, you'll find lines here much shorter than they are at the Boudin at Fisherman's Wharf.

⑥ New Montgomery Street

Before the quake of '06, the area south of Market Street, or SoMa, was an over-crowded, filthy depository for the working class, famous for block upon block of tumbledown homes. This area was known as "South of the Slot," a reference to the cable-car route that then plied Market—think of it as the "wrong" side of the tracks. The fire following the quake claimed nearly everything in SoMa, and the area was rebuilt with equally depressing warehouses and factories. To this day, despite some notable developments (such as the open spaces at the Yerba Buena Gardens a block away from here at 3rd and Mission sts.), the area's mood still suffers.

The handsome, bulky building on the corner, at 50 New Montgomery St., is the famous Palace Hotel, which, upon its original construction in 1875, was the best and grandest hotel in America west of the Mississippi, and an icon of San Francisco wealth and pride. Every room had its own bathroom, a novelty even among luxury properties, and rooms could communicate by interconnected pneumatic tubes. A

who's who of the Gilded Age stayed here, including Oscar Wilde, Ulysses S. Grant, and Teddy Roosevelt. Tenor Enrico Caruso was famously sleeping here on the night of the quake, and King David Kalakaua, one of Hawaii's final monarchs, died here, ultimately delivering the kingdom into the hands of the United States. The building survived the quake intact and might have weathered the subsequent fire—it had its own cistern but employees were too liberal with the water, leaving little for the firemen.

The present building, built in 1909 (anyone is welcome in its lobby, so go on in to explore), is still plenty grand, and it isn't without its own colorful history. The luncheon celebrating the establishment of the United Nations was held in its Garden Court, under its spectacular, 63,000-paned glass ceiling. In 1923, President Warren G. Harding died (many say mysteriously) in the Presidential Suite upstairs and was embalmed in its bathtub. Near the left-hand end of the Grand Promenade, which runs from Market Street to Jessie Street in back, a pair of escalators takes you up to the Mezzanine, where about 20 framed antique photos depict the grand old lady at her peak. If the tales of the hotel's turn-of-the-century opulence intrigue you as they do me, you'll be glad to know that City Walks (p. 126) conducts a near-daily tour of the building's grandest public areas; I highly recommend it. This would also be the time to check out the gorgeous Maxfield Parrish mural located behind the hotel's Pied Piper Bar inside Maxfield's (p. 208). The door to the bar is beside the Market Street entrance. The line of whiskey bottles beneath the painting looks as if it, too, is following the Pied Piper. Just outside its entrance in the Promenade, you'll find a case displaying memorabilia about the mural, including the original 1909 commission for $6,000. That was money well spent: The artwork is now worth around $2.5 million. Rooms upstairs, for their part, go for around $400 a night.

Exit the hotel at Market Street and turn left.

❼ Lotta's Fountain

A little further on, at 703 Market St., the stone tower was built in 1898 as the fantastically ornate Call Building, and, for a few years, it was the tallest building west of the Mississippi and a symbol of the city. But during the '06 fire, it burned from the top down. Watching it go was, for many locals, a confirmation that their wonderful and powerful city was doomed. Because of a steel frame, the shell of the Call survived enough to be filled in again, albeit without its domed top and most of its ornamentation. Today's it's the rather boring Spreckels Building, named for a magnate of the old days.

Cross Market to check out the little column at the confluence of Market, Geary, and Kearny streets. It's Lotta's Fountain. The sign here would lead you to believe that the reason to cherish this column is because a once-famous opera singer performed here one day in 1910, but in fact, this is the oldest monument in the city, erected in 1875 as a gift by a singer and dancer, Lotta Crabtree, who rose to fame performing for gold miners. And for many years, this intersection was so much considered the center of town that its three major newspapers were headquartered here; survivors of the '06 quake also met here annually until there were none left alive. Today, sadly, this once-central icon, although recently rehabilitated, has sunk into obscurity with locals. It is, though, on the National Register of Historic Places.

Turn right at Kearny Street and walk the short block to Maiden Lane. Turn left onto it.

❽ Maiden Lane

If you were here 125 years ago, you'd find a thoroughfare for prostitution (hence, the winking name—its original name was Morton Street) along Maiden Lane. It has risen substantially in the world. Today, it's a desirable address for top-of-the-line labels and boutiques. Once strictly for ladies of the evening, it's now the domain of trophy wives.

Halfway down this block on the right, stop in front of the tan, brick, windowless edifice with fanned brickwork around its doorway. This building, built in 1948, was Frank Lloyd Wright's only San Francisco effort. Today it houses a fine-arts dealer specializing in Asian antiquities (it welcomes visitors), and has a ramped interior that even those who aren't students of architecture can recognize as clearly a forerunner to Wright's Guggenheim Museum in New York City.

Walk to the end of Maiden Lane to Stockton Street. A park is directly in front of you. Turn left to the intersection of Geary Street.

❾ Union Square

Unlike New York City's Union Square, an important plaza which was named for the fact that it sits at the confluence, or union, of several major avenues, this one was named just before the Civil War to demonstrate support for the Union of American States—California was never a slave state. The granite Corinthian column in the middle, the Dewey Monument, was dedicated in 1903 by Teddy Roosevelt to commemorate the war dead of the Spanish-American war, and it somehow made it through the 1906 disasters untoppled. But both Union Squares were and are

The Great Quake

There are always earthquakes in San Francisco, and there always will be, but there is only one that can be called the Quake with a capital Q. The disaster that earned this capitalized shorthand was no ordinary shaker. It was a cataclysm that destroyed an entire city, something unimaginable by most modern minds. You'll hear a lot about it on your visit, but talk of the Quake is not simply tourist-friendly theatricality. I don't think it's possible to underestimate its importance; nearly everything in today's San Francisco has roots in that awful period, and even today, you can trace its aftermath everywhere.

The earthquake, which lasted for less than a minute at 5:12am on April 18, 1906, was rough, but contrary to belief, it was not the most destructive aspect of the day. Even the mayor went back to bed afterward, thinking it was routine; he had to be roused later by citizens who filled him in on just how bad things were. No, San Francisco's real downfall was fire. In that age, natural gas was a primary fuel, and the earthquake snapped lines across town. Snapped with them were the water mains, leaving firemen mostly without resources. Back then, San Francisco was mostly a wooden town with buildings thrown up by profiteers—relatively few buildings, aside from commercial ones around Market Street and some mansions, were made of stone and stood much of a chance.

What started as a few fires quickly whipped into a true nightmare. At the wrong moment, the winds changed, fanning already-monstrous blazes into one mighty firestorm in which the air itself was so hot that it caused everything in its path to spontaneously combust. Few living souls have ever witnessed a phenomenon like this. People who had been trapped by the earthquake but remained alive were now consumed by the conflagration. Troops were called in, suspected looters shot on sight. And to stay the flames' advance, whole city blocks were blown up—but as fate had it the troops, lacking high explosives, had to use low explosives, which caused even more fires. No structure, no matter how well-built, could seal itself from something so unprecedented.

Imagine an entire city reduced to charred fields and scattered crumbled walls, like Hiroshima after the blast. Nearly everything from the Embarcadero west to Van Ness Avenue, the biggest dynamite barrier, was gone, as was SoMa, then a warren of wooden tenements. The tops of Russian Hill and Telegraph Hill mostly escaped, but the Mission and Hayes Valley, both west of Van Ness, were also consumed after citizens, not understanding the extent of the earthquake's damage, tried cooking their breakfasts under chimneys that weren't structurally sound (one massive blaze was dubbed the "Ham and Eggs Fire").

"San Francisco is gone," wrote Jack London, who was there. "Nothing remains of it but memories."

Four days later, the fires burned themselves out. Some 200,000 (out of 410,000 residents) found themselves homeless, some 522 city blocks were obliterated. About 3,000 people died, but we'll never know the true number. It took weeks for even the safes to cool down enough to open, but too often, even the fortunes within those was reduced to ash.

The great urban planner Daniel Burnham just happened to have recently drawn up a grand map of San Francisco that drew inspiration from the grand avenues and plazas of Paris and the waterfront parks of his Chicago plan. With everything swept away, the city had a virtually blank slate and they could dream their own future. But the recent past proved too traumatic for dreams, and the capitalists of San Francisco were impatient. They wanted a rebuilt city and they wanted it now. Twisted streetcar lines had been repaired within days in the effort to return life to a semblance of normalcy, and reconstruction on homes and offices began within weeks. Burnham's plan was discarded and a golden opportunity was lost.

So what evidence will you find of the Quake? Not much, except that nearly every old building in town was constructed or heavily rebuilt in the years immediately after. A precious few structures, like the outer walls of the Old U.S. Mint (5th and Mission sts.) and Old St. Mary's Church (Grant Ave. and California St.) have outer shells that made it through the apocalypse. North Beach's wooden Saloon (p. 205) survived because, it's said, its proprietors gave free booze to exhausted firemen during the blaze.

There are countless other aftereffects. Pervasive corruption among city leaders (including that sleepy mayor) was exposed by the disaster, and to this day, San Francisco's citizens pay close attention to the doings of their elected officials and are civically active at a much higher rate than in most other American cities. There is also a strong local tradition of organizations designed to help other people, an outgrowth the post-Quake charity. Some sociologists believe Los Angeles's modern dominance among West Coast cities came because investors grew skittish about investing in the Bay Area. Countless Americans who are descended from Chinese homesteaders owe their lives here to the Quake because, in 1906, the migration records were lost, permitting even illegal residents to pass off their families back home as legal Americans. The borders of the town were changed after the Marina district was fashioned out of rubble to provide land for a World's Fair held in 1915. And, of course, all modern buildings are now constructed with sophisticated features designed to foil earthquakes, from hidden springs to layers of shock-absorbing oil. But that doesn't mean that we should ever be truly comfortable with man's arrogance when it comes to technology. Even in 1906, 6 years before the sinking of the *Titanic*, buildings that advertised themselves as "fireproof" were soon consigned to memory along with the grand, powerful, sophisticated city that they belonged to.

important gathering places for the city residents in times of stress. After the quake, thousands of residents camped out here as their city burned down.

Even if you don't spend a cent, duck into the Neiman-Marcus that stands opposite you, kitty-cornered to the park; its gorgeous stained-glass dome was salvaged from the City of Paris department store that stood here previously (and was destroyed after an epic city protest to preserve it). Beneath that dome, on the building's top floor, you'll find a ritzy cafe that costs more than many other Niemen cafes around the country, but would make for a genteel coffee or tea break.

On the opposite side of the square, on Powell Street at Geary along the cable-car tracks, you can't miss the proud bulk of the luxury St. Francis Hotel (the main building was erected in 1908; a tacky, incongruous tower was added in 1971), which like the Palace has long occupied a prestigious position in city culture and is now a Westin. Like the famous Astor Hotel in New York, the St. Francis in its heyday was known for a clock that stood in its lobby, which became a well-known public meeting place. Unlike the demolished Astor, though, the St. Francis still has it; the hotel is undergoing endless renovations and changes, but at press time, this handsome Austrian timepiece was standing just inside the entrance to the main lobby. Explore its ornate marble-and-mirror lobby—the hotel employs a staff historian who keeps the walls stocked with vintage photographs (including several by Ansel Adams), thank-you notes from luminaries, and newspaper stories.

It was in a suite at the St. Francis where silent film star Fatty Arbuckle, who rivaled Chaplin for fame, hosted a party that ended in a young actress's death; although Fatty wasn't there at the time, the massive trials and their publicity ruined him, and modern movie censoring was instituted in response to the public fear of Hollywood debauchery. Here, too, was where, in 1950, one of the next greatest stars of the era, Al Jolson, died while playing cards in his suite. And in 1975, revolutionary Sara Jane Moore fired at President Gerald Ford as he left the building; she got out of prison in 2007.

Inside the park on its west side, you'll find the half-price-theater ticket booth (p. 194), so if you'd like to go to a show tonight, now's the moment to plan. On the other side of the same little building, there's a branch of See's Candies, a well-known local brand.

From here, many of the best sights of the city are just blocks away. Six blocks Stockton Street (although because of the tunnel, it's less noxious to take Grant, 1 block east) is Chinatown. Down the slope of Powell is the busiest cable-car turnaround and the destination-shopping Westfield shopping mall.

Walking Tour 2: Chinatown & Lower North Beach

> **Start:** At the Chinatown Gateway located at Grant Avenue and Bush Street
> **End:** Washington Square, North Beach
> **Time:** About 75 minutes, not including time spent shopping or eating
> **Best time:** Daylight hours, 7 days a week
> **Worst time:** Nighttime, when many shops close

Walking Tour 2: Chinatown & Lower North Beach

1 Chinatown Gateway
2 Old St. Mary's Church
3 Empress of China
4 Buddha's Universal Church
5 Ross Alley
6 Stockton Street
7 Pacific Avenue
8 The Condor
9 City Lights
10 Beat territory
11 Washington Square

Take a Break
Cable car

San Francisco's Chinatown claims to be the largest one in America, an assertion I would dispute; Manhattan's has been spreading for years. But there is no questioning that it's one of the liveliest, most colorful sections in all of San Francisco, easy to visit and get to know, and the neighborhood as a whole is more established than many American cities, having begun around 1850. Each of the district's two main avenues, a block apart, offers a different take on the same culture; Grant Avenue is all about antique stores, jewelers, and emporia, while Stockton Street, 1 block west, is a rich food experience of exotic groceries and dim-sum houses. You can pick your Chinatown to suit your mood, although this walk will bring you through both. And at the end, we'll nibble at the southern end of historic North Beach, where the Beat writers drank and the American music culture was called in the 1960s.

❶ Chinatown Gateway

Many Chinese villages have their own gateways and, bowing to tradition, so do many Chinatowns around the world. This one, to me, is very much an emblem of San Francisco's Chinatown. That's because it's not even Chinese, but Pan-Asian. It was a gift from modern-day Taiwan. Astute observers of Asian life will notice, as they walk these streets, a blurring of national and cultural lines; although many of Chinatown's residents are, indeed, of Chinese extraction, the wares and services are spread a little more around the map of the East.

Stroll slowly up Grant Avenue, past the souvenir shops and statuary houses, and I'll fill you in on how this all came to be.

Before rampant landfilling, this area was closer to the wharves, and Chinese residents could easily get back and forth from here to work on the docks. In 1849, there were only 54 Chinese here, but by 1876, there were 116,000 in the state. They mined for treasure. They broke their backs building the railroad. For their pains, they were despised, overtaxed, and excluded. Sometimes segregation begins with good intentions—when illiterate Asian young men were being placed in schoolrooms with Western girls half their age, it seemed logical to the government to simply solve the impropriety by establishing separate schools. But too often, living separate lives fostered a "yellow peril," or fear of Asian invaders, and the Asian population was despised for reasons of economic jealousy—that they were poaching too many jobs.

And as is so often the case, those not in power were seen as sexual quarry by the overclass. In the late 1800s, this area teemed with prostitution, along with diseases. Many of the tales are too harrowing to detail here, but much of it was forced upon young girls who had been tricked into slavery by crooked businessmen, and, by their late teens, many were tossed aside, their health broken and their futures finished. Chinatown was a hotbed of hot-sheet operations.

As for the men, they were worked hard. These so-called "coolies"—a bastardized word derived from the Chinese words for "rent" and "muscle"—had slightly more protection in the form of benevolent societies, where acclimated Chinese helped them negotiate for jobs. But to booming San Francisco industry, these men were just as disposable as the girls.

Moral crusaders fought an uphill battle for their liberation, but the quake of '06 did what they couldn't—the whole district was wiped out. The rebuilt Chinatown was more civilized than the old one, full of benevolent societies and churches rather than opium dens and saloons—although the buildings were still mostly owned by Western men, not Chinese. A local businessman named Look Tin Eli recognized that the squalor of the old Chinatown gave his neighbors an image problem, so he arranged to make buildings more tourist-friendly, decorating them with false pagodas and sloping roofs. At a time when the vast majority of Americans never left their home country, coming here felt like venturing to the Orient. The ruse worked, and today Chinatown retains both its stage-set appearance and its fascination for visitors.

Knowing this background, you'll now understand why you'll see in Chinatown a higher-than-normal incidence of hospitals, churches, and society headquarters. The area is still largely home to elderly and poor immigrants, and the housing remains less than palatial—many Chinese-born immigrants also choose to live in the city's western areas instead—although the chances of being abducted in a Chinatown alley are now all but nonexistent. Thank goodness, because I'm going to take you down a few.

The next 2 blocks are all about souvenir stores, probably because this section is closest to the tourists of Union Square. I find the inventory too inauthentic for my tastes. (T-shirts with Mao on them would be considered in poor taste in Beijing.) Still, since you're currently in the part of Chinatown that's richest in gifty purchases, you should take a few minutes to peruse. Prices in this stretch (which we'll remain until we reach Jackson St.) aren't always great, but the shopkeepers are keenly aware of their competition, so haggling is easy if you have the

nerve—don't be afraid of doing it, because here it's expected. I won't stop you much here, so spend your time shopping. Keep going up Grant until California Street, where the cable-car tracks run.

Cross California Street to the church at its northeast corner.

② Old St. Mary's Church

Here stands the state's first building to be built as a cathedral, which it was from 1854 to 1894. Because the city began with such meager resources and fires were rampant, the oldest churches here are not the prettiest. The interior of this one is no exception, mostly because it was gutted by two catastrophic blazes—one of them after the quake of '06; there are several famous archival photos of the building standing amidst the smoke. The shell of the building is original, but the inside dates to the days of Donna Reed.

It's no accident, to me, that the symbol of the city of St. Francis (the patron saint of the environment) is the phoenix, because the story of this town is all about rising from the ashes. St. Mary's rebuilt in another part of town. When that burned, too, it constructed a third version, and that remains today on a hill high above the Tenderloin (p. 72). This place is now just a sweet parish church with a long history. It was here, in 1902, that America's first mission for indigent Chinese immigrants was established; food was served, English taught, and charity otherwise available for anyone who was suffering in the New World. On Tuesdays at 12:30pm, there's usually a $5 classical music concert (www.noon timeconcerts.org).

Opposite Grant from Old St. Mary's, that rather tan pagoda-ed four-story building is the Sing Chong Building, built after the quake as a sort of showplace for Asian commerce.

Originally, it was full of exciting stores and functioned a bit like a multi-floor bazaar of the sort that's still popular throughout Asian cities.

Continue up Grant Avenue.

❸ Empress of China

You should be between Clay and Washington streets now.

I can never walk Chinatown without humming the song "Grant Avenue" from Rodgers and Hammerstein's generally forgotten musical *Flower Drum Song* (1958), which was set here and which tackled the tension between traditional Chinese immigrants and their free-spirited American-born kids. That show reflected the Chinatown of the 1940s, a world of nightclubs and brassy Asian showgirls. Oscar's lyric makes Chinatown seem like Vegas on the Bay:

> "You can eat if you are in the mood
>
> Shark fin soup! Bean cake fish!
>
> The girl who serves you all your food
>
> Is another tasty dish!"

This dinner-show-era of Chinatown ended even before R&H wrote that song, but it lingers, or at least echoes, at Empress of China (833 Grant Ave.), a classy and eternally popular dining spot in the roof garden of this building, the China Trade Center. It's not the sort of place where I'd suggest you grab a cheap bite (the Dungeness crab is $41, lunch mains about $17), but it's where corporate vice presidents might dine when they're in town.

As you go, notice the details above street level, such as the unchanged '50s and '60s signage and the way laundry hangs to dry in some upper-floor windows. It's a glimpse into how, because of low income, this neighborhood is forced to cling to many of the ways of the past.

At Washington Street, turn right (east) and walk past Walter U. Lum Place. Look across the street.

❹ Buddha's Universal Church, 720 Washington St.

Before you judge this hideous box of a building, from 1963, you may be swayed by its origins. A nightclub stood here before, and, when it went out of business, a cash-strapped Buddhist congregation purchased it. Soon, they learned they'd bought a lemon. It had to be torn down. So, the congregation—and this is my favorite part—spent 11 years literally holding bake sales to raise enough money for a home of their own. This ugly building, built on cookies, now houses the city's largest Buddhist congregation. The church also owns what's said to be a shoot from the bodhi tree under which Buddha received enlightenment some 2,500 years ago. You can't walk in without an appointment, so we'll move on.

The grand-looking multitiered pagoda near you was built in 1909 by the phone company, which wanted to construct an exchange for its operators that would fit into the local culture. Today, it's a bank.

The little park at the corner of Grant and Washington, Portsmouth Square, is pretty much the only green patch in Chinatown, so it's where locals gather early each morning to practice their tai chi together. It was here, on this plaza, that the American flag was first raised over this land, in 1846.

Return to Grant Avenue and cross it. One short block later, at Waverly Place, turn left. At 125 Waverly, you'll find the building housing **Tin Hou Temple.** Founded in 1852, it's the oldest Chinese temple in America. Visitors are welcome, although it's polite to remove your shoes when you go inside to inspect its carvings, traditional architectural details, and altar, portions of which survived the 1906 blaze. It's customary to leave a few dollars in the red envelopes on the front table. The temple, serene and wafting with incense, is on the top floor and there's no elevator. (By the way, this kind of house of worship isn't so common here; there are more Chinese Christians in Chinatown than there are Buddhists.)

Return to Grant Avenue and go left. Continue past Sacramento Street. Continue up Grant. At Jackson Street, turn left.

⑤ Ross Alley

Once you leave Grant Avenue, the kitschy red lanterns and hokey hyper-Oriental flourishes dribble away, delivering you into a much more authentic community at work.

You'll pass an alley on your left, and at the second one, Ross Alley, turn left. In here is the Golden Gate Fortune Cookies Co. (p. 138), worth a stop if only for the glimpse of workaday Chinatown that is so rarely afforded to outsiders. These alleys, in the bad old days, were rife with gambling, brothels, drug dealing, and worse, and it was these dark and dangerous dens that seemed to mortify reformers the most. Duncombe Alley, across Pacific, was famous for its opium dens. St. Louis alley, on this side of Pacific, was known for its slave market, where naked girls were auctioned off to pimps. It's all so hard to picture today, and thankfully it's over. Enjoy a cookie instead.

A few steps down the alley, at no. 50, the Sam Bo Trading Company deals in Taoist and Buddhist religious items, such as fake paper money designed to be burned at funerals—it's a good place to pick up a few offbeat souvenirs for merely a few dollars.

Return to Jackson Street, turn left, and continue to Stockton Street. Then turn right.

⑥ Stockton Street

This is my favorite part of Chinatown, and the part that most closely resembles a typical urban street in an older Chinese city, with sidewalk produce stands, fish markets, and bakeries. Some of the greasy spoons display the roasted meats of the day in their windows, head and all—the sight repulses some Westerners, but many Chinese customers know how to tell at a glance whether the quality of the inventory is high today. You'll also notice that the signs in the shop windows aren't in English as often as they are on Grant Avenue; that's because this is an active shopping street for everyday sundries, particularly for older Chinese-born residents.

Here, you should take your time and wander into the groceries to see what non-endemic produce is for sale. You'll find durian, star fruit, lychee, and other fruits they don't have at your local Winn-Dixie, and you'll have to swim through crowds of Asian folks to get to them. Happily, shopkeepers, though displaying a businesslike manner, are generally willing to explain any product for which you can't read the label.

At 1121 Stockton St., on the top floor of a building marked 1908 near its cornice, is the century-old Tung Sen Benevolent Association, one of many groups, such as the famous Chinese Six coalition, that were organized to ease the transition into American society, battle the ghetto's gangs, and assist the poor in getting a leg up. Back in the day, these groups had far more power than today and they functioned like labor unions–cum–legal counsel, fighting discrimination. These days, they tend to arrange festivals and scholarships and ensure local history is preserved.

After 2 blocks on Stockton Street, stop at Pacific Avenue.

❼ Pacific Avenue

The specific ethnicity of Chinatown stops abruptly around Pacific Avenue. Within a few steps more, you'll be on the lower fringe of Italian American North Beach, historically the Italian part of town. Because of the city's quirky topography, you may also be enjoying better weather than you did at the start of your tour—this area is less likely to be cloaked in fog than other parts are.

In the 1800s and very early 1900s, Pacific Avenue (look right, toward the Bay) was considered to be the spine of the notorious Barbary Coast area. Think of a wooden shantytown leading down to a bustling, curved wharf, which, in its earliest days, was called Yerba Buena Cove. Over time, the settlement grew, but it always retained its male-heavy population and its rough, low-class profile. From the gold rush, respectable men with families didn't come out West to seek their fortunes; that was the province of drifters, opportunists, and poor laborers. San Francisco was founded by these men.

This hellish hamlet, in its early days called both Sailortown and Sydney-Town (after an Australian gang that once brutally ruled it), was a den of sin, pleasure, and crime. Routinely, young men on a night of carousing at the saloons and opium dens would pass out and wake up the next day on a ship already well out to sea, where they'd be forced to join the crew for months on end until they'd be able to return home. This impression-by-kidnapping method was called being "shanghaied," which meant it often involved drugs slipped surreptitiously into beer, and it was so common

that the police barely kept track of incidents. The brilliant underworld journalist Herbert Asbury, famous today for his book *Gangs of New York,* wrote in *The Barbary Coast* that the period was "the nearest approach to criminal anarchy that an American city has yet experienced."

Pacific was the first street in these parts to be cut through to the water (it now stops 2 blocks short), so it became a vital thoroughfare. By the ragtime era, the neighborhood got classier, if only by a notch. It hopped with dance halls, street barkers, "working" women, and worse. It was a vigorous, often sleazy, thoroughly dangerous, cavalcade of pleasure for San Francisco's considerable working-class population. San Francisco, a city at the end of a frontier, was a place without limits.

The Barbary Coast is now gone. Because of the fire, barely a plank of the original place remains, and even the neighborhood name fell out of favor around World War I after local campaigns succeeded in shutting most of the straggling merriment down. The land is also no longer on the coast, thanks to subsequent landfilling. But the Barbary Coast's 70-odd-year reign gave San Francisco its dominant reputation as a devil-may-care town of hedonistic inclinations, a reputation it no longer deserves but which persists among people who have never actually visited.

Proceed 1 block to Broadway and turn right. Go 1 block to Grant Avenue and cross the short block to Columbus Avenue.

❽ The Condor

The old Barbary Coast frolic hasn't completely died out—it limps along here, along Broadway between Columbus Avenue and Montgomery Street, where a fleet of XXX stores and go-go houses continue to attract men at all hours. Strange to think of a porno-shop block as having a long and established heritage, but this one does.

The city's topless scene got its start in 1964 on the opposite (northeast) corner of Broadway, Columbus Avenue, and Grant Avenue at the Condor, the tan building with green cornice and a lower floor of arched brick. The owner, looking for something to liven up his club, asked the chief of police if his waitresses could loosen their bikini tops. They did, and toplessness wasn't far behind. The mayor at the time tolerated it by saying, "Fun is part of our city's heritage."

Within days, every club in the vicinity had also gone topless. But the person who gets the most credit, to this day, is the copiously chested Carol Doda, who danced a dozen shows nightly at the Condor and was profiled in Tom Wolfe's *The Pump House Gang*. Only around 20 at the time, Doda is still a fixture on the San Francisco scene, now as a chanteuse and the owner of a lingerie store in the Marina (at 1850 Union St.). Her specialty? Bras.

In these more prudish days, the tops—or at least, the pasties—are back on, and the Condor is outrageously overpriced. The strip of prurient emporia past the Condor—Big Al's, Roaring 20s, and the Hungry I Club—will give you a limited feel of what a party zone Pacific Street was during the Barbary Coast's heyday.

In the 1960s, that stretch of Broadway was a prime entertainment area where you could catch the likes of up-and-comers like Bob Marley, the Grateful Dead, Tony Bennett, James Brown, Lenny Bruce, Barbra Streisand, John Coltrane, and other greats. The look of the place, and the illuminated vertical marquees, still give a sense of those glory days, but the entertainments within are either lame or not what your mother would want you to see.

⑨ City Lights

Look right, down the slope of Columbus, and you'll get a gorgeous long view of the avenue and of the famous Transamerica Pyramid at its end—one of the best views in the city. Two blocks down, where Kearny intersects Columbus (stay here for now), you can see a green-skinned building with a cupola. That's Columbus Tower (also known as the Sentinel Building), which survived the quake by virtue of being under construction at the time. The Kingston Trio owned it in the 1960s, when it went to seed; at the time, the basement contained a recording studio where the Grateful Dead recorded their second album. The movie director Francis Ford Coppola owns the building now; upstairs are the offices for the production company he started (now co-owned by his son Roman and his daughter, *Lost in Translation* director Sofia). Downstairs, he sells his Napa county and Sonoma county wines (p. 242 and 247), and there's also a little slightly overpriced but good European-style bistro, Café Zoetrope ($12 for pasta or pizza).

Directly on your right, at Broadway and Columbus, you'll find one of the best and most historic bookstores in the country, **City Lights** (p. 184), whose triangular building is stuffed on three levels with volumes, particularly hard-to-find ones by fledgling presses. Back in the 1950s, its owner, Lawrence Ferlinghetti, decided that good books didn't have to be expensive, and he set about publishing new writers who he thought deserved to be read. One of his choices was *Howl and Other Poems* by a young writer named Allen Ginsberg. The book's homoerotic overtones scandalized some, and the resulting obscenity trial (which the poet won) made Ferlinghetti's bookstore nationally famous among both literary types and civil liberties defenders. By the 1960s, the Beat writers, a restless lot, had moved on, mostly taking their jazz-and-poetry evenings with them, but North Beach was indelibly stamped with their reputation.

You can take a break now and combine an extended browse with a beer at the eclectic **Vesuvio** (p. 205), a bar with a gas-fired chandelier and slightly absurdist decor next to the bookstore and across the alley. Or you can wait a few minutes more while I take you to an authentic Italian cafe for an espresso.

Cut through the alley (named for Jack Kerouac) to Grant Avenue and turn right. Cross Grant, and then cross Broadway and follow Grant to Vallejo Street. On the corner is the stop in the next box.

TAKE A BREAK

I have brought you to Caffe Trieste (p. 85), which is generally acknowledged to be the king of the North Beach cafes. It makes a mean espresso—in fact, it claims to have served the first one in the neighborhood back in the 1950s when it opened. Its paneled dining area is the kind of place where you're encouraged to linger for hours, and many do. Some of the Beats hung here, shaking off their hangovers, and Francis Ford Coppola is said to have fashioned the screenplay to *The Godfather* at the tables. So take a load off and get a homemade pastry.

⑩ **Beat territory**

The block up Grant Avenue to Green Street was, in the 1950s and 1960s, rich with cabarets and cafes popular with the era's most iconic talents. At Coffee and Confusion, once at 1339 Grant, Janis Joplin made a major splash in 1963, and years later, an unknown Steve Martin tried out his fledgling act there. Probably because of the aftereffects of the marginal offerings of the Barbary Coast, this neighborhood was then a cradle for daring entertainment, new names, and experimental forms of at. It's pretty much all gone.

From the cafe, continue left down Vallejo. The Gothic Revival, twin-towered church is the St. Francis of Assisi; it, too was gutted by the quake and fire, but its shell dates to 1860.

Continue to the short block to Columbus Avenue and turn right. Two blocks later, you'll arrive at a park.

⑪ **Washington Square**

The Romanesque church on its northern side, Saints Peter and Paul Church (1924), is most often cited as the background of some shots of Marilyn Monroe and Joe Dimaggio (who grew up about a block from here) after their wedding in 1954. (They actually got married at City Hall—the images were just for publicity.) In true literary North Beach style, the Italian motto on the facade quotes not the Bible but Dante's *Paradise,* from *The Divine Comedy.* About a third of the congregation these days is of Chinese extraction.

The statue of Ben Franklin in the square—why are there so few statues of Ben in America, by the way?—was a gift in 1879 from a dentist, Henry Cogswell, who made a mint in the gold rush. An avid teetotaler, he built such statues, fitted with fountains, across the country in an effort to get people to drink water instead of beer or liquor. North Beach was lucky; usually, the statue was of him, glass of water proffered in an outstretched hand.

So where's the beach of North Beach? Gone. When sailors first got here, the shoreline was actually around Taylor Street, 2 blocks west. So deep beneath your feet, North Beach's beach, now dry, still lies. Landfill erased it, but the name stuck.

Where Are the Painted Ladies?

Not everything was crisped by the quake and fire of 1906. Thanks in part to the line of dynamited buildings along Van Ness Avenue north of Market Street, much of Pacific Heights was saved, despite the fact that it was (and remains) a tinderbox of redwood homes dating mostly from the latter 1800s. This one-time middle-class enclave is now distinctly for the wealthy, and following a period in which these old handsome houses were disdained as déclassé, the current owners lavish great attention and resources on their restoration and maintenance. Walking up and down these civilized streets is a marvelous way to enjoy San Francisco, its distinct architectural style, and its rare way of blending urban living with suburban rhythms and ease.

Although you find pockets of Painted Ladies all around town, from the Mission to the Western Addition to Presidio Heights, perhaps the densest concentration of the best-maintained and prettiest ones is in the 120 square blocks of Pacific Heights bounded roughly by Sutter Street to the south, Union Street to the north, Van Ness Avenue to the east, and Scott Street to the west. Just south of those boundaries, Alamo Square at Hayes and Scott streets provides that postcard-perfect perspective of a row of Painted Ladies in foreground of the distant Downtown skyline.

Your walking tour is over, but your tour of North Beach can be just beginning, if you like, for this park is its unofficial heart, and there are dozens of shops, bakeries, and restaurants in the blocks around here. **Columbus Avenue** is known for its string of sidewalk cafes—although for me, just sitting on one of the park benches and watching the characters go by can be like a meal unto itself. If you have any juice left at all, you can also head up the stairs on **Filbert Street** (which runs in front of the church) to reach the stellar city view of Telegraph Hill and Coit Tower (p. 111). Following Columbus Avenue north, away from the direction you've come, will bring you to Fisherman's Wharf in 8 blocks. And a block west of here, at **Mason Street,** you can catch the famed cable car as it plods the hill back to Powell and Market Streets.

TAKE A BREAK

Eastern Bakery (720 Grant Ave.) is a long-running (since 1924), seriously old-school bakery good for carb-tastic snacks that'll get you through the rest of this walk; you can fill a bag for just a few bucks. The options are many: radish cake, mooncake, *tikoy* (a sort of globular rice cake popular during Chinese New Year), custard tarts and BBQ pork buns that cost less than a dollar. This is one of the only bakeries in town to make *ngow yee daw,* which are thin, crispy, snacky sorts of chips sold by the $3 bag. Keep pointing at goodies without worrying much about the cost, because it won't amount to much. In about 25 minutes, I'll have you at a historic beer hall, and then an Italian cafe for coffee, so don't fill up *too* much—get a to-go bag.

Walking Tour 3: The Castro & The Mission

Start: Castro station (Castro and Market streets; BART and Muni; the F streetcar stops 1 block east)

End: Church Street station (Church and Market sts.; BART, Muni, F streetcar)

Time: About an hour, not including shopping and restaurant stops

Best time: Business hours, Monday through Saturday

Worst time: There is no worst time, but evenings are slightly less preferable because Mission Dolores will be closed and Mission Street will feel less safe.

Through the first half of the 20th century, Eureka Valley was an average, blue-collar neighborhood typical of countless other San Francisco areas. But in the 1960s, when the Haight was overtaken by hippies and partiers, Eureka Valley's residents got spooked. Rather than battle the tide that they thought was headed their way, they sold out and headed for the suburbs, as so many working-class families were doing across America. Seizing the moment, within in about 2 years some 20,000 members of the gay population were able to buy homes here for cheap, creating an enclave of their own. And a new district, now called the Castro after its main thoroughfare, was born. Today, young gay people from around the world come to San Francisco to visit the place they consider to be a crucible for modern gay culture.

On this walk, I'll take you on a stroll through the heart of the Castro, past the mission that was the first permanent settlement in modern San Francisco, and into the eclectic Latin-inflected Mission District. By the end, you'll have a firm feeling for what everyday life is like for two very different types of permanent residents of the city.

① Harvey Milk Plaza

As you come up out of the Muni station, you'll be in Harvey Milk Plaza. It's not much of a public space—really just a roadside bricked area and a stairway that leads into the station. But in this case, it's the thought that counts—Milk was honored because of his importance to gay rights.

No retelling of the Castro's history—indeed, no retelling of San Francisco's history—would be complete without the name Harvey Milk. Milk, a born Long Islander, spent his early years as a buttoned-up financial-industry man in Manhattan before finding himself swept up in the promise of social change that the late 1960s introduced to American culture. He moved to San Francisco and, with his partner, opened a camera shop on Castro Street. Before long, this charismatic, cocky, and visionary man got into politics, and, after several attempts, he finally won a seat on the city's powerful Board of Supervisors—the first openly gay man to serve such a large population. He successfully worked to implement several changes that raised the ire of the city's more traditional, working-class types. Seeing one of their own rise to power was inspiring to the long-downtrodden gay population. Watching him effect changes that made San Francisco more equal for all its residents gave them hope for the future. Just a decade earlier, gay folks were being arrested simply for hanging out at bars together,

Walking Tour 3: The Castro & The Mission

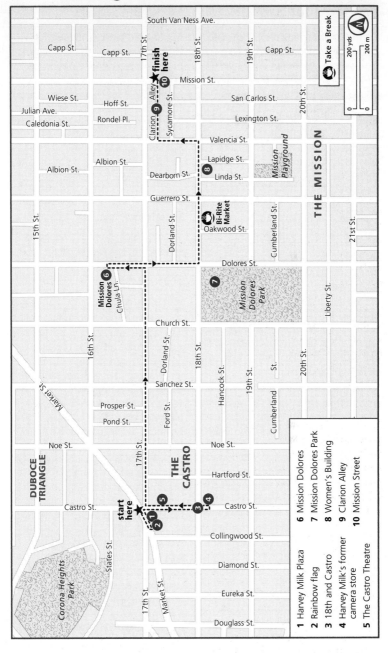

South Van Ness Ave.

★ finish here ⑩

Capp St.

Capp St.

17th St.

18th St.

19th St.

Capp St.

Mission St.

Wiese St.

Hoff St.

Clarion Alley ⑨

Sycamore St.

San Carlos St.

20th St.

Julian Ave.

Rondel Pl.

Lexington St.

Caledonia St.

Albion St.

Albion St.

Valencia St.

Lapidge St.

THE MISSION

15th St.

Dearborn St.

⑧ Linda St.

Mission Playground

Guerrero St.

Bi-Rite Market

Dorland St.

Oakwood St.

Cumberland St.

21st St.

Mission Dolores ⑥

Chula Ln.

Dolores St.

⑦

Mission Dolores Park

Liberty St.

16th St.

Church St.

Dorland St.

18th St.

Market St.

Sanchez St.

Hancock St.

19th St.

St.

20th St.

Prosper St.

Ford St.

Cumberland

Pond St.

DUBOCE TRIANGLE

Noe St.

17th St.

Noe St.

THE CASTRO

Hartford St.

Castro St.

start here

⑤

④

Castro St.

②①③

Corona Heights Park

States St.

17th St.

Market St.

Collingwood St.

Diamond St.

Eureka St.

Douglass St.

Take a Break

N

200 yds

200 m

1 Harvey Milk Plaza	6 Mission Dolores
2 Rainbow flag	7 Mission Dolores Park
3 18th and Castro	8 Women's Building
4 Harvey Milk's former camera store	9 Clarion Alley
5 The Castro Theatre	10 Mission Street

and now an openly gay man was a trusted city leader.

Milk might have been just a footnote in the history books were it not for a disgruntled former police officer, Dan White, who had been Milk's adversary on the board before he himself quit. Historians disagree what pushed White over the edge—political jealousy is posited by some, latent homosexuality by others—but in 1978, he slipped into City Hall through a basement window, foiling the metal detectors, and assassinated both Milk and then-mayor George Moscone, a hero of ethnic San Francisco, at point-blank range. Nine shots altogether, split between the two men in two areas of the second floor, plus time to reload. (Current U.S. Senator Dianne Feinstein was a horrified witness.)

Naturally, the gay population was crushed and enraged. After years of having to skulk around in secret, they'd felt like they had achieved some political parity, and the hope had been snatched from them.

But what came next pushed the community over the edge: In court, White claimed that he did it because he ate too much junk food and sugar—dubbed in the press as the "Twinkie Defense." The verdict came down: White got off easy, with just five years for manslaughter. The resulting outrage by the people in this neighborhood was swift and violent. A tide of furious citizens swept to City Hall, gradually boiling over with anger and overturning and burning a dozen police cars, in what is now called the "White Night" riots. In retaliation, the police swarmed into a Castro gay bar, the Elephant Walk, trashing it and beating patrons regardless of whether they had been involved. But this time, gay people

didn't bow to the abuse. Things had suddenly changed. They decided they would not permit themselves to be stepped on and insulted again; the modern gay-rights movement was instantly galvanized.

White killed himself in the mid-1980s, but Milk's fame seems to grow each year; in 2008, his bust was placed under the dome of City Hall. This plaza was named for him in 1997, two decades after his election to the Board of Supervisors.

Face Market Street and look left.

❷ Rainbow Flag

Standing high above Market Street, you can usually see an enormous (20×30-ft.) rainbow flag flying; erected in 1998, its monumental size and placement were intended to function as a kind of balance to the Ferry Building tower that anchors the other principal end of San Francisco's most important avenue. Like all good flags, the gay rainbow flag is a political manifesto unto itself. The spectrum of colored stripes has nothing to do with Dorothy and that rainbow; they actually illustrate the concept that many different types can live together in harmony.

The gay flag's design goes back only to 1978, which because of the assassinations (and other irritants, such as Anita Bryant's hateful "Save our Children" campaign in Florida) was perhaps the most pivotal year for gay rights here in the Castro. After those indignities, the community assumed a "we're not gonna take it anymore" resolve which it has retained ever since. And that decade, a too-brief celebratory period after the darkness of gay oppression and before the nightmare of AIDS, was the heyday for the outspoken, if somewhat insular, gay culture that centered here.

At the western end of Harvey Milk plaza, at the junction of 17th and Market streets (if you head over there, be careful of traffic and backtrack to this spot afterward), is a small, leftover parcel of land known as Pink Triangle Park, dedicated to the memory of the gay men persecuted by the Nazis. Each of the 15 granite pylons represents about 1,000 of the estimated 15,000 souls exterminated by the Third Reich simply because of their orientation.

Directly across Castro from Milk Plaza, facing Market, you'll see the Twin Peaks Tavern (named for the hills just west of here), a long-running, friendly place with picture windows. Notice that you can see, even here from across the street, the faces of the customers inside. Back in the 1960s and before, gay-oriented establishments usually cloaked their businesses with painted or covered windows; this one, open since the Nixon Administration, was one of the first to operate like any other American business, without hiding or shame.

Turn right (do not cross any streets) and slowly walk downhill.

❸ 18th & Castro

The wood-frame, three-story buildings of this neighborhood are typical of San Francisco in general; without its second layer of history, the Castro might be anywhere in town. In the early days of the 20th century, it was known as an enclave for Scandinavian arrivals, and by its middle decades, for Irish Americans and some Italians.

Back in the 1970s, dozens of gay bars lined this street, not necessarily because gay men are any randier than any other men, but because for the first time, homosexuals were permitted to fraternize with their peers without a significant fear of abuse. The liberation created a bar boom. At the time, gay residents of this area formed a firm community—many of the more outgoing characters from the period are still spoken of with affection and reverence, and there are people who can recall, shop for shop, what the district looked like in 1975, the way others can recall the lineups of the New York Yankees. A few gay bars are left, especially on the side of the street where you're now walking, but there's just a fraction of the number that the early '70s supported.

Today, of course, young people in American cities don't live in fear of expressing their sexuality. Because modern young people rarely feel the need to voluntarily ghettoize themselves, the importance of the Castro as a refuge has greatly diminished. Many of the area's residents are long-time residents—now getting up to Social Security age—and the Castro is too prosperous for very young settlers to afford. When younger gay people venture here at all, it's usually to patronize one of the neighborhood bars.

When you reach 18th Street at Castro, stop briefly. This intersection is considered the heart of this district, and it was in the building housing the bistro/bar Harvey's across 18th from you and the Walgreens now, that the Elephant Walk bar was once located.

Cross 18th Street. Then cross Castro and walk down it a little more.

❹ Harvey Milk's former camera store

A city landmark, at 575 Castro St., this is where Harvey Milk's camera store (opened in 1973) was once located. At the time, he lived upstairs. There's a bronze plaque in front commemorating him.

In early 2008, the Castro received a remarkable renovation as the Hollywood movie biography *Milk* filmed on location here; for about a month, the 2-block stretch of Castro from here to Market Street was largely restored to the way it looked in 1977. Stores' signs were re-created exactly as they once were, bars that had been closed for nearly 30 years were re-marked in their former locations with their old logos, and the faded Castro Theatre was restored to glory. Many longtime residents were deeply moved (and slightly freaked out) by the transformation, as you can imagine you'd be if you woke up and your own neighborhood had been turned back 30 years.

Return to 18th Street and cross it, continuing up Castro back to Market Street.

❺ The Castro Theatre

The next block is full of survivors from the old days. **A Different Light** (p. 185) is one of the last gay-oriented bookshops in this city. **Cliff's Variety** (p. 192), a general store on your right, started in this neighborhood in 1936 and has been serving its changing population ever since. Further on at no. 429 is the **Castro Theatre,** one of the many surviving neighborhood single-screen theaters in San Francisco, but one of the only ones still in daily operation. While the exterior is in Mexican/colonial style, to honor Mission Dolores, inside its decor is a mix of Spanish, Italian, and an unspecific Asian, and it's remarkably unchanged since the cinema's 1922 opening. The Castro attracts film buffs from across the city, regardless of their sexuality, and it's worth seeing an old flick here and hearing its live organist play; read more about its regular movie programs on p. 199.

In the late 1970s, Armistead Maupin, a local newspaper scribe, wrote a serialized fiction column for the *San Francisco Chronicle* that was peppered with topical references and comically ripe with soap-opera bluster. The columns were later published as the *Tales of the City* series of books. The stories touched on the landmarks and institutions of the entire city, from Grace Cathedral (p. 109) to the End Up bar (p. 209), and many of its scenes were set in a garden apartment complex on Russian Hill, but probably because its main character, Michael Tolliver, was gay, Castro locals took the stories as their own. The stories' depiction of that lost decade has come to be synonymous with life in San Francisco and with modern gay history, covering the brief celebratory period after the darkness of sexual oppression and before the nightmare of AIDS.

The Castro was decimated by the disease. For a number of its early years, sufferers were both misunderstood and neglected, as scientists had no clue what was going on (could you catch it from a toilet seat?) or how to treat it (many a poisonous drug hastened patients' declines). Many, too, viewed Washington in general and Reagan in particular as indifferent to their plight, and before the 1980s were done, countless were dead. In many circles, more than half perished. The panic and fear that gripped San Francisco then is difficult to imagine now, and unfortunately for the progress of gay rights, many politicians chose to approach the phenomenon as a social issue rather than a medical one, closing bathhouses and bars rather than focusing on known methods of prevention. Today, of course, the disease (its prevention and its treatment) is seen as a way of life rather than an outright death sentence. But the melancholy and terror of the period will never be truly forgotten by the survivors who lost many of their friends.

At Market, Castro joins with 17th Street. Turn right and walk down. In about 5 blocks, past Church Street, you'll reach Dolores Street. Turn left and go 1 block to 16th Street.

❻ Mission Dolores

Just a week before the Declaration of Independence was dated—June 29, 1776—the first Western settlers said their first Mass on this land, which was then a marshy plain near a small pond. There were no settlements in San Francisco yet; these missionaries would prove to be the pioneers and the modern city would grow up around them. By 1791, Spanish missionaries (well, their Indian slaves) had finished the building you see on the corner now—a squat chapel in adobe, with walls 4 feet thick; it's the oldest building in the city. Although standing here now, you'll feel no sense of the wilderness this area once was, you will see a rare vestige of California's early days. A survivor of fires, earthquakes, and (most devastating of all) development, Mission Dolores has miraculously survived to see modern civilization fill the space around it.

Spanish and Mexican control of the building ended in 1834, but 20 years later, the Catholic Church made it a parish, which it remains today. Religious services are held next door at the unremarkable basilica, preserving the older building as one of California's most important historic sites. But for a few dollars (see p. 112 for details), you can go into the more historic building's basic, serene sanctuary, sit on a simple wooden pew, and admire the Mexican hand-carved altar and figurines. Through an attached museum, you'll be delighted to find a cloistered garden that contains the oldest cemetery in town.

The Mission (which, yes, gave the name to the district we're about to enter) is now crowded on all sides by modern buildings, streets, and parks. For the first half of its life, it functioned as a sort of plantation house, with active fields and graveyards around it. There's no telling how many bodies are buried beneath the surrounding apartment buildings and churches today, but it's no small figure, since some 5,000 Native Americans died as they lived here and toiled for the church. Across Dolores from the Mission, in true Mexican/Spanish style, there was even a bull ring, where bears battled bulls until the mid-1800s.

❼ Mission Dolores Park

Also called Dolores Park, this patch of green is one of the few oases around this part of town that doesn't require a backbreaking climb up a hill to attain. Here, thanks to San Francisco's quirky weather, you're also more likely to encounter sun than in other parks in town. On pretty days, especially weekends, it seems like half the surrounding neighborhoods—lots of gay folks, plenty of hipsters—pour into the park for picnics and sunbathing.

The southern part of the park, near 20th Street, has some decent views of Downtown. Also at the intersection of 20th and Dolores, there's an antique fire hydrant that is painted gold every year. Why such an honor? It was the only one around which functioned during the '06 quake and fire, and this single unit saved countless buildings to the south of it. There's a public restroom in the park for potty breaks, but be warned: It's filthy. Still, it's your best option around here unless you try to sneak into a restaurant's facilities.

TAKE A BREAK

Especially along 18th Street leading east from Dolores Park, you'll find a few cafes catering to loafers. But I love the cramped, deservedly busy **Bi-Rite Market** (3639 18th St.; ☎ 415/241-9760), a grocery that looks from the outside to be a postwar transplant but in fact is a gourmand's paradise that sells all manner of top-quality meats, truly fresh produce, sauces, wines, and dips. Its cheeses, sourced from some of the best Bay Area dairies, are particularly delicious. Assemble a picnic here. Or, across 18th Street and slightly closer to the park, stop into the ice-cream shop, the Bi-Rite Creamery (p. 79) operated by the same owners.

Continue east, away from the park, down 18th Street.

❽ Women's Building

Three short blocks east of the park on the south side of 18th between Guerrero and Linda streets, you can't miss the Women's Building (built in 1910), which houses about a dozen nonprofit organizations designed to assist women. In 1994, a collection of artists got together to cover two sides of its exterior with the sometimes historical, sometimes psychedelic *MaestraPeace Mural,* covering themes of female empowerment and multiculturalism. The artwork makes the place a tourist destination unto itself. Inside, you can pick up a key to the faces and symbols—or buy postcards and T-shirts depicting the building.

This social-services center marks the beginning of the Mission District, which contains the city's densest concentration of Latino residents. Nearly half the people living here either were born in a Latin American country or can trace their lineage to one within a generation or two. Many an immigrant has arrived, penniless, in the Mission, and social services such as this one have helped many of them pull themselves up by their bootstraps to chase the American Dream.

Ebullient and accomplished murals, interestingly, enjoy strong support in this part of town. Born out of the seemingly ancient urban practice of graffiti, which can be seen as a temporary visual exclamation, the murals around the Mission usually dwell on the kinds of subjects important to the often-marginal populations that live here: diversity, traditions, and the simple pleasures of life.

The services inside the Women's Building are designed for locals, not visitors, so after you've enjoyed the artwork, just keep walking down 18th Street until Valencia Street, and turn left. I have one more thing to show you before I unleash you to explore at your own pace. Walk up Valencia for most of the block. Before you reach 17th Street, you'll see Clarion Alley to your right. Enter it.

❾ Clarion Alley

Clarion Alley is another one of those hidden pockets where the public mural tradition is left alone to thrive. Unlike the Women's Building, it isn't designed to last for posterity or even to showcase a single artist. Instead, it's meant to be an ever-changing canvas for civic expression. One artist's work will inspire the next, older works will be overpainted in favor of current ones, and over a few months, the works will be different. If you come here in a year, it will be a new Clarion Alley—and that's just the way the artists want it. (Another famous mural alley, Balmy Alley, is located east of Folsom Street at 24th Street—about a 25-minute walk from here.)

Go straight through to Mission Street.
Turn right.

⑩ Mission Street

When it isn't far from the Civic Center,
the Mission Street of SoMa makes a turn
south and morphs into a Main Street for
the Latin population. This Mission
street can be a real blast to wander down.
Like Broadway in Los Angeles, it may be
litter-strewn and lined with buildings
that haven't seen a new coat of paint in
thirty years, but it also has a carnival flavor. Here, jumbled discount shops, produce markets, and sidewalk stalls
producing a cheap banquet of pan-Latin
delicacies clamor for your attention. The
energy (and, yes, some of the down-and-
out denizens) may unsettle some visitors
used to more subdued shopping streets,
but give it a few blocks and it'll grow on
you. Mission Street is one of the liveliest
places in the city, and its busy sidewalks
mean that although you might be
uneasy at first here, you'll almost certainly be safe.

Stroll down it for as far as you like,
soaking up the affordable, low culture.
There are BART stations at both 16th
Street and at 24th Street. The walk to
24th will take you about 15 minutes if
you don't dally; from there, you can just
hop the subway to go downtown. The
Mission is also renowned for its cheap
Latin foods, and it would be a shame to
leave town without trying to stuff one
of the Mission's famously giant burritos
in your belly. So if you can't find anything you like in the multiple greasy
spoons lining the avenue, allow me to
direct you to two hugely popular burrito vendors, La Cumbre (p. 75) and
El Farolito (p. 75), which are described
in the dining chapter. But I encourage
you to nose around and find your own
culinary miracles—despite sometimes
bedraggled appearances, the restaurants
in this part of town are held to the same
health standards as every other establishment in the city.

I like to take Mission in one direction of a walk, and then head one long
block west to Valencia Street, which
also runs north-south. Contrasting the
Latin vibe of Mission Street, Valencia
has a young, intentionally hip personality, giving the Mission neighborhood a
second, parallel life. Over the past
decade or so, thanks to the infusion of
cash generated by the dot-com boom,
Valencia has seen a growth of cafes and
stores. That hasn't overpowered the
Latin blowout a block east, but it
has turned the Mission District into
an important shopping and nightlife
destination.

8 Attention, Shoppers!

Fill your bags without emptying your wallet

San Francisco is not really known as a place for major shopping deals. Food? It's top of its class. World-renowned postcard views? Check. Computers? Definitely. But very few renowned clothing labels, for example, originate here. Many of the people who live and work in San Francisco are doing quite well, thank you very much, and finding a deal is not the competitive sport it can be in New York or Los Angeles.

Once you accept that it's not a discount wonderland, it's easier to have a good time with the simple sport of finding stuff you like. This is a place where shoppers will be rewarded by ducking into countless boutiques spread around town. The major names are located around Union Square, but fashion-forward types will be rewarded by investigating the off-the-beaten path neighborhoods (see "The Main Drags," p. 182) for little stores worth a gander.

Most stores open at 9am (10am if they're small), and they close at around 6pm. Around Union Square, the hours are likely to be more extended, and stores tend to close around 9pm. Most shops, if they do close one day a week, will do it on a day or two, Monday through Wednesday, so that they can stay open on Sunday. On all goods, with the exception of most edible grocery-store items, 7.5% sales tax is charged.

DEPARTMENT STORES

At the foot of Powell Street at Market Street, the brass-and-marble mega-mall **Westfield San Francisco Centre** ★★★ (www.westfield.com/sanfrancisco) is the fallback shopping attraction for nearly every day-trip visitor to the area. The space is gorgeous—check out the unusual curved escalators that wind in front of the five-story Nordstrom, and on the other end of the mall, a 100-foot glass-and-steel dome has been a city landmark since 1908, when it was first built. Along with the usual well-groomed suspects (Victoria's Secret, Kenneth Cole, Club Monaco, Banana Republic, Bloomingdale's, and so on), there's a mighty Borders bookstore and a state-of-the-art multiplex to fill out those many rainy afternoons.

You're not likely to have a pressing need for most of the things on sale at the luxury retailer **Gump's** ★ (135 Post St., btw. Kearny and Grant; ☎ 800/766-7628; www.gumps.com); its stock in trade is housewares and wedding gifts, mostly. But it's also a San Francisco institution—has been since 1861—and there's only this one store. Any list of the great shopping destinations in town would be lacking without it. Prices are stratospheric across the board; the most affordable things will probably be stuff you don't need, like $50 corkscrews. But that fact doesn't diminish the window-shopping fun of a stroll through its floors. Don't miss the giant carved gilt-wood Buddha on the first floor; the store swears it's the largest of its kind outside a museum. Even if it's not, it certainly sets the rarified and exotic tone.

INDIVIDUAL STORES YOU'LL WANT TO VISIT

ANTIQUES

I know you're unlikely to tote old furniture home with you after your vacation, but most places arrange shipping for large pieces. There is no one district for the pursuit of antiques, but you're most likely to run across other stores along Jackson Square in the Financial District and on Fillmore between Jackson and Geary.

The **San Francisco Antique and Design Mall** ★★★ (701 Bayshore Blvd.; ☎ 415/656-3530; www.sfantique.com; daily 10am–5:30pm) is a 37,000-square-foot warehouse stuffed with some 200 booths where independent vendors sell every conceivable category of bric-a-brac, flea-market-style. There are several benefits to this setup: there's plenty of competition to keep prices down, and much of the inventory will be small enough to get home easily. The bummer is that it's located a few miles south of the meat of the city, near where the 101 and U.S. 280 intersect. But look at it this way: You're far more likely to find a cheap "find" here than you are at the gentrified shops in the middle of the city.

What looks at first like an undisciplined, more-than-bizarre junk store is actually curated by a man who does inventory search at the markets of Europe: **Aria Antiques** ★ (1522 Grant Ave., at Union; ☎ 415/433-0219) in North Beach stocks the kind of stuff that a designer dreams about. Think chandeliers, anatomy posters, wooden toys, doll parts, and other ephemera. The longer you stay, the more you see.

The Mission's **Gypsy Honeymoon** (3599 24th St., at Guerrero; ☎ 415/821-1713) is a fantasia of Victoriana, from stuffed birds to lace doilies, alabaster to feathers. The lineup ranges from jewelry-size to full furniture, plus some soaps and other modern notions to fill out the choices.

The eclectic **Timeless Treasures** (2176 Sutter St., at Steiner; ☎ 415/775-8366; www.timelesstreasuressf.com), just west of Japantown, is quite unlike any other store you might have seen. It sells a selection of stationery and candles, sure, but its real fame is in letters—of every font, size, and purpose. If you need a huge G—say, if you live on Sesame Street—this nook, a decorator's dream, is the word for the alphabet.

CDS, MOVIES & BOOKS

This is a profoundly literate town, so this list is by no means complete. Seemingly every neighborhood has its own adored bookstore or used-book shop—the way most other American neighborhoods have mini-groceries or laundromats—you shouldn't feel nervous about ducking into any place that seems interesting. But these stores are generally acknowledged as the biggest or most established, especially among places that sell new volumes.

Perhaps it's ironic that the Bay Area, which supports the computer industry that fostered the explosion of online downloading, should also have a music store as comprehensive as **Amoeba Music** ★★ (1855 Haight St., at Stanyan; ☎ 415/831-1200; www.amoeba.com), where Haight Street meets Golden Gate Park. Housed in a former bowling alley, the too-cool-for-school Amoeba has perhaps an overabundance of VHS tapes in its movie section, but no one's complaining about the healthy selection of vinyl or its well-stocked listening stations. Most CDs are $5 to $11, new and old, while DVDs (there are plenty, too) hit for around $7 to $19. The flagship location

The Main Drags

One of the great unspoken charms of San Francisco is its affection for private business, and that affection has created a city rich with little boutiques. To my mind, one of the principal ways to enjoy an afternoon here is simply to pick a shopping street and crawl from store to store—there's always something original or unique for sale (although it may not always be affordable, because San Francisco is such an affluent city).

Just as the city is more about little boutiques than it is about giant wonder stores, San Francisco also doesn't really have a central shopping district. Some people might say that Union Square would be it, but in fact that area is host (mostly) to major corporate chains found in malls across America. That, to me, doesn't make it necessarily desirable. Here's some advice on Union Square, plus some other good areas to troll, along with how to reach them.

Union Square

The unofficial center of town, and the place most neophytes think of when they think of shopping in the city, is packed with enormous versions of well-known stores such as Virgin, Macy's, Nordstrom, and others. Even Kenneth Cole has two stores in the area. Because of the multitude of well-known brands, kids will probably find the most to interest them (read: be least bored) accompanying their parents around Union Square.

Chestnut Street

Bus no. 30 from Union Square to Scott Street. Serving the upper-middle-class denizens of the Marina and their growing brood, Chestnut Street offers a pleasant smattering of well-known brands (Body Shop, Williams-Sonoma) as well as small local finds (best for books, kids' clothes).

Union Street

Bus no. 45 from Union Square. Chestnut Street's more restaurant-heavy cousin, just a few blocks uphill, Union Street has a similar selection of upscale home shops and clothing boutiques. It's easy to combine a visit here with one to Chestnut.

Fillmore Street

Bus no. 2 on Sutter Street. Fillmore Street is like Chestnut Street with more beer. Stores are upscale in an aspirational way, such as Rachel Ashwell

is still located in Berkeley (2455 Telegraph Ave., at Haste; ☎ 510/549-1125) where the shop began, but you should be satisfied with this equally voluminous, more convenient outpost.

Although its personality comes across as more hard-core, dare I say punkier, than Amoeba's, I must say I've always found the staff at **Rasputin Music** ✪✪✪ (69 Powell St., at Ellis; ☎ 800/350-8700; www.rasputinmusic.com) to be friendlier

Shabby Chic, home of the post–Laura Ashley bedding and pillow designer. Its patrons are certainly wealthy, but the smattering of pubs and coffee bars relaxes the vibe.

Hayes Street

Bus no. 21 from Union Square. Centered on its intersection with Gough Street, the 3-block-long stretch of Hayes is light on corporate stores and heavy on cute boutiques selling bath products, decorative knickknacks, sake, and upscale clothes for kids. There aren't many bargains, but there are lots of original items.

Haight Street

Bus no. 7 or 71 from Union Square. Most tourists make at least one pilgrimage to this avenue and then, having arrived, wonder what to do here. The answer is to be on the lookout for secondhand duds, because a number of shops along this famous street (between Stanyan St. and Masonic Ave.) deal in hipster clothes. You'll also find the colossal Amoeba Records at its shabbier western end. Famously, a Gap was recently unable to survive here, yet there's still a Ben & Jerry's at the corner of Haight and Ashbury, so the district clearly isn't as anti-corporate as its old rep might indicate. Golden Gate Park anchors its western end.

Grant Avenue

The spine of tourists' Chinatown, a short walk up Stockton Street from Union Square, Grant Avenue is packed with stores selling bric-a-brac, sculpture, cheap silk apparel items ($1.88 T-shirts!), teas, and other Asian-made goodies. The tiny chirping "birds" in cages fascinate kids and torment their parents.

Valencia Street

BART to 16th Street or 24th Street. Two blocks west of Mission Street, Valencia has gone from a questionable ghetto to a city capital for bohemianism. It's slightly thinner on shops than other streets, but what it has is usually quite interesting, from the death-and-garden boutique Paxton Gate (p. 191) to an assortment of clothing and bookstores. There are lots of cafes here at which to spell a spree.

and more eager to help. The multi-floor layout is confusing; you'll need to rely on the hipster elevator operators to shuttle you around, sort of like a grungy version of the old department stores. It, too, has a location in Berkeley (2401 Telegraph Ave., at Channing Way; ☎ 800/350-8700) to feed off Cal students, and at that location, there are semi-frequent in-store appearances and performances. Prices are similar to Amoeba's.

When you're in the Ferry Building, stop at **Book Passage** ✦ (1 Ferry Building, Embarcadero at Market; ☎ 415/835-1020; www.bookpassage.com), a deeply admired and fiercely independent bookstore that has a second, larger location in Marin County's Corte Madera, too far away for a casual visit. The selection here is big on travel of all types, Bay Area concerns, and food and wine. For me, the real appeal are its excellent author events; this store is more likely than any other around to host a big-name author or even a literate comedian, and its selection of signed first editions is unparalleled. The store will send you updates about what's scheduled if you sign up at its website, which is so loaded with events and upcoming conferences that it reads more like a site for a community center. In August, the stores host a well-attended travel writer's conference.

William Stout Architectural Books (804 Montgomery St., at Jackson; ☎ 415/391-6757; www.stoutbooks.com) is remarkably well stocked: 20,000 volumes on two floors. Some of the books are so unusual that they cost a pretty penny, but most of the others are simply pretty. This is the best place in town to go for coffee-table books, artists' monographs, and those eye-popping German books full of arty photos.

Despite the sound of the name, **Stacey's Books** (581 Market St.; ☎ 800/926-6511 or 415/421-4687; www.staceys.com; closed Sun) isn't run by some middle-school girl who dots her I's with hearts; it was started by Mr. Stacey in 1923. Its beginnings were as a medical-book supplier but, over time, it grew to become the respected megastore it is today, with 150,000 titles of every subject—professional medical tomes, though, are still a specialty. It hosts (and promotes) regular events with authors, so check the schedule online.

One of the last gay-themed bookstores in a major American city to remain in business (gay people feel decreasingly like they need a safe space in which to buy

The Bookstore that Changed America

Co-founded in 1953 by poet Lawrence Ferlinghetti, **City Lights** ★★★ (261 Columbus Ave., at Broadway; ☎ 415/362-8193; www.citylights.com) is probably the most famous independent bookstore in America. Once the first place in the country to sell all paperbacks, it now comprises three floors of both paperback and hardback books, many grouped in political or socially aware categories such as "muckraking." It even publishes its own books, with around 100 titles currently in print that range from great thinkers including Noam Chomsky and Tom Hayden to that old Bay Area stalwart, noir. This monument of the Beat generation isn't quite the hive of activity it was back in the day, and I find the staff rather stuck-up, but I always seem to go home with some hard-to-find title, and the store is still a required stop for the literary-minded. Happily, you're encouraged to browse as long as you like, and even to read a little. As you might expect, this destination bookstore schedules about 10 events a month, from author readings to awards announcements. You can pick up a list of what's upcoming at its front desk or check it out online.

books about them), **A Different Light** (489 Castro St., at 18th; ☎ 415/431-0891; www.adlbooks.com) has perhaps a diminished stock—people are buying their queer-studies and gay lit at Borders and the like—but it's worth a browse.

Is it shameful to admit that I dash into **Borders** (400 Post St., at Powell; ☎ 415/399-1633; www.borderstores.com) to browse the wares even if I don't always intend to buy anything? I'd be upset if I saw someone doing that to my own books. But its cafe overlooks Union Square and a scenic stretch of Powell, and I just can't resist. There's another Borders a few blocks south in the Westfield mall (845 Market St., at Powell; ☎ 415/243-4108). I have, I admit, made substantial purchases at both. The city's main **Barnes & Noble** (2550 Taylor St., at Bay; ☎ 415/292-6762; www.bn.com) is located 2 blocks inland at Fisherman's Wharf.

NEW CLOTHING

Some of these places also sell used stuff, but enough of their stock is fresh to justify inclusion as new-clothing stores.

Union Square, Tenderloin & Civic Center

The discount chain **H&M** ★★★ (150 Powell St., at O'Farrell; ☎ 415/986-4215; www.hm.com) has steadily been spreading across America, so it's not the fashion revelation that it used to be, but it's still worth popping into the IKEA of clothing to browse its terrific selection of wearable, well-cut, and incredibly affordable duds. Offerings could be better fabricated, but for great-looking stuff you may only wear a year or two and then not feel guilty about tossing, H&M is hard to beat. Another location (150 Post St.) sells only women's clothes, and a third location inside the Westfield mall (845 Market St., at Powell) also has a kids' section.

From new and designer pieces and heaps and heaps of denim to wearable shoes and even a bunch of vintage, **American Rag Cie** (1305 Van Ness Ave., at Bush; ☎ 415/474-52143; www.amrag.com) seems to have casuals to please everyone. Everything is organized by vintage or by the type of clothing it is, making perusing easier. Cheap? No. But much of what's on the racks will not be duplicated at other stores.

Cow Hollow, the Marina District & North Beach

The Marina's **City Clothing** (3251 Pierce St., at Chestnut; ☎ 415/345-9326) has a dull presentation to match its uncreative name, but it's one of the best places in town to score attractive trendy-casual basics from the likes of James Perse, Ella Moss, and Juicy. The owners are honest about how clothing fits you and they don't blow smoke. Prices can be a little high, but not early in the year, when sales of 20% to 50% off are thrown.

The closest thing San Francisco has to a "sample sale" warehouse is **Porto** ★★ (1770 Union St.; ☎ 415-440-5040; www.portoboutique.com), an American outlet for fashions by up and coming Italian designers (there's also a store in Milan). The clothes are only for women and can be unusual—shirts often have purposefully asymmetrical hems, pants are less likely to be brown or black than deep purple or rust—but the fabrics used are so rich, and the cuts so flattering, even the most conservative dresser should be able to find something tempting. Best of all, prices are very reasonable as you're buying the samples that were either worn by models or sent around to department stores for a look see (don't worry, they usually haven't been worn; and they come in all sizes).

Like the sign says, lady, **Warm Things** (3063 Fillmore St., at Filbert; ☎ 415/931-1660; www.warmthingsonline.com) sells, well, warm things. Down comforters, overstuffed pillows, and jackets that could preserve a bowl of ice cream are among the many markdowns, which are regularly 40% to 50% off normal retail rates.

If you like something high-quality resting on your noggin, toupees are passé. You want something from **Goorin Hats** ★ (1612 Stockton St., at Union; ☎ 415/402-0454; www.goorin.com), which makes some of the coolest head-toppers in town. Fedoras, porkpies, all in a classy, old-school setting with shelves up and down the walls, right across the street from North Beach's Washington Square. It also does a few casual hats, but its real claim to fame since 1895 has been the manufacture of dapper brimmed hats that you can brag about.

SoMa & the Mission

Rolo ★★ (1235 Howard St., btw. 8th and 9th; ☎ 415/355-1122; www.rolo.com) does clothes, particularly denim, that's a season or two old, not that you'd know the difference from fresh-off-the-mannequins. Brands you'll find at up to 75% off include Earnest Sewn, G-Star, and Rag & Bone.

Although the trendy sneaker brand recently opened a flagship store on Powell near O'Farrell, the real place to score some **Skechers** (2600 Mission St., near 22nd; ☎ 415/401-6211; www.skechers.com) is in the Mission, where an outlet store is tucked among the district's junkier clothing shops. If you don't already know the Skechers (*Sketch*-ers) brand, you'll still recognize the style: skaterboarder-y sneakers and retro shoes, plus the odd boot and classic leather shoes. Everything's fairly casual, and prices start around $25 per pair—sometimes half what they cost at the mainline Skechers shops or at department stores.

In the pricey world of camping and adventure outfitting, **REI** ★ (840 Brannan St., btw. 7th and 8th; ☎ 415/934-1938; www.rei.com) is a cut above because customers have the option of becoming members, and members receive about 10% of their annual purchases back each year in the form of a dividend redeemable for merchandise. And some of its gear is stylish enough to wear off the hiking trail, as long as you're aware that sizes here run large.

Noe Valley's **Isso San Francisco** ★★ (3789 24th St., at Church; ☎ 415/920-9149; www.issosf.com) specializes in stuff that was "made, found, or designed in the San Francisco Bay Area" and is known for carrying local lines Nopal (women's apparel adorned with intricate hand-drawn designs), Anne Cook Vintage Jewelry, and Nicacelly (an Oakland label combining hip-hop and quilting). In early 2008, it opened a second store in the Mission (3608 19th St., at Guerrero; ☎ 415/865-0969; closed Tues) that's slightly more accessible to BART.

Hayes Valley

One of the most interesting boutiques around, where looks are unlikely to be duplicated anywhere else, is the admirable **Residents Apparel Gallery (RAG)** ★★★ (541 Octavia St., at Grove; ☎ 415/621-7718; www.ragsf.com), a one-room storefront dedicated to fostering local fashion talent. Some 65 rising designers—folks who can't yet command backbreaking prices—sell their experimental designs here, and some of them have gotten so popular they've graduated to opening their own stores. I've seen chenille knit wraps for under $100 and some eclectic San Francisco–themed tees that put the standard tourist tat to shame. Selections are haute but not pretentious—enough to pique jealousy but not to drain the purse.

Right nearby, **Lemon Twist** (537 Octavia St.; ☎ 415/558-9699; www.lemon twist.net) is a good second stop in the area for shoppers seeking local-made casual clothing that, by virtue of its originality, your friends will never be able to copy; everything is made in San Francisco.

The Haight

Hoodies, sweatshirts, tees with left-leaning inscriptions, shoes, and other implements of hipsterdom fill the rails at **Villains** ★ (1672 Haight St., at Cole, ☎ 415/626-5939; www.villainssf.com), one of the Haight's largest and most established clothing shops (since 1986). The store calls its ethnic "street style," but I like to think of the look you get here as "stylish slacker." Bargains of 25% to 75% off are in the back and to the right. Across the street, **Villains Vault** (1653 Haight St., at Belvedere; ☎ 415/864-7727) carries a similar style but with designer labels, giving it a higher price point.

Installed in a fabulous early 20th-century building left over from the street's early days as an amusement center, **Wasteland** ★★ (1660 Haight St., ☎ 415/863-3150; www.thewasteland.com) repeats the Haight formula of mostly affordable hipster wear, except in designer-y vintage—$20 pants, $15 shirts, and $40 designer tees are the norm. There are interesting selections of jewelry and shoes, too. The deals aren't amazing, although the selection is diverse. Staff is daffy, to put it kindly, and on its own planet.

For more "stylish slacker" stuff—things you'd see a wealthy skateboarder wear—there's **VA** (1485 Haight St., at Ashbury; ☎ 415/701-7822; www.rvcaclothing.com). Do your best to see past the pretentious preening with which it presents its products as artistically sound; it claims to be "free from passing trends" when it's anything but. However, one-of-a-kind tees are $40 and well-cut shirts are $80, which isn't too bad in these parts.

USED CLOTHING

If consignment stuff is your bag, a run up and down Haight Street near Ashbury will do you good, because it's the city's unofficial seat of used clothing.

Those capricious clotheshorses of Russian Hill and Pacific Heights cast off their perfectly good, barely worn couture to **CRIS** ★ (2056 Polk St., at Broadway; ☎ 415/474-1191), where they're resold in a fancy environment that belies the 50%-plus discounts you're actually getting. Cris, the owner, is expert at helping customers put together looks that suit them. The stock changes per the whims of its former owners and what they're weary of wearing, but Prada, Chanel, Gucci, and Versace are typically in rotation.

Samples, clothes from past seasons, items used in window displays and ads—they all end up at **Jeremy's** ★★ (2 South Park, btw. Bryant and Brannan; ☎ 415/882-4929; www.jeremys.com), where clothes are not pre-worn but cost as little as if they were. You can find some amazing stuff from Jimmy Choo, Dolce & Gabbana, Prada, and other high-end, dressy labels you never thought you could afford, plus more middle-ground names like Jill Sander and Vera Wang. I've received word that one woman found a gown for $299 that was selling 8 months earlier at the same designer's flagship store in Manhattan for $14,000. You can also find menswear and accessories. The hours are a bit annoying; it opens at 11am and closes at 6pm Monday through Saturday and at 5pm on Sunday. There's another location in Berkeley (2967 College Ave.; ☎ 510/849-0701) that perhaps stocks a few more casual items.

A Haight boutique that deals in true antique clothing—stuff spanning the late 1800s to the Swinging Sixties—**Decades of Fashion** ✹ (1740 Haight St., at Cole; ☎ 415/668-8202) is one of the most well-rounded vintage shops in town. The shoes are often in remarkable condition for being so old, and the '60s items retain their otherworldly vibrancy. If you want something junkier, there's a Goodwill five doors east, but here, you'll find items that were as cool in their time as they are now. Like so many vintage shops, it carries much more for women than for men.

Nice stuff at thrift-store prices keeps the minor chain **Crossroads Trading Company** (2123 Market St., at Church; ☎ 415/552-8740; www.crossroadstrading. com) popular. Its habitués know that they'd rather spend $35 on a pair of resale jeans that cost $200 a few months ago at the big stores. The wares lean toward the glam, but casual is the dominant mode. Search out the half-price rack, where the already cheap duds are priced even lower—some real deals can be found there. Other locations: (1901 Fillmore St. at Bush; ☎ 415/775-8885) and (1519 Haight St. (at Ashbury; ☎ 415/355-0555).

California has 20 **Out of the Closet** (100 N. Church St.; ☎ 415/252-1101; www.outofthecloset.org) thrift stores, and all of them support health services for HIV and AIDS patients. Think of it as a Goodwill for the fabulous, where you're as likely to see feather boas and sequined gowns as you are old blue jeans and record players. Even the mannequins in the window are sometimes cross-dressed. Purchases are tax-free. There are three other locations—at 1295 Folsom St., 2415 Mission St., and 1498 Polk St.—but the Church Street location is right off the streetcar line.

COSMETICS & BEAUTY

San Francisco has Sephora, of course, as nearly every city does, and it also has an outpost of expensive Kiehl's and of the soapy Lush chain on Powell near Market. But finding a privately owned beauty store that doesn't charge ridiculous prices is a challenge; you're more likely to find cool beauty products for sale on the back shelves of general boutiques.

Nancy Boy (347 Hayes St.; ☎ 888/746-2629; www.nancyboy.com) does a tidy business online selling its line of beauty and skin-care products derived from natural plant oils, not chemicals. It works with a family-owned pharmaceutical-grade lab in Berkeley and this—a modest room perfumed with peppermint and lemongrass—is the only store where the resulting products are sold. The company claims to spend some seven times more on ingredients than its salon competitors, but final retail prices aren't crazily high. The men's stuff is most affordable, at $4 to $10 for most items, and locals swing around to stock up on laundry powder ($30 loads for $16). The store also dabbles in modernist furniture finds.

FOOD & DRINK

The city is full of great places to buy food, from boutique groceries to gourmet charcuteries to generations-old butchers. And in chapter 4, you'll find sources for delicious desserts as well as a lineup of markets where farms for miles around bring their pure, home-raised products for sale. Below, I've listed places where comestibles are likely to be good gifts to bring home; and where you might pick up a quick nosh as you're rushing around town.

PlumpJack Wines ★ (3201 Fillmore St., at Greenwich; ☎ 415/346-9870; www.plumpjackwines.com) is one of the biggest wine dealers in a city that cares deeply about the beverage: Some 900 wines are in its cellars. An unusually plentiful selection of them are priced under $15. The main intention, claims the company, is to remove pretension from wine, although this place's style, flash, and large inventory may still intimidate many. Besides running this Cow Hollow store, the brand operates as a kind of boutique titan in the area, from running restaurants, to running some upscale lodges in Wine Country, to successfully launching a wine label at its own Napa winery. The founder of this smart-and-sassy outfit was none other than Gavin Newsom, the dashing can-do man who went on to become San Francisco's love-him-hate-him mayor.

One of the reasons that San Francisco's Little Italy, North Beach, has (in my opinion) edged out New York City's is the continued survival of great little Italian grocery stores like **Molinari Delicatessen** ★★★ (373 Columbus Ave., at Vallejo; ☎ 415/421-2337), where cheeses, meats, olive oils, and other ingredients—often in hard-to-find varieties—pack a small, old-school corner deli. It's in the heart of the neighborhood, and over time, it's become something of a local emblem. Custom-made sandwiches using their fine breads and meats are $6 to $8—don't neglect to grab a number when you come in. If you'll have a kitchen in the city, avail yourself of the homemade pastas.

Many of the finer restaurants around town get their focaccia-style bread from one place: the long-running **Liguria Bakery** ★★★ (1700 Stockton St., at Filbert; ☎ 415/421-3786), a no-frills corner takeout store that specializes in that one product. And what a product—spongy, touched with oil, topped with various choices like mushroom or onion, cut in enormous inch-thick planks and wrapped in paper, and always sold fresh for around $3.50 each. The hours are funny because the owners don't live to work; getting here early in the morning (perhaps before you wait on the breakfast queue for Mama's, p. 58, across the street?) is wise.

If Liguria is out of bread (a possibility), head a block south to **Italian French Baking Company** ★★ (1501 Grant Ave., at Union; ☎ 415/421-3796), another no-nonsense elder in the world of North Beach bakeries. It also does huge slabs of focaccia and some other terrific breads and sweets, almost always under $3. The 19th-century brick still in daily use is locally renowned; ask, and they'll let you in the back to have a peek. For sourdough bread, take a peek at the write-up of the Boudin bakery on p. 137.

If the temperature goes above 70°F, the owner of **XOX Truffles** ★ (754 Columbus Ave., near Greenwich; ☎ 415/421-4814; www.xoxtruffles.com) won't make his chocolate bonbons. That's because he doesn't want to ruin his confections with waxy ingredients like hydrogenated oils that hold cheaper chocolates together. His hand-rolled artworks are 90¢ each in a variety of flavors, but buying a box of 20 for $9 brings the per-piece down to a more tolerable 45¢ each. Rich hot chocolate (real cocoa, not that sugary Swiss Miss junk) is a steal at $3. It tastes so good to be a chocolate snob.

If you're a *sake* (Japanese rice wine) person, it's not always easy to find stuff beyond a few core labels, and those, true aficionados will tell you, are usually not the best-tasting. But the stylish **True Sake** (560 Hayes St., at Laguna; ☎ 415/355-9555;

www.truesake.com) in Hayes Valley sells nearly a hundred varieties of the good stuff. Claiming to be the first sake-dedicated store outside of Japan, they give sake the respect that a Frenchman might give a cabernet.

HOMEWARES

If I were shopping for nifty stuff for my own mantelpiece, I might start on Hayes Street in Hayes Valley, where there are lots of smart shops. And if those places didn't make me smile, I'd head down to Chestnut or Union in Cow Hollow/the Marina, where there are more shops selling one-of-a-kind housewares, though not usually for low prices.

Biordi Art Imports ★ (412 Columbus Ave.; ☎ 415/392-8096; www.biordi.com; closed Sun) capitalizes on the Italian heritage of its North Beach location by importing fine painted ceramic Maiolica pottery, a long tradition from the Boot. The store has been in business since the 1940s, and in its current hands (of owner Gianfranco Savio) since 1977. Every piece of pottery is distinct, unique, and hand-painted—some in a rustic style, and some according to the whims of the individual artist—and prices are as good as, if not better than, what you'd pay in Italy—only without the shipping costs. You'll pay about $70 for a countertop storage pot for your kitchen.

Guess what the material of choice is at **Alabaster** (597 Hayes St., at Laguna; ☎ 415/558-0482; www.alabastersf.com; closed Mon)? Not just the translucent mineral, of course, but also housewares, furniture, and pretty things to hang on the wall. Like Paxton Gate, it sells dead bugs, but in this case, they're artfully framed rainforest butterflies. The store, whose design ethic is modern American but using an antique vernacular, also designs its own lighting, also for sale. There are some really cool vintage pieces, too, especially in furniture, transferware, and pressed glass.

Fans of Asian cuisine, and people who would like to get into cooking it at home, might find something worth bringing back to their kitchens at **The Wok Shop** (718 Grant Ave., at Sacramento; ☎ 415/989-3797; www.wokshop.com), in Chinatown. Wares include crockery, woks, steamers, teapot sets, and even sushi kits. Its staff is generally eager to help visitors understand the tools of the trade and to match-make them with items they might need for any cuisine they plan to undertake.

TOYS & CHILDREN'S CLOTHES

Where else can you find a shop devoted to kites but in a windy, seaside location like San Francisco? The tiny, adorable **Chinatown Kite Shop** ★ (717 Grant Ave., at Sacramento; ☎ 415/989-5182; www.chinatownkite.com) is small, but as you can imagine, as a specialist, it has kites of every type imaginable, from pirate ships to more complicated geometric shapes it would take a village to operate.

Lynne Gallagher, onetime designer for the rock 'n' roll set, runs the adorable **Wee Scotty** (1807 Divisadero St., at Bush; ☎ 415/345-9200; www.weescotty.com), a vibrant kids' clothes boutique that doubles as a training ground for young would-be fashionistas. The clothes for sale are cute and well made, and might be enough to satisfy someone wanting to dress her kids, but it also organizes intermittent "Project Junior Runway" events in which kids design, fabricate, and present their own fashions.

Asian Shopping, Beyond Chinatown

In chapter 6, I tell you about the **Japan Center** ★★★ (Post St. at Webster), an unusual development in the Japantown section of town, where you can find all manner of souvenirs, foods, housewares, and other stuff specific to Japanese culture or imported—usually cheaply—from Japan. A stroll through this sprawling complex, past its sliding screens and giggling groups of ice-cream-eating schoolgirls, is like a being handed a mini-education on Japan, only without the 11-hour flight.

Among the coolest stores, most of which sell stuff you'll never find else-where without a struggle, are **Taiyodo Record** (☎ 415/885-2818), big on Japan pop music; **Tokaido Arts** (☎ 415/567-4390; www.tokaidoarts.com), for woodblock prints; **Townhouse Living** (☎ 415/563-1417), for tatami beds, paper lamps, and other authentic housewares; **Japantown Collectibles** (☎ 415/563-2970), for pop-culture ephemera such as trading cards and models; and the large **Kinokuniya Bookstore** (☎ 415/567-7625; www.kinokuniya.co.jp), with lots of books in English about Japan and still more in Japanese, including comics.

If you dig Asian art and antiques, also check out the gift shop at the Asian Art Museum (p. 114), which has some excellent high-end replicas and objets d'art.

God bless a city with a strong Asian contingent and with lots of Asian tourists—it can support a store as whacked-out as **Sanrio** (865 Market St., at Powell; ☎ 415/495-3056; www.sanrio.com), purveyor of everything kooky and cute. This leader of the Japanese *kawaii* movement (the one where cute little things sell like hotcakes) deals in Hello Kitty goodies, pencil cases, toys, and other cartoon merchandise. Ask if they still have the toasters that burn Hello Kitty's ghostly image onto your breakfast.

GIFTS

Grown-up toys are found at **Good Vibrations** ★★ (603 Valencia St., at 17th; ☎ 415/522-5460; www.goodvibes.com), a sex shop with a sleek look and no creepy or sleazy personality issues. While there isn't nearly the wide selection you'd find at the XXX emporia in North Beach or on mid-Market, the items it does carry don't stink like poisonous cheap plastic either; most of them have been carefully selected by the respectful and knowledgeable staff, which also owns the store. Women may find the wares more exciting than men will; there's a decided lesbian bent, although people of all persuasions shop here. It's something of a sexual landmark in town. A second store is located at 1620 Polk St. (at Sacramento).

One of the strangest and most interesting stores you're ever likely to peruse, the wildly eccentric **Paxton Gate** ★★★ (824 Valencia St., at 19th; ☎ 415/824-1872; www.paxtongate.com) is the only store I've ever been to where I could buy a porcupine skull if I so desired. A baroque wonderland for taxidermists, or Addams family rejects, it's also a delightfully macabre place to snoop around even if you're not. For the squeamish, there's also a giant garden shop, some architectural salvage, and a wide selection of cool-looking housewares, such as bell jars and perfume bottles that are cut from the classic mold. The shop also runs classes, such as a recent one on "insect mounting"; that was $60 and included a bug.

A beloved resident of the Castro since the 1930s, **Cliff's Variety** ★★ (497 Castro St.; ☎ 415/431-5365; www.cliffsvariety.com), in the heart of the gay district, is technically a hardware store first, but over time it has expanded to sell a huge range of interesting and fun items, from greeting cards to housewares to novelty toys. It'll put you in mind of a smart version of the Woolworth's of your youth.

Open since 1990, when the Castro was going through much darker days, **Under One Roof** ★ (549 Castro St., near 18th; ☎ 415/503-2300; www.underone roof.org) is a boutique whose wares go toward supporting AIDS causes—to the tune of 100% of profits. Unlike Out of the Closet, its stuff is mostly new and interesting, and it focuses mostly on gift items and housewares, not clothing. In August, the store sponsors a "summer merchandise sale," usually somewhere off-site, that marks down post-season stuff.

A surprising number of Australians are wandering the streets of San Francisco—it's a primary stopping point for long-haul flights to Europe—which may explain, partly, the survival, since 1980, of **Australia Fair** (700 Sutter St., at Taylor; ☎ 415/441-5319; www.ausfair.com), which deals in Aussie stuff. Bronco hats, R. M. Williams boots, Tim Tam cookies, Cherry Ripe candy bars, and that old standby Vegemite are sold here (and online by the same store).

Japanese snack food, cheap little gizmos, and other fascinating Asian doodads are shipped by the cargo-container-load from Japan to **Ichiban Kan** ★ (22 Peace Plaza, Suite 540; ☎ 415/409-0472; www.ichibankanusa.com), the Japanese equivalent of a dollar store, except crammed with curious Japanese products that you probably won't find many other places. It sells a little bit of everything, from Japanese sweets (Pocky rules!) to bizarre plastic gadgets, usually for around $1. It's got the same plastic smell that American dollar stores have, but many of its wares are distinctly Asian. It's hard to come away with at least a few low-priced goodies. Everyday staples such as batteries can be found for cheap here, too, so don't overlook it just because you're all set on key chains.

An eight-strong chain with a sole San Francisco branch, **Flight 001** (525 Hayes St.; ☎ 415/487-1001; www.flight001.com) is a bright, hyper-colorful shop selling the latest high design as it applies to travel. The funky luggage tags, passport holders, alarm clocks, and other travel-ready stuff on sale here will make your luggage stand out at the baggage claim. Its colorful and florid designs may appeal more to trendy women than to the average male, but it's still fun to peruse what they've got.

San Francisco Nightlife

There are a hundred reasons to continue exploring the city by night

SAN FRANCISCO IS, AT HEART, A SMALL CITY, A MODEST CITY, AND IT DOESN'T have a central role in calling the tunes of American culture the way it once did. That modesty translates to its evening diversions, too, in that there are very few major venues that couldn't be swallowed up by similar ones in other cities.

There's something endearing and soothing about this humility, to say nothing of the adventurousness it fosters in artists. And when you're out in these intimate settings, you can feel like you're partying with friends. Which is exactly what most locals do—it seems that most folks are satisfied to go out together to a wine bar or a nice restaurant or hit one of the city's sophisticated theaters, as opposed to partying all night long like college kids. Sure, there are plenty of places where you can dance yourself into a sweaty lather, too, or hear new music (the city has a bustling underground music scene that seems to morph into something new every few months), but in general, San Francisco's nightlife is a bit more grown up.

THEATER

San Francisco's theater scene support dozens of little companies that might do two to four short productions a year. Seats at these shows, which are often experimental, homegrown pieces mounted with passion, can cost around $7 to $20. The excellent website **Theatre Bay Area** (www.theatrebayarea.org) lists current productions, including some dance productions, as does that old entertainment standby *SF Weekly.*

Also, don't neglect the major Broadway-style venues, the Curran, Orpheum, and Golden Gate theaters, where major temporary runs are sometimes booked. Seats farthest from the stage start at $30 at matinees, $45 weekend evenings, and top out at $80 ($20 less than Broadway's current top rate). Although regular discounts are hard to come by for the major Broadway road shows (use the half-price ticket booth, p. 194, for your best chances), they do consider San Francisco an important stop on their tours. These days, many that end up on Broadway, such as *Wicked* and *Legally Blonde,* get their earliest public airings before the less critical audiences here, and others that have already struck success in New York (such as *August: Osage County*) have elected to begin their national tours here for the same reason. Check **SHN** (www.shnsf.com), which runs the three aforementioned theaters, to see what's playing.

Even people who don't know much about theater agree that **American Conservatory Theater** ★★★ (415 Geary St., at Mason; ☎ 415/749-2228; www. act-sf.org), west of Union Square, is one of the best companies in the country, with peerless acting, design, and show selection chops. Its home is its beautiful namesake theater, which was constructed in 1910, lovingly restored since, and has seen some of the finest performers of all time, including Sarah Bernhardt, Laurence Olivier, and Isadora Duncan. You may not have heard of some of the actors today, but chances are you will; in the past, students at its associated drama school who also appeared on stage have included Annette Bening, Denzel Washington, Danny Glover, Anika Noni Rose, and Benjamin Bratt. ACT's artistic director, Carey Perloff, is considered American theatrical royalty. Although full-price seats for its Mainstage shows are $55, prices go as low as $15 for balcony seats; considering it's an old house, the view isn't too bad and acoustics are good. Some shows, particularly new works, are often mounted at the **Zeum Theater in the Yerba Buena Center for the Arts** (221 4th St., at Mission; ☎ 415/777-2800). Check to see if there's an upcoming Koret Visiting Artist Series panel; they're free, and recent discussions have included one with luminary Tom Stoppard.

Berkeley Repertory Theatre ★★ (2025 Addison St., Berkeley; ☎ 510/647-2949; www.berkeleyrep.org) was founded in 1968 and has been mopping up awards ever since. Shows are conducted in two houses: the 600-seat Roda Theatre, a proscenium stage, and a 400-seat Thrust Stage. Programming is a mix of worthy classics *(Mother Courage, Our Town)*, world premieres and commissions, and even some acclaimed one-man shows (in the winter of 2008, Carrie Fisher and Danny Hoch both appeared). The company also brings in occasional co-productions with other esteemed theaters, such as Chicago's Steppenwolf. Preview performances, held early in the run, are $33 to $37; otherwise, expect to pay $33 to $69, with lower prices on weekdays. Students and seniors can get another $10 off with ID 1 hour before curtain, cash only. Those under 30 can also score half-price tickets, especially for weekday shows. One Tuesday and Thursday at 7pm, the theater gives free half-hour talks about the play being performed, and it also sometimes does a post-show discussion, too, so ask about upcoming dates. BART's Downtown Berkeley station is right around the corner, making an outing easy.

Seats for Half Off, Every Day

At a booth in Union Square facing the Westin St. Francis Hotel and the Victoria's Secret, half-price theater and cabaret tickets are sold by **Tix Bay Area** (www.theatrebayarea.org; AE, DC, MC, V). Expect a service fee of $2.25 to $6, but you can get a 50¢ discount if you pay with cash. On any given day, expect at least 20 different shows to be available, particularly in the morning when there's a better selection of seats. You don't actually have to stand in line to snare seats; they're also sold online through the Tix website. Do be alert, though, about where your theater is located, or you may find yourself holding seats for something playing in Oakland or some other distant place that you'll get lost in.

In the weeks before you leave home, also consider signing up for the free e-mail alerts from **Goldstar** (www.goldstar.com), which promotes and discounts events and performances, especially for last-minute events that need to sell unsold seats for a song.

Your Seats, Sirs

Several theater companies in town have been known to request volunteers to help seat theatergoers in exchange for the right to watch the show themselves, free. Pack black pants, shoes, and a white shirt—the usual usher's uniform—in case you score. Another good place to check for appeals for ushers is the Volunteers section on craigslist (http://sfbay.craigslist.org/vol).

Give **American Conservatory Theater** (☎ 415/439-2349) 2 weeks' notice and you stand a chance of being asked to help theatergoers to their seats in ACT's historic house.

Call the **Eureka Theatre** (☎ 415/255-8207; www.eurekatheater.org) and ask which upcoming performances (a mixed slate of one-off productions by independent producers) require ushers. You may luck out and see a free musical, although the house programs lots of concerts, too, which won't need your services.

It's first-come, first-served at the **Herbst Theatre** (401 Van Ness Ave., at McAllister), one of the city's go-to houses for lectures, shows, concerts—just about anything, every night. The only shows that are out are the SFJAZZ concerts, which provide their own volunteer ushers through (☎ 415/398-5655, ext. 114). Present yourself at the door to the left of the box office an hour and a half before showtime (wear black and white; men should wear a black tie), and have a little flashlight with you.

Also **The Marines Memorial Theatre** (☎ 415/441-7444) and **The Post Street Theatre** (☎ 415/321-2909) rent out their space to a wide variety of companies for short-run performances, and their erratic schedules translate into a need for temporary staff.

The Magic Theatre ★ (Fort Mason Center, Building D, 3rd Floor; ☎ 415/441-8822; www.magictheatre.org), which largely presents new works at its home in the Marina's Fort Mason, does $10 tickets for students, seniors, teachers, and people under 30 a half-hour before showtimes—otherwise, the first three categories get $5 off with ID. Wednesdays are "sliding scale" days in which early bookers can snare tickets as low as $5 to $25, if they're quick. The company, which uses two intimate houses, has been around since 1967, and Sam Shepard has been a longtime artist in residence; his *True West* and *Fool for Love* both had their world premieres here, and many of its other selections are equally strong.

Named for the mother of African-American drama, the **Lorraine Hansberry Theatre** (620 Sutter St., at Mason; ☎ 415/474-8800; www.lorrainehansberry theatre.com) is true to its calling, producing major works by African-American playwrights, from James Baldwin to August Wilson, along with some smart adaptations along black themes. The space is intimate, so no seat is a loser. Sunday matinees are as inexpensive as $18 a seat, but Saturday nights can cost up to twice that figure.

For something different, sometimes maddeningly so, there's **CounterPULSE** (1310 Mission St., at 9th; ☎ 415/435-7552; www.counterpulse.org), a space dedicated to helping local performers, dancers, and artists create and mount new, daring stuff. It's a fairly high-minded enterprise, with language thrown around that includes "multidisciplinary," "community-based art," and other terms that tell you the curators are smart people. You may not understand what you saw, but you'll likely think it was something unrepeatable. Weekends are the busiest time for shows, which are free to about $20, and on Wednesdays from September through March, there's a free series of lectures that largely concern local issues and history, from the Spanish era to the city's current Arab population.

Crowd-pleasing plays that you ought to know (like *Cabaret* and *Six Degrees of Separation*), plus some premieres by worthy young playwrights (such as 2008 Pulitzer winner Tracy Letts), distinguish **SF Playhouse** (533 Sutter St., at Powell; ☎ 415/677-9596; www.sfplayhouse.org), a 100-seat house that uses Equity performers for a high standard. Tickets are usually $38, but if you catch productions in their first few days, you can score the "preview" price of just $20.

The company's self-definition of "queer live theater" might put off some neophytes, but in practice, what that really means for **Theatre Rhinoceros** (2926 16th St.; ☎ 415/861-5079; www.therhino.org) is that productions are about people on the outside of American society, and that there may be swearing or adult themes. One recent show, for example, was a docu-play about the last "wild Indian" alive in America. The intimate space also presents solo shows and some premieres of daring productions. Wednesday performances are cheapest ($15), and weekends are $25. Students and seniors can secure $5 discounts.

COMEDY

San Francisco has long been a prime starting ground for live performance. Name a major comic who became famous in the 1960s and 1970s, and you'll find his gig history full of local cabarets and underground coffee bars. Steve Martin, Robin Williams, and Ellen DeGeneres all got their starts by tearing down the house in San Francisco, but that was a different time, when there was a still a comedy circuit that both performers and audiences could progressively visit over an evening. Today, many of the great spaces are no longer in operation, but the city still hosts more regular comedy nights and bricks-and-mortar clubs than any other place of its population level. And the hippest names in comedy still make a point of passing through San Francisco on their tours.

Some of the hottest names—Sarah Silverman, Craig Ferguson, Tracy Morgan—are drawn to **Cobb's Comedy Club** ★ (915 Columbus Ave., at Lombard; ☎ 415/928-4320; www.cobbscomedy.com), where there's probably not a bad seat in the house. Cover is around $20 for most comics, although the bigger names from TV command around $35, and there's a two-drink minimum. Owners really pack them in for the most popular acts, so arrive up to an hour ahead. Drinks, unfortunately, are far weaker than the lineup.

Comedy aficionados can catch recent, respected acts—Dom Irrera, Emo Philips, Louis C.K.—and other traveling workhorses at **Punch Line San Francisco** ★★ (444 Battery St., at Washington; ☎ 415/397-7573; www.punchlinecomedyclub. com). It's even been known to unexpectedly host a legend, such as the time Dave Chappelle showed up and did a multi-hour set on the fly. Admission is usually around $20 with a two-drink minimum, the city standard, but make sure you buy tickets ahead of time if you really want to go, because the club is intimate and there's no assigned seating. On Sundays at 8pm, $8 plus a two-drink minimum buys you entree to check out SF Comedy Showcase, a roster of fresh, local talent.

Born out of the improvisational-comedy craze that swept America in the '80s, **BATS Improv (Bayfront Theater at Fort Mason; ☎ 415/474-6776; www.improv.org)** is one of the last West Coast companies standing. Its weekend shows sell some 11,000 tickets a year. It's a little different from the *Whose Line Is It Anyway?* style of improv (that show's Greg Proops is an alum) in that shows are geared toward assembling a coherent story, not just 2-minute bursts of weirdness, even as the audience calls out subjects and ideas. Regular shows are Fridays and Saturdays at 8pm and Sundays at 7pm. On the first, second, and fifth Sunday afternoon of each month, the "Sunday Players," students in the group's classes, take the stage in a sort of game show, in which the audience gives points for the best performances and a winner is ultimately declared. That's just $5 in advance or $8 at the door, or about half the usual price ($12/$15).

Located below an average Italian restaurant, Caffè Macaroni, **The Purple Onion (140 Columbus Ave., at Jackson; ☎ 415/217-8400; www.caffemacaroni.com)** has been a North Beach institution for years, although it's only just now climbing out of a long decline. Wednesdays at 9pm, the weekly Something People Like comedy show is a mixed bill of young up-and-comers, short movies, and, sometimes, sur-prise big names (Robin Williams has been known to slip in the back, observe the show that's underway, and take the stage to test new material). Cover then is $8, but there's no drink minimum. Most other nights of the week, the room is dead (although its owner would love to build it back into an A-list club), but check its schedule because fun one-off comedy events do crop up.

OPERA

Staging huge productions from September to early July, **San Francisco Opera (War Memorial Opera House, 301 Van Ness Ave.; ☎ 415/864-3330; http://sfopera.com)** is the second-largest opera company on the continent. Productions span the clas-sics to new works, such as an adaptation of local novelist Amy Tan's *The Bonesetter's Daughter* in 2008. Although prime orchestra seats are $150, spots in the back few rows of the second balcony are just $25. From 11am on perform-ance days, $25 seats are sold to students, $30 seats to seniors age 65 or older and to current military personnel; call before heading down to the box office to check availability. The company shares its space with the San Francisco Ballet, so there's not singing there every night.

GENERAL INTEREST

Many different companies, including the City Arts & Lectures, book fascinating one-off events into **The San Francisco War Memorial and Performing Arts Center (www.sfwmpac.org)** at the Civic Center, which comprises the Louise M. Davies Symphony Hall, the Herbst Theatre, War Memorial Opera House, War Memorial Veterans Building, and the Green Room, a gold-leafed reception hall–cum–performance space. These city-owned spaces are collected along Van Ness Avenue on the western side of City Hall, and because they often host one-night-only events, some of these tickets are among the city's hottest, such as world-famous artists in town for only one night. All the various upcoming events, which include lectures, concerts, and performances, are listed in collected form online, so it's a good idea to check ahead rather than find out once you're in town and risk being shut out.

DANCE

Lots of little companies present one or two chamber performances a year; check the resource BayDance.com for listings of upcoming choices. Also check to see if there's a hot international company visiting town through San Francisco Performances (listed above).

The venerable **San Francisco Ballet** (War Memorial Opera House, 301 Van Ness Ave.; ☎ 415/861-5600; www.sfballet.org) is, believe it or not, the oldest ballet company in the United States, and its 2008 season marked its 75th. If you know anything about most ballet companies, you won't be surprised to hear that attending a performance is expensive. That is, unless you're a student or senior (age 68 or older) or you're in the military, in which case you should call or visit the box office at least an hour before showtimes for $10 to $25 tickets. Standing room is also typically available for $10, but that goes fast. Typically, you can't get in the orchestra for less than $55, although $95 is more like it. The company does an annual *Nutcracker* that sells out, plus a host of mixed repertory and tribute programs. Call ahead at ☎ 415/865-2000 and they'll tell you if you stand a chance of getting in.

Smuin Ballet (300 Brannan St.; ☎ 415/495-2317; www.smuinballet.org), a smaller ballet outfit that has been around since 1994 with the goal of not being snooty, offers occasional "pay-what-you-can" nights. It performs at several venues around town. Its leader, Michael Smuin, was one of the most respected ballet directors in America with roots both in ballet and Broadway, and despite his sudden death in 2007, his company plans to continue to stage accessible works, although its mettle has yet to be re-proven. Its signature piece is an annual "Christmas Ballet."

The ODC Theater (450 Florida St.; ☎ 415/863-9834; www.odctheater.org) both rents itself to a variety of modern-dance companies for one-off productions and fosters its own modern-dance company called **ODC/Dance** (www.odcdance.org), whose holiday tradition, going since the 1980s, is a production of *The Velveteen Rabbit* at the Yerba Buena Center for the Arts in SoMa, a larger space than this one. In late spring, the offbeat **Fresh Meat Festival** (www.freshmeatproductions.org) is held here; it strives to tell stripped-down narrative-style stories about off-the-mainstream people using only movement, and usually creates three or four pieces that get the local dance world buzzing.

For an erotic treat, twice (7:30pm and 9pm) on Thursdays at Latin-American/Bolivian restaurant **Peña Pachamama** (1630 Powell St., at Union; ☎ 415/646-0018; www.penapachamama.com; Wed–Sun 5:30–10:30pm; reservations recommended) the flamenco dancers of **Theatre Flamenco** (www.theatreflamenco.org) take the wooden floor with musicians and put on a 90-minute show. Dinner and sangria is served (entrees are $17–$20 and big on roasted and grilled meats), and the cover is just $10. You don't have to have a full dinner, but you're expected to eat *something*—tapas are just $7.

FILM REVIVAL HOUSES

If you're a film buff, San Francisco is one of the best places in the country to hook up with rare and generally unseen titles. Catching a classic movie in a real big-screen revival house is part of the culture here—remember that scene in *Foul Play* when Goldie Hawn's date dies at one?

A classic single-screen cinema from the grand old days of the movies, the 1,400-seat **Castro Theatre** (429 Castro St., at Market; ☎ 415/621-6120; www.castrotheatre.com) is the revival house that every city used to cherish before TVs took over. Every night, there's at least one classic film being shown, usually in double-feature dollops, and many of them aren't available on DVD. A live organist is also on hand—well, he levitates out of the stage floor, really—to stitch the evening together on a gorgeous Wurlitzer instrument. Programming is often supplemented by mini-festivals, such as one celebrating a single Hollywood studio's oeuvre or another dedicated to film noir. You might also find some excellent Q&A's with world-renowned film-industry names. In early 2008, the theatre's facade and long-broken neon sign received a restoration by the makers of the movie *Milk*, which filmed in front of it, bringing the building back into vitality. With it, a onetime neighborhood theater was transformed into a bona fide city landmark. Entry is $9, even for double features, but there are frequent bargain matinees for $7.

While the Castro fulfills the tarnished-Hollywood programming role that TV's *Late Movie* used to fill, **The Roxie New College Film Center** (3117 16th St., at Valencia; ☎ 415/863-1087; www.roxie.com; $9) is more about unusual documentaries and small films that might otherwise never have an audience or surface on PBS in two years' time. The theater opened in 1909 and served time as a porno house before finally being acquired by a local college (hence, the odd compound name) and today, it prides itself on showing nonfiction film. The roster is usually supplemented by a title that's currently popular, so don't expect to just show up and see something rare—check the schedule.

For a less dramatic but more eccentric environment, **Red Vic Movie House** (1727 Haight St., at Cole; ☎ 415/668-3994; www.redvicmoviehouse.com) is another neighborhood institution that, like the Roxie, arranges screenings of popular films and worthy unknown titles alike. Probably because it's a co-op, and partly to be defiantly anti-corporate, there's something of a thrown-together, neighborly thing going on here—coffee arrives served in ceramic mugs, popcorn in wooden bowls. Arrive as doors open if you want to stand a chance of snagging one of the big comfortable couches (tickets for shows go on sale 20 min. beforehand), otherwise, you may land on a lumpy seat or, worse, a pew. Seats are $8.50 (7:15pm and 9:15pm shows, usually) except for 2pm shows, when they're $6.50. No doubt about it: This place has character. But the other revival houses are easier on the hindquarters.

LIVE MUSIC

San Francisco loves its music, and audiences here are passionate and daring, supporting one of the widest palettes of options in the country. When it comes to rock and more adventurous styles, a portion of the action happens at smaller clubs and spaces in pop-up performances. See "A Clubbing Crib Sheet" (p. 202) for websites you can use to learn lineups from home.

CLASSICAL MUSIC

Michael Tilson Thomas, or "MTT," is perhaps the most celebrated living American conductor, and he is the musical director at **San Francisco Symphony** ★★ (☎ 415/864-6000; www.sfsymphony.org). Thanks in part to his leadership, the roster is full of world-class soloists, world-premiere pieces, and high-quality performances. Tickets are usually $35 to $125, but rush tickets are often issued during business hours on the day of performances for $20; only two per person are permitted, and availability is heralded on a special phone line: ☎ 415/503-5577. Check out the upcoming schedule of the Youth Symphony Orchestra—they're in training on full scholarship to graduate to the main symphony and yet their performing experience rivals most adults and they book appearances around the world. Tickets for them are much saner, from $12 to $30.

The esteemed **San Francisco Performances** (☎ 415/398-6449; www.performances.org) aims to bring the best rising and lesser-known artists in the world to the Bay Area and, in that quest, mounts some 200 nights year-round, bringing in impressive talent in jazz, classical music, chamber music, modern dance, and other skilled disciplines. Every week, there's something new. Among the artists who have had their first Bay Area airings with SFP are cellist Yo-Yo Ma and soprano Dawn Upshaw. The biggest names fetch ticket prices from $25 to $82, but most performances are in the upper $30s to low $40s. Performances are held at spaces across town, but most often at the Herbst Theatre (p. 195), seating just 918, so even the least expensive seats are good.

Several times a week when school is in session, there's a performance—usually free—at the **San Francisco Conservatory of Music** (50 Oak St., at Van Ness; ☎ 415/864-7326; www.sfcm.edu), a school for the crème de la crème of musicians and performers. It's easy to get a handle on which performances are upcoming, because they're listed in the "Calendar" on the home page of the school's website. The best time to catch free performances is late April and early May, when seniors and graduate students perform their final recitals and the doors are thrown open to the public.

LARGE VENUES

Mezzanine (444 Jessie St., at 6th; ☎ 415/625-8880; www.mezzaninesf.com) is pretty chill for a mega-club, and there are plenty of bars to go around at this two-story, high-ceilinged venue. The programming is as diverse as the crowd, from music to comedy, but still favors acts you might have heard of over up-and-comers. I'd rather see a musical show here, because when it gets packed, the columns can mar sightlines for performances by solo acts. Tickets are $12 to $25.

Concert promoter Live Nation has cheapened the value of its name by appending it to its other venues around the country, but there's still only one place you can honestly call **The Fillmore** ★★★ (1805 Geary Blvd., at Fillmore; ☎ 415/346-6000; www.thefillmore.com). It's a treasure of San Francisco history. In the 1960s, it was the heartbeat of the San Francisco counterculture, where legendary promoter Bill Graham booked the likes of the Grateful Dead, Jefferson Airplane, Janis Joplin, and Led Zeppelin. While it's no longer a crucible of what's next, it's still an excellent place to see a show, and small enough (1,250 capacity for most shows) so that you can stand in the back, near the bar, and still be satisfied. If your concert sells out, they pass out free posters designed by specially selected artists, a long tradition with the Fillmore. Amusingly, there's also a tub of free apples available at the door of every show.

Once a prime booker of vaudeville acts, **The Warfield** (982 Market St., at 6th; ☎ 415/567-2060) still has a streak of the vaudeville in it, as it hosts high-value specialty acts (like Margaret Cho, Katt Williams, KT Tunstall, and Sasha & John Digweed) at market concert prices. The orchestra area is general admission, while the balconies offer assigned seating.

Acts and audiences alike dig **The Great American Music Hall** (859 O'Farrell St., at Larkin; ☎ 415/885-0750; www.musichallsf.com), a saloon-like ballroom (opened in 1907), which is sized just right to enable you to stand, sit, or hang out on a chair in the balcony. Tickets are affordable ($10–$15) for an excellent selection of acts—some would say that its programming is as solid as the venue itself. Add another $25 to your ticket, and they'll serve you a fully coursed supper and you can keep your seat in the balcony for the show.

INTIMATE VENUES

A valued indie-band lounge, **Cafe du Nord** ★ (2170 Market St., at Church; ☎ 415/861-5016; www.cafedunord.com; cover $10–$20) was built in 1907—then again, most of modern San Francisco was, too—and during Prohibition, it was known as a down-and-dirty speakeasy. It still retains many of its Victorian touches, including lots of moody wood and a 40-foot-long mahogany bar. Today, you can slip in legally, without a reservation, and catch live music 7 nights a week. The picks are mixed, from bluegrass to singer-songwriters to jazz. Food's served but you don't have to eat, and there aren't many tables anyway. Upstairs, the cafe runs a larger space, the **Swedish American Hall,** where bigger names appear in a balconied dance-hall-type room. A detailed online calendar of events for both is well maintained, including information concerning which upcoming shows have sold out.

Nightly after 9pm, there's free music at the laid-back **Revolution Café** (3248 22nd St., at Bartlett; ☎ 415/642-0474; cash only), including jazz, folk, Mac-powered experiments—even classical sometimes. Call it hipster bait if you will, but the heat-lamp-warmed patio is a pretty relaxed place to spend a few hours. It's friendly and hardly stands on ceremony: You order at the bar before seating yourself. That is, if you can find a seat; show up before 8pm if you want a sporting chance.

The intimate and eclectic **Amnesia** ★ (853 Valencia St., btw. 19th and 20th; ☎ 415/970-0012; www.amnesiathebar.com), in the Mission, programs bluegrass on Monday (when getting in is free), gypsy jazz (think Django Reinhardt), and a Sunday night featuring a wide range of styles from klezmer to burlesque, a music style suited to the red curtains and bordello chandeliers of the decor. It's the kind of place where the musicians wear fedoras. Covers are generally charged only on weekends, and even then, they usually top out at $8. Tuesday is karaoke night. Hard liquor isn't served, but there is Belgian beer.

Perhaps the most stylish place to catch a musical performance, **Bimbo's 365 Club** ★★ (1025 Columbus Ave., at Chestnut; ☎ 415/474-0365; www.bimbos365 club.com), lushly draped in curtains and evoking a 1940s dance hall, books a wide variety of acts, from old-school crooners to well-known rock bands. This place has been open since the music it favors was new, in 1951, and folks consider it an

A Clubbing Crib Sheet

It's tough, as a visitor, to get a handle on who'll be appearing at which club. For that, head over to **SF Clubs** (www.sfclubs.com), which rounds up the upcoming events. Another smart place to look is *SF Weekly*, a free newspaper distributed in boxes around town; its listings section is online at http://entertainment.sf weekly.com. The *Guardian* (www.sfbg.com) is also useful. Clubs usually close around 2am, by law, unless they have a rare after-hours license from the state. Expect last call at about 1:30am, and don't be surprised if bouncers snatch your drink from you at 2am sharp to avoid getting into trouble.

institution. Seating is first-come, first-served, and it's tiered, which means most spots will be good. You can buy your ticket (usually $25 or less) with a credit card, but after that, it's cash only.

Opened by venerated Mississippi bluesman John Lee Hooker in the last years of his life, **Boom Boom Room** (1601 Fillmore St., at Geary; ☎ 415/673-8000; www.boomboomblues.com) started life as not just his venture, but also as one of his favorite hangouts—in the mid-20th century, Fillmore Street was the most important scene for West Coast blues—and it still has street cred as a blues hall, with a simple stage at the back. Dim, cozy, unpretentious, it attracts all types and colors. Acts, which by no means are restricted to blues, are about $15.

Because it throws frequent 18-and-over nights in addition to ID-insistent over-21 nights, **Bottom of the Hill** (1233 17th St., at Missouri; ☎ 415/621-4455; www.bottomofthehill.com; cover $8–$15) can tend to attract a more juvenile clientele. However, its programming (indie punk, rockabilly, hard rock, funk, other alternative forms, and plenty of foreign bands) is popular with its crowd, the dance floor is jammed right up against the stage, and the place remains one of the city's better venues in terms of elbow room and sound system.

There's someone on every night at 8pm and 10pm at the respected **Jazz at Pearl's** ★ (256 Columbus Ave., at Pacific; ☎ 415/291-8255; www.jazzatpearls.com; cover from $20) in North Beach, where a speakeasy atmosphere is cultivated. Light tapas dishes are also served, if you want, but there are only 25 tables, so get in early if you want to sit; otherwise, you'll be standing. Jazz is a musical form that came from the lower classes; yet, today, to enjoy the good stuff, it seems that you have to spend a lot for a night out—on top of the cover charge, there's a two-drink minimum here. Good thing you get quality performances in a romantic atmosphere. Locals freaked out in the spring of 2008 when it briefly looked like it might close, which only served to cement its esteem in the civic mind.

Overpriced drinks but spot-on blues and jazz are served up at **Lou's Pier 47 Restaurant and Blues Club** (300 Jefferson St., at Jones; ☎ 415/771-5687; www.louspier47.com). Some people eat here—the menu is a Creole-type riff ($8–$20)—but there are better places to do that. The cover charge starts at 4pm ($3–$5) and jumps at 8pm ($5–$10), when the place starts functioning more as a bar.

It was once known as the best place to sample acid jazz, but now, the two-level **Elbo Room** (647 Valencia St., at 17th; ☎ 415/552-7788; www.elbo.com) books live bands and DJs, playing a mix of funk, soul, Afro-Cuban, hip-hop, and other alternative music. Daily from 5pm to 9pm, draft pints are just $2. Show tickets are generally $6 to $10.

Good bands in a boring building; that's the winning formula at **The Independent** ★★ (628 Divisadero St., at Grove; ☎ 415/771-1421; www. independentsf.com), one of the most reliable places in town to catch a band. Facilities are small and simple, with a good sound system, excellent sightlines, and tickets usually top out at around $25 but usually cost less. Sometimes there are movie nights.

CABARET

You'd think that an artsy city like San Francisco would have lots of rooms hosting classy, often throwback musical performances akin to the great hotel performance rooms of New York. But ever since the York Hotel, now the Vertigo, converted its performance space into a tony Tyler Florence restaurant, there's really only the **Rrazz Room at the Hotel Nikko SF** ★ (222 Mason St., at Ellis; ☎ 866/468-3399; www.therrazzroom.com), located in a comfortable space on the ground floor of a bland executive hotel. It books singers like Maureen McGovern, Oleta Adams, Mary Wilson, and Diane Schuur, plus TV comics, the odd famous drag queen, and famous names trying out cabaret shows. The space was just getting on its feet at press time but, nevertheless, was taking bookings a year ahead. Tickets are $20 to $55, depending on how big the name is.

Dark and brooding, with a super-tiny upstairs cabaret-style room for performance, **House of Shields** (29 New Montgomery St., at Stevenson; ☎ 415/975-8651; www.houseofshields.com; closed Sun) has been likened to a Mafioso bar. Others think its intricate flooring and narrow booths make it seem like a bank. That's a nice sentiment, in a theatrical kind of way, but the clientele here is actually more like post-work 20-somethings. Pabst Blue Ribbon is sold on tap for just $2, and Thursday through Saturday, there's usually a musical performance squeezed into the space for a $5 cover.

As you might imagine from its fun name, a tongue-in-cheek take on a slurred drink order, **Martuni's** ★ (4 Valencia St., at Market; ☎ 415/241-0205) is cheerful, inclusive, and serves from a long list of well-poured martinis and other drinks. Skilled singers and piano players hold sway in back, making it the best place to catch casual but classy cabaret-style performance in the city; there's a different style of music every night. It's also a great place to bring friends.

DANCE CLUBS

Ruby Skye (420 Mason St., at Geary; ☎ 415/693-0777; www.rubyskye.com) delivers a big but somewhat impersonal experience, which can work, considering there are 15,000 square feet and four rooms to get lost in. The beautiful Art Nouveau space, dating to its original incarnation as an 1890 theater, invokes a pleasingly baroque energy, even if some of the details have been obliterated by misguided renovation and the dancing crowd is pure Saturday night. If you can name any DJs as if they were mainstream celebs, it's the scene for you. It's also the

The Party Coach

There's little that's more alienating (and possibly dangerous) than stumbling bewildered around a strange city after a few drinks. Here's a novel service for shuttling you between several clubs on one night: The **Mexican Bus** (☎ 415/546-3747; www.mexicanbus.com; $38) zips you around three clubs on both Friday and Saturday night, and all cover charges are included. You pile off the elderly bus at three well-chosen Latin or salsa clubs, dance, and just when it starts getting old, you pile back onto the bus (with your DJ host); as the party continues onboard (no drinks are served, but that doesn't stop passengers from toting a cocktail), you drive to the next locale. A similar service without the Latin theme and with a plusher vehicle, **Three Babes and a Bus** (www.threebabes.com; Sat only; 5 hrs.; $39) also takes you to three clubs that change weekly and spends about an hour at each one. Considering that so many of the city's clubs are in junky parts of town, having wheels is a real boon. The services can be economical if you would have otherwise been taking lots of taxis, but the value also depends on the cover charges at the clubs you choose to go. They're popular with groups, especially women, having nights out together.

place that lazy out-of-towners choose, given its central location, which accounts for why the cover is often a ridiculous $30 on weekends. (Depending on the event, tickets can be had for around $15.)

A well-rounded club with a good mix of friendly, attitude-free people and music, from minimal techno to hip-hop, **Mighty** (119 Utah St., at Alameda; ☎ 415/762-0151; www.mighty119.com) is in the middle of a grim industrial district, but it's still crowded, and it swings many nights until 4am. The dance floor, while not huge, is one of the larger ones in town.

There's no dress code per se at **Milk** (1840 Haight St., at Shrader; ☎ 415/387-6455; www.milksf.com), but everyone wears the Haight uniform anyway of jeans, hoodie, T-shirt, and sneakers. Hip-hop is the dominant music style, music is spun by DJs, and several changing monthly parties (B.A.S.S. is for female DJs, Good Times for uplifting tunes) spice up the offerings. Everything's tiny, from the dance area to the bathrooms.

Bootie ★★ (DNA Lounge, 375 11th St., at Harrison; www.bootiesf.com; $12 cover), a bimonthly Saturday night party, is like a microcosm of everything San Francisco—people of every ethnicity, age, and sexual preference. The music chosen, too, a mash-up of pop music from the past 30 years, satisfies the hipster's feel for the ironic. Count on lots of nooks and crannies in this multilevel club, but don't count on having them to yourself, because this joint's deservedly popular. The venue isn't all that popular the rest of the time. Check its website for the next dates, but it usually falls on the second and fourth Saturdays of each month.

GOOD DRINKIN'

There is no shortage of bars in town. San Francisco started its life as a den of iniquity, a place where sailors could drink their weight in whisky. The city's habits are more dignified these days, but locals still enjoy a hearty pour. These are some of the most distinctive, fun, historic, or gimmicky places to pull up a bar stool. Needless to say (I hope), these aren't places where you ought to tote along a kid.

A generous pour, a trinket-stuffed decor, a cozy vibe, and a friendly attitude despite its illustrious history all make **Vesuvio Café** ★★★ (255 Columbus Ave., at Broadway; ☎ 415/362-3370; www.vesuvio.com) a go-to North Beach drinkery. Vesuvio was opened in 1948, just in time to catch all the dissolute Beat writers as they staggered in and out of City Lights, located directly across Jack Kerouac Alley from its front door. In fact, this is where Kerouac spent many a night toxifying his liver. I guess that makes this bar a monument to alcoholism—how many bars wear that rep with honor? If you can get a table upstairs, do, because it overlooks the bar below, making it prime for people-watching, and it's romantic and secluded, making it prime for nuzzling.

One of the more amusing lounges in town, **Hobson's Choice Punch House** ★ (1601 Haight St., at Clayton; ☎ 415/621-5859; www.hobsonschoice.com; AE, MC, V) specializes in that old-fashioned quaff: rum. There are more than 100 available, served in a frilly environment that recalls a Victorian-era English pub, complete with etched-glass light shades and seating upholstered in blue velveteen. Each month, a new trio of inventive cocktails is introduced (not all of them are rum-based, by the way). Doors open at 5pm weekdays, noon Saturdays, and 8am Sundays (yes—the sinners!). Happy hour ($2.50 specials) falls weekdays from 5pm to 7pm.

A true dive, **The Saloon** ★ (1232 Grant Ave., at Fresno; ☎ 415/989-7666) is supposedly the oldest bar in the city, and it looks (and smells) like it. Floors are but worn planks, staff is grizzled and hairy as biker-gang members (even the women), and the story goes that this place managed to survive the conflagration following the 1906 quake by offering all firefighters free booze. Knowing which side their bread was buttered on, they saved the building, and I don't think it has changed much since then. There's live music every night of the week ($5 cover most of the time)—mostly blues and jazz. Don't come expecting a cruisey scene; come for down-and-dirty music and cheap whiskey. Cash only, and beer's mostly in bottles, but served cold.

It's touristy and lacks ambience, but what at Fisherman's Wharf doesn't? The claim to fame at **Jack's Cannery** (2801 Leavenworth St., at Beach; ☎ 415/931-6400; AE, MC, V), which used to serve wharf workers, is a long wall lined with draft beer taps—68 by my count along some 25 feet of bar space. Most of them are unusual choices you may never have heard of before, like Moose Drool Brown Ale. El Toro IPA, a bartender favorite, often runs out. Pints are $6, which isn't cheap, but on that you can hang out in the huge wainscoted pub room for hours. On weekdays, the kitchen (pub food like a $10 T-bone dinner) may close at 8pm if it's quiet, but on weekends, when the Wharf is thronged, this place bumps until late night. Otherwise, it's the sort of place where the fancy rum bottles gather dust and where to get off your feet after navigating the crowds of the Wharf.

It's considered a modern tradition to visit **Buena Vista Café** (2765 Hyde St., at Beach; ☎ 415/474-5044; www.thebuenavista.com) to order a $7.25 Irish coffee (coffee and whiskey), which was conceived here in 1952 by a local travel writer (hurrah!). This punch-packing quaff lures hordes of tourists before they wobble toward the cable-car turnaround across the street. You may not want to hear how the bartender gets the cream to float—it's aged for two days before use. Some 2,000 are served each day in high season, which means you'll probably have to wait for a table on a weekend afternoon (better, probably, to come at night; it's open until 2am). These beverages are indeed delicious, and the publike setting is classic without being snooty, but the high price is questionable. Stop at one.

Exposed brick and lounging downstairs in the Krug Room, DJ upstairs at **The Bubble Lounge** (714 Montgomery St., at Columbus; ☎ 415/434-4204; www. bubblelounge.com; closed Sun and Mon), a temple to champagne and sparkling wine. Drinks will cost you, but there's not usually a cover.

A loft-like blend of bar, art space, and performance venue, **111 Minna** ★ (111 Minna St., and 2nd; ☎ 415/974-1719; www.111minnagallery.com) consists of two areas, each with its own bar, and an eclectic crowd. Skip the $10 cover by coming Monday through Friday before 9pm, when happy hour's on. The artwork on display changes so often, it's like visiting a different space each time you go.

For a spirited glimpse of how remarkably diverse and accepting the city can be, there may be no more apropos drinkery than **Zeitgeist Bar & Guesthouse** (199 Valencia St. at Duboce; ☎ 415/255-7505). What started as a rough biker bar is now a beloved dive bar that welcomes a broad range of patrons, from urban professionals to leather-bound gay folk to simple amblers who like their beers cold and their afternoons long. And, yes, there's still a line of motorcycles out front, although the chances of getting clocked with a beer bottle inside are slim to none—particularly because pitchers (just $12) are favored here. The bar's backyard patio, larger than the barroom, is busy late into the night, and on weekends, its picnic tables are snapped up early in the day. The under-the-freeway neighborhood isn't much to write home about, and in fact, it can be too edgy for comfort. (If this is your milieu, here's a tip: There are rooms for rent upstairs if you're staying for a few weeks or more. They're simplicity defined, embellished with a bed, desk, sink, and the occasional blare of cycle mufflers. Get on the waiting list and you may end up scoring a place for $30 a night. A great deal for those with youth, patience, and/or tolerance.)

DRINKS WITH A VIEW

A 19th-floor bar doesn't sound like much when compared with the 52-story high Carnelian Room (p. 208), but considering in this case it's in a building that's already atop Nob Hill, and adding the fact that it's one of the most famous bars in the country, both the view and the mood are high at **Top of the Mark** ★ (999 California St., at Mason; ☎ 415/616-6916; www.topofthemark.com). Floor-to-ceiling windows take in the kind of panorama that makes people want to move to this city: Golden Gate Bridge, Coit Tower, Alcatraz, and beyond, all in a smart, upper-class setting. The operators regularly close the space for private parties, so call ahead to make sure it's open on the night you want to go. From Tuesday through Saturday, musical acts are booked—mostly jazz or other styles that make nice background—and covers are surprisingly cheap ($5 Tues, depending on the name, but $10 is more common). Dinner is served as well, but since it starts at $60 a seat, you're better off just coming for drinks. Those are $10 each, at least, so make sure the clouds have lifted in town before arriving for a view that isn't there.

The namesake of **Harry Denton's Starlight Room** (Sir Francis Drake Hotel, 450 Powell St., 21st Floor, at Sutter; ☎ 415/395-8595; www.harrydenton.com; AE, MC, V) isn't some socialite dandy who was kicking up his spats in the 1930s, although you won't be strongly disabused of the image. He's alive, spunky, and not even that old—he just decorates and runs his romantic aerie, atop an antique hotel over Union Square, as if he expects Dick Powell and Joan Blondell to stroll in. There are few better places to raise a stylish drink with an unspoiled panorama of one of the world's great cities. Along with drinks, there's a menu more about comforts than fine cuisine (filet mignon sliders, mac and cheese, all under $18), and once the live music starts at 8:30pm, a cover charge of $10 weekdays/$15 weekends, but if there's no band, there's no cover. If you don't want to swing the price of dinner and dancing, you can still enjoy exciting western views from the bar area. On Sunday, it's the scene of one of the best brunch bargains in the city: an all-you-can-eat buffet (including made-to-order omelets and sliced-to-order roast beef), an incredible view, and live performances by a trio of hysterical drag queens—all for $30 (2 shows: noon and 2 or 3pm).

Bless Those Little Cocktail Umbrellas

My favorite place to chill after a long day of tackling the hills, the sublime and one-of-a-kind **Tonga Room Restaurant and Hurricane Bar** ★★★ (Fairmont Hotel, 950 Mason St., at California; ☎ 415/772-5278; AE, MC, V) has my heart for being totally ridiculous. Every half-hour in this dim, Polynesian-themed fantasia decorated with rocks and 12-foot tikis, lightning strikes, thunder rings out, and rain falls above the pond in the middle of it all (once the hotel's indoor pool). Of course, it's a gimmick and, naturally, you'll pay a lot for a cocktail here ($9-ish), but it's fun anyway. During happy hour, Monday through Friday 5 to 7pm, there's a list of strong, tropical cocktails sold for $7.50, and if you throw down just another $9.50 after buying one drink, you get unleashed on the heat-lamp-lit all-you-can-eat buffet of egg rolls and other grub, served beneath rigging on the deck of an imaginary ship. There's a full menu, too, at higher rates (reserve ahead), but people tend to take advantage of that later in the evening, when musicians take the stage in the middle of the pool. Couples should order the Lava Bowl, a $13 punch-bowl-sized serving of something rummy and delicious served with two long straws. If every bar in the world were like this, I'd develop a habit, because this place is Disney-ready, 1960s-kitsch silliness. The hotel is where the two cable-car lines intersect.

Every skyscrapered city has a pricey cocktail lounge atop something tall, and **Carnelian Room** (555 California St., at Montgomery; ☎ 415/431-7500; www.carnelianroom.com), on the 52nd floor of the drab Bank of America Building, fills the bill. Like so many such places it's all about the view, which includes the Golden Gate Bridge and the Transamerica Pyramid. Though you may not want to down too many drinks in this costly spot, one at sunset is a great way to kick off the evening and feel like you're celebrating.

At this bar, the view isn't of the skyline, but of a fine work of art. It's not an inexpensive outing, but seeing as it's one of the most famous bars in the city, you should at least raise a ginger ale at **Maxfield's Pied Piper Bar** ★★ (Palace Hotel, 2 New Montgomery St., at Market; ☎ 415/512-1111; www.maxfields-restaurant.com; AE, MC, V), where one of the city's greatest art treasures, a mural of the Pied Piper by Maxfield Parrish, presides over the woody, dusky bar. Keepers know how to mix a classic drink here, but I hope they also know jujitsu, because the painting behind them is now valued at $2.5 million. The back room serves as a restaurant, but do you really want to spend $23 on a burger? It's bad enough that a simple vodka martini drains your account by $10.

GAY & LESBIAN NIGHTLIFE

San Francisco being San Francisco, there's no shortage of gay venues. Unlike in other cities, though, gay-catering bars and nightclubs haven't yet blended very far into the mainstream. Most gay clubs are not mixed venues for Generation Y, as they largely become in cities across America. Each one has its own "type," meaning customers are usually looking for something particular in their fellow customers. Dress the type—doormen and management throughout the Castro routinely shoot themselves in the foot by being snippy to guests who don't fill the bill.

For more ideas, check out **SFgay.org,** where upcoming events are listed for venues around town. Other good sources for community information, events listings, and bar tips include **Castro Online** (www.castroonline.com) and **Castro SF** (www.castrosf.org).

IN THE CASTRO

These aren't the only options, of course, but they are some of the most welcoming. Once you arrive in the 'hood, which radiates from the intersection of Castro and 18th streets, just ask whomever you meet at the first bar which other establishments you might like.

440 Castro (440 Castro St., btw. 17th and 18th; ☎ 415/621-8732; www.the 440.com) attracts a manly crew; wear jeans and/or leather to fit in.

SF Badlands (4131 18th St., near Castro; ☎ 415/626-9320; www.sfbadlands. com) is a place people tend to outgrow by their mid- to late-20s, but for those into the scene, and if you like to dance with your hands over your head, it's one of the liveliest dance floors and bars in town. If this is your world, the blissfully shallow scene at **The Bar on Castro** (456 Castro St., near 18th; ☎ 415/626-7220; www.the barsf.com), around the corner, will also do. **Esta Noche** (3079 16th St., at Mission; ☎ 415/861-5757) is cheap, loose, and in a shifty part of town, but it's where to go for a Latin crowd.

Harvey's (500 Castro St., at 18th; ☎ 415/431-4278; www.harveyssf.com) often hosts popular and busy gay-themed stand-up nights; it's usually free with a one-drink minimum. It's also the place to catch the only drag show in the Castro, *The Monster Show,* usually held the second and fourth Saturday of each month. During the day, Harvey's is popular for bistro-style food, particularly weekend brunch (about $10/plate), and for wide windows where patrons can watch the denizens of the Castro pass by.

Midnight Sun (4067 18th St., btw. Hartford and Castro; ☎ 415/861-4186) is a video bar, meaning that, when it isn't showing Madonna, it's projecting the big TV shows for crowds at night. If your hotel-room TV isn't showing *Project Runway,* you can join the audience here.

Mix (4086 18th St.; ☎ 415/431-8616; www.sfmixbar.com) proves that gay bars have evolved quite a bit; this one is a no-attitude sports bar that packs the fans for football, hockey, and other sports events. The chummy patio grill is open weekends, when the indoor bar with pool tables also opens at 6am.

Moby Dick (4049 18th St., at Hartford; no phone; www.mobydicksf.com), dating to 1978, is the quintessential friendly neighborhood bar: not sleazy (despite the name), with pinball machines and plenty of places to sit and lean and raise a pint. The drink specials, available daily, can be incredibly cheap.

Twin Peaks (401 Castro St., at Market; ☎ 415/864-9470; www.twinpeaks tavern.com) will give you a taste of the Castro of old; clients are generally long-term residents of a certain age who have survived it all. They watch the street life along Market from this corner pub's windows.

SOMA

The Eagle Tavern (398 12th St., at Harrison; ☎ 415/626-0880; www.sfeagle.com), in SoMa, is a sleazy biker bar—one of the last of its kind in America, and a gay SF institution. The rough junk-shop interior scares off the folks who couldn't handle it anyway. In truth, the guys look tough, but because there aren't many actual gay biker gangs, you'll find them to be mostly teddy bears looking for release. Thursday nights, bands perform, and at the Sunday beer bust, $10 buys you all the beer you can drink and all the sex-minded freaks you can stare at. The back patio is one of the most fascinating places to drink in town. You may see things here that you can't shake from your memory—at the least, stuff your mama never even thought to warn you about. For a smaller, more homey gay biker bar (if that's possible), head over to **Hole in the Wall Saloon** (289 8th St., at Tehama; ☎ 415/431-4695; www. holeinthewallsaloon.com), also in SoMa.

The Endup (401 6th St., at Harrison; ☎ 415/357-0827; www.theendup.com) is so named, in part (wink, wink) because it's where you "end up" after the other bars close; here, the DJs and their house music are plugged in until 4am to 6am. It's not cheap (after midnight, cover can fly to $15–$20) or very cheerful (most of the patrons seem high), but this dance party is quite literally storied in the local gay world; in the *Tales of the City* books, it's where Michael Tolliver wins an underwear contest and repels his boyfriend in the process. That can be you!

Lone Star Saloon (1354 Harrison St., between 9th and 10th; ☎ 415/863-9999; www.lonestarsaloon.com), in SoMa, is famous for its strong drinks and its huge barrel of peanuts that drinkers can dip into anytime. That, and for a shirtless, hairy, tattooed patronage that is known in gay parlance as "bears." If you're a bear, an otter, or a cub, don't go to the zoo—come here instead, where anything goes among your type. The crowd is friendlier than you might guess.

The Stud (399 9th St., at Harrison; ☎ 415/863-6623; www.studsf.com) may be the quintessential San Francisco gay bar, complete with a friendly crowd, good bartenders, and go-go boys whose underwear just *happens* to slip off when they're oil wrestling in the kiddie pool. Tuesday night at midnight is the outrageous *Trannyshack* drag show ($8).

OTHER AREAS

The Cinch (1723 Polk St., at Clay; ☎ 415/776-4162; www.thecinch.com) in seedy Polk Gulch pleases out-of-towners and straight folk alike. Many think it's the best gay bar in America in terms of festive fun. Perhaps it's the free Ms. Pac-Man machine. There's a vibrant, neighborhood feel, a diverse crowd, a strong pour, parties during every holiday, and both pool tournaments and over-the-top drag shows (Fri are for an award-winning one called *Anna Conda*).

Lexington Club (3464 19th St., at Valencia; ☎ 415/863-2052; www.lexington club.com; closed Sun) is a friendly lesbian bar in the Mission. The energy is homey, and there's not just pool but also frequent strip action.

10 The Wine Country

Raise a glass, not the budget

PEOPLE HAVE BEEN GROWING GRAPES IN THE MOUNTAINS NORTH OF San Francisco for about as long as the city to its south has been habited. But it went through some rough times: Plant plagues and Prohibition both knocked back the area's progress for a century until finally, a generation ago, a handful of mavericks figured out a way to turn wines from Napa and Sonoma counties into internationally respected brands. Now, the region is booming. It has mostly left behind its grubby farming personality and borrowed no small measure of European prestige and style in the journey.

The rolling green hills and pocket ponds of this region are so beautiful they could be considered draw enough, but of course, the main reason you come here is because you love food and drink. The foodie-ism is contagious. Within 2 or 3 days of arriving, even someone who knows zip about wine will start to talk about what he's drinking as if they were born experts. It's fun to watch the people you love transform themselves into gourmets before your eyes, even if they're only mouthing the words in excitement.

Get ready to hear a lot of stories from the wineries you visit about what brought the owners to the Wine Country. They usually go like this: He was a lawyer and decided to chuck it all to make wine the way his grandfather did in the Old Country. Words like *legendary* and *greatness* are bandied about with abandon. (I don't understand why people think hearing about the winemaker's good fortune should make the product taste better.) Whatever the area's faults, though, there's no denying that there's a lot of good stuff to taste. Even in winter, as you drive past vineyard-covered mountains carpeted with bright yellow mustard-plant blooms, it will be hard not to feel lucky for being able to spend time here. In summer, when breezes are warmer and everything sings with green, you could believe, after enough wine, that you've rediscovered Eden.

Yes, the Wine Country is all about the good life, and you may find yourself developing a desire to drop everything and move there to stomp grapes.

But you'd better bring your wallet, because affluent visitors are the focus market—a budget hotel room here costs just as much as it does in the big city of San Francisco, and meals at most restaurants cost even more than they do an hour south. This is a region committed, in essence, to making and selling luxury products. Honeymooners come here to live like royalty for a few days amongst the greenery and gardens. The expectations foster a spendy experience, but there are some ways to taste and experience the Wine Country's Good Life without paying for it for the rest of yours.

A QUICK LAY OF THE LAND

Picture the whole area as a long uppercase U in which the two top tongs are pinched together around a light mountain range.

On the "left," or western tong, of the U is Sonoma County, where the principal north-south road is U.S. 101, which goes straight to the Golden Gate; in Napa County, the eastern half, the main road is Highway 29, which can be slow going, especially around rush hour.

At the bottom of the U, the town of Sonoma connects to the town of Napa, 30 minutes east, via 121/12. That's also where the 37 links Napa County to the 101, as well as to Vallejo and I-80; either road can take you back to the city, although the 101 is probably faster.

North from Napa, the principal towns, which gradually grow smaller and quainter, are Yountville, Oakville, St. Helena (all adorable but relatively expensive towns of boutiques and wineries), and finally the Main Street town of Calistoga (known for hot springs). Not far north from that, 29 turns into 128 and links up with Geyserville, at the tippy top of the Sonoma wine region.

From there, heading south through Sonoma County, you hopscotch between populous towns and quiet hamlets. First is Healdsburg (a cute weekenders' town square good for strolling), and Santa Rosa (bigger and with cheaper motels, but no wineries to speak of within it; there is an airport here). Route 12, also known as Sonoma Highway, branches off to the east there, taking you through Kenwood and the charming town of Glen Ellen, and finally Sonoma, the county's historic seat. West and southwest of Santa Rosa along 116 are the towns of Sebastopol and Forestville, and, finally, Guerneville, where the thick redwood forests begin in what's called the Russian River Valley. The vibe here is more laid-back, and in summer, the big pastimes are canoeing and swimming. Guerneville is also a well-known gay resort town, particularly in summer, although you won't find that it rages often with parties; the visitors tend to be a bit more middle-aged and settled. For a resource on gay-friendly and gay-specific resorts and restaurants, go to www.gayrussianriver.com.

The character of the two counties varies slightly. Whereas Napa is mostly verdant farmland and some small towns, Sonoma has a few larger communities (Santa Rosa) and its topography is much more varied. There's rolling hills and farms in the east, which gives way to deliciously damp redwood forests in the middle west, to wild and undeveloped seashore. (Remember Hitchcock's *The Birds?* It was shot in Bodega Bay, on the Sonoma Coast. It's still just as rustic now, although it's about 30 minutes' drive through forests from what is considered Wine Country.)

I don't personally think it matters where you start, because loveliness and good wine can be found everywhere in the region.

Important note: Both counties possess towns of the same name; when I'm talking about the town, I leave off the "County," and of course, when I'm talking about the county, I specify it.

WHEN TO GO

Because the area is a major draw from the cities in the Bay Area, you'll find that crowds build when people are normally vacationing. Summers, when tourism and accommodations prices are at their highest, are ludicrously busy, and the lines of

Should I Choose Napa or Sonoma?

First of all, it's not a choice—you should visit both. They're right next to each other, after all, and linked by plenty of safe roads. But when it comes to affordability, especially in lodging and in food, Sonoma wins. Napa long ago caught wise to the value of wine tourism—in fact, many of its biggest successes have been modeled on imitations of the European gentry—and it's tough to find a hamburger for less than $11, let alone a hotel that won't break you if you stay more than 3 nights. Even the nightly bed tax is 3% higher in Napa.

So why does Napa have a great cachet (and higher prices) than Sonoma? Much of it has to do with the rules of appellation. It was a collection of Napa wineries, eager to make a name for Northern California wines, that beat French wines at a blind tasting contest in Paris in 1976. Locals still talk about the so-called "Judgment of Paris," in which Napa wines won against European ones in a blind taste test by French judges, and in 2006, they even reenacted it on its 30th anniversary. Sonoma was left out of the prestige . . . that time.

More of a problem is the fact that each county guards its turf jealously, and almost all the maps, brochures, and even reservations agencies you'll find cover either one or the other despite the fact that most visitors want to see both. So the counties will tempt you into sticking to one or the other by withholding information from you, but in fact, you can travel between the great sights of both in about 40 or 50 minutes.

Lastly, picnicking is against the law at most, but not all, wineries in Napa (really—blame the restaurant lobby), while in Sonoma, it's more easily done. And since picnicking is one of the essential pleasures of a Wine Country sojourn, why go without it?

All that said, I generally prefer to stay in Sonoma, because I find I get the full Wine County experience there—great food, nuanced wine—but without the feeling that I'm getting squeezed for every last dollar. And I just love to veg out with the redwoods.

cars and endless traffic on the counties' two-lane roads can truly try your patience. Still, the land is simply gorgeous in summer with the grapes sprouting on the vine; it's the season for garden tours, as well. Fall, when the grapes are harvested and squeezed, can also be maddening, because so many people want to witness some of the rare action involved in winemaking. I'm a fan of visiting in winter: Tourists tend to stay away then, and prices are at their best. You'll get much more attention and education from the vintners—in summer, the line at the tasting counter can be three-deep—although the vineyards will be in their annual woody brambly stage. Spring, in my mind is a close second in terms of seasons, because the area bursts with green. It's never terribly cold—Wine Country everywhere, by definition, is mostly mild, because that's what makes it good for grape growing.

For most innkeepers, high "summer" rates start in April and last through October. Prices are almost always higher on the weekends, when city folk pour in. So if you only plan to go for a few days, make them weekdays—you'll not only pay less for lodging, but you'll also contend with far fewer drivers.

WHERE TO STAY

In Napa County, you could feasibly stay anywhere I mention and be within reach of most of the county's wineries. In Sonoma County, because of the forested Russian River area to the west, proximity is less clear-cut because it's possible to sleep deep in the trees, which would put you about 30 minutes (on a day with minimal traffic) from the bulk of the wineries. That means that a few places in Sonoma County will not be ideal for intense winery-going unless you don't mind braving dark and windy forest roads after dark.

I think the best place to stay, for a balance of geographic convenience and price, is around Sonoma town, because from there, you can drive into Napa in about 35 minutes over a pretty road. It's a lovely, historic location with plenty of cute restaurants, and it's easy to stroll around. You'll also find ample budget accommodation in Napa town, and for that, the commute is reversed: 35 minutes or more to Sonoma's attractions. However, Napa town is much more populous and consequently much more urban, diminishing its small-town appeal. There is no one place to stay that will not require about 35 to 45 minutes' drive to *somewhere* if you intend to tour both counties. Do you want to stay in one county for a few days and another for the balance of your vacation? It's not a bad idea for a week's stay in the region, but for a few nights, you might as well just stay in one spot and not shuffle your stuff around.. I have done research in Napa County many times while I was staying in Sonoma, and vice versa.

Although there are many hotels I think are worthwhile and in which I would gladly stay, renting a home or apartment is my favorite way to see the region. It's a hugely popular method for visitors here. Probably because there are plenty of affluent Bay Area residents who bought second homes here but rarely come to stay, leaving them to rent them out to make some money back, there's a large inventory on hand. Unfortunately, given the popularity of Wine Country, they can charge—and get—high rates. Many owners rely on agencies, listed below, to take care of the reservations for them. Prices are best if you agree to stay longer (they seem to hit a sweet spot around 6 nights), so use that as a bargaining chip.

And having a kitchen to use transforms a Wine Country experience, where food is such a huge component of the draw. You'll be tempted all day long to buy good fresh food, and if you don't have somewhere to prepare it, you'll have wasted your money—not to mention the fact that almost every restaurant around is hideously expensive, and those $90 bills add up quickly unless you do something to mitigate them. Rentals also usually include a living room in which to pop open a bottle and unwind—it's just not as fun to sit on the edge of a hotel bed and sip your wine. Unless otherwise specified, also expect perks in your rental that include cable TV and phone. Generally the standard of decor and amenities in these units remains high across the board.

A few reservations services exist, but be warned that most of their inventory leans strongly toward the expensive. When you call any reservations agency with multiple offerings, you'll always want to stress that you're looking for something affordable. To keep costs low, reserve a place with a size suited to your party. Generally, properties in or close to the towns of Sonoma or Napa are the most affordable of these companies' holdings, and because these population centers are pleasant and not urban, they often constitute a good score. I'm combining both counties in one list since these companies may offer properties across the county lines.

About 30 properties, all in the charming towns of southeast Sonoma County (in Sonoma town, Glen Ellen, and Kenwood) are repped by **Go Sonoma Valley/ Glenelly Properties** (☎ 707/996-6720; www.go-sonoma.com), which keeps a close eye on quality. The firm has been known to post discounts on its website, so always go there first. Besides, that's where each of the listed homes is shown in plenty of photos and described in generous detail. These are on the expensive side, but they're top quality. Rates start at about $250 a night for a one-bedroom, but three-bedrooms start just over $300, which means this firm is more economical for couples' retreats, girlfriends' weekends, and so forth. Each place was decorated by its owner, but all of them are fully stocked with everything you need to pretend it's yours for a while. Some even have pools, although hot tubs are more the norm.

Perhaps more likely to hook you up with the least expensive properties in the southeast of the county, **Stay Sonoma** (☎ 866/647-8888 or 707/996-1888; www.staysonoma.com), like all these companies, has mostly places that charge for around $350, but there are a few affordable winners in its stable. Its president, Wendy Newman, has been in the lodging biz for decades, and its website is better-organized than Go Sonoma's, enabling you to see in a list which properties you can afford and even which will be booked on the dates you want. Among the least expensive: $175 to $190 for a studio cottage at Palmer Place, although if you have lots of people with you, paying $475 for a four-bedroom (which is what lots of places charge for a one-bedroom) isn't a bad deal. That's a little under $125 per bedroom. Also ask about the Sonoma Oak Hideaway, a new property, priced at $175; it would fit three for $200; and about Alexandra's Plaza Suite, an unfussy and cozy cabin, conveniently right off the main plaza in Sonoma, that goes from $165 to $185.

To stay amongst the redwoods of the Russian River area, contact **Russian River Vacation Homes** (☎ 800/997-3312 or 707/869-9030; www.riverhomes.com), the rental wing of a long-running property-management company. It has about 60 places, and its website lets you search by price. Rates in this neck of the woods are lower in general, probably because it's a 20- to 30-minute drive to the thick of the wineries (albeit through gorgeous forest and farmland): $150 to $225 for most of its one-bedrooms and studios. There is a $20 booking fee.

Early in your search, check out **VRBO.com**—it stands for **Vacation Rentals By Owner**—a booming, generally reliable site where, as the name suggests, people who want to rent their cottages post descriptions and enticements for your business. At any given moment, there are several dozen properties listed in a dedicated "Wine Country" section, with prices and photos clearly announced to make your search quicker. A few of the properties I single out below, such as Acorn, list there. The price range is varied, but the quality is generally high. You will, though, have to vet the properties and renters yourself, although the fact there's a fee to post a listing seems to weed out the tricksters and the poorer candidates. Another spot to check is **Keys for Rent** (www.keysforrent.com), but note that you'll have to do separate searches for Napa and Sonoma counties there; at

Accommodations in Napa/Sonoma Counties

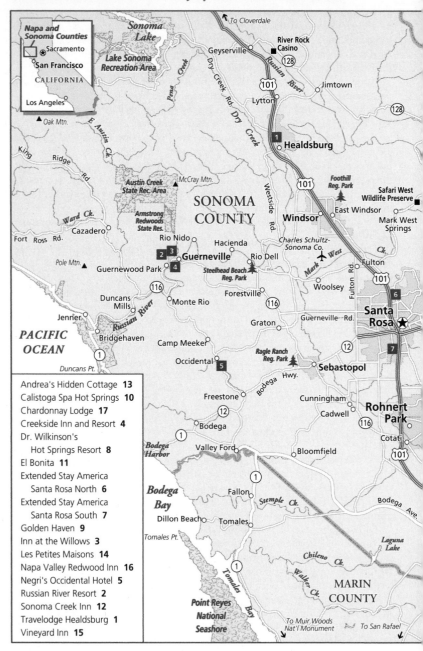

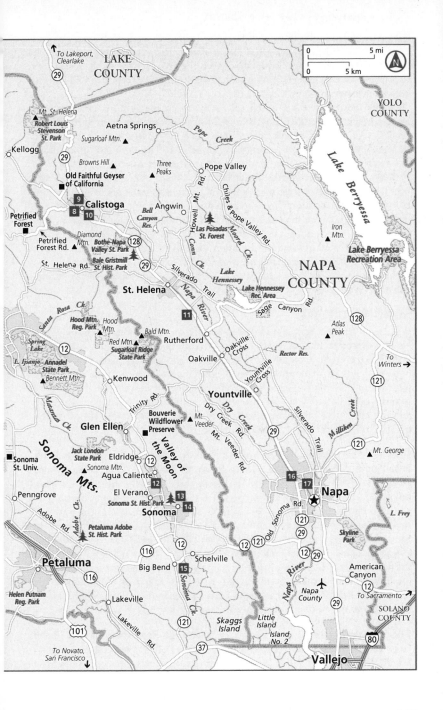

last count, it had listings for about 35 places combined. One reliable place to find a rental is our old friend **craigslist** (http://sfbay.craigslist.org/nby), which as I've noted before in this book, is heavily used in the Bay Area, probably because it's free. You'll have to research and do your own background checks on your own, because no one's minding the store there.

As for hotel and B&B rooms, given that even the simplest establishment charges well into three digits for the night, you should prepare yourself to take the smallest room they have. Sometimes, a place charging $350 a night to capture the honeymooners and venture capitalists will have a $169 room stashed up the stairs in a renovated attic—or some similar civilized arrangement.

Napa Valley Reservations Unlimited (☎ 800/251-6272 or 707/252-1985; www.napavalleyreservations.com) is a local outfit that arranges reservations in everything, from motels to B&Bs to hotels, and may be able to find you some of these smaller rooms in the cushier properties. Its home page has a link for "Xtra Value Rates," which is a gimmicky way of saying "deals."

Make sure to ask if there's a minimum stay; lots of places impose minimums of at least 2 nights, particularly on weekends. Also, Sonoma County has a 9% nightly tax; Napa, 12%. For the scale of what the dollar signs preceding listings mean, go to p. 21.

SONOMA COUNTY

Because the area has several midsized towns that are large enough to host a number of well-known budget brands (Extended Stay America, Motel 6, Quality Inn, Ramada, Travelodge), the lowest-priced end of the accommodations market in Sonoma tends to be dominated by the corporations. Check those companies' websites for lodging in Santa Rosa and Petaluma, where most of the cheapest rooms are. Make sure you visit their websites to make sure you're not passing up a stellar value. You won't have a bucolic experience, but the rates, almost always under $100, could make a Wine Country jaunt possible.

$–$$ One of those established national chains is **Extended Stay America Santa Rosa South** (2600 Colby Ave., Santa Rosa; ☎ 800/804-3724; www.extended stayamerica.com; AE, DC, MC, V). You know the drill: fully equipped kitchens, unlimited local calls, Wi-Fi, and no personality. But if you can stomach staying in a busy town rather than nearer the countryside, you'll often have to pay only $79 to $99 a night to stay here, even in summer. There's a second property in north Santa Rosa (100 Fountain Grove Parkway; ☎ 707/541-0959; www.extended stayamerica.com) that goes for another $20 per night, or around $99; it's probably the noise of the 101 and the unappealing surroundings nearby that account for the lower rates. The northern location is also near a big strip mall where supplies are readily available. Both properties are in a city setting, so don't expect to rise and see the mist over the vineyards through your window. Just expect to save money.

$–$$ I make no promises of beauty for **Travelodge Healdsburg** ★★ (178 Dry Creek Rd., Healdsburg; ☎ 800/499-0103 or 707/433-0101; www.travelodge.com; AE, DC, MC, V)—it's in a blah industrial part of town with no bucolic appeal. (Of course, in these parts, bucolic appeal is always just a 2-minute drive away.) But I can vouch for the rates of $89 a night, and what's more, I can say that they've done an excellent job in renovating and in running this place. It's clean, it's of standard size, and it's an excellent fallback in an expensive area, even if it totally lacks glamour (and if the parking lot is too cramped). I'm always a little nervous when I stay at a super-budget chain like this because repeat business isn't important to some roadside locations, but this place is run very well.

$–$$$ An excellent value for the price, the **Sonoma Creek Inn** ★★ (239 Boyes Blvd., Sonoma; ☎ 888/712-1289 or 707/939-9463; www.sonomacreekinn.com; AE, DC, MC, V) is cutely decorated (colorful bedspreads, fun lampshades, the odd tile mosaic in the wall), starting at $79 weeknights/$109 weekends in winter to $129/$169 in peak season. Rooms are a tad more spacious than they are at other converted motels that are a bit older. There's also a little cafe on the grounds, which makes evening meals easy when you're pooped. Another $20 buys you a balcony or a pleasant walled patio with your own fountain, a terrific touch. Its street is a little noisy (well, for Sonoma), and its neighborhood is strictly farm community—meaning it needs some grooming but isn't unsafe—and you'll have to drive a minute or two to get anywhere else in town. Check the website's special offers—in low season, I've seen 3 nights for $160.

$–$$$ **Negri's Occidental Hotel** (3610 Bohemian Hwy., Occidental; ☎ 877/ 867-6084 or 707/874-3623; www.occidentalhotel.com; MC, V), a two-level motel-style facility backed up against a stretch of rich forest in western Sonoma County, isn't flashy, although there is a swimming pool. Mostly, it's just a simple crash pad, in need of updating but respectable, and popular with scrimping visitors. Rates from $85, although on its website, you can find a Sunday-through-Thursday deal for $80. Suites, which have kitchens, go from $140.

$$–$$$ I like staying in the Russian River Valley, primarily because I find the thick redwood forests so soothing and at odds with the open farmland I experience all day. The excellent **Creekside Inn and Resort** ★★ (16180 Neeley Rd., Guerneville; ☎ 707/869-3623; www.creeksideinn.com; AE, MC, V) is a complex of apartments of varying sizes, all built on stilts above the forest floor. There are two options: an individually themed and designed bed-and-breakfast room (mostly $98–$105; the waffles you'll get are marvelous), and cottages with full kitchens ($125 for 2, $165 for 4; most have gas fireplaces). The staff here is genuinely friendly and laid-back, and there's also a pool. The pubs and coffee cafes of downtown Guerneville are a short walk away over a pedestrian bridge.

$$–$$$ The **Russian River Resort** (16390 4th St., Guerneville; ☎ 800/417-3767 or 707/869-0691; www.russianriverresort.com; AE, MC, V) is a gay-specific inn that parties more than its neighbors. Need proof? There's an annual "Buns and Baskets" competition that has nothing to do with baked goods. In summer, its semi-rustic appeal is combined with a lively social scene that is patronized by people, gay and straight, from town—its nickname in these parts is the "Triple R." There's an on-premises restaurant, plus a bar that sees action until the wee hours. In winter, it's quiet and prices drop to $70; the rest of the year expect to pay between $90 and $155.

$$–$$$ A sweet little inn right on the river, with views to match, **Inn at the Willows** ★ (15905 River Rd., Guerneville; ☎ 707/869-2824; www.innatthewillows. com; AE, MC, V) starts its prices at $99 for its "roadside rooms," in a self-explanatory building that isn't all that noisy, and move to $149 for a room with a terrific river view where the water is flat and soothing. It's in quite good shape, overall, and advertises itself as a "place of inclusiveness," which means gay folks are more than welcome—the place doesn't judge its guests' romantic proclivities.

$$$–$$$$ The perfectly adorable **Les Petites Maisons** ✯✯✯ (1190 E. Napa St., Sonoma; ☎ 800/291-8962 or 707/933-0340; www.thegirlandthefig.com; AE, MC, V) were once grubby workmen's cottages for field hands. But the people who run the girl & the fig restaurant waved a magic wand over them, turning them into terrific mini-homes for tourists, candy colored and sweet, with equipped kitchens, living rooms, big bathrooms, wide wood floors, outdoor seating areas, and a security gate for the parking area. Their location, 2 miles east of Sonoma, makes for an ideal home base to explore both counties. Rates start at $175 in winter and peak at $250 per night when it's a weekend in harvest, but for that money, you get enough space for a family of four to six, and the maintenance standards couldn't be higher. Weekly rates are just above $1,000 most times of year.

$$$ Perhaps a good choice for visitors from San Francisco who won't have much time to drive deep into the counties, the **Vineyard Inn** (23000 Arnold Dr./ Carneros Hwy., Sonoma; ☎ 800/359-4667 or 707/938-2350; www.sonoma vineyardinn.com; AE, MC, V), located at the south of Sonoma County, is a cute, good-value lodging based in a renovated 1950s motor court. Some rooms are tiled, some carpeted, and the often-outdated decor lets you make no mistake that this is a family-run place in the farmland, but there's also no denying it's private, cozy, and well-located near the road that zips into Napa. The continental breakfast is generous (including local fruits), and, although the bathrooms are shower-only, there are granite touches instead of cheap counters. Rates start at around $159 weeknights/$179 weekends for a queen-size bed, which is a little high, but the owners can be talked down during slow periods.

$$$–$$$$ A brief mention of three of the least expensive rentals around: At $190 a night, is **Acorn House** ✯ (☎ 707/833-2134; www.acornhouse.org; cash or check only), which sounds like a rehab center but is actually is an unpretentious cottage on a little country lane in Kenwood. The house is packed with useful extras such as movies and books, a continental basket breakfast, and a free bottle of local wine; plus, there's a little hot tub. It's in an area that's particularly full of fun wineries, so you won't have to drive a lot if you don't want to. Just a one-bedroom cottage off Sonoma's restaurant-lined plaza, **Andrea's Hidden Cottage** ✯ (138 E. Spain St.; ☎ 707/939-7070; www.andreashiddencottage.com; cash or check only) is cute and well-equipped with a kitchen, utensils, a barbecue, and a private patio. It's situated in a small private vineyard, and when you check in, you—yup—get a free bottle of wine. Summer rates are $127 weeknights/$155 weekends; winter, $110 weeknights/$125 weekends. Also close to Sonoma Plaza, **Lisa's Garden Cottage** ✯ (☎ 707/933-8804; www.lisasgardencottage.com), too, leaves a bottle of wine for guests, and it's simple and sweet, but its calling card is its lush, private, enclosed garden and the ability to walk down to a little creek at the back. It's $160 weekdays/$185 weekends, per night.

NAPA COUNTY

$–$$ A relatively new owner has injected a large measure of quaintness into the 19-room **Chardonnay Lodge** ★★ (2640 Jefferson St., Napa; ☎ 707/224-0789; www.chardonnaylodge.net; AE, DC, MC, V), where each room has its own personality, some an inoffensive modern hotel style and others gussied up with things like throw pillows and, in some rooms, murals on an Italian theme. Although the building is an old motel, units are very well-maintained and have been recently renovated, and someone is paying a lot of attention to the flowers growing all around the yard. I wouldn't want to squeeze a whole family into one of the rooms, but for couples, it works well, and the free bottled water and snacks are a nice touch for the sensational price: $85 for a queen-size bed (these rooms go first, so book early), $98 for a king, and $110 for a room with two double beds, which *is* big enough for families. The rose garden is several cuts above the kind of perks you get for a place this cheap. When it's busy, prices may go up about 40%. Of the motels around here, this is my top choice.

$–$$$ Or perhaps you'd prefer a nice Chablis? The two-story **Chablis Inn** ★ (3360 Solano Ave., Napa; ☎ 800/443-3490 and 707/257-1944; www.chablisinn.com; AE, MC, V) is another motel-style accommodation very much like the Chardonnay: Simple, nothing fancy, but updated and clean in a way that proves owners are paying attention, and at a price that other places in town refuse to beat: $130 to $159 in the high season. Like the wine Chablis, it's a very satisfactory, cheaper substitute for something fancier and more expensive, and it does the trick. There's a cloistered pool/patio area with a hot tub, and rooms have mini-fridges, but its location, too close to the hubbub of Highway 29, brings it down just a notch for me.

$–$$ A cute wooden building on the main street of town, **Calistoga Inn Restaurant & Brewery** ★★ (1250 Lincoln Ave., Calistoga; ☎ 707/942-4101; www.calistogainn.com; AE, MC, V) has one thing against it and one big one going for it. The negative is that its 18 rooms are above a popular local restaurant and brewpub run by the same folks. The place doesn't rage—places that charge $26 per plate generally don't—but some people may be annoyed by the nightly (Mar–Nov) live music on its patio. Me, I join in. The positive news is the extreme low price: $75 weeknights/$100 weekends November through March; $89/$139 April through October. That gets you a clean, bright room with fresh furniture and an in-room sink, but with a shared bathroom down the hall—one bathroom for men and another for women. It also puts you smack on the homey main drag of Calistoga, one of the most charming streets in the area.

$$ Another very simple motel that sets itself apart by being new and clean, if unexciting, the **Napa Valley Hotel and Suites** (853 Coombs St., Napa; ☎ 707/226-1871; www.napavalleyhotelandsuites.com; AE, DC, MC, V) is a Travelodge in downtown Napa, making finding food easy, and it's not very far from COPIA (p. 259), a lavish center where food and wine experts speak and hold demonstrations every day, should that be something you want to follow up on. For $129 (double bed) to $149 (king bed), you get a place where the conveniences of the boutique-filled downtown are all within a quick stroll, although that also comes with the feeling that, well, you're downtown. There's a pool, and the three-story motel is built in a courtyard form around it.

$–$$$　The one-story, motel-style **Wine Valley Lodge** (200 S. Coombs St., Napa; ☎ 707/224-7911; www.winevalleylodge.com; DC, AE, MC, V) was, not long after being built in 1953, famous for hosting the cast of the Elvis Presley movie *Wild in the Country* during filming. (Elvis slept at a fancier inn up the road, thankyou-verymuch.) Although its 56 rooms have been renovated with care several times since then, make no mistake: This is an old-style motel, close to the highway. I include it because it's hardly a horror show, and the value is strong: $89 single, $139 double, including continental breakfast with fresh waffles. One benefit of staying here is that you'll be close to the town of Napa, making eating cheaply and buying groceries much easier than it is the farther out you go.

$–$$$　Simple, small, rooms in an unattractive green two-level roadside structure at **Napa Valley Redwood Inn** (3380 Solano Ave., Napa; ☎ 707/257-6111; www.napavalleyredwoodinn.com; DC, AE, MC, V) are what you get for your $75 to $150—an excellent price for Napa. It's right around the corner from the main drag up the county, making it convenient for winery touring, and because it's in Napa proper, you'll be able to find grocery stories to feed yourself so that you won't have to break the bank at all the gourmet restaurants; there's a little shopping center right across the street for that. If you've ever stayed in a motor inn, you'll get what's being delivered here: Facilities won't change your life, but for many people, the price may make it possible to see Napa at all. Expect your room to have a stand-up shower but not a bath, and also for it to come with a continental breakfast in the morning. The area, too, is not the best Napa has to offer, but it's not too bad (nothing here is).

$$–$$$　**El Bonita** ★★ (195 Main St., St. Helena; ☎ 707/963-3216; www.elbonita.com; AE, DC, MC, V) is a simple, clean, family-run motel built in the old drive-in style; it was once a religious retreat in the 1940s, but now, people mostly fall on their knees here in thanks for a good room that isn't $500 a night. Although it's on the main road, it's not really that noisy, especially if you get one of the rooms in the newer building that was put up behind the classic one. Rooms are smallish, but thoughtfully done for the price: The king beds are four-poster, and many bathrooms have been fitted with heated tile floors. Prices leap around according to the time of year and the day of the week (the usual rules apply), but expect a queen-size bed facing the pool (again, not too noisy, since people don't come here to swim) for $112 to $189. Upgrade to a "homestead" with a kitchen for around $200.

$$–$$$　Rooms start at $109 at **Dr. Wilkinson's Hot Springs Resort** (1507 Lincoln Ave., Calistoga; ☎ 707/942-4102; www.drwilkinson.com; AE, MC, V), an institution among the Calistoga spas, where that money buys you a simple room with a queen-size bed, an armoire, a little dining table, and, for $18 more, a kitchenette. Although the buildings are distinctly 1950s motel (standard room sizes, walls made of era brick tile, and the neon sign out front deserves to be in an Americana museum), the resort has gone to extra lengths to recently renovate the rooms to a more refreshed standard. The patios and outdoor courtyards have been well-groomed and are fitting places to unwind before walking out to the shops and food along Lincoln. If you stay here, you can avail yourself of a standard pool plus a pair (indoor and outdoor) of pools fed by mineral water. Then, of course, there's this place's famously medicinal mud-bath spa (p. 257). The resort also maintains a few cottages nearby; those start around $170.

$$–$$$ More motel-style accommodation, renovated to a Wine Country–appropriate standard, can be found at **Golden Haven** (1713 Lake St., Calistoga; ☎ 707/942-8000; www.goldenhaven.com; AE, MC, V), which, like Wilkinson's, is a mid-20th century motel (built at a time when Napa County didn't have much going for it) that now doubles as a spa, so mineral pools come as part of the package. Its fanciest room, at $165 to $219, comes with a whirlpool fed by natural springs (it's within reach of the bed, so no horseplay), but the way to save the most here is to take a room on the second floor of the building—they cost $99/$135 versus $135/$169 for the larger rooms on the first floor. But since that $40 a night you save upstairs could buy you an unforgettable dinner in these parts, is having a dressing area really that important? Check out the specials on its website; many dates, it's possible to score a couples' mud bath plus a room for $99—a fantastic deal considering the bath alone is $75.

$$$ The homey rooms at the two-story **Inn on Randolph** ★ (411 Randolph St., Napa; ☎ 800/670-6886; www.innonrandolph.com; AE, DC, MC, V), in downtown Napa, are everything you imagine a B&B room might be when it's in an old wooden home like this one is. The appeal of historic downtown Napa—boutiques, restaurants, gold-rush-era buildings—is right outside the front door. Rates start at $139 for two of the rooms, called "Spring" and "Summer," but $189 is the usual starting point (the "Summer" room is better—it has a little private deck), so you have to book early to get the lowest prices. There are private baths and breakfast is big, but there are no TVs. Three cute cottages line its garden, and they can be rented, too, but for prices that start another $100 higher.

$$$ The rooms could use some updating, but for the price, I'm satisfied with **Calistoga Spa Hot Springs** (1006 Washington St., Calistoga; ☎ 866/822-5772 or 707/942-6269; www.calistogaspa.com) because its rooms, which aren't luxury, have little kitchens with fridges, cooktops, and dishes and utensils. Given that it's in Calistoga where thermo spas are cool, there are also four pools of varying sizes and temperatures, and mud baths are administered. Rooms are usually around $135, and the motel is fairly convenient to Healdsburg, in Sonoma County, via the Alexander Valley.

DINING FOR ALL TASTES

Food is everywhere in the Wine Country. Affordable food isn't. This is a place where even a deli sandwich costs upwards of $8. Let it also not be forgotten that some of the finest and most expensive tables on Earth (such as Yountville's $200/meal French Laundry, where nights book up months in advance) are located here—that's the playing field. It's obvious you could use a little help finding a delicious sit-down meal.

If it's fancy foods you crave, my strongest suggestion is to grab tastes of fine meats and cheeses not as table-service meals, but at one of the many upscale groceries scattered around the two counties (I round up a few of the best in the box on p. 232). Nibbling your way across the vineyards is perhaps not only the cheapest way to see them, but also the most fun, and this style of eating affords you the widest exposure to interesting flavors grown and made in the valleys. Restaurants serve $25 cheese-sampler plates, sure, but you can buy the same stuff for yourself for half that. All you'll be missing is the wine pairing suggestions.

Dining in Napa/Sonoma Counties

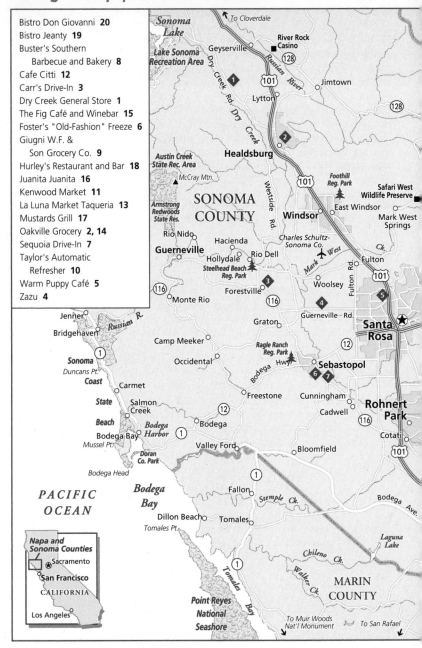

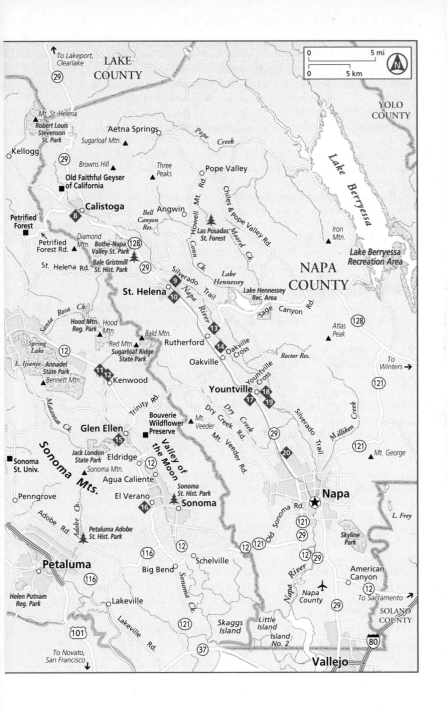

Here's some more important guidance: Lunch is drastically underrated here. At lunch, many places use the same chefs, the same ingredients, and often, the exact same menu—but for less than dinner. If you don't mind cutting into your wine-touring time (aw, come on, how many places can you visit in a day, anyway?), do your gourmandizing at lunch and go easy on dinner.

I don't include places that specialize in breakfast, because many B&Bs offer continental breakfast. If you want to break the bank, there are plenty of opportunities—including the French Laundry, named by countless millionaires as literally the best restaurant in the world—and everyone you meet will suggest that you visit three or four of these expensive places without really stopping to consider how much you'll be paying.

If a restaurant listed here has three or more dollar signs listed with it, then there's probably a *corkage fee,* charged for opening a bottle of wine that you don't buy from one of them. Those start around $15, so don't presume that you'll be saving money by bringing your own wine.

In addition to these places, the not-very-famous-but-ought-to-be burrito carts (p. 228), used by many vineyard workers, are also a prime resource.

AROUND SONOMA

$ Just one room with a few tables and a diner-style counter, **Juanita Juanita** ★★★ (19114 Arnold Dr., Sonoma; ☎ 707/935-3981; www.juanitajuanita.com; Wed–Mon 11am–8pm; cash only) is a terrific find for a wide range of flavorful Mexican food. The cook seems to never simply throw things together: The chorizo is crumbled and perfectly charred, the enchiladas smooth and full of moist meat (in fact, they're so good that they sometimes sell out by around 7pm). Anything costing more than $6 will be so massive you may regret ordering it, but staff is friendly and doesn't sniff at packaging leftovers. Don't be put off by the slogan: "Food isn't properly seasoned unless it's painful to eat." That's more a cute promise to people who like it spicy than it is a mantra that you'll find in every dish. Dinner wraps up by 8pm, so don't plan a long evening.

$ No, they don't serve warm puppies at **The Warm Puppy Café** 🐾 (1667 W. Steele Lane, Santa Rosa; ☎ 707/546-7147; www.snoopyshomeice.com; Mon–Tues 11am–6pm, Wed 11am–5pm, Thurs–Sun 11am–9pm; AE, MC, V). It's really just the resident food counter at the Snoopy's Home Ice skating rink—you know: pizzas, burgers, and other snacks it feels good to eat when you come off the ice. In fact, countless parents do eat here as they watch their kids frolic on skates through the plate-glass windows. This was *Peanuts* creator's Charles Schulz's daily breakfast habit from 1969, when he built this place, to 2000. His favorite table, the round one to the right of the fireplace, is still held in his honor. I think this place is pretty great because it's so homey and has such a strong community feel. Order the Snoopy special, a hamburger served with fries inside a dog dish, or the Peppermint Patty, which is a mint hot chocolate. The museum dedicated to Schulz's legacy (p. 225) is right across the street.

$–$$ The roadside Italian joint **Cafe Citti** ★★ (9049 Sonoma Hwy./Route 12; ☎ 707/833-2690; www.cafecitti.com; Sun–Thurs 11am–3:30pm and 5–8:30pm, Fri–Sat 11am–3:30pm and 5–9pm; MC, V) is the kind of place popular with local office workers and retirees who want a solid meal without paying a lot for it—the

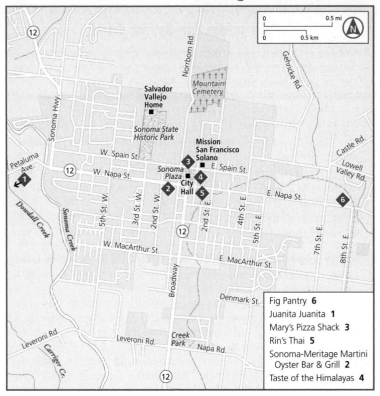

Fig Pantry	**6**
Juanita Juanita	**1**
Mary's Pizza Shack	**3**
Rin's Thai	**5**
Sonoma-Meritage Martini Oyster Bar & Grill	**2**
Taste of the Himalayas	**4**

simple dining area is nothing flashy, and, as a bonus, the tables in front get a mountain view through the windows. Choose from among eight pasta sauces for four different pastas, get a sandwich for $7 to $9, or grab a salad for $4.50 to $7. Make sure to take stock of the daily special, which includes Northern Italian–influenced meals such as egg and leek frittata on focaccia. Local beers, many with names like racehorses (Pliny the Elder, Damnation) are also poured for about $4.50 each. Even better for picnickers, everything is available for takeout. If you decide to dine here, know that you might make some new friends: The clientele is local and friendly all the way. Just make sure to pronounce the name correctly—it's as in *Chitty Chitty Bang Bang,* uncomfortably close to swearing, but the prices are certainly dignified and the food is very good. In busy seasons, the closing time may be extended to accommodate the crowds. This family runs a nice place.

$$ I've been to a number of Thai places on the road, and I never expect much, but I'm happy to report that **Rin's Thai** ★★ (139 E. Napa St., Sonoma; ☎ 707/ 938-1462; www.rinsthai.com; Sun–Thurs 11:30am–9pm, Fri–Sat 11:30am–9:30pm; MC, V) is pretty terrific. The menu offers all the standards ($9–$12), but extremely well done, and with special attention to the level of spiciness that the guest prefers.

Wrap It Up: The Burrito Carts

A tourist in the wine region could be forgiven if he's lulled into the belief that everyone in the area is rich, white, and of Italian or Spanish descent. But the locals know better. Many of the people working the land—the ones who prune the vines and make the wine happen—are immigrants (some legal, some not) from Mexico, Colombia, and other Latin countries. And do you think that in the evening, after a hard day spent in the dirt, that they make reservations at places serving fig compote or smoked salmon? Heck no.

For some real local flavor, go where the locals go: one of the several take-away burrito cart locations popular with workers. What's that? A little kitchen in a specially refitted RV where a hard-working cook dishes up some incredibly large, deeply tasty Mexican treats. Burritos start at $4.50, and the $6 "super" version is the *biggest* one I have ever seen in my life—at least 12 inches long, heavy as a Duraflame log. One could feed three average people. Quesadillas are $5, and stuffed. And tangy chorizo tacos go for a mere $1.25 served with fresh lime. Each cart posts its county-approved paperwork, including health inspections.

Obviously, since these carts are by definition transient, there's no promise where they'll always be. But several carts are so established that they tend to appear in the same places every day. Just north of Sonoma on 12, in the lot of Cavenaugh's Auto Care Center at Boyes Boulevard, is one of the more popular ones near Sonoma town (☎ **707/235-9492**). In Guerneville (Sonoma County), you'll find another trusted one in the front parking lot of the Safeway supermarket in the center of town.

If you don't find yourself near those, any local will know where you can find a good one. Ask supermarket clerks, wine-room attendants, and anyone else who actually lives in the area where the goodies are currently parking.

And Napa? What about there? In Rutherford, head to the back of the **La Luna Market Taqueria** (1153 Rutherford Rd., Rutherford; ☎ 707/ 967-3497; daily 8am–7:30pm). In the hind end of a grocery store, cooks whip up a huge range of authentic Mexican classics, like a killer *carne asada,* although for slightly more than by the carts of the west. It's not as down-and-dirty as Sonoma's carts, but it'll get you through a burrito jones.

Don't mess around, though, because if you request your order made brutally hot, you'll get it that way. The restaurant is in a former house, lending a comfortable vibe, and in good weather the outdoor patio is a terrific place to hang out.

$$–$$$ And now for something completely different: You might expect something portentous out of a restaurant serving something so different from its rivals, but **A Taste of the Himalayas** ✦ (464 1st Street E., Sonoma; ☎ 707/996-1161;

daily 11am–2:30pm and 5–10pm; AE, MC, V) is cheerful and well-priced, and the food is of higher quality than the bashed-out stuff you're more likely to actually get in Nepal. Try the *momos,* which are bread stuffed with meat or vegetables, or the samosas. If you're more used to Indian-style food, they do that, too; curries and tandoori chief among them. Everything comes with *dal,* a staple soup of lentils and spices that everyone eats with every meal there. Sometimes, there's a lunch buffet for $10. In season, it's smart to make a reservation.

$$–$$$ Although dinner at the celebrated girl & the fig restaurant in Sonoma is a huge and unquestionably mouthwatering splurge, the owners also run this smaller, cheaper cafe, **the fig cafe & winebar** ★★ (13690 Arnold Dr., Glen Ellen; ☎ 707/938-2130; www.thegirlandthefig.com; Mon–Fri 5:30–10pm, Sat–Sun 9:30am–2:30pm and 5:30–10pm; AE, MC, V), in the adorable town of Glen Ellen, right up the road. Main dishes are in the upper teens (about $10 less than at the other place, but with fewer cheese plates), and they approximate many of the more expensive flavors at the flagship restaurant. The menu changes to accommodate seasonal ingredients, but expect thin-crust pizzas, salads, risotto, duck confit, and some simple French-style dishes.

$$–$$$ If you have kids clamoring to eat something they can pronounce, **Mary's Pizza Shack** ★ [kids] (8 W. Spain St., Sonoma; ☎ 707/938-8300; www.maryspizza shack.com; Sun–Thurs 11am–10:30pm, Fri–Sat 11am–midnight; AE, MC, V) fills the bill for a no-nonsense family joint. In fact, it's a 17-location Northern California chain with its headquarters just west of Sonoma, so although it's not very charismatic and has the manufactured character of a much larger chain, it's local in its way. Parents won't be bored, though; its wine selection is local, its pomegranate martini is popular, and the dessert of choice is the Bemba, a colossal ball of peanut-butter gelato plugged with caramel and encased in chocolate. But the real call here is the pizza; a six-piecer is about $14. For $21, you can get a medium pie with two toppings, salads, and drinks. This is the sort of cavernous place where local high schoolers (they're well-behaved) come, and it's a pubby atmosphere for watching the big-screen TVs, turned low, as you dine. It's also a place that values ranch dressing so much that it makes its own. God bless America!

$$$$ A sceney hangout for local winemakers and foodies in the know, **Zazu** ★★★ (3535 Guerneville Rd., Santa Rosa; ☎ 707/523-4814; www.zazurestaurant.com; Wed–Sun 5:30–9:30pm, Fri–Sat 5:30–10:30pm; MC, V) has a menu that changes daily to suit the notions of its chef-owner couple, John Stewart and Duskie Estes, and to harness the seasonal crops of the moment. Think star anise-rubbed duck, fried green tomatoes, and cider-glazed Cornish game hen, all for the mid-$20s to low $30s. Not cheap (you can stick to a selection of the "small plates," which cost half as much, to avoid a budget calamity), but delicious and casual. The roadhouse-style space can be deafeningly loud with chatter, and it's not just because the copper-top tables create echoes: This place simply encourages celebration. Wednesday, Thursday, and Sunday, it does its "Pizza and Pinot," during which the kitchen makes specialty pizzas (about $19, but shareable) designed to be paired with pinot flavors, which are included by the flight. And there's always one selected wine available for just $5 a glass.

Where Grease Is the Word

Probably because the area hosts a large number of summer visitors—and partly because people eventually feel overfed on gourmet dinners—the region retains several old-fashioned drive-in burger joints that date back to a time when the area was strictly agricultural and families might have piled into the pickup for a comfort meal on a summer evening. If you're a fan of streamline architecture and home-cut french fries, several heart-clogging doses of nostalgia await. None of them actually employs roller-skating girls, but they're quintessentially local. After all, this is the land where *American Graffiti* was filmed.

Carr's Drive-In (6533 Covey Rd., Forestville; ☎ 707/887-7053; Mon–Sat 10am–7:30pm, Sun 11am–7:30pm; cash only) serves malts, burgers, and other treats that would get a cardiologist clucking. Also, try **Taylor's Automatic Refresher**, St. Helena (p. 230).

The specialty of **Sequoia Drive-In** (1382 Gravenstein Hwy. S./116, Sebastopol; ☎ 707/829-7543; www.sequoiadrivein.com; Mon–Thurs 10am–8:30pm, Fri 10am–9pm, Sat 8am–9pm, Sun 8am–8:30pm; MC, V), besides the usual burgers and fries, is "barrel chicken" cooked in weird-looking, handmade ovens.

Fosters Freeze (935 Gravenstein Hwy. S./116, Sebastopol; ☎ 707/823-1644; www.fostersfreeze.com; daily 10am–9pm; AE, MC, V) is a California chain. Its claim to fame is classic drive-in food, from burgers (its "Big Boss" is topped with fried onion rings) to soft-serve ice cream.

$$$$ Another source of excellent, carefully sourced and prepared dishes, one that won't skin you alive or make you feel like you don't belong, is **Sonoma-Meritâge Martini Oyster Bar & Grill** (165 W. Napa St., Sonoma; ☎ 707/938-9430; www.sonomameritage.com; Wed–Mon 11:30am–3pm and 5–9pm; reservations recommended), a labor of love off Sonoma Plaza by chef Carlo Cavallo. Oysters and fresh seafood are, as you can tell by its name, its specialty, and it also has a list of excellent (and reasonable—$8) specialty cocktails. For dinner, the menu is full of French and Italian influence, such as a few pasta choices (starting at just $11), slow-roasted wild-boar ribs, risotto with scallops with a spicy tomato sauce, all in the mid-$20s. At lunch, the dishes are simpler—upscale sandwiches, entree-size salads, and the like—but they're made from the same fine local ingredients that Cavallo cares about, and they're priced at only around $10 each. The olive tapenade that comes with the focaccia bread may be reason enough to book a seat here.

AROUND NAPA

$–$$ The original drive-in that spawned the popular outpost in San Francisco's Ferry Building, **Taylor's Automatic Refresher** ★★★ (933 Main St., St. Helena; ☎ 707/963-3486; www.taylorsrefresher.com; daily 10:30am–9pm; AE, MC, V)

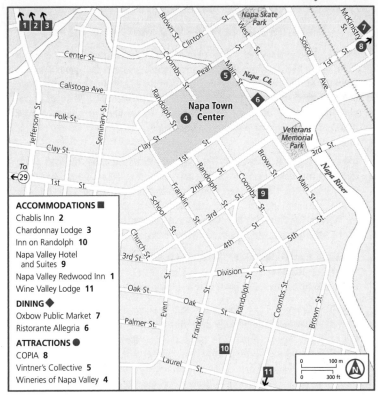

ACCOMMODATIONS ■
Chablis Inn **2**
Chardonnay Lodge **3**
Inn on Randolph **10**
Napa Valley Hotel
and Suites **9**
Napa Valley Redwood Inn **1**
Wine Valley Lodge **11**
DINING ◆
Oxbow Public Market **7**
Ristorante Allegria **6**
ATTRACTIONS ●
COPIA **8**
Vintner's Collective **5**
Wineries of Napa Valley **4**

does classic comfort food with clean ingredients, served in an old-style counter-service setting. It's been slinging meat since 1949 and looks like it. Eating here is a nice break from the balsamic vinegar and goat cheese served seemingly everywhere else. Burgers go from $6 to $9, fries and rings are $4 but cooked with care. There are a few non-greasy choices such as a rare seared ahi burger ($14) and a few chicken sandwiches. Don't skip the milkshakes, served with both spoon and straw, since they're something it's known for. The menu and prices are identical here to the Ferry Building. Beware if it's cold or rainy, because every seat is outdoors and not every one is sheltered. A third branch, pressed from the same mold, opened in early 2008 at the Oxbow Market in central Napa (p. 223).

$–$$$ Situated in a former bank, **Ristorante Allegria** (1026 1st St., Napa; ☎ 707/254-8006; www.ristoranteallegria.com; Mon–Sat 11:30am–2:30pm and 5–10pm, Sun 5–10pm; AE, MC, V) does steady Northern Italian standards for not too much money: antipasti for $8 to $12, salads around $8, six pasta selections for around $16 (like the wild mushroom ravioli), and a list of grilled meats and salmons done well, for $17 to $28. The space is stylish without being hokey. Spectacular? No. But it provides a dignified, affordable meal at the end of a long day of moving around.

Don't Be Any Sandwiches Short of a Picnic

I wouldn't rely heavily on the winery shops for food supplies. Too many of them call a halt to their offerings after fancy jams and European sausage. Instead, go to the cute supermarkets and cafes spread around the area, some of which are actually well known in their own rights. Most little grocery stores close by 6pm; only the giant fluorescent-lit chains, always found in town, will be open past dinnertime.

Sonoma County

Dry Creek General Store (3495 Dry Creek Rd., Healdsburg; ☎ 707/433-4171; www.dcgstore.com; Mon–Sat 6am–6pm). Like the Napa County version of Oakville Grocery, this wooden roadside store has been going since this was pioneer country, and although it still looks like it, its prices are more in line for modern San Francisco folk. Come during nice weather to get the most out of the beer garden, which has marvelous views of a nearby valley.

Kenwood Market (8910 Rte. 12/Sonoma Hwy., Kenwood; ☎ 707/833-5053; Mon–Sat 6:30am–8pm, Sun 7am–7pm) sells five or six types of sandwiches in its deli, plus has a full grocery that locals themselves use.

Oakville Grocery (124 Matheson St., Healdsburg; ☎ 707/433-3200; www.oakvillegrocery.com; daily 8am–6pm) is the Sonoma County sister of the original Oakville Grocery in Napa County. Here you'll find a big room full of fancy potato chips, a busy deli counter where sandwiches and pizzas are prepared, and lots of olive oils and marinades. How yuppie is it? It even bottles its own mineral water. The grocery does box lunches from $18 that include a sandwich, pasta salad, fresh fruit, and a cookie. Everything else in the place is about as affordable. It's located on Healdsburg's town square, ideal for strolling.

Napa County

The original location of **Oakville Grocery** (7856 St. Helena Hwy., Oakville; ☎ 707/944-8802; www.oakvillegrocery.com; daily 8am–6pm), off a busy

$–$$ When you drive east on Calistoga's Lincoln Avenue, you'll notice a bluish cloud of smoke rising against the trees. That could be your dinner in the works if you choose **Buster's Southern Barbecue and Bakery** ★ (1207 Foothill Blvd., Hwy. 29 and Lincoln Ave., Calistoga; ☎ 707/942-5605; www.busterssouthernbbq. com; Mon–Sat 9am–7:30pm, Sun 9am–6pm; MC, V), a real, honest-to-goodness, slabs-of-ribs-on-the-open-grill kind of place. All the greats are here, from pork loin to baked beans to coleslaw by the quart. (Frankly, I'd almost rather fill up on sides—pints are around $5.) The dining area is as rustic as Buster's old-school cooking method: a covered patio where you'll want to sip beers for a while. A full dinner, which includes a hefty meat portion and comes with garlic toast and two side dishes, goes for around $10—a top value.

highway, is harder to visit (or, more precisely, harder to rejoin traffic from after a visit). There's been a store in this cute wooden building since 1881, and some locals still pick up their mail in the tiny post office that's attached. It's not inexpensive (salads are $9), but it's a good place to buy locally made products, ready-made and made-to-order sandwiches, and fussy ingredients.

Right next door to COPIA (p. 259) across a parking lot, the $11-million **Oxbow Public Market** (610 1st St., at McKinstry, Napa; ☎ 707/226-6529; www.oxbowpublicmarket.com; Tues 9am–8pm, Wed–Mon 9am–7pm, restaurants Mon–Wed to 8pm and Thurs–Sun to 10pm) is a newly built (late 2007) fancy-foods mall devoted to local and artisanal food producers, most from within a 100-mile radius. Its founder ran the Oakville Grocery for 2 decades, and he chose the vendors for San Francisco's Ferry Building Marketplace. In addition to a third Taylor's Refresher (burgers, fries); there's Pica Pica Maize Kitchen for delicious pressed Venezuelan *arepas* ($5–$8); and Rotisario for roasted meats. Those are just a few of the prepared-food outlets; you can also get cheese, raw meats, organic ice cream, spices, oysters, chocolate, and coffees at many of the other stores, as well as culinary antiques at Heritage.

There's a ritzy Dean & Deluca in St. Helena for people who don't mind spending $12 on a pot of mustard, but I recommend the overstuffed, nostalgic **Giugni W. F. & Son Grocery Co.** (1227 Main St., St. Helena; ☎ 707/963-3421; daily 9am–4:30pm; cash only), another long-runner, where the sandwich routine goes like this: From a case of a couple dozen meats and a couple dozen cheese, you point out which ones you'd like to try, and a meal is made. Eight bucks is standard. It's known for its secret ingredient: Guigny (*Joo*-nee) Juice, a homemade vinaigrette.

$$–$$$$ Excellent, ethical food mostly at reasonable prices is served at the casual/arty **Mustards Grill** ★★ (7399 St. Helena Hwy., Yountville; ☎ 707/944-2424; www.mustardsgrill.com; Mon–Thurs 11:30am–9pm, Fri–Sat 11:30am–10pm, Sun 11am–9pm; AE, DC, MC, V), a place that has been around for a generation on the main drag through Napa County at Yountville. The idea here is what it calls "farm-to-table" food, meaning it draws from the farms around town. Sandwiches are hefty (half-pound burgers, $12), salads wittily garnished (one with blue cheese dressing and candied pistachios, $10), and it makes a production out of its desserts, such as the lemon-lime pie with a towering brown sugar meringue ($8.50). It's when you order something cooked in the wood-fired grill that the prices leap into the $20s. Some of the produce served is raised in a small garden just outside the restaurant. Naturally, the wine list is long.

$$$$ I wish Napa would just admit it: It wishes it were Europe. Most of the wineries are pretending they're in Tuscany, and most of the vintners are obsessed with the French. At least **Bistro Jeanty** ★★ (6510 Washington St., Yountville; ☎ 707/944-0103; www.bistrojeanty.com; daily 11:30am–10:30pm; MC, V; reservations recommended) makes no bones about it; it's French all the way. Its chef, Philippe Jeanty, came from Champagne, France, in 1977. Delicious fare like escargots ($12), steak tartare ($18 with fries), frites for ($4.50), and coq au vin ($17—a fine deal), fully creamed and buttered, would please any Continental. There are also some more offbeat choices, such as pike dumplings with lobster sauce ($13) and rabbit pate ($13). The patio, shaded by trees, is magnetic. It calls itself a "bistro," which is why its decor leans toward bent-cane chairs and ceramic roosters, I guess, but that cutesy banality says nothing about the fine food. Best of all, it's hard to find a main dish that breaks the $20 mark—a rarity, especially in Yountville.

$$$–$$$$ Another "bistro," this one with more of a villa feel and a marvelous view, the busy **Bistro Don Giovanni** ★ (4110 Howard Lane/Hwy. 29, Napa; ☎ 707/224-3300; Sun–Thurs 11:30am–10pm, Fri–Sat 11:30am–11pm; MC, V; reservations recommended) does both Italian and French classics. Don't fear the cheesy name. Pastas (there are six choices) go from $14 to $22, while wood-oven pizzas (four selections, including one with fig and gorgonzola) are $13. To give you a sense for the casual-but-quality market they're going for, there's a Caesar salad ($9.50), not usually on the very finest restaurant menus, but it's made of whole romaine leaves, not cheap shredded iceberg lettuce. All nights of the week people like to sit out on the patio, where the aromas of the garden waft in and where, in winter, a fireplace warms the customers. Some of the olives it serves are grown on property.

$$$$ This is what I wish Napa had a lot more of: approachable California cuisine places, priced within reason, where you can eat a delicious meal made by a chef who cares as deeply about craftsmanship as the chefs who charge twice as much. That's **Hurley's Restaurant and Bar** ★ (6518 Washington St., Yountville; ☎ 707/944-2345; www.hurleysrestaurant.com; daily 11:30am–midnight; AE, MC, V), an outpost of affordability in normally backbreaking Yountville. A long-established local chef (he used to cook at Domaine Chandon) started this place to have his way with local produce. Wild game, local wines, a martini bar, and a casual, white-tablecloth atmosphere all attract locals who care about food. In warm weather, the patio, with wrought-iron details and a fountain, is a happy place to raise a glass. The menu is ever-changing, but mains like horseradish-crusted salmon and braised wild boar—dishes in which you can taste the quality of the ingredients—cost $18 to $29. The best deal, as is often the case, is served at lunch: a two-course (appetizer, entree) *prix fixe* for $18, served from 11:30am to 4pm.

WHY YOU'RE HERE: WINERIES

The fact is, you could tour wineries for months. In Napa County alone, there are some 100 wineries to visit. So don't approach winery circuits the way you might the great museums of Paris or the rides at Disneyland. You can't hit everything, so don't try. The key is to find places that deliver the experience that you want. And that experience may be only partly about the flavor of the wine. Flavor is highly

Getting from Winery to Winery

The most important tool for a day or week of wine tasting is a good map. They're not too hard to find, since they're distributed at restaurants, wineries, and anyplace tourists are likely to tread. Get one that has all the wineries labeled, because sometimes a place is located off a main road and is only easily locatable with help. Also look for a list of all the county's wineries, because that way you can take stock of the smaller, family-run places that may require you to phone ahead to visit. It's typical rivalry: Both regions produce their own maps, leaving off their neighbor completely. For Sonoma, my favorite map for its ease of use is *The Official Visitors Map* put out by **Sonoma County Tourism Bureau** (☎ 800/576-6662; www.sonomacounty.com). For Napa, there are downloadable maps at www.napavalley.org, the site run by the Napa Valley Conference & Visitors Bureau. Its office in Napa (1310 Napa Town Center, Napa; ☎ 707/226-7459) is full of brochures. Don't believe at first glance the prices for accommodations that are quoted on either of those tourism sites. I usually find that, in reality, they're as much as 40% higher, and in periods of leaner visitation, you can often talk innkeepers *down* off the posted rates, too.

If you can't download maps before you arrive, don't fret, because they're distributed widely and for free. Also check out the brochure "Visitors Guide from the Sonoma Valley Visitors Bureau" (453 1st St. E., Sonoma; ☎ 866/996-1090; www.sonomavalley.com). It lists winery after winery and their entry policies and is published by Preiser Key; they want you to spend more than $12 to have them mail you a booklet, but in truth, it's given away for free all over the place once you arrive.

Besides that essential winery map, you'll also need discipline. It's easy to get pretty drunk during a wine-tasting day, even if you think you're not having much, which would only be your problem if you didn't have to also drive a car. That's why all wineries keep a little spittoon on the bar that's meant for you to use. Don't gulp down wine—taste it in little sips and, if you want, spit it out. (Frankly, you'll rarely see anyone use the spittoons—wineries take precautions not to over-serve you instead—but they're there.) If you drink too much, which is unlikely given the small shots of wine each place doles out, call Vern's Taxi (☎ 707/938-5885). There are companies in San Francisco that, for hundreds of dollars, will drive you around the area in a limo, but coming here for just one day, as you'd have to do including commute times, is no way to get to know it and to kick back to enjoy the afternoon with a drink or meal, which is half the appeal. Most of those programs only take you to the most touristy places, although you can pay even more money to customize some tours. It seems to me to be a high price to pay just to be able to drink, especially since you can buy any wine you see for home consumption.

Wine Country Wineries & Attractions

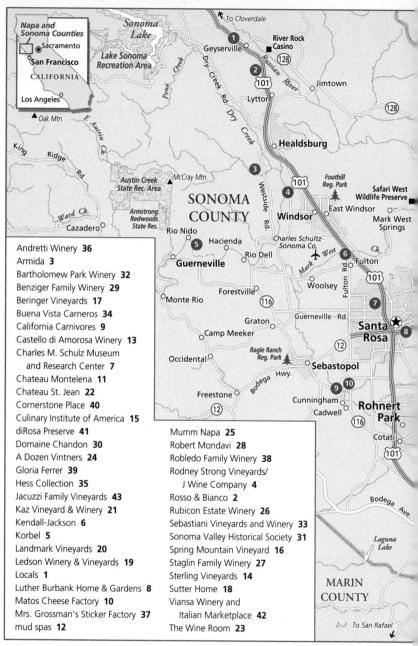

Napa and Sonoma Counties

Sacramento
San Francisco
CALIFORNIA
Los Angeles

▲ Oak Mtn.

Sonoma Lake

Lake Sonoma Recreation Area

To Cloverdale

Geyserville

River Rock Casino

128

Jimtown

101

Lytton

Russian River

Healdsburg

128

King
Ridge
Rd.

E. Austin Ck.

Ward Ck.

Austin Creek State Rec. Area

▲ McCray Mtn.

Armstrong Redwoods State Res.

Cazadero

Rio Nido

SONOMA COUNTY

Westside Rd.

Foothill Reg. Park

Safari West Wildlife Preserve

East Windsor

Windsor

Mark West Springs

Charles Schultz-Sonoma Co.

Hacienda

Rio Dell

Guerneville

Mark West Ck.

Fulton

101

Forestville

Woolsey

116

Monte Rio

Graton

Guerneville Rd.

Santa Rosa

★

Camp Meeker

12

8

Occidental

Ragle Ranch Reg. Park

Fulton Rd.

Bodega Hwy.

Sebastopol

Freestone

Cunningham

9 10

Rohnert Park

12

Cadwell

116

Cotati

101

Bodega Ave.

Laguna Lake

MARIN COUNTY

To San Rafael

Andretti Winery **36**
Armida **3**
Bartholomew Park Winery **32**
Benziger Family Winery **29**
Beringer Vineyards **17**
Buena Vista Carneros **34**
California Carnivores **9**
Castello di Amorosa Winery **13**
Charles M. Schulz Museum and Research Center **7**
Chateau Montelena **11**
Chateau St. Jean **22**
Cornerstone Place **40**
Culinary Institute of America **15**
diRosa Preserve **41**
Domaine Chandon **30**
A Dozen Vintners **24**
Gloria Ferrer **39**
Hess Collection **35**
Jacuzzi Family Vineyards **43**
Kaz Vineyard & Winery **21**
Kendall-Jackson **6**
Korbel **5**
Landmark Vineyards **20**
Ledson Winery & Vineyards **19**
Locals **1**
Luther Burbank Home & Gardens **8**
Matos Cheese Factory **10**
Mrs. Grossman's Sticker Factory **37**
mud spas **12**

Mumm Napa **25**
Robert Mondavi **28**
Robledo Family Winery **38**
Rodney Strong Vineyards/ J Wine Company **4**
Rosso & Bianco **2**
Rubicon Estate Winery **26**
Sebastiani Vineyards and Winery **33**
Sonoma Valley Historical Society **31**
Spring Mountain Vineyard **16**
Staglin Family Winery **27**
Sterling Vineyards **14**
Sutter Home **18**
Viansa Winery and Italian Marketplace **42**
The Wine Room **23**

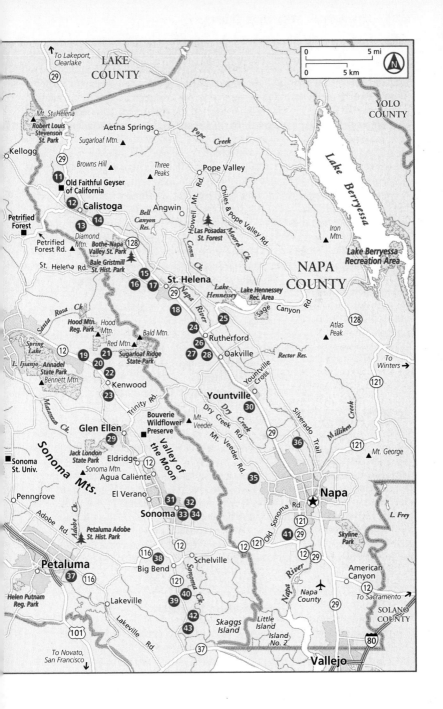

subjective matter, after all, and what I like will not necessarily please even the person standing next to me. That's why, in the pages that follow, I don't spend much time discussing the quality of the wine in each place. I think roaming the wineries, tasting what's on offer, and deciding on your favorite is half the fun of a trip to Wine Country, so I'll let you draw your own conclusions. It's perfectly possible to enjoy a trip to the region without knowing a thing about wine (although it's hard to come away from one without a little bit of knowledge and appreciation) and it's even possible to have a blast without ever tasting a single drop of *vino*.

If that's true, why name any wineries at all? The places I've chosen to highlight possess that extra something that makes them fun or pleasant places to be. Some of them have terrific views, and some have an unusual or rich history, some have exceptionally affordable wines, some have excellent art displays, and some provide the better tours in the region. But there are literally hundreds of wineries in the region, so by no means do I consider my list exhaustive, and by no means should any interested tourist, if he's into visiting wineries, stop with the places that I name here. Like restaurants, wineries are a matter of personal choice, so you should ask everyone you meet which wineries you should go to. And take a look at Chapter 12, which has basic information on the most popular varietals in Wine Country, how to taste wine and more.

And don't feel pressured! Remember that most casual tourists, particularly ones who fly into the Bay Area and can't carry back lots of luggage, don't necessarily go to wineries to purchase wine—although plenty of people do buy bottles at the places that strike their fancy—they go mostly for the atmosphere. So don't feel like you have to buy any wine at all. You don't. That said, it's a lot harder to find free tastings than it used to be because of the number of freeloading, *vino*-guzzling tourists who come and depart without buying a thing.

SONOMA COUNTY

One of the busier wineries in Sonoma due to its long history and easy-to-reach location right off the main town square, **Sebastiani Vineyards and Winery** (389 4th St. E., Sonoma; ☎ 407/933-3230; www.sebastiani.com; daily 10am–5pm) has been run by the same family for four generations, and is extremely tourist savvy. That means it's not a terribly rustic or adorable place, and the old men who lead the indoor winery tours could use a few lessons in theatricality. A trolley tour goes around the grounds (which are somewhat industrial) at 11am, 1pm, and 3pm, but only when the weather is good because the vehicles are open-air. But the well-oiled machinery of this place might make it a good first stop for nervous newbies—just let yourself be carried along and you'll start to get the hang of how winery tours

Timing Your Tastings

Try to get a head start on your day; most wineries open to the public at 10 or 11am (they aren't always reliable about this, so it pays to call ahead), and serve their last by 4:30 or 5pm. Unless I specify otherwise, listed wineries don't require advance reservations.

work without feeling much pressure to interact or purchase. One tasting (a chardonnay or a merlot) is free, and then you pay $5 for three more. Consider it the big dog of Sonoma.

Grapes have been planted on this property since the 1830s, and in 1857, Hungarian nobleman Agoston Haraszthy took over the 833 acres of land in one of his several attempts to establish winemaking in California; he used European cuttings. That original parcel of land, buried back in the woods and of a different character than the wide-open English topography common elsewhere, has been split into **Bartholomew Park Winery** ★ (1000 Vineyard Lane, Sonoma; ☎ 707/ 935-9511; www.bartpark.com; daily 11am–4:30pm) and Buena Vista next door (see below). The vineyards are certified organic. Take-away food isn't for sale here, but the property includes some good hiking trails over the hill above the town. The winery, which is now owned by a trust, maintains a good (but usually unpatronized) museum about the history of winemaking in Sonoma and Carneros, the microclimate that this winery falls into. My favorite exhibit is the set of stereoptic images taken by Eadweard Muybridge in 1872, when the area was rural in the extreme. But it's also hard to forget this little tidbit about the adventurous Mr. Haraszthy: He was probably eaten by a crocodile in Nicaragua in 1869. I'd have stayed in Wine Country.

For those interested in the history and origins of winemaking in Sonoma, also be sure you visit **Buena Vista Carneros** ★ (18000 Old Winery Rd., Sonoma; ☎ 707/ 938-1266; www.buenavistacarneros.com; daily 10am–5pm), where the buildings actually date to Haraszthy's age. This isn't a place to buy food, but it's a lovely setting for picnics—a creek, a stone bridge, leafy trees, and rustic stone buildings. Upstairs in the tasting room, there's a brief self-guided history tour that tells much of the same story as the museum at Bartholomew Park. Tastings start at $5 for four, and bottles at $22. Don't neglect the old wine vault, which Chinese laborers carved into the hill; you can't tour it, but you can peer in.

One of the best historical tours is at **Korbel** ★★★ (13250 River Rd., Guerneville; ☎ 707/924-7000; www.korbel.com; May–Sept daily 9am–5pm, Oct–Apr daily 9am–4:30pm), the best-selling premium champagne maker in America that, for reasons that are still not entirely clear to me, claims it is permitted to call itself a champagne maker (usually only wineries in the Champagne region of France may do so) and does not call itself a maker of "sparkling wine" (as most other wineries have to). It's been doing it here since 1882, started by a Czech cigar-box maker who got in trouble back home for political unrest. His mom snuck him out of prison by smuggling civilian clothes under her skirts during a visit. That story is interesting enough, but the place is full of stuff like that. For example, the cleared area in front of the work buildings was once the site of the train line to San Francisco, 70 miles south, and 50-minute tours of the property start in the old railway station. Call them whistle-stop tours, then: The old winery is now a history center, with lots of period winemaking implements and photographs, including some fascinating snaps of the property when it was full of redwood stumps. (They called Guerneville "Stumptown" then. There are none left.) Guides keep things witty and fresh, even if some of the language is overblown in that giggle-worthy Wine Country fashion, but you'll learn a lot about the tools and the process of champagne making wrapped in a mini-history of the area. They run tours every hour on the hour from 10am to 3pm in winter, or every 45 minutes in summer, from 10am to 3:45pm. From mid-April to mid-October, Tuesday through Sunday at 11am, 1pm, and 3pm, there's also a rose-garden tour of more than 250 varieties of roses, many of them antiques planted by the first Czech immigrants. Interestingly, although 1.3 million cases a year are made here, there are only eight people working in the factory, which probably means your tour will outnumber them. There's also a little deli and market where sandwiches and salads cost $7.50—not bad.

If your pockets are nearly empty and you lack for activities, this smaller vineyard, which has set up a few things for skinflints to do, is for you. Damaris Deere Etheridge, an heir to the John Deere fortune, is one of the patrons of **Landmark Vineyards** (101 Adobe Canyon Rd., Kenwood; ☎ 707/833-0218; www.landmark wine.com; daily 10:30am–4:30pm), which explains the bright green tractors sitting in places where you might think they shouldn't. In addition to the free tastings, which come with a souvenir glass, there's a small pond where catch-and-release bass fishing is allowed. The winery will lend you a rod. What's more, it will let you borrow equipment for its "Vinolympics," a collection of pastimes such as horseshoes, croquet, volleyball, and bocce ball. Remember that if you avail yourself of these activities, it's customary to buy a bottle or a few glasses of their wine in repayment. The gravel-lined courtyard isn't much for picnics, but **Sugarloaf Ridge State Park** (2605 Adobe Canyon Rd., Kenwood; ☎ 707/833-5712; call for hours; free), with about 25 miles of hiking and horseback-riding trails, is about a mile farther down the road that passes the winery.

It looks like some guy's house because it is: **Kaz Vineyard & Winery** ★★★ (233 Adobe Canyon Rd., Kenwood; ☎ 877/833-2536; www.kazwinery.com; Fri–Mon 11am–5pm; tastings $5). Richard "Kaz" Kasmier makes only 60 barrels a year, but he does it with care and with 10 times fewer sulfites than his competitors. Some say that you really need more sulfites to balance out the flavor, but the many people who are made ill by sulfite-heavy wines will find his efforts useful. His winery is strongly family oriented—the swing set on his property is for his grandkids, but he encourages any visiting shorty to play on it, and to feed the fish in the koi pond out back. Kaz doesn't take the area's pretentiousness very seriously; when I first called to ask if his winery was open to visitors, I was told, "Yes, but only if you're the right *kind* of visitor." They were kidding, of course, a dry wit made even clearer by the amusing names of his wines: Say "Rah," Red Said Fred, and Moo Vedra among them. Tastings are $5 for six. You'll find it a little down the turn-off from Route 12 where you'll also find Landmark Vineyards.

The facility at **Ledson Winery & Vineyards** (7335 Sonoma Hwy./Rte. 12, Kenwood; ☎ 707/537-3810; www.ledson.com; daily 10am–5pm), though built to imitate an old French Normandy mansion that looks like a house but isn't (it hosts lots of weddings, though), is too perfect in that way that gives away its recent construction. The building makes me think of a mansion where a dating reality show might be shot. It's still beautiful and surely cost a lot, with carved wood ceilings and a foyer that will drop you in your tracks. There's a small garden in back where you can nibble on the cheeses and other light snacks on sale along with the pottery and whatnot. The winery is so small-scale, it's not distributed to retail stores, so this is your chance to get a few bottles. Five-glass tastings are $5 to $15, with whites being cheapest; you'll have had one full glass by the end. The winery also runs a six-room hotel charging $400 a night. As if!

Two weeks before my last visit to this winery, I was sipping a **Chateau St. Jean** (8555 Sonoma Hwy./Rte. 12; ☎ 707/833-4134; www.chateaustjean.com; daily 10am–5pm) in the Caribbean aboard Cunard's luxury *Queen Victoria* ship. That says more about the quality of the wine than about me, by the way. The building, set back from the main road, is signified by a cupola and looks at first like it might be a country boarding school. When you first enter, the regular wines are to the left, and the pricier ($15/5 tastes) reserve selections are to the right. If you go online ahead and have a printer, you can get a two-for-one tasting pass (normally $10/5 tastes). A limited selection of cheeses, meats, and chocolates are also sold, but mostly the store peddles books and gifts. At press time, winery tours were in flux as the owners tried to figure out how to accommodate guests in wheelchairs. Garden tours of the grounds' formal greenery, planted in 2000, are held daily at 11am and 2pm, but call ahead to make sure. Also make sure you say the name of the place correctly; it's Jean, as in blue jeans.

If you go to **Kendall-Jackson** (5007 Fulton Rd., Fulton; ☎ 707/571-7500; www.kj.com; daily 10am–5pm) because you've heard of the label, be warned that this French-style chateau, though pretty, is just a showplace. The company's operations are elsewhere, although most of the wines poured here are exclusive to this tasting room. The real reason to come is to tour its garden, which was cultivated by famed English horticulturalist Adrian Bloom. Free, 20-minute tours go at 11am, 1pm, and 3pm daily in good weather and take in 2½ acres, including a sensory garden and one growing plants destined for the dinner table. Santa Rosa Junior College also operates a Californian viticulture exhibit here, with 16 different trellis systems on display (more than the average person has room for in his brain for). Tastings are $5 for four, but the best bargain is a $25, 40-minute food-and-wine pairing (stuff like chocolate and caviar; not enough for a meal, but satisfying). The compound is pretty, but the whoosh of Highway 101 is audible throughout. The winery also runs a small tasting room in the center of Healdsburg (337 Healdsburg Ave., Healdsburg; ☎ 707/433-7102), but the Fulton location is where you're able to picnic.

Benziger Family Winery ★★ (1883 London Ranch Rd., Glen Ellen; ☎ 888/490-2739; www.benziger.com; tours daily 11:15am and 2:15pm) offers one of the better tours: a $15 tram run that concludes with four tastings (sorry, tours don't come cheaper if you don't want wine). This all-organic, sustainable winery is doing things right, and it's fun to see how they go about making good wine without despoiling the land. In winter, sheep wander the property, eating the grass around the vines (when grapes are going, said our guide, "they can't be trusted"). All organic waste is recycled, and the winery even runs an "insectary" where beneficial bugs are encouraged to breed. The tram tour whisks you about to show the general layout of the property, which occupies a microclimate specific to its valley, and takes you into wine caves that are some 70 feet under the hillside; among the racks of French and American barrels, it's in the mid-60s all the time. You'll also hear about the *cooperage* (barrel making), although you won't see a demonstration. All in all, it's one of the most well-rounded tours on the market, and something about the family-run facility, or maybe its idealism, doesn't make you feel like you're being herded from site to site.

The family that owns **Gloria Ferrer** ★ (23555 Arnold Dr./Hwy. 121, Sonoma; ☎ 707/933-1917; www.gloriaferrer.com; daily 10am–5pm) is powerful in

Catalonia, Spain, and at this, their 17th property, they're not doing too shabbily either; there are 210 acres here and another 125 acres 3 miles up the road. The focus here is the $10 tour, usually daily at 1pm, which takes about a half-hour and finishes with two tastings. It's worth taking, because you'll see its fifth-mile of dark, moody wine caves—55,000 bottles spend 6½ years in there, waiting for a party. Beyond that, a flight of pinot noir is $8 and a flight of sparkling wines is $15. Bottles are mostly under $40, and some are under $20. The champagne grapes for sparkling wine are harvested around mid-August, earlier than many other types; merlot comes last, in October. Unfortunately, there's a dairy farm next door, so when the wind shifts and comes from the north, the fragrance changes slightly.

The quiet **Robledo Family Winery** ★★★ (21901 Bonness Rd., Sonoma; ☎ 707/939-6903; www.robledofamilywinery.com; visits 10am–5pm by appointment) is one of the great personal success stories of the area. The family patriarch came to America from Michuacuan, Mexico, in 1968 and worked as a laborer for the Christian Brothers, respected winemakers, before working his way up, bit by bit, to finally owning his own spread. There are "live barrels" in the tasting room, which means they're full of aging wine, and the smell throughout the former dairy barn is marvelous. They don't do tours, but because one of Mr. Robledo's kids is usually on duty and not many tourists come through, you're bound to have a truly interesting and possibly inspiring conversation. Tastings are $5, and bottles, which you can't buy anywhere else, start at $16. I love the fact that tour buses are highly unlikely to come through here and that it's a place where you'll really get the story from locals with a fascinating tale to tell. Make sure you meet Zorro, the fat, friendly Chihuahua. This winery received a huge honor in early 2008 when Mexican president Felipe Calderón, on the first visit to the region by any Mexican president ever, chose Robledo and no other winery for an appearance. He, too, is from Michuacuan.

When you drive into **Rosso & Bianco** ★★ (300 Via Archimedes, Geyserville; ☎ 707/857-1400; www.rossobianco.com), you pass through a triumphal arch that says FRANCIS FORD COPPOLA PRESENTS. Yes, this is the winery owned by the legendary director, and the experience here is as much about his movies as his wine. Here, you'll find a glass case full of his awards, including several Oscars (such as the ones he won for *The Godfather*), two Golden Globes, and two Directors Guild of America awards. You'll also see a giant bamboo cage used as a prop in *Apocalypse Now*. The twice-daily tour (12:30pm, 2:30pm; 45 min.) is a good deal; for $15, you see the vineyard, learn about the vintner's grape philosophy, pop into the barrel room where you taste wine right out of barrels, and wind up with a sampling of some reserve wines. Even without the tour, tastings are free (for 3 pours). This is also one of the few wineries where you'll find picnic tables that are actually in the vineyards rather than in some area by a parking lot or something like that. The winery's cafe has an outdoor patio with a terrific view of forests, mountains, and vineyards—one of the better settings around. The food's not bad, either, particularly for brunch or lunch, when pastas and fish go for around $15. Even the shop is a little more interesting (and down-to-earth) than the average; copies of his favorite movies on DVD are sold, as are copies of *Zoetrope: All-Story,* his omnibus fiction magazine that attracts submissions from some of the best living American writers. Add to all this the fact that the staff is more welcoming than at many no-name places, and I have to say that Rosso &

Bianco, despite the vanity venture, is one of my favorites wineries to visit. Although Rubicon, in Napa (another Coppola property), has a longer history and is certainly as pretty as a coffee-table book, it charges $25 to get in. This place is free, and it also gives you glimpses at some movie memorabilia. Another boon: It's yards off the 101 (but not close enough for its pollution), making this a top choice for people who hate navigating country roads. It's under renovation until 2009, so one or two elements of this review may not be up and running when you visit.

Some of the best views at any winery in the region can be had at **Viansa Winery and Italian Marketplace** ✱ (25200 Arnold Dr./Hwy. 121, Sonoma; ☎ 800/ 995-4740; www.viansa.com; daily 11am–4pm), atop a hill south of Sonoma. Sure, it's a Disneyfied version of a Tuscan estate, made to look old, but there may be few places better suited to a picnic with a supreme panorama of vivid green hills, neighboring vineyards, and even a slice of the Bay. Tastings of its Italian varietal wines—its specialty—are $5 for four glasses, and tours are $10, but they're mostly historical and not about the process. Intelligently, the owners have placed plenty of picnic tables outside, where you can watch the birds of prey circling the valley below at eye level. And the deli sells a selection of foods you'd actually want to eat, including $3 risotto cakes, $3 baguettes, and cheese and salads for $7.

Next door, at the bottom of the same hill, **Jacuzzi Family Vineyards** (24724 Arnold Dr./Hwy. 121; ☎ 707/931-7575; www.jacuzziwines.com; daily 10am–5:30pm) is equally theatrical, but for different reasons. Here, the grounds are done up with the bombast of rustic Italian stone manse; little surprise, since it's based on the Jacuzzi family home in Italy. Tastings are free, and although there's no wine production on the premises, which are just for show, the winery does own vineyards around the area, and daily at 11am, 1pm, and 3pm, there's a production tour of a facility across the street. A separate part of the shop area is dedicated to fancy olive oil, mostly by local maker The Olive Press; squeeze some out of a soap-style dispenser and dip a little bread in to taste. Some oils are made here; peer through the glass window at the back to see if anyone's busy today. In the piazza-style courtyard, Italian opera is gently piped in, and inside the church-like events hall, which is flanked by two grapes-carrying figures, there's a triptych that came from a cathedral in Lyon, France (mind you, it's not very old). All of this is brought to you by the family that brought you the trademarked spa tub (still doing their bit for romance, I see), and the shop carries lots of vanity products such as books dedicated to their self-celebration.

You'll need to bring a few supplies to **Armida** ✱✱✱ (2201 Westside Rd., Healdsburg; ☎ 707/433-2222; www.armida.com; daily 11am–5pm)—meaning a camera for the fab view and some food to eat on its fab patio. People come from miles around—at least, people in the know do—to sit out on its generous wooden deck, which overlooks a man-made reedy pond and an excellent vista beyond. There, you can sit in the sun or in the shade, eat whatever you've brought, and hang out for as long as you like. The winery just asks that you only drink their wine on property. (If you don't, as they explain it, "it upsets our dog.") The tasting center, for its part, is relaxed and non-aggressive, and the winemakers don't take the scene too seriously; one of its wines is called PoiZin (as in "the wine to die for"—they must also mean it's a budget-killer, since it's $90/bottle) and the wine club is called Wino. There's a list of six wines that are available to taste for free, or pay another $10 to try its specialty and limited-release wines. It sells a few

Wine Clubs & Your Budget

At nearly every winery you visit, there will be two sets of prices, and often, two sets of pouring facilities. One will be for walk-in visitors, and the other for members of its "wine club." This is simply a fancy mechanism for drumming up guaranteed business. Club members usually "subscribe" to receive a certain amount of wine each year. Membership can get you discounts on wine, in part because you'll be buying by the case. Obviously, this isn't an arrangement you'll want to enter into at many wineries, especially since you have to pay shipping costs, so before you sign on the dotted line, make sure you *love* that winery. I mean, really *lurrrrve* it. For wineries without distribution connections to liquor stores, and there are a lot of them, clubs may be the only way to secure some bottles on a regular basis without a fuss.

Just so you're warned, most wineries are only permitted by law to ship wine to Alaska, California, Colorado, Florida, Hawaii, Idaho, Illinois, Iowa, Michigan, Minnesota, Missouri, Nebraska, Nevada, New Hampshire, New Mexico, New York, North Carolina, North Dakota, Oregon, South Carolina, Texas, Vermont, Virginia, Washington, West Virginia, and Wisconsin.

Domaine Chandon (p. 249) is one of the few places where you might actually consider casually joining the wine club, because some of varieties of membership are free but still grant you discounts on purchased wine. In fact, if you know you want to buy a case of something anywhere, look into joining the place's membership club (just about everyone runs one), and because if it's free, you may save cash.

cheeses and salamis, but in truth, you'll want to bring your own nibbles, and they don't mind if you do. There are no tours (the company is too small), but Armida (Ar-*meed*-a) also sells a savvy line of Ed Hardy–style, skateboarder-ready souvenir clothing. Locals clearly come here to hang out on weekends; on one recent visit, I watched a mom and her son, who was around 10, play with the bocce balls on the course below the patio. It's a warm-hearted atmosphere without a slice of pretension. Meanwhile, folks chatted, accompanying dogs smiled, and a general sense of good vibrations prevailed. Most of their products aren't as expensive as PoiZin and cost $19 to the upper $30s.

What sets **Rodney Strong Vineyards** (11455 Old Redwood Hwy., Healdsburg; ☎ 800/678-4763; www.rodneystrong.com; daily 10am–5pm with tours at 11am and 3pm) apart is the fact that it's housed in a sort of segmented circular 1970 building that more or less carves off different functions of winemaking into different wings. In its time, it was a bold experiment in industrial architecture, but as such things often are, it was quickly outgrown by success. Visitors make a self-guided circuit in a loop of the various aspects (except the "crush pad," which was moved away years ago), inhaling the warm aroma let off by the wine holding tanks. The grounds here aren't so interesting—more like a corporate park—but the mode of touring is different from the Wine Country norm. Two tastings are free, and beyond that, you'll pay $5 for four—a good bargain. Tours of the rest of the grounds are also free (11am, 3pm), but in winter or in bad weather they may not go regularly, so you'll want to book ahead. In summer (June–Sept), the winery presents a series of outdoor concerts, but you'll need tickets; check online for the lineup.

Exactly next door to Rodney Strong (you could walk, but no one does), you'll find **J Wine Company** (11447 Old Redwood Hwy., Healdsburg; ☎ 707/431-3646; www.jwine.com; daily 11am–5pm), another arresting early-'70s concrete architectural experiment that fans of the genre might enjoy. The wine here is expensive, tastings start at $10, and its Bubble Room is just silly ($55 flights served with foie gras, paddlefish caviar, gnocchi with truffle emulsion, and other trappings of culinary pretension). But the tour here has a point of difference. It's free, and it takes in one of only two *coquard* presses in America; this piece of equipment, established in France's Champagne region, is one of the gentlest grape presses in existence. The press is enclosed, so it doesn't put on a show. The winery also makes a pear liqueur, which being a distilled spirit cannot be sold online, so this is the place to try it and take some home.

NAPA COUNTY

The oldest continuously operating winery in Napa Valley (established in 1876) is **Beringer Vineyards** (2000 Main St., St. Helena; ☎ 707/967-4412; www.beringer.com; May 30–Oct 23 daily 10am–6pm, Oct 24–May 29 daily 10am–5pm), which is right off the main road and easy to duck into. This highly tourist-savvy winery supplies visitors, who come by the busload in summer, with wine education but not really a relaxing day out, since there's no picnicking. The grounds are beautifully tended, though. The Info Center's back wall is lined with placards announcing the day's myriad tour and tasting times as if it's a day at the zoo, which, during crazy high season, it might as well be since the place is right on the main road, Highway 29. The 30-minute "Introducing Beringer" tour (usually 10:30am, 2pm, 2:45pm), gives you some light wine-aging tutorials and a vineyard history, costs $15, and includes three tastings and a glass to keep. Upgrade to the "Taste of Beringer" for another $5 and you get an hour's tour with more information and four tastes (11am, noon, 1pm, 3:40pm). This place sells a variety of other tour and tasting permutations, too, but I have no evidence that the more expensive ones have any appeal other than to wine snobs. All the gifts here are about 50% more expensive than in other places; I saw a set of glasses here for $20 that I also saw at Ledson for $11. Fortunately, you'll get a 20% discount on everything on the same day you take a tour. *Tip:* Several tasting areas line the warehouses that make up the winery; tastings are cheapest in the one marked OLD BOTTLING ROOM, where full bottles are $20 to $40; the one marked BERINGER WINERIES is more for pricier reserve bottles.

Despite the fact the label has become a supermarket titan, the operators of **Sutter Home** ★ (277 St. Helena Hwy., St. Helena; ☎ 800/967-4663; www.sutterhome.com; daily 10am–5pm) like to pretend they're still just an aw-shucks family winery. You could almost believe it from this pretty layout. The perfumed garden dates to 1874 and, in season, blooms with 100 varieties of roses and 40 of daylilies. There's a camellia tree that was planted in 1876, and if the palm trees seem odd, you should know they were brought from the Canary Islands in the mid-20th century. The wine is dirt cheap—bottles go from $5 to $8, and four tastings are free. There are a few ports and sherries to try, too. I imagine this label, known as a drinkable wine but not an award winner, takes a lot of flak from the boutique vintners in the region, which may account for how friendly the customer-service staff is here. You can benefit from that overcompensation.

On the flip side of Napa cachet is the swanky **Robert Mondavi** ★★ (Hwy. 29, Oakville; ☎ 888/766-6328; www.robertmondaviwinery.com; daily 10am–5pm), started by the acknowledged pioneer of modern-day California winemaking who died at 94 in 2008. There's a sign off the visitor's parking lot directing trucks for GRAPE DELIVERY—if your winery needs one of those signs, you're not growing everything yourself on-site, and you're big. The grounds are laid out like a preppy college campus you wish your parents had the money to send you to. As you drive up, you're greeted by a handsome bronze-and-glass-mosaic statue of St. Francis by Beniamino Bufano, and from there, the Mission-style buildings open up into a view of the vineyards and the hills beyond. This may be the most theatrical winery that also makes wines that connoisseurs care about. Check into the Visitors Center, to the left, for a highlight history of the winery and to arrange a tour. There are hourly 80-minute tours ($25) from 10am to 4pm, and the noon tour also accommodates kids who are too young to drink but older than 13 ($10). You can't roam the vineyards, although you'll be sorely tempted to, but you can stroll around the building; to the right, you'll encounter a collection of more chunky Bufano works; my favorite is the walrus. Benny Bufano was famous for chopping off his trigger finger and mailing it to President Woodrow Wilson rather than fight in World War I. His digital protest didn't seem to affect the power of his art. The tasting rooms generally offer about 10 types that are exclusive to the winery, and the Appellation Room charges $10 for 3 tastings. All summer long, the winery hosts outdoor concerts on its grounds, something it's been doing since 1969, 3 years after Mondavi kicked off Napa's post-Prohibition rise. It's wise to have tickets in hand, since big names like Lena Horne and Tony Bennett have been lured in the past.

Just when people begin to accept that Napa has its own American identity quite distinct from the European vineyards, someone goes and builds something like this, which fetishizes Europe in a way that would embarrass a Continental. The exuberant, over-the-top European pretensions of some of the area's landlords is on no more immoderate display than at the sublime **Castello di Amorosa Winery** (4045 N. St. Helena Hwy., Calistoga; ☎ 707/942-8200; www.castellodi amorosa.com; Dec–Feb 15 daily 9:30am–5pm, Feb 16–Nov daily 9:30am–6pm), a fake medieval castle—completed 2007—of 107 rooms, 121,000 square feet, a basement dungeon outfitted with antique torture devices, and a 72-foot-long Great Hall with a 22-foot-high coffered ceiling. Its reputation is more for a tourist attraction than for its quality wines, which are only sold here. Entry fees are in place at $10, which includes a tasting, or $5 for the underage. Combined tours and tastings (1hr and 45min) go for $25 weekdays and $30 weekends, reservations required. I guess he's gotta pay for his white elephant somehow. It's no Biltmore or Breakers, but there's nothing else like it around, making it at least worth a drive-by. Its owner, Daryl Sattui, also runs the V. Sattui Winery in St. Helena, which is popular with picnickers.

Hollywood & Vines

Although *Sideways* (2004) is considered the quintessential movie about California winemaking, it was set and shot farther south in the state, around Santa Barbara. However, the 2008 film *Bottle Shock,* about the Judgment of Paris in 1976 led by Chateau Montelena, was shot in the region (mostly, ironically, in Sonoma). It was only the most recent of many flicks that lensed in the area. Hollywood, and Hollywood types, can't seem to get enough of Napa and Sonoma. A sampling:

The 1961 Elvis movie *Wild in the Country* (1961) was shot in and around Calistoga and the Victorian-style **Ink House** hotel (1575 St. Helena Hwy., St. Helena; ☎ 707/963-3890; www.ila-chateau.com/inkhouse; from $179/night). Its French Room still has the bed he slept in.

Spring Mountain Vineyard (2805 Spring Mountain Rd., St. Helena; ☎ 877/769-4637 or 707/967-4188; www.springmtn.com) stood in for *Falcon Crest* on the 1980s primetime soap opera of the same name. These days, it doesn't encourage visits from outsiders, and you have to make reservations and pony up $25 per person to get in.

You might have seen photos of **Staglin Family Winery** (☎ 707/944-0477; www.staglinfamily.com; reservations required to obtain address; closed weekends) in the background at the weddings of both singer Christina Aguilera and *American Idol* mastermind Simon Fuller. The organic winery's privacy and its Earth-first principles have made it popular with entertainers.

Petaluma was where the kids trawled Petaluma Boulevard in their cars in *American Graffiti* (1973), and the city's still getting mileage out of the memories. The **Petaluma Visitor Center** (210 Hwy. 116, Petaluma; ☎ 707/769-0429; www.visitpetaluma.com) provides a tour of the locations on its website.

The idyllic suburbs of the thriller *Scream* (1996) were played by Santa Rosa, Healdsburg, and Sonoma; the Sonoma Community Center on East Napa Street played the serial killer-afflicted high school. Hitchcock also shot in Santa Rosa for *Shadow of a Doubt* (1943) and, more recognizably, in Bodega Bay for *The Birds* (1963).

In opposition to Francis Ford Coppola's visitor-friendly estate in Sonoma, he also owns **Rubicon Estate Winery** (1991 St. Helena Hwy., Rutherford; ☎ 800/782-4266; www.rubiconestate.com), founded as Inglenook in 1880 and now restored with *Godfather* money to feel like some movie director's fantasy of what the good life is like. This glorious chateau, the centerpiece of 235 acres, is a paragon of over-the-top fabulosity—grand staircase, hardwoods from Belize, and a $25 fee to enter. It's as pompous and as overblown as, well, a Coppola movie.

Another gimmicky wine visit, but one your camera will love anyway, is **Sterling Vineyards** 😊 ⭐ (1111 Dunaweal Lane, Calistoga; ☎ 800/726-6136; www.sterlingvineyards.com; daily 10:30am–4:30pm), where a $20 aerial tram ($10 for under-21s) takes you to and through some fantastic views over the area. The main building sits on a hill some 300 feet above the valley floor and the parking lot. Obviously, to visit it completely, you'll need to budget plenty of time and go on a clear day. You've got to pay the fee even if you don't want to ride the ram, but the price also includes a tour (self-guided, not narrated) and a five-wine tasting at your own table. Interesting side note: the bells in the tower used to hang in St. Dunstan's of Fleet Street London, which was destroyed in World War II. There are not a lot of places where kids will be welcomed or engaged in the wine country, but because of the tram, I'd take hard-to-please kids here. Picnicking is allowed.

True wine nuts will have to hit **Chateau Montelena** ⭐ (1429 Tubbs Lane, Calistoga; ☎ 707/942-5105; www.chateaumontelena.com; daily 9:30am–4pm except major holidays and 3rd Sat in May). It was a product from the people behind this winery that, in 1976, won a top honor among white wines at the Judgment of Paris. The basic tasting is $15 for five. If you're deeply interested, set aside 45 minutes for its Library Wine Tasting (10am, 11:30am, 1:30pm, 3pm; $25). This isn't a place well laid out for hordes of casual gawkers, even if the ivy-covered stone-castle-like winery building (built in 1882) is pretty and the Chinese garden and 5-acre pond, Jade Lake, make for a lovely place to sit for a few minutes. The people pouring here (they're in the modern ranch-style building) know their wine, and they're still proud of the victory that put Napa on the serious wine drinker's map. In fact, if you've seen the movie *Bottle Shock* (2008), a retelling of the Judgment of Paris, this is the central winery in that story. Look carefully for the easy-to-miss driveway; as you're driving to the winery, if the road you're on starts giving way to hairpins and ever-climbing altitude, you've gone too far, and you're on a mountain pass.

It looks like it would be a marvelous restaurant, what with a patio overlooking green fields and blue hills in the distance, but no, **Mumm Napa** ⭐ (8445 Silverado Trail, Rutherford; ☎ 800/686-6272; www.mummnapa.com; daily 10am–5pm) doesn't serve food—it's about tastings ($7/full glass, limit 2 per person) and art, and a genteel place to sit with some bubbly, which is what Mumm does best. There are 75-minute tours, but it's of a demonstration vineyard for the method of making sparkling wine (the real plants are off-site)—instead, spend your time in the store, which sells some unusual *flutes* (champagne glasses). Also stroll through the free and well-curated Ansel Adams Gallery, where the theme is arts in nature, and where there are five large windows looking into an aging room full of over a million bottles. Recently, legendary musician Carlos Santana joined with Mumm to create Santana DVX Sparkling Wine, a 50-50-mix of pinot noir and chardonnay.

Another top choice for art lovers is **The Hess Collection** ⭐⭐ (4411 Redwood Rd., Napa; ☎ 707/255-1144; www.hesscollection.com; visitor center daily 10am–5pm), an excellently chosen set of modern art collected by a wealthy Swiss guy, Donald Hess, who normally loans his goodies to top museums. He grants his support for about 20 living artists, saying he'll reassess when they either die or become "well established." Now, I'd say Robert Motherwell (displayed here) is already on the established list, and Francis Bacon's dead, but I see his point, and the stuff he has is arresting, and the way the place mixes winery and high-end art gallery is satisfying.

If you have to choose only one champagne/sparkling wine maker in Napa County, productions don't get more elaborate than **Domaine Chandon** ✗ (1 California Dr., Yountville; ☎ 707/944-2280; www.chandon.com; Nov–Apr daily 10am–6pm, May–Oct Mon–Thurs 10am–6pm, Fri–Sun 10am–7pm), which has its own local radio station, 88.1 FM, to orient you as you drive onto its property. (You don't need it, but it demonstrates what caliber of tourist operation we're dealing with here.) The winery, which focuses on sparkling wines, was founded in 1973 by the French outfit Moët-Hennessy in an effort to make sparkling wine in the French way, called *champenoise*. That means it's just like champagne, even if for tangled winemaking rules, they can't actually call it that. This place is everything a modern champagne palace ought to be; after parking, you cross into the main building, which gives the sense of a conference center, over a stream swimming with ducks, and you'll pass a fascinating field of mushroom sculptures by artist Richard Botto, a local. There's a media room screening a mini-documentary about the place (mostly public relations pap, nothing too informative), tastings are $15 for two to four (depending on which pours you pick) with a flute you take home. Tours cost $10 for 35 minutes, and they're honed to a science based on the number of bus tourists that come through here. The facility was the first in the

---

Picnicking in Napa

Most wineries in Napa County forbid picnickers. But a few don't. Know that it's customary, if not downright required (are you listening, Clos du Val?) to buy a bottle of that vineyard's wine to drink over your lunch. Never bring your own. Check out these properties, not all of which sell food, or just head to Sonoma, where nearly every winery will welcome your basket and your ants:

Chappellet (1581 Sage Canyon Rd., St. Helena; ☎ 707/963-7137; www.chappellet.com; reservations required). Serene view high over the valley.

Clos du Val (5330 Silverado Trail, Napa; ☎ 800/820-1972; www.closduval.com; $5/picnic). Flat vineyards, olive grove.

Cuvaison Estate Wines (4550 Silverado Trail N., Calistoga; ☎ 707/942-2468; www.cuvaison.com). Proto-suburban, like lunch in a garden.

Diamond Oaks (1595 Oakville Grade, Oakville; ☎ 707/948-3000; www.diamond-oaks.com). Midlevel view over the valley.

Rutherford Hill Winery (200 Rutherford Hill Rd., Rutherford; ☎ 707/963-1871; www.rutherfordhill.com). Shaded hillside.

Summers Estate Wines (1171 Tubbs Lane, Calistoga; ☎ 707/942-5508; www.summerswinery.com). A tiled patio in the valley.

V. Sattui Winery (1111 White Lane, St. Helena; ☎ 707/963-7774; www.vsattui.com). Shade trees, 2½ acres of lawn.

The Wino Awards

Of the wineries I write about in this guide, here's how they break down in terms of the experiences they offer.

Best All-Around Tour: Benziger Family Winery (p. 241), an organic, sustainable winery

Best for Wine History Buffs: Chateau Montelena (p. 248)

Best for Over-the-Top Ostentatiousness: Castello di Amorosa Winery (p. 246), a 107-room castle with a stocked dungeon

Best for Champagne: Korbel (p. 239)

Best Place to Hang Out and Enjoy the View: Armida (p. 243), where locals meet, relax, and chat on the patio

Best Place for Movie Buffs: Rosso & Bianco (p. 242), Francis Ford Coppola's winery

Best for Kids: Sterling Vineyards (p. 248), home of the aerial tram tour

area, in 1977, to open a four-star restaurant on its premises, and it's still one of the only ones to have a kitchen serving casual visitors. It's still operating, although dishes at Étoile are $25 and up. Better to visit the tasting room, which overlooks the soothing grounds—an artful mix of lawns, trees, and sculpture—and which serves a few light bites for $7 to $17. Check out the carpeting, which is a clever design that subtly imitates champagne bubbles in gray. Domaine Chandon is something of the McDonald's of posh quaffs; there are also locations in Spain, in Argentina, and outside Melbourne, Australia.

Another made-to-look-old Tuscan-style winery, **Andretti Winery** (4162 Big Ranch Rd., Napa; ☎ 707/261-1717; www.andrettiwinery.com; daily 10am–5pm) is co-owned by racecar driver Mario Andretti and one of his friends, who used to be in charge of Kmart, although the gift shop is remarkably restrained about the celebrity worship and focuses on wine. The winery, in a little grove surrounded by vineyards and flatlands, also comes across as a low-key operation, as if your uncle ran a place and allowed people to come wander around whenever they wanted. Tastings are $10 for four, or $14 for four with a free Andretti tasting glass. No tours are given, but they'll let you wander outside the buildings and check out the eight metal tanks used in winemaking. Strangely, there's a house in the middle of everything—presumably the winemaker's, not Andretti's. Most bottles cost $20 to $35.

GROUP TASTING ROOMS

Not every winery can afford to run a regular tasting room, is located near town, or can employ a hospitality staff. For them, you go to a tasting room that serves all kinds of wine from a variety of wineries. Good ones are scattered around the region.

Samples of 62 wines from 10 wineries are free at **Locals** (Geyserville Ave. at Hwy. 128, Geyserville; ☎ 707/857-4900; daily 11am–6pm; www.tastelocalwines.com), where the favored method is a tasting of wine in flights of similar grapes/wine types, so that visitors can make direct comparisons. (Believe it or not, such a method isn't very common.)

An artsy mini-mall for antiques, wine, and art, **Cornerstone Place** (23570 Hwy. 121, Sonoma; ☎ 707/933-3010; daily 10am–5pm; www.cornerstoneplace.com) hosts five wineries, some sharing a room. My favorite is the ultra-hip **Roshambo,** which was created as a reaction against pretentious wine companies. The tasting room staff is warm and fun. Their wine is gradually becoming famous for putting on an annual "rock-paper-scissors" competition in June. The wine's tasty, too, but you gotta have a gimmick. Cornerstone itself has a good gimmick: a 9-acre garden (closes 4pm) designed by a bunch of envelope-pushing landscape architects, sculptors, garden designers. Sometimes there's a $9 fee (a lot, right?), but when things are quiet, such as on non-summer weekdays, it's free. There's also a cheap and tasty cafe, the **Blue Tree** (☎ 707/935-1681), where sandwiches are along the lines of the Sgt. Pepper, which is turkey and Jack on a warm croissant with strawberry chili jam, for $5.50. It's otherwise hard to find inexpensive meals in this stretch of the county.

The Smothers Brothers (yes, *those* Smothers Brothers) have been producing wine in the region since 1977, and they built the **Wine Room** (9575 Sonoma Hwy./Rte. 12, Kenwood; ☎ 707/833-6131; www.the-wine-room.com; daily 11am–5pm) on an easy-to-find main road. Their wine is known as Remick Ridge, but you can also taste stuff by five other smaller local outfits, including Friendly Dog Winery, Moondance Cellars, and Orchard Station. "Meet the Winemaker" events are commonly scheduled, although Tom and Dick are not usually in attendance; call ahead.

In downtown Napa, where you can walk off a tasting session by window shopping, **Vintner's Collective** (1245 Main St., Napa; ☎ 707/255-7150; www.vintners collective.com; daily 11am–6pm) has a handsome home: an 1875 sandstone building, once a brothel, that has been restored past any previous glory. Some 18 wineries are represented, and the makers often drop by to mingle with potential customers.

One mile north of St. Helena on the main highway, **A Dozen Vintners** (3000 St. Helena Hwy./Rte. 12, St. Helena; ☎ 707/967-0666; daily 10am–5pm; www.adozenvintners.com) delivers exactly what its name promises. Most of the little wineries it represents are from Napa, but there's one from central Sonoma.

Another upscale collective that is geared to casual visitors in that it makes by-the-glass sales a big part of its model, **Wineries of Napa Valley** (1285 Napa Town Center, Napa; ☎ 707/253-9450; www.napavintages.com; Mon–Thurs 11am–6pm, Fri–Sat 10am–7:30pm, Sun 11am–6pm) is a little harder to visit because its location in a downtown shopping mall means you'll probably have to park in a nearby garage. Particularly in late afternoons from Thursday to Sunday, the room often arranges small special events (reserve tastings, cheese pairings) or free canapés.

WHAT TO SEE BEYOND THE WINERIES

There isn't much in the way of historic sights of depth, because most of the attractions are wineries. But there is some fun stuff.

Don't bother with the touristy wine train that traverses Napa County; it's a trap on which you're required to eat their food, and you can't get off and on as you wish (and as would actually be useful).

SIGHTS ON THE DRIVE THERE

It will take about 60 to 90 minutes to go from San Francisco to the heart of Sonoma's town square. Most people take the opportunity to drive over the Golden Gate Bridge itself, on which the major route to the Wine Country, the 101, travels. Try to travel outside of rush hours, because Marin County is full of people who work in the city and who clog the roads at key hours.

An unexpected but wholly original sight just off the 101 on the waterfront in Sausalito, the **Bay Model** ★ (2100 Bridgeway, Sausalito; ☎ 415/332-3871; www.spn. usace.army.mil/bmvc; free admission; Tues–Sat 9am–4pm) is a hangar-like space filled with a working, wet model of the entire Bay Area. Built in 1957 by the U.S. Army Corp of Engineers to help scientists understand the complex patterns of the water currents and the tides, it's capable of duplicating, at a smaller time scale, the way flow works. Buildings aren't represented, but major landmarks such as bridges are identifiable as you walk around the space, which is about the size of two football fields, or 1½ acres. Water, which is shallow throughout, is studded with some 250,000 copper tabs that help re-create known current patterns. The facility, the only one of its kind in the world, hasn't been used for research since 2000, leaving it to educate school groups and the odd visitor about Bay conservation; the gift shop is strong on the subject of ecology. A visit is quite relaxing; many days, you'll be one of the only guests there, and the only sounds in the enormous room will be the faint sound of the water pumps, still working away. The model sits on the site of an important World War II shipbuilding yard, called Marinship (Ma-*rinn*-ship). Tucked away to the left of the exit (don't miss it) is a terrific exhibit, full or artifacts and including a video, that chronicles the yard, where an astonishing 93 ships were built in 3½ wartime years.

Twelve miles north of the Golden Gate and well-marked, **Muir Woods** ★★★ (☎ 415/388-2596; $5 adults over 15; www.nps.gov/muwo; 8am–sunset) is heralded as one of the best forests for admiring redwoods—thousands of them. Teddy Roosevelt himself consecrated it as a National Monument in 1908—with good reason, too: It's the only primordial redwood forest remaining near the city. Of course, it's not just about 350-foot-tall redwoods—you can find Douglas firs, bik-leaf maple, tan-bark oak, and many others, but the mama redwoods, longer across than your dining room table, impress the most. In the 1800s, redwoods were so plentiful here that people thought they'd never run out, and pretty much every single building in San Francisco and beyond was built of the trees, which are the tallest living things on Earth. You could argue that the trees got their revenge on the city, when anything made of them went up in smoke in the fire after the quake of '06, and today, Muir Woods is one of the last groves of the trees (primordial or otherwise) in the area. There are three trails totaling 6 miles, from a half-hour one to one that takes 90 minutes if you take your time. I strongly suggest that you do, because the sense of stillness that you'll find even just a few yards down the well-maintained trails can approach a spiritual experience. If you'll be heading up to Guerneville, in western Sonoma County, you may find that the Armstrong Redwoods State Reserve (p. 254) usually makes for a much more secluded visit; Muir Woods tends to attract large numbers of city dwellers and tourists (some three quarters of a million annually). In summer, Memorial Day to Labor Day, a free shuttle bus runs from the Sausalito Ferry, which means that those without cars can feasibly travel there from town. Schedules are available at http://goldengate.org. If you do go to Muir, avoid it on weekends, when worka-day people throng it and spoil the peace. Also, bring a jacket, because the moist air inside the ecosystem brings fog and temperatures to between 40° and 70°F.

SIGHTS IN NAPA & SONOMA

Some 2,200 works of art are kept on 900 stunning acres, centering on a 35-acre pond, at **diRosa Preserve** ★ (5200 Carneros Hwy./Hwy. 121, Napa; ☎ 707/ 226-5991; www.dirosapreserve.org; gallery Tues–Fri 9:30am–3pm; tours April–Oct Tues–Fri on the hour 10am–1pm, Sat on the hour 10am–noon; free Wed), whose philanthropist owners are dedicated to both nature and, of course, expression. The works here are delightfully fractured, wild, avant-garde experiments, many of them kinetic and every one of them by Bay Area hands and minds. It's gratifying to see someone supporting risky art in any format—Cars hanging from trees? Who'd risk it?—but you have to take exception with the expensive, elitist ticket-ing system: There are three tours offering three levels of access to the grounds, which is sort of a ridiculous concept that even the Louvre doesn't try on visitors, but I think that the $10 "Introductory" version, a 1-hour overview of the high-lights, including the core of the collection, will do almost everyone. Pay up to $5 more, and you can see the diRosas' home and a few more thoroughly sumptuous sculpture gardens. Better yet, spend just $3 and you can enjoy the manageable rotating selection of art in the Gatehouse Gallery without a tour of the grounds, pretty as they are. (All this price quibbling doesn't apply on Wed, when everything is free.) Students of landscaping and architecture won't want to miss it, nor will fans of eccentric contemporary art. Others may leave scratching their heads. But no one departs without sighing over the greenery at least once.

Horticulturalists will also be drawn, or should be, to the **Luther Burbank Home & Gardens** (Santa Rosa Ave. at Sonoma Ave., Santa Rosa; ☎ 707/ 524-5445). The name doesn't ring a bell for most, but gardeners revere him for developing more than 800 new varieties of plants, particularly roses. His old home is now a national historic landmark. The surrounding acre of land, free and open until sunset, is still tended and contains many of his concoctions. His house and the little museum, though, is only open April through October, and tours are conducted by a recording that you call on your cellphone. Downtown Santa Rosa is also confusing to navigate and choked with traffic, so only come here if you intend to pay respects.

Just north of Sonoma Plaza, there's the overlooked **Sonoma Valley Historical Society** (270 1st St. W., Sonoma; ☎ 707/938-1762), a museum stuffed with intriguing artifacts, such as the painted stage curtain from the long-gone Union Hotel (now a modern bank on the southwest of the square), complete with era ads painted onto it. It was found rolled up in a barn. The women in charge of the place are generous and enthused; ask to hear the 1850s Swiss music box and they'll tune it up for you. Not all the exhibits in this museum are labeled, so just ask questions—they love telling tales here.

The Historical Society is my favorite of the attractions a stone's throw from the **Sonoma State Historic Park** (363 3rd St. W., Sonoma; www.parks.gov.ca), which consists of six sites in the same immediate area Three of these sites open regularly (usually daily 10am–5pm, though they close earlier in winter if no one shows up). They are:

- **The Mission** (☎ 707/938-0560), which was built in 1823 as part of a network that stretched up and down the coast; this was the northernmost.
- The adobe-built **Barracks** (☎ 707/939-9420), also on the north side of the main square in Sonoma, which dates to 1840. It garrisoned soldiers in the Mexican General Vallejo's ongoing attempt to put the local Native Americans underfoot. (There's a small museum in both, but truth to tell, it's tough to keep all the names, religions, and national affiliations straight, so you may not want to linger for more than 20 min. or so.)
- A 3-minute drive away, **Vallejo's Home, a.k.a. Lachryma Montis** (☎ 707/938-9559) is the pretty two-story house that the famous general lived in, and it's almost exactly as it was when he was there. There's a case of archaeological finds from the mid-1800s—pipe bits, as usual, plus an 1840 half-dollar, a loss that must have pained its original owner.

A ticket to one of the above three museums will get you into the others on the same day; if I had to pick one, I'd probably go with Vallejo's Home, which, with its many old furnishings, seems to come alive a little more, but maybe that's real-estate envy; the drive along the tree-lined driveway helps a visitor get a sense of why these old-timers chose this green, pleasant region. Try to come on weekends around lunchtime; that's when the docent-led tours tend to occur.

The 805-acre **Armstrong Redwoods State Reserve** ★★★ (☎ 707/869-2015; www.parks.ca.gov; 8am to 1 hr. after sunset; $6/vehicle), 2 miles north of Guerneville, is a place of peace, silence, and very big redwood trees—some of them are more than 300 feet tall and at least 1,400 years old. The moistness of the air means that, when the sunlight does manage to break through the density of the ecosystem, it can draw steam off the bark of the mighty trees, creating a seriously beautiful environment. This is one of the places in Wine County that I most dream about after I return home. Save the entrance fee by parking at the visitor center and walking in. There are a few trails, but overall, it's not busy, so it's often pin-drop quiet, putting it ahead of the larger Muir Woods in my book.

The famous writer's ashes are buried at **Jack London State Historic Park** (2400 London Ranch Rd., Glen Ellen; ☎ 707/938-5216; www.parks.sonoma.net/JLPark. html; Mon–Fri 9:30am–5pm, Sat–Sun noon–4pm; $6/vehicle), where he spent his final years and his wife stayed on afterward. London's study, in the cottage, contains some artwork from his stories and stuff he picked up on his travels, and elsewhere on the property is a ruin of a magnificent house he tried to build—it burned down before it was done. There's an easy half-mile trail through the bucolic surroundings. On weekends, docents show up at 11am or 1pm to give tours. Between this and the shrine to Robert Louis Stevenson over in Napa, this one has more to offer, and the town of Glen Ellen is adorable.

Jack London isn't the only writer to have escaped to this corner of the world. Scotsman Robert Louis Stevenson spent most of his life trying to get away from people and maintain his poor health; in 1879, he wound up here and stayed briefly, when this area was empty. He and his wife honeymooned at Stevenson House at **Robert Louis Stevenson State Park** (Rte. 29, 8 miles north of Calistoga;

Paean to Peanuts

Anyone who loves the *Peanuts* comics and TV shows will spend a few hours in happy absorption at the surprisingly lavish **Charles M. Schulz Museum and Research Center** ★★★ (2301 Hardies Lane, Santa Rosa; ☎ 707/579-4452; Mon–Fri 11am–5pm, Sat–Sun 10am-5pm; $8 adults; $5 seniors, students, and kids; www.schulzmuseum.com). Sparky, as he was called, made ungodly amounts of money off the licensing of his creations, so his estate has the financial wherewithal to burnish his reputation at this two-story facility, which would be worthy of any major artist.

There's lots to see and do at this two-level gallery-cum-library. Of course, there are tons of strips from the entire run of the series—always the original, never copies—and biographical information about Sparky, who died in 2000 (this place opened in 2002). Even more interesting are the many tributes to the strip by other artists, such as a life-size Snoopy made of Baccarat crystal, Christo's *Wrapped Snoopy House,* and a wall mosaic of 3,588 tiles by Yoshitero Otari. The museum preserves Schulz's work room, with its worn drawing board, Higgins ink, and unremarkable book selection. Also fun is the nonstop slate of showings of classic TV specials and movies in a screening room. (Kids will particularly enjoy that, as well as the play area outside.)

But in all honesty, the biggest lesson that I came away with is that *Peanuts* is one seriously depressing strip, a catalogue of human cruelty and misery. The characters are constantly demeaning and insulting each other. (Think I'm crazy? Have a look at some old strips for yourself.) It's fascinating that something as dark became such a mainstream kids' property.

Many visitors don't realize it, but the Schulz experience continues across the street at the Redwood Empire Ice Arena, also known as Snoopy's Home Ice, which Schulz built himself as a gift to Santa Rosa. As random as it may seem to have a Snoopy-themed ice rink, there's a real sense of community here. Public skating costs $9 to $12, including skate rental, but call ahead (☎ 707/546-7147) to find out when the rink will be free, because it's popular with a variety of local clubs and it's usually crawling with kids. It's also closed on Tuesdays in winter. The gift shop next door far surpasses the inventory of the little closet they run in the museum, so make sure you stop here. The canteen at the rink is called the Warm Puppy Café (p. 226), and Sparky used to eat there every day.

☎ 707/942-4575; www.parks.ca.gov; sunrise–sunset). You'll find just a few artifacts from the man, including what are supposedly the last words he ever wrote. It's mostly an undeveloped park with a fire road that affords a good view from atop Mount St. Helena.

Farmer for a Day

Like wineries, the list of farms in the area is long. Check out **FarmTrails.org** and request a map and guide of all the places in the area visitors can buy fresh fruit, vegetables, and meats right where they were produced.

When you drive up to **Matos Cheese Factory** ✹ (3669 Llamo Rd., Santa Rosa; ☎ 707/823-4454), you'll swear you're in the wrong place. Roaming roosters and a dirt road? But the reception is friendly; as you enter the work area, a deafening alarm rings and doesn't stop until the door's closed again. A lady comes out from the back and immediately slices you a sizable hunk of St. George Cheese, for free. You don't even have to ask. It's light, moist, and full of little holes, but overall the effect is Havarti-like. It's good stuff, ideal for snacking as you make the rounds at the wineries, and it's just $5 a pound. This is a very unusual food provider, and a fun stop to make.

Three fascinating factory tours aren't located too far away: Jelly Belly (p. 140) and Anheuser-Busch (p. 141) are both about a half-hour's drive east; they're covered in chapter 6. Same with Six Flags, a nearby amusement park (p. 131).

There's also **Mrs. Grossman's Sticker Factory** (kids) (3810 Cypress Ave., Petaluma; ☎ 800/429-4549; www.mrsgrossmans.com; $3; closed weekends; reservations required) open during business hours in Petaluma. This homegrown outfit, which has nationwide distribution, makes a dizzying array of stickers destined for greeting cards, scrapbooks, and the tops of exemplary student reports. Don't expect a major production—door to door, the experience is 1 hour, but that includes a glimpse at how stickers are made, a pass through a museum of every decal the place has made, and a few minutes in a craft gallery where kids can create their own artwork with stickers.

MUD BATHS

In the 1800s, people didn't really care too much about the process of making a nuanced wine. It was just wine. People just drank it. Instead, the big draw in the region was its hot mud baths. The quake of 1906 shifted the location of many of the springs, wiping out most of the wells that then existed in Sonoma County as well, so that today, the best place to participate in a geothermal treatment is Calistoga, in Napa County. Like bungee jumping or hot-air ballooning, it's a once-in-a-lifetime vacation treat that is only available in a special location.

Most places mix the mud and hot springs water (which is a little over 100°F) with clay, peat, and volcanic ash from nearby St. Helena volcano, and it may stain some swimsuits, so don't wear your best one (or, like most people, don't wear anything at all). These treatments used to be touted as an excellent treatment for arthritis, but modern marketing laws being what they are, they're now meant mostly as stress relievers (supporting scientific studies show that arthritis suffers may, in fact, find some relief). At the least, after the various substances wash over it, your skin can't help but be cleaner.

It's a Mud, Mud, Mud, Mud World

What's taking a mud bath like? I recently went to Dr. Wilkinson's, which provides a straight, no-frills mud bath in an institutional environment complete with plain tile walls and antique spigots. I had flashbacks to my middle-school gym, preparing for a scoliosis check. (Most other spas are much more feminine and genteel.) In gender-separated areas, there are two side-by-side tubs (at some places, they're private; at others, in a common area) full of mud that's rinsed with 180°F water and then cooled before you get naked (yes, at Dr. Wilkinson's you have to get naked in front of the attendant) and settle in, awkwardly. It feels like being buried in sulfured coffee grounds or hot oatmeal, and moving the limbs gets harder. I'm not normally claustrophobic, but when they put cucumber slices and a cool, moist washcloth over my eyes, I began counting the minutes until it ended. Still, I got over my nakedness quickly—my attendant had been doing this for a decade. Then you shower, sit in a whirlpool, take a steam bath, and get a blanket wrap, during which you all but fall asleep in relaxation. If a tour bus is in, you may see a lot of dangly bits, but late in the afternoon, it's more likely to be empty. In the final analysis, my nudity was as big of a rush as the bath itself. I don't know if my attendant would agree with the feeling.

All these day-spa facilities include mud baths—the most "local" of the treatments. Some of these baths will be thick, others soupy; some will start as mineral-water baths before having ash mixed in (to prove it's fresh, I suppose), and others will have a tub premixed before you begin. There's no proven difference between any style. Your place's water should be mineral water, which means drawn hot from the earth. Each maintains a full list of massages, treatments, and other spa procedures from Swedish massage to hydrotherapy, always for a surcharge beyond the mud-bath rate. They list their treatments online.

Dr. Wilkinson's Hot Springs Resort (1507 Lincoln Ave., Calistoga; ☎ 707/942-4102; www.drwilkinson.com), in a delightfully 1940s motel complex, has been a player in Calistoga for generations and does a range of treatments, but it's basic in the classically medicinal sense that spas once had. The mud bath described in the "It's a Mud, Mud, Mud, Mud World" box (above) is $89 and takes a little over an hour. Wilkinson's also has 42 rooms of reasonably priced simple lodging, which in winter rent for around $100.

Golden Haven (1713 Lake St., Calistoga; ☎ 707/942-8000; www.goldenhaven.com) costs $74 per person for two (unusually, it has tubs in which couples can fit, making it the honeymooners' choice), but often you can score an appointment for $50 via its website. You can also have one done in a private treatment room. It has motel rooms, which go from $135 to $175; the rooms' hot-water spas are fed with natural hot springs mineral water.

Lavender Hill Spa (1015 Foothill Blvd., Calistoga; ☎ 707/942-4495; www. lavenderhillspa.com) does everything with Asian flair and additives (a Thai Bath uses milk; the mud bath, kelp), and its mud is thinner than at other spas. One-hour treatments are $70.

Lincoln Avenue Spa (1339 Lincoln Ave., Calistoga; ☎ 707/942-2950; www.lincolnavenuespa.com) might be the choice for severe claustrophobes, because they won't have to get into the thick, mucky baths that alarm some people. Instead, they apply mud onto themselves in a private room—with a loved one, if desired—followed by time in a less-constricting steam capsule. That's $85 for an hour, minus a 10% online booking discount.

ACTIVE SONOMA

Because of a relatively tranquil climate, hot-air ballooning is a possible pursuit here. You've got to get up before dawn to try it (you'll be airborne as the light appears), and the path changes depending on weather patterns. **Napa Valley Aloft** (www.nvaloft.com) offers several different baskets fitting between four and eight people; the latter cost $225 to $245 per person. As with so much, it's cheaper in Sonoma: the company **A Balloon over Sonoma** (☎ 707/546-3360; www. aballoonoversonoma.com) charges $195 per person, $165 for kids 6 to 12.

I can't think of a much more pleasing way to pass an afternoon than on horse-back on a 90-minute walk through the moist redwoods of Armstrong Redwoods State Reserve. That's what's offered by **Armstrong Woods Pack Station** (☎ 707/ 887-2939; www.redwoodhorses.com; $70, $65 for kids under 18), run by husband-and-wife team Jonathan and Laura Ayers. A 4-hour ride to the top of McCray Mountain, where there's a vista of Sonoma County, is $175. The Ayers also do rides through the Austin Creek State Recreation Area (same pricing as Armstrong Woods), which has a less-dense flora and a topography consisting of hills and thinner forests. **Triple Creek Horse Outfit** (☎ 707/887-8700; www.triplecreek horseoutfit.com) does slightly more expensive tours (1 hr. for $60, 90 min. for $70), but their three riding locations, split between three state parks in both Napa

---

Slip on Your Tevas

Because there's so much relatively wild natural beauty around them, Bay Area residents are some of the most outdoorsy folks in America, and they hike and bike with a regularity that rivals going to the mall or movies for the rest of us. Countless books have been written to round up the best locations, how to reach them, and the (usually) supremely low costs that get you into them.

If you're into hiking, a terrific Web resource for ideas and information is **Weekend Sherpa** (www.weekendsherpa.com), a (usually) weekly, short, easy-to-read e-mail that rounds up places to hike and things to see that might appeal to the fresh-air crew.

Hiking trails are also set up in the state parks; the major ones include Armstrong Woods (p. 254), Robert Louis Stevenson (p. 254), and Sugarloaf Ridge (p. 240).

and Sonoma counties (Jack London, Sugarloaf Ridge, and Bothe-Napa Valley), offer a more "traditional" view of the wine lands than the forests of Armstrong Woods. If anyone in your party weighs more than 200 pounds, he may be excluded from the ride for the health of the animal.

Cycling fans will find support from **BikeSonoma** (☎ 707/545-0153; www. bikesonoma.org), which hooks athletes up with advice, resources, and maps. **Rincon Cyclery** (4927 Sonoma Hwy., Santa Rosa; ☎ 707/538-0868; www.rincon cyclery.com) rents mountain bikes for $7 per hour or $25 per 24 hours..

THE "OTHER" WINE COUNTRY

In a way, when you come to enjoy the wineries of this region, you're already learning all about Wine Country from a local's perspective. After all, what is a winery tour but, essentially, a backstage industrial tour where you learn how the local product is produced? And since nearly every winery puts its history and the aspirations of its owners and operators front and center in any introduction to visitors, you'll spend time learning about the locals and their roots. Every day here can be an education, but there are a few other places you might want to check out where you can get an even deeper understand of the production of food and wine.

In 2001, a group of Napa winemakers and foodies got together to open **COPIA** ★★ (500 1st St., Napa; ☎ 707/259-1600; www.copia.org; daily 10am– 6pm), said to have cost some $70 million. Think of it as a mini-university for food and wine, with days full of tastings and lessons in one of several seminar theaters. If you're nervous about your lack of wine knowledge, I suggest taking its daily "Wine Tasting 101" at 10:15am (30 min.), where your tasting skills will be sharpened to the point where you won't feel like an idiot when you set out for the wineries, but you won't be made to feel stupid if you don't get it right away. (It's very gentle: "What are you tasting?", you'll be asked. "What's your mouth's reaction?") You'll even learn useful information that's new to lots of people, such as how a decanter works. Frankly, given a choice between paying $15 for yet another winery tour and paying $15 for a class here, I'd come here, where I know I'll get an introduction to local ingredients and come away with information that will last.

Outside of peak season, free entry is likely most of the time, which is a terrific, recently instated deal that has saved the enterprise from ruin after a few lean first years. In 2008, TV chef Tyler Florence was brought in to revamp the facilities' offerings just as an upscale Westin hotel opened nearby, but the gist and purpose is expected to remain the same. Sometimes, such as during the spring Mustard Festival, there's an extra entrance fee to cover all the extra events on the schedule. All visitors pay for are the programs they want to take—most of the time, that's about $15 for an hour's program—and the generally small class size means you'll be meeting people from around the world and the area. Also, see what's on at the Meyer Food Forum, a classroom set up like a Food Network kitchen, with overhead cameras catching everything your instructor's doing. (I did a chocolate course last time I was there; we made flavored marshmallows and learned about cooking candy—it was like the most fun science lesson I've ever had.) Not just food and wine is addressed; how to shop for produce, growing methods, and other subjects are on the menu, so you could really spend a day or two here, absorbing new information.

Celluloid & Cellulose: Movies & a Meal

COPIA's on-site gourmet restaurant, Julia's Kitchen, is named for Ms. Child and operated by celeb chef Tyler Florence. It's not cheap, although a lower-priced bistro section is in the planning for late 2009. Until that opens, there are two ways to snag an affordable meal here:

1. Search the Copia website for discounts and promotions
2. Attend Friday night movies, where three to four truly gourmet courses are served, and a classic flick is shown, for $29—one of the best bargains around.

The grounds, as you might expect, are beautiful, so make sure you roam the backyard, and there's a random but high-quality food-oriented museum on the second floor that's also worth a look. Make sure you pick up one of its Wine Country passports, which includes discounts at wineries all over Napa. While you're there, walk across the parking lot to Oxbow Public Market (p. 233) for some lunch or dinner. There are big doings in this part of town; a new 315-room Ritz-Carlton is planned for next door; that should tell you a lot about the kind of patron COPIA is shooting for.

Another gold mine for foodies who want to learn about quality cuisine without having to enroll in a 6-week course, **The Culinary Institute of America** ★ (2555 Main St., St. Helena; ☎ 707/967-2320; www.ciachef.edu/california) runs a West Coast branch at Greystone, a most impressive, castle-like building (once a winery) about 30 minutes north of Napa. Unlike COPIA, it's aimed mostly at food professionals, and most courses take at least a few days to complete. But the most affordable and practical way to dip into this institution's knowledge base is to go to the institute's theater, where one of the school's chef-instructors conducts regular culinary demonstrations for as little as $15, including tastes and receipt of the recipe (which changes every few days, so you can go twice). Those usually fall Monday and Friday at 1:30 and 3:30pm, Saturday and Sunday at 10:30am, 1:30pm, and 3:30pm. Like COPIA, there's also a pricey restaurant here, in this case under the *Wine Spectator* rubric.

During the active harvest period (Aug for whites, Sept–Nov for reds), most wineries will automatically gear their tours toward including one or two show-and-tells (always paid, about $35–$70) which walk visitors through the process as it's happening. Don't expect to be asked to get your feet purple in an old-fashioned stomp—Lucy Ricardo notwithstanding, there are machines for that nowadays. Wineries that have their own on-premises vineyards, especially, will be able to show you the process from plant to press (many properties, even the most illustrious ones, actually buy their grapes from farms with no visitor facilities, depriving you of the fruit-picking portion of the process), so ask your prospective winery if the grapes are grown on-site.

Perhaps the cheapest way to participate in the harvest and crush is to attend the packed **Sonoma County Harvest Fair** (www.harvestfair.org; $6), held in Santa Rosa the first weekend of October. The highlights: a competition between some

1,000 wines and a rowdy "crush" contest in which shoeless stompers try to juice the most grapes in open-topped barrels.

To learn about *blending*, or the art of mixing different varietals to create a custom beverage, there's no more affordable place than COPIA, which often schedules (especially on weekends; about $65) afternoon-long workshops. You'll use the same tools that modern winemakers use—including ones more appropriate to a chemistry lab (pipettes, beakers) than one would think—to mix a balanced wine. COPIA gives you a bottle of your custom blend at the end—no promises on how it'll taste—plus a personalized label.

A few wineries offer occasional blending seminars, too, including **Ravenswood Winery** (18701 Gehricke Rd., Sonoma; ☎ 888/669-4679 or 707/933-2332; www.ravenswood-wine.com), a relaxed winery that mounts 1-hour sessions yielding a free 375mL (about a Coke can's worth) bottle of wine, for $50 on Fridays at 11am. Another is **Mayo Family Winery** (13101 Arnold Dr., Glen Ellen; ☎ 707/938-9401; www.mayofamilywinery.com), which offers an appointment-only seminar ($35) of about 2 hours in which three types of wine are mixed to taste

---

Developing a Crush

Unfortunately for visitors, learning how to make wine yourself isn't as easily done as learning how to appreciate the finished product. Many of the area's vintners mastered their craft either by years of on-the-job training or through months of college courses. And because the winemaking process is split between seasons (harvest and pressing in fall, blending and bottling in spring), you can't get a full, hands-on sampling of the art without at least two trips. But if you're willing to put in the effort, here are some options:

The upscale **Hope-Merrill Bed-and-Breakfast** (☎ 800/825-4233 or 707/857-3356; www.hope-inns.com), located in two adorable Victorian houses in Geyserville, is known for organizing **"Pick and Press"** events. These furnish four all-day lessons (2 in Sept, 2 in May—the price includes both stays) in which guests pick grapes by hand and then press them, with guidance from an expert, on old-fashioned equipment. The $1,500-per-couple price includes all meals, lodging at the B&B, and wine. That price seems at first blush to be as back-breaking as grape-picking work is, but it in fact breaks down to about $170 per person, per day, and it includes two cases of your homemade wine. The downside, of course, is that you'll have to come twice in a year to get the full education.

In late September for the same price ($1,500/couple, including meals and 2 nights' lodging; $200 more for solo travelers), the Sonoma County Winegrape Commission holds its popular annual **Grape Camp** (☎ 707/522-5860; www.sonomagrapecamp.com), which gives you much the same experience but without bottling your blend, which won't have had time to ferment.

Little Shop of Carnivores

Sonoma is, at heart, an agricultural region, and, as a consequence, it supports some offbeat agricultural experts you'll never find anywhere else. One amusing stop is **California Carnivores** 🅺 (2833 Old Gravenstein Hwy. S., Sebastopol; ☎ 707/824-0433; www.californiacarnivores.com), which sells America's largest selection of carnivorous plants. Kids love the pitcher plants, Venus flytraps, and bladderworts, and if you're lucky, you'll catch a feeding (call a few days ahead if you want to be sure to catch one—these plants don't eat very often). Proprietor Peter D'Amato is an expert on the subject, having written the well-received book *The Savage Garden: Cultivating Carnivorous Plants* (Ten Speed Press, 1998), and he loves sharing his knowledge about these weird botanic oddities. So although it's technically a greenhouse store, it's one well worth a visit and one that will welcome and inform you.

and the resulting wines may be purchased for about $45 each, with a six-bottle minimum. There are also a variety of do-it-yourself crush facilities where you're walked through the blending process in much greater detail, but unfortunately you're expected to buy in volume. Prices start at around $3,000 a barrel (or about 24 cases/288 bottles, the minimum), with around $5,000 the norm—you can't do just a bottle or a case.

Finally, many wineries augment their regular tours with other programs designed simply to celebrate wine. The most common events pair fine foods with wines and are catered by chef-artists who take the opportunity to show off and tease palates. Each winery does things its own way—you can find combo lobster boils/tastings, straightforward how-to's, and launch parties for new vintages. Rarely do you get enough food to fill your belly—just enough to taste. One of the least expensive pairings (most cost $60–$120) are held at **Cakebread Cellars** (☎ 800/588-0298; www.cakebread.com; $40/30-min. sampling; reservations required) in Rutherford. For info on all kinds of events, go to **Sonoma County Vintners** (☎ 707/522-5840; www.sonomawine.com), a nonprofit group of winemakers working together to promote themselves; online, it posts its members' upcoming events for the next few months. (Its counterpart, Napa Valley Vintners, at www.napavintners.com, isn't as good at tracking events but does include some good general resources.)

NIGHTLIFE

Napa and Sonoma mostly shut down after sunset. People would rather go out and have a nice meal, it seems, than brave the dark roads when it's dark, and for locals, there's a lot of work to be done in the fields and the cellars the next day. If you're not the type to go straight to bed after a long meal, try the following choices.

Evenings at **Bounty Hunter Wine Bar** (975 1st St., Napa; ☎ 707/226-3976; www.bountyhunterwinebar.com) are like Old Home night for the area winemakers. They come in droves to mingle here—attitude is minimal and lips can be loose.

The convivial atmosphere and casual drinking vibe are draw enough. However, the list of 400 wines, 40 served by the glass and many of them highly elusive or little known, guarantees a social night amongst this crowd. Even *Wine Spectator* has discussed the way winemakers come here from all over the area to "recount harvest stories." There's a bar where you can sit and eavesdrop on the latest from the grapevine. There's food, too, served until midnight—the signature dish is the Beer Can Chicken—it serves two, with salad and bread, for $24.

For first-run movies, I recommend a visit to the **Sebastiani Theatre** (476 1st St. E., Sonoma; ☎ 707/996-2020; www.sebastianitheatre.com), a cinema built in 1993 that makes for a nostalgic anchor to Sonoma Plaza's east side: island box office, original bowed marquee aglow with neon, and unusual Italianate details for a place built in what was then essentially an agrarian backwater. It's used as a center for community events, too, so don't come unless you know there's a film on.

Summer is high time at the **Calistoga Inn Brewery** (1250 Lincoln Ave., Calistoga; ☎ 707/942-4101; www.calistogainn.com): There's jazz on its relaxed outdoor patio, on the banks of the Napa River, April through October; from March through November, there's dancing to R&B from 9pm to midnight on Friday and Saturday nights. All year, on Wednesdays from 8:30pm, an open-mic night encourages locals to come in and perform—more fruitful than you might think, since many people move to this part of the world because they want to dedicate themselves to a more creative life. Beer comes from the microbrewery stashed in the old water tower.

In Petaluma, the **Cinnabar Theater** (3333 Petaluma Blvd., Petaluma; ☎ 707/763-8920; www.cinnabartheater.org) is the only venue in Sonoma County to mount a year-round slate of drama and opera. It also hosts the odd one-off event (a chili cook-off?) in a converted two-room schoolhouse north of town. It's rare to find a ticket for more than $22.

11 The Essentials of Planning

BECAUSE SAN FRANCISCO IS SUCH AN IMMENSELY POPULAR CITY WITH domestic and international visitors alike, you won't find many obstacles to visiting it easily. In fact, because of excellent transportation services, getting the best of San Francisco is easier than in lots of other places. Its weather, too, is mostly agreeable and mild, its calendar is full of interesting events, and the best attractions beckon year-round. But you may have important questions, such as how to get in from the airport and which airlines have good prices, so for those matters, there's this chapter, designed to help you plan.

Throughout this book, I've included the websites of all the attractions, malls, restaurants, and tour operators so that you can take a little time to plan ahead. Don't forget that the Bay Area is where the dot-com boom hit most, and so compared to the rest of America, companies are much more ahead of the curve than the national average. You'll find pretty much every establishment and attraction maintains a website stocked with useful information.

The San Francisco Convention & Visitors' Bureau (www.onlyinsanfrancisco.com) lists tons of restaurants and hotels, but what's particularly useful is its calendar of upcoming events. You may not find it to be comprehensive mostly because it's one of those offices that is sponsored by its members (albeit some 1,800 of them—plenty to get you started) and not by tax dollars, so its recommendations stick to its membership and not to all available options. The CVB runs a storefront which it calls **Visitor Information Services** (900 Market St., at Powell; ☎ 415/391-2000; Mon–Fri 9am–5pm, Sat–Sun 9am–3pm, closed Sun Nov–Apr) that supplies information and reservations to drop-in tourists. It's a great place to stock up on leaflets. You'll find it in the sunken plaza that feeds into the Powell BART station beside the cable-car turnaround.

A rich source for events that you might not otherwise hear about is *SF Weekly*, a free giveaway paper available around town. You can also find it, and its event listings, online at www.sfweekly.com. It even has a blog about restaurants, deals on meals, and other fun developments. *The Examiner* is another free paper, although its listings section is not as comprehensive: www.examiner.com/san_francisco.

WHEN TO VISIT

The table below charts seasonal weather shifts, although in San Francisco, the forecast can change moment to moment and neighborhood to neighborhood.

San Francisco's Average Temperature & Rainfall

	Jan	Feb	Mar	Apr	May	June	July	Aug	Sept	Oct	Nov	Dec
Temp (°F)	43–56	46–59	47–61	48–64	51–67	53–70	55–71	56–72	55–73	52–70	48–62	43–56
Temp. (°C)	6–13	8–15	8–16	9–18	11–19	12–21	13–22	13–22	13–23	11–21	9–17	6–13
Rainfall (in.)	4.5	4	3.3	1.2	0.4	0.1	0.1	0.1	0.2	1	2.5	2.9

You may have heard prior complaints about San Francisco weather. The accompanying table collects rain and temperature data valid for the entire year, and you'll probably agree that it's pretty appealing most of the time. The famous quote, erroneously attributed to Mark Twain, is "The coldest winter I ever spent was a summer in San Francisco." He didn't actually say it, and even if he did, it'd be hyperbole, because summers aren't all that cold, but they aren't sweltering either. The hills and sea air of town wreak havoc on the weather patterns, so it's almost useless to even give a blanket prescription for the whole city's forecast. When there's fog at the Golden Gate, it may be sunny on Twin Peaks. For a few days in September or October, the temperature may soar above 100, but it passes quickly. When there is fog, it usually clears by lunchtime.

One warning: The amount of rain in January in our chart is not a misprint; bring an umbrella if you plan to visit around then, because the downpours can be intense. Most of the rest of the year, precipitation fizzles as a drizzle. And likewise for summer, come prepared with layers, because the temperature can and will dip lower than you're used to for a July day.

San Francisco Visit-Worthy Events

One of the cool things about San Francisco is that there's almost always something going on. The marquee stuff is named below, but you'll also find that locals are constantly throwing amusing one-off parties and festivals with very little warning and with no intention of making them annual events. To wit: a mass pillow fight on Market Street, or the one-day-a-year How Weird Street Faire (www.howweird.org), a peace-themed festival with nine musical stages. How do you get wind of these events? First, consult *SF Weekly* (www.sfweekly.com) and *The Examiner* (www.examiner.com/san_francisco), but also drop in at hipster blogs such as SFist (www.sfist.com).

January

New Year's Eve: Unlike in, say, New York City, there's not one place where everyone goes for midnight. Locals tend to gather to celebrate the New Year at Union Square, at Ocean Beach, or, now that its clock is working again and there's not a highway in front of it, in front of the Ferry Building. However, in recent years, the city has permitted free rides all night long on Muni, so you can pick your perfect spot without spending too much, if the above three don't work for you.

Dine About Town: Dozens of gourmet restaurants participate in this weeklong mass price-cutting during which a three-course meal costs $22 at lunch or $32 at dinner. Not dead cheap, but less expensive than you'd usually pay, and at places you might not otherwise find affordable to visit. A second week is usually also held in mid-June. Go to www.onlyinsanfrancisco.com/dineabouttown for more information.

February

Chinese New Year: One of the city's most family-friendly public events, this 2-week celebration parties in the streets with food stalls, martial-arts demonstrations, fireworks, art displays, a beauty pageant, and, of course, a parade so elaborate (lions, firecrackers, costumes) that bleacher seats are sold for it starting in December. Secure a hotel room early. Check out www.chineseparade.com.

March

St. Patrick's Day Parade: St. Patrick's Day parades everywhere have turned mostly into an occasion to drink heavily, and this one is no exception. It falls sometime around the 17th, but not always right on the day, and its centerpiece is a parade from 2nd and Market to the Civic Center, where a stage and food booth are set up. (☎ 415/395-8417; www.sfstpatricksday parade.com)

Sisters of Perpetual Indulgence Easter Celebration: Gay men dressed up as nuns flit about Dolores Park blessing the people and absolving them of sins of which they are probably not remotely guilty—until they cheer along to the Hunky Jesus look-alike contest.

April

Northern California Cherry Blossom Festival: Held two weekends in mid-April in Japantown with tea ceremonies, flower arranging demonstrations, a food bazaar, and an elaborate parade. Most events are free. Check out www.nccbf.org for more information.

May

Cinco de Mayo: San Francisco's sizable Latin community comes out to the Civic Center parks for this shindig—music, parades, fireworks—which celebrates Latin culture in the way that other holidays honor other nationalities. Get good food and tequila, and party in the street.

Bay to Breakers foot race: Held at 8am on the third Sunday in May, this 12km race is one of the city's institutions, having been started in 1912, and it's typical of the city's carefree, thumb-nosing attitude. Anything goes, from dragging a beer keg alongside you to dressing up like a mariachi band to (gasp!) actually trying to take it seriously and run it in a decent time. It goes from the eastern end of Howard Street through Golden Gate Park all the way to Ocean Beach, a clear cut across town. (www.ingbaytobreakers.com)

Carnaval: Latin and South American cultures combine in the Mission for this Memorial Day street fair of drum performances, scantily clad performers, traditional foods, and lots and lots of dancing. Attendance usually numbers in the hundreds of thousands. (www.carnavalsf.com)

Uncorked! San Francisco Wine Festival: Better show up early for this festival, because it'll be over in 5 hours. Still, those 5 hours, held at Ghirardelli Square, are packed with tastings, seminars, chef demonstrations, and participation from dozens of local wineries. The fest tends to fall on the third Saturday of the month (but check www.localwineevents.com for the exact date when you visit).

June

Haight Ashbury Street Fair: The '60s, to which this neighborhood clings, come back in force during this 1-day street festival, where some 200 booths sell hippie clothes, pot pipes, and other accoutrements of the lifestyle. Early June and Sunday, usually. (www.haightashburystreet fair.org)

North Beach Festival: One of the most worthwhile neighborhood parties is the one specializing in quality Italian foods. This 2-day event at Washington Square Park, which has been going for generations, promises food stalls, music, animal blessings by a local church (seriously), and even a celebrity pizza-dough-tossing demonstration. Mid-month most likely. (www.sfnorthbeach.org)

Union Street Festival: It seems like every city neighborhood wants to throw its own festival day; in this case, it's the yuppie drag Union Street, which mounts this "Eco-Urban" (whatever that is) carnival of gourmet food stands and artists' stalls. The folks in this 'hood care about their fine foods, so it's a great chance to throw some top chow down your gullet. (www. unionstreetfestival.com)

San Francisco LGBT Pride Celebration Parade: No city knows how to throw a gay parade like San Francisco. Outrageous costumes, huge floats, some half a million celebrants, and glad-handing politicians (in this town, they court the gay vote) make this the most inclusive of any of the annual festivals. You don't have to be gay, or even if you are, you don't have to be campy, to enjoy the spectacle. Last weekend in the month. (www.sfpride.org)

July

Fourth of July Waterfront Festival: Live entertainment, food booths, and, of course, a huge fireworks show mark this, the biggest of the Independence Day festivities in town. It's held at Fisherman's Wharf.

August

San Francisco Marathon: The 26.2-mile course visits just about every great landmark and neighborhood in the city, including a crossing of the Golden Gate Bridge—twice. In this race, though, participants are not encouraged to do things like dress like chickens, the way they do at the Bay to Breakers. First Sunday of the month. (www.runsfm.com)

Nihonmachi Street Fair: Usually held on the second weekend of August in Japantown, this celebration of all Asian culture features a range of musical styles and cuisines, and performances that go from drums to Lion Dances, with lots of stalls selling unique crafts. Happily, Japanese cuisine lends itself to noshing on little bites of food as you stroll along. Second weekend of August, most likely. (www.nihonmachistreetfair.org)

September

How Berkeley Can You Be? Festival: Berkeley is famous for its liberal attitude, and this parade capitalizes on and magnifies that reputation—crazy floats made of food, outlandish costumes, and other over-the-top festivities. Think of it as Mardi Gras for physics students. Usually held on the last Sunday of the month.

Folsom Street Fair: Leave the kids at home for this one: A bawdy, anything-goes fair celebrating the leather sexual fetish and its pornography, particularly as it applies to gay men. It attracts men from around the country because most of their own cities won't tolerate similar public nudity. Don't be shocked if you witness people having nooky in the street—if you attend, you asked for it. Often held on the last Sunday of the month. (www.folsomstreetfair.org)

October

Castro Street Fair: As a contrast to Folsom, this is a family-friendly event with arts and crafts, information booths, and the open support of the city. It was begun by Harvey Milk back in the day when gay folks needed the positive exposure. Expect the street to be packed and several music stages, including (surprise!) a country-and-western one. Early October. (www.castrostreetfair.org)

Halloween San Francisco: The city is trying to stamp out this informal October 31st tradition of people packing the Castro in their costumes. Police already ban alcohol, and the pubs close early to squeeze out troublemakers. Many locals are happy to go along with the changes because in 2007, nine people were shot at the event. Scary! So ask around to see where the party has moved; the city is working to move the whole shebang to the Civic Center, but we all know you can't force these things.

November

Dia de los Muertos: Fans of folk art will dig this pre-Columbian procession, which is more sober than the raucous Cinco de Mayo. Folks dress up as skeletons to symbolize both death and rebirth, and they move down 24th and 25th streets in the Mission. It falls around Halloween, and there are usually some adjunct events such as art shows and craft demonstrations. (www.sfmission.com/dod)

Neighborhood Associations

It isn't just the city itself that maintains a presence for tourists. Many neighborhoods in town present their own faces to visitors; check these websites for tips on restaurants, shopping, and events.

Castro: http://castroonline.com

Fisherman's Wharf: www.fishermanswharf.org

Haight Ashbury: www.haightashbury.org

Japantown: www.sfjapantown.org

The Mission: www.sfmission.com

North Beach: www.sfnorthbeach.org

Union Street (Cow Hollow): www.unionstreetsf.com

Yerba Buena District (SoMa): www.yerbabuena.org

ENTRY REQUIREMENTS FOR NON-AMERICAN CITIZENS

Be sure to check with your local U.S. embassy or consulate for the very latest in entry requirements, as these continue to shift. Full information can be found at the **U.S. State Department's** website, **www.travel.state.gov.**

VISAS

Citizens of western and central Europe, Australia, New Zealand, and Singapore need only a valid machine-readable passport and a round-trip air ticket or cruise ticket to enter the United States for stays of up to 90 days. Canadian citizens can also enter without a visa as long as they show proof of residence. Do check with your government, though, because the U.S. Department of Homeland Security has been ornery in recent years and rules are apt to change.

Citizens of all other countries will need to obtain a tourist visa from the U.S. consulate. Depending on your country of origin, there may or may not be a charge attached (and you may or may not have to apply in person or wait weeks on end for the paperwork to clear). You'll need to complete an application and submit a 1½-inch square photo, and your passport will need to be valid for at least six months past the scheduled end of your U.S. visit. If an interview isn't mandated (South Africans, for example, have to appear before a bureaucrat), it's usually possible to obtain a visa within 24 hours, except during holiday periods or the summer rush.

PASSPORTS

To enter the United States, international visitors must have a valid passport that expires at least six months later than the scheduled end of their visit.

For residents of Australia: You can pick up an application from your local post office or any branch of Passports Australia, but you must schedule an interview at the passport office to present your application materials. Call the **Australian Passport Information Service** at ☎ **131-232,** or visit the government website at www.passports.gov.au.

For residents of Canada: Passport applications are available at travel agencies throughout Canada or from the central **Passport Office,** Department of Foreign Affairs and International Trade, Ottawa, ON K1A 0G3 (☎ **800/567-6868;** www.ppt.gc.ca). *Note:* Canadian children who travel must have their own passports. However, if you hold a valid Canadian passport, issued before December 11, 2001, that bears the name of your child, the passport remains valid for you and your child until it expires.

For residents of Ireland: You can apply for a 10-year passport at the **Passport Office,** Setanta Centre, Molesworth Street, Dublin 2 (☎ **01/671-1633;** www.irl gov.ie/iveagh). Those under age 18 and over 65 must apply for a 123€ 1-year passport. You can also apply at 1A South Mall, Cork (☎ **021/272-525**) or at most main post offices.

For residents of New Zealand: You can pick up a passport application at any New Zealand Passports Office or download it from their website. Contact the **Passports Office** at ☎ **0800/225-050** in New Zealand or 04/474-8100, or log on to www.passports.govt.nz.

For residents of the United Kingdom: To pick up an application for a standard 10-year passport (5-yr. passport for children under 16), visit your nearest passport office, major post office, or travel agency; or contact the **United Kingdom Passport Service** at ☎ **0870/521-0410.** You can also search its website at www. ukpa.gov.uk.

MEDICAL REQUIREMENTS

No inoculations or vaccinations are required to enter the United States unless you're arriving from an area that is suffering from an epidemic (cholera or yellow fever, in particular). A valid, signed prescription is required for those travelers in need of **syringe-administered medications** or medical treatment that involves **narcotics.** It is extremely important to obtain the correct documentation in these cases, as your medications could be confiscated; and if you're found to be carrying an illegal substance, security officials tend to lock you up first and ask questions later. You could be subject to significant penalties.

CUSTOMS REGULATIONS FOR INTERNATIONAL VISITORS

Strict regulations govern what can and can't be brought into the United States—and what you can take back home with you. The rules mostly concern restricted substances such as booze and tobacco, so I wouldn't get too worried, unless fresh citrus was part of your plan.

WHAT YOU CAN BRING TO SAN FRANCISCO

Every visitor over 21 years of age may bring in, free of duty, the following: (1) 1 liter of wine or hard liquor; (2) 200 cigarettes, 100 cigars (but not from Cuba), or 3 pounds of smoking tobacco; and (3) $100 worth of gifts. These exemptions are offered to travelers who spend at least 72 hours in the United States and who have not claimed them within the preceding 6 months. It is forbidden to bring foodstuffs (particularly fruit, cooked meats, and canned goods) and plants (vegetables, seeds, tropical plants, and the like). Foreign tourists may carry in or out up to $10,000 in U.S. or foreign currency with no formalities; larger sums must be declared to U.S. Customs on entering or leaving, which includes filing Form CM 4790. For details regarding U.S. Customs and Border Protection, consult your nearest U.S. embassy or consulate, or **U.S. Customs** (☎ **202/927-1770;** www.customs.ustreas.gov).

WHAT YOU CAN TAKE HOME FROM SAN FRANCISCO

This is an important thing to research, particularly if you plan to buy bottles of wine on your trip.

For a clear summary of **Canadian** rules, write for the booklet *I Declare,* issued as publication no. RC4044 by the **Canada Border Services Agency** (☎ **800/ 461-9999** in Canada, or 204/983-3500; www.cbsa-asfc.gc.ca).

For information, **U.K. citizens** contact **HM Customs & Excise** at ☎ **0845/ 010-9000** (from outside the U.K., 020/8929-0152), or the website at www.hmce.gov.uk.

A helpful brochure for **Australians,** available from Australian consulates or Customs offices, is *Know Before You Go.* For more information, call the **Australian Customs Service** at ☎ **1300/363-263,** or log on to www.customs.gov.au.

Most questions regarding **New Zealand** rules are answered in a free pamphlet available at New Zealand consulates and Customs offices: *New Zealand Customs Guide for Travellers, Notice no. 4.* For more information, contact **New Zealand Customs,** The Customhouse, 17–21 Whitmore St., Box 2218, Wellington (☎ **04/473-6099** or 0800/428-786; www.customs.govt.nz).

GETTING TO SAN FRANCISCO

With all those tourists and conventioneers on the move, San Francisco is served by lots of airlines coming from all directions. In recent years, fixed-cost airlines such as JetBlue and Virgin America, on which prices rise by a formula as seats are sold, have added service to the city, too, making it relatively easy, with advance planning, to score an affordable ticket. How affordable? Well, that's a relative term, but for cross-country flights from the East Coast to the West Coast, a rate of $250 each way is common as long as you book several months ahead. Here are some other tricks to finding decent airfares:

* **Look at the low-fare carriers.** Airlines such as **JetBlue, Southwest, AirTran, America West Airlines, Spirit Airlines, Sun Country, and Virgin America** sometimes have better fares than the larger airlines like American, Delta, and United, but they may not be searched, or at least displayed in an obvious place, if you go to a site such as Expedia. So use a search tool such as **Sidestep.com, Kayak.com**, or **Mobissimo.com**, which search airline sites

directly, adding no service charges and often finding fares that the larger travel sites miss. Book at far ahead as possible for the best fares, because all airlines raise prices as seats sell. I personally prefer JetBlue or Virgin America because their seatback TV sets make the time go faster. If you're flying from Europe into the United States, take a look at the fares from British Airways, American, Continental, Delta, United, Virgin Atlantic, Lufthansa, Icelandair, Martinair, and Iberia, as these carriers tend to have the lowest rates for international travel. **Mobissimo.com** and **CheapFlights.uk.com** are good for searching fares that don't originate in the U.S.

♦ **Fly when others don't, and take an itinerary the biz travelers don't want.** As much as the rules of airfare change, one thing stays true: Those who fly midweek and midday, and who stay over a Saturday night, will generally pay less on the standard carriers than those who fly at more popular times. This price difference is becoming less pronounced as airlines pack more people onto each flight, but it still exists. Tuesday and Wednesday are also good days to fly because fewer people are going then. If you jigger your days and you're still finding that prices are high, perhaps a major convention is starting on the day you want, bumping up traffic. The same goes for hotel rates. To save the most, try to be flexible with your arrival and departure dates.

♦ **Book at the right time.** Consider booking on a Wednesday, traditionally the day when most airfare sales come out. These usually fall around four to six weeks before departure, but you've got to be vigilant if you're going to rely on this tactic; if for some reason the news about a sale doesn't reach your ears, by the time you get to booking your ticket, many of the flights could be full and prices could be high. Be sure to monitor such sites as Frommers.com, SmarterTravel.com, and the Kayak.com "Buzz Feed," all of which highlight fare sales. If you don't want to live your life looking out for sales, the best rule is to book as many months ahead as you can reasonably manage.

♦ **Try booking through a consolidator.** Those traveling from another country may wish to use a consolidator or "bucket shop" to snag a ticket. These companies buy tickets in bulk, passing along the savings to their customers. If you reside in Europe, the best way to find one that services your area is to go to the website **www.cheapflights.co.uk**, which serves as a clearinghouse for bucket shops both large and small. Many will also advertise in the Saturday papers and in London-based *TNT Magazine,* a backpacker bible that posts its entire publication—ads by international sellers of cheap flights and all— online at www.tntmagazine.com/emag. Be careful, though: Some charge outrageous change fees, so read the fine print before you purchase your ticket. Bucket shops will not be useful for those flying within the U.S., because they are not generally able to undercut standard pricing on domestic travel.

San Francisco is one of the West Coast's two major gateways to Asia and Australia, so lots of people from that part of the world use the city to break their journeys from or to those places. If you doubt the breadth of destinations, you may be surprised to learn there is even a nonstop flight to Dubai from SFO. Given a choice between breaking a journey in Los Angeles and breaking one in San Francisco, I'd pick the Bay Area every time, and not just because it's much easier to get into and around San Francisco from its airports than it is Los Angeles.

With low-cost carriers as relatively cheap as they are, no domestic company operates regular commercial charter flights to San Francisco, and there are precious few online packagers who will combine discounted hotel stays with scheduled airfare on a regular basis. Generally, though, these packagers are not American and they cater to the foreign market. **Virgin Holidays** (www.virginholidays. co.uk) is a huge player, with lots of on-the-ground customer-service reps available in case things go wrong. North Americans should check the major players in air-and-hotel combinations, including (in no particular order) Travelocity.com, Orbitz.com, and Expedia.com, as well as some of the vacation packaging wings of major airlines like Southwest, Delta, American, and Northwest—but only after having done their own checks for good airfare and hotel rates individually, because the package prices offered by these sites are not always lower than what you'd get if you booked components on your own. Remember that you won't need a car unless you have definite plans to head out of town for the duration of your visit.

Lastminute.com, which used to operate as Site59.com, specializes in airfare-inclusive packages of less than 7 days that depart within the next 2 weeks. The prices you get depend on how full the hotels are and what the whims of the air-lines are that day, but deals along the lines of airfare from the East Coast plus 3 nights' hotel can be had for about $415 per person based on two traveling together. (Be ready to agree to take the first flight of the day in order to get the best rates.) And for about $100 more for the whole trip, the choice of hotel can move from three stars to five stars—a good deal.

San Francisco is a major tourist's town, so you'll also frequently find deals at sites such as Hotwire.com, Hotels.com, and Priceline.com. Hunt around, because you'll find that different prices have been negotiated by different websites. Services like Sidestep.com and Kayak.com are useful because they canvass dozens of different sites at once for you, cutting out much of the legwork.

ARRIVING OR LEAVING BY TRAIN OR BUS

The national rail system **Amtrak** (☎ 800/872-7245; www.amtrak.com) doesn't stop in San Francisco; the nearest station is in Oakland, and there's also one in Richmond, which is also across the Bay. BART is accessible to both. Even then, the main route serves Sacramento, but you'll have to change trains to go anywhere else in the country. So it's not a convenient option well-suited to reaching the city on major cross-country journeys. The **USA Rail Pass** is the American equivalent of the Eurail Pass in Europe—although our national rail system hardly compares to the European system. The pass allows foreign visitors to travel extensively within the U.S. for one set (and fairly reasonable) rate. It's *only* for those living outside North America (Canadians and Mexicans are not eligible). The passes are good for 15 or 30 days of travel, and work either within a region (Northeast, East, or West) or, if you shell out more, throughout the entire United States. The cheapest pass is a 15-day pass for off-peak rides along the Northeast Corridor ($299); the most expensive offers 30 days of peak-time travel throughout the U.S. ($599). The pass covering the West of the country starts at $329 for 15 days of validity and goes to $359 for 30 days. That doesn't mean you get 15 days of travel; it means that once you validate your pass, you'll have a little over two weeks to get all your movements in. There is also a 30-day North American pass, the grand poobah of passes, which includes Canada's not-much-better VIA Rail system; it costs between $709 and $999 (the higher price is for travel between May and October and over the December holidays). Given how you'd have to keep moving to get the most value out of your pass, it isn't the most economical bet.

For bus travel, **Greyhound** (☎ 800/231-2222; www.greyhound.com) covers the United States, and the company's prices, both for individual trips and for the passes, are equivalent to what you'll find at Amtrak. The conditions aboard these buses are bottom-of-the-barrel—cramped conditions, smelly bathrooms, and frequent traffic delays—making this a less pleasant option. **Trailways** (www.trailways.com) is a collection of privately owned bus systems across the country and its rates are usually similar to Greyhound's. If faced with a choice between bus and train, choose the train, because at least on the rails you'll be able to stand up and move around as you plod across the enormity of the U.S.

Another option that bears mentioning, and is doable for Americans as well as foreign visitors, are the low-cost shuttles that zip around California. They're intended for backpackers and students, but anyone may take them. **Green Tortoise** (☎ 800/867-6647; www.greentortoies.com), the popular backpackers hostel and adventure travel company, runs shuttles to Vegas and L.A. from June through October for $39 (L.A.) and $59 (Sin City) each way. The buses are like traveling common rooms, with bunks for resting, lounges for socializing, and entertainment systems for passing the time. Reservations are only accepted a week ahead. For similar prices ($39–$43 with a 7-day advance purchase), **Greyhound** operates express buses to Los Angeles, as well as to Las Vegas. But the Greyhound station is in a truly unsavory part of town, and many people don't feel comfortable going there or taking the bus with people who do.

Another newish option is **Megabus** (☎ 877/462-6342; www.megabus.com). The appeal of Megabus, which takes the 8-hour trip to Los Angeles four times daily using comfortable luxury coaches, is that, if you're among the first few people to book a seat, tariffs are just $1 each way; they top out at $36 for last-minute bookers. A rate of $15 to $20 is most likely. A marginally more expensive option is **California Shuttle Bus** (☎ 800/387-3319 or 626/336-0027; www.cashuttle bus.com; $45 each way), which departs daily at 1pm from near Union Square.

HOW TO GET TO & FROM THE AIRPORT

The region's subway system, Bay Area Rapid Transit (BART) is mostly designed for commuter use, but a few years ago it finally hooked up with the city's main airport, making it a cinch for tourists to use upon arrival and departure. Catching BART from SFO airport to the city is easy enough. The station is attached to the International Terminal, so if you fly into a different terminal, just take the free AirTrain elevated tram to the right place. Once there, you stick a credit card or cash into the machines and pull out a ticket that you'll keep using until the cash you've put on it has been depleted. You can keep using the same ticket to get around on BART during your visit. The default charge is usually $20, which, unless you plan to ride BART a lot (you probably won't), is too much, so make sure to tap the button that brings the charge down by a few dollars, because machines don't give more than $4.95 in change. Riding the train to Powell (for Union Square) or Embarcadero will cost $5.15 each way and take about 30 minutes. (If you plan to visit the Mission from Union Square during your stay, budget

Airport Art

The evidence that San Francisco is a dignified city presents itself the minute you arrive at its main airport, SFO. **San Francisco Airport Museums** (www.sfoarts.org) has outfitted the terminals with a range of pieces by well-known artists. Some are before security, some after, but you can find a brochure listing artists and locations at the information centers near baggage claim. There are also changing shows scattered throughout the terminals. A recent one was a retrospective of 130 years of audio-related inventions, co-curated by Dolby, and another on model trains. There's even an **Aviation Museum and Library** (☎ 650/821-6700; Sun–Fri 10am–4:30pm; free admission) including more than 6,000 books and 5,400 artifacts to do with aviation history. There aren't too many cities that invest their transit ports with as many high-culture benefits.

around another $4 per round-trip visit, but otherwise resist the urge to load up your ticket, because BART doesn't go many places once you're in town. You can always put more value on the card later.) Keep your ticket handy during your ride, because you'll need it to get out of the station again. Most stations have escalators, so you won't have to fight your luggage too much. Finding the right train at the airport is easy enough, but when you take BART back to SFO, make sure you board the correct train: You want Dublin/Pleasanton-SFO/Millbrae, in the direction of Millbrae. It's the blue line on the maps.

From Oakland (OAK), you can also take BART, but it involves the quick, free AirBART shuttle bus that goes every 10 minutes to the station. From there, the fare is $3 to Embarcadero, and the train trip takes about 25 minutes. Ultimately, it's an easy way to go, and although the shuttle is a slight pain, if the airfare to OAK is markedly cheaper than it is to SFO, there's no reason you shouldn't fly here instead.

Taxis to town from SFO cost $40 to $50; from Oakland, $30. Of course, plenty of shuttle companies will take you into town for a higher fee. **SuperShuttle** (☎ 800/258-3826; www.supershuttle.com) operates shared-ride vans door-to-door to the city for $17 each way ($27 to Oakland's airport). You can have your own car through the company for $60. If you have a reservation with a hostel, ask about transfers; many offer ones for cut rates.

Important note: You may be tempted to fly into San Jose. Don't be. It's not well situated for casual visitors to San Francisco, and unless you rent a car, you'll pay dearly ($120/taxi ride) to get to town. There are enough airfare bargains between SFO and OAK to keep you limited to those airports, which are easily reached by rail.

I warn you strongly against picking up a **rental car** at the airport unless you plan to immediately drive out to the countryside. San Francisco has one of the worst parking situations of any American city, and I pity the fool who drives into that city with an intention of parking. San Francisco is one of the few American cities that you can easily tour without using your own car, so take advantage of that. Finding a paid space will hit you for huge amounts of money, tangling with the cable cars and streetcars is enough to frazzle even the coolest head, and if you do manage to score a rare free curbside space, you must know how to position your wheels (turned away if you're pointed uphill, toward the curb if you're going downhill) to avoid being ticketed. If you need a rental car for trips out to the Wine Country, pick up your car the morning you leave from a city-based rental office.

Now, let's say you will have a car and there's no getting around it. My advice is to book a low-cost room at one of the city's several but little-known motor-court-style inns; there are several in Cow Hollow and a few more around North Beach, and they provide free parking in their courtyards. They're listed in the chapter 3, and believe me, using them will save you tons of cash. You can also save cash by canvassing the cheapest gas rates using the user-generated site www.san frangasprices.com, which keeps track of which service stations charge what price per gallon.

Should you crave a rental car anyway, the usual renters are operating, but go for the smallest vehicle you can, not just for the sake of parking, but also for the sake of mileage. The local **Rent-a-Wreck** (☎ 800/732-7368; www.rentawreck.com) out-fit isn't at either airport, but it's in the industrial part of town in Potrero Hill. Take a cab there; rates start around $24 a day for a compact, which is low for the city. However, you're more likely to score an online deal in advance with the major renters, and for the ease of just picking up your car at the airport, that's my pref-erence as long as the price quote is reasonable to me.

TRAVEL INSURANCE—DO YOU NEED IT?

Yes, you do, principally because you're spending so much money. If you need to cancel your trip before you leave, travel insurance can buffer you from a large financial loss. But does that mean you need to buy some? Not necessarily—you may already have it.

If you're a domestic tourist, your existing medical coverage, for example, may include a safety net that will cover you even though you're traveling; ask so you're sure. The credit card you use to make reservations may cover you for cancellation, lost luggage, or trip interruption; again, the only way to be sure is to ask your issuer. Most hotels will issue refunds with enough notice, but a few of the cheap ones won't; ask what the deadline for cancellation is when you're booking.

So what else may you want to insure? If your medical coverage and credit cards don't lend a hand, you may want special coverage for **accommodation rentals,** especially if you've plunked down a deposit, and any **valuables,** since airlines are only required to pay up to $2,500 for lost luggage domestically, and not every hotel provides in-room safes (and even the ones that do have safes too small to hold much).

If you do decide on insurance, you can easily compare available policies by vis-iting **InsureMyTrip.com**. Or contact one of the following reputable companies:

> **Access America** (☎ **866/807-3982;** www.accessamerica.com)
> **CSA Travel Protection** (☎ **800/873-9844;** www.csatravelprotection.com)
> **MEDEX** (☎ **800/732-5309;** www.medexassist.com)
> **AIG Travel Guard** (☎ **800/807-3982;** www.travelguard.com)
> **Travelex** (☎ **800/228 9792;** www.travelex-insurance.com)

MONEY MATTERS

You know how Murphy's Law works: Most **ATMs** that you'll find are run by third parties, not your bank, which means that you'll be slapped with fees of around $2 per withdrawal. But the good news is, they accept pretty much anything you can stick into them. There are tons of banks in the Financial District north of Market and between Embarcadero and Montgomery, so to improve your chances of avoiding that fee, hunt for your bank around that part of town. For other locales, ask the FDIC; the agency insures deposits in America and maintains a free Web database of bank locations nationwide: www4.fdic.gov/IDASP/main_bankfind.asp. Smarter yet would be to contact *your* bank before you leave home and obtain the addresses of its branches in the city. Make sure to ask the names of "partner" banks that, unbeknownst to you, might offer fee-free ATM privileges, and get their locations as well; for example, Citibank and 7-Eleven have a deal in which Citibank customers can draw cash at the convenience stores without paying a fee (not that there are many 7-Elevens in San Francisco, but your bank may inform you of a similar surprise that saves you money).

Sitting down to do that will afford you the chance to tell your **credit card** issuer that you plan to be on the move. Before you leave home, let your credit card issuer know that you're about to travel. Many of them, guarding against potential fraud, get antsy when they see unexpectedly large charges start appearing far from your home, and they often freeze your account in response. It has happened to me despite the fact that I've told them repeatedly that I'm a travel writer, and my spending history proves it. There's no one minding the ship at most of these companies, and your requests must always be re-lodged every few months.

By the way, credit cards are nearly universally accepted. I think you could strut off the plane with just a Visa or American Express card and live in style for your entire trip. In fact, you *must* have one to rent a car. Your only problem would be how to pay the highway tolls. The majority of places accept the Big Four: American Express, MasterCard, Visa, and Discover. A few places add Diners to the mix, and some smaller family-owned businesses subtract American Express because of the pain of dealing with the company.

European card users who are acclimated to chip-and-PIN technology will be shocked at how lax American clerks are about security. Not only will they almost always neglect to check the purchaser's identification, but also, in some stores, credit card charges under $25 or $50 often don't even require signatures. You just swipe and go. Furthermore, compared to their European counterparts, American merchants rarely request ID when purchases are made. Knowing this, you should keep your cards even closer, since it's possible for strangers to dine out on your dime.

Try not to use credit cards to withdraw cash from ATMs. You'll be charged interest from the moment your money leaves the slot. If your credit card allows for online bill paying through links with your bank account, set up that capability before you leave—at the very least, you can pay off your withdrawals within hours, cutting your losses. Using an ATM card linked to a liquid bank account, like a debit card, is far less expensive.

Traveler's checks are also widely accepted, even if they're slipping from favor. This is a city that sees large numbers of international tourists, so you won't get any blank stares when you present one—although, because redeeming them can

What Things Cost

San Francisco's cost of living never seemed to settle back down into realistic proportions after the dot-com bust. People still seem to be living high on the hog, despite tough times. So if you plan to enjoy the high life, you'll still have to pay high prices.

Bus or streetcar ride: $1.50

Cable-car ride (one-way): $5

Daily parking in a garage: $20–$35

Meal at a diner-style restaurant, without drink: $9

Main dish at a fancier restaurant: $18

Glass of wine at dinner: $8–$12

Pint of beer: $5–$6

Evening movie ticket: $9.50

involve time-consuming paperwork, you may hear exasperated sighs from people in line behind you. Too bad for them.

Several creditors have come up with **traveler's check cards,** also called **prepaid cards,** which are essentially debit cards encoded with the amount of money you elect to put on them. They're not linked to your personal bank accounts, they work in ATMs, and if you lose one, you can get your cash back in a matter of hours. If you spend all the money on them, you can call a number or visit a website and reload the card using your bank-account information. American Express used to offer a prepaid "cheque card," but it discontinued them. That leaves the **Visa TravelMoney** (www.allaccesstravelmoney.com) version, sold through AAA offices (☎ 866/339-3378); it costs $10 and keeps a little over 1% of everything you load onto it, plus all the regular international transaction fees. Basically, if a place takes Visa, it'll take this, too. It also charges you $4.95 a month if you keep it longer than 7 months. It's not ideal, but it's a relatively safe way to travel with money.

MONEY EXCHANGES

Does anyone still use these anymore? Like travelers checks, changing cash is on the outs, and good riddance, since exchange rates are often usurious. Because ATM withdrawals give much better exchange rates, old-fashioned exchange desks are few and far between these days, although you'll still find a few willing to do the deed upon landing at the airport or at the front desk of the larger hotels. If you need to change money, take advantage of the better rates offered by banks during regular banking hours (9:30am–4pm). There's practically a bank on every corner in the Financial District, and most of them are quite beautiful buildings worth a visit on their own merits.

HEALTH & SAFETY

San Francisco has one of the worst homelessness problems in the country—so much so that most visitors are both appalled and terrified at what they see. One reason for the problem is the weather: Because the city is such a mild, temperate place to be, people are attracted here. The local government seems paralyzed when it comes to handling this issue. You'll see the highest numbers of homeless in the Tenderloin district, followed by the Mission, and these are areas you need to be cautious in when walking alone or at night.

Still, despite such high vagrancy rates, petty crime is not as common as you'd think. Pickpockets exist in all neighborhoods, of course, but especially where groups of distracted tourists wander. Be vigilant about any bags you're carrying, such as fanny packs and backpacks, especially on the cable cars, which are usually crammed with ogling visitors who pay far more attention to the views than to their purses. Use your hotel room's safe, if there is one, but remember many of them are too small to contain most laptop computers. If you're truly concerned about theft, consider assembling a "fake" wallet containing a few expired credit cards and a few bucks which you can part with in lieu of your real goods. Keep it in an obvious place like your back pocket, and hide the "real" one in a money belt or in your front pocket. By the time a villain, rare as they are, realizes he got a decoy wallet, he'll be long gone.

Don't leave anything of value in your car, ever, not even in the trunk. Cars are a popular target here just as they are elsewhere.

Nuisances such as mosquitoes are unheard of here, and rare is the day so sunny that you'll be burned; the usual common sense applies.

Which brings us to earthquakes. They actually happen all the time, although you're unlikely to feel most of them. If a big shaker does hit, don't run outside. Instead, just go into a doorway, lean against a wall, and stay away from windows, which can shatter. Don't freak out. And when you finally are able to go outside, be alert for power lines; the city is crisscrossed with them, and it's easy to run afoul of them. If you're in a car when a quake hits, get off bridges, overpasses, elevated highways, or anything else that could prove unstable. If you're walking outside when one strikes, stay away from the sides of buildings, because architectural ornamentation and masonry have a way of coming loose.

PACKING

For the latest rules on how to pack and what you'll be permitted to bring as a carry-on, consult your airline or the Transportation Security Administration (TSA) at www.tsa.gov. Also be sure to find out from your airline what your checked-baggage weight limits will be. Even airlines that previously were lax with the limits, like JetBlue, now impose maximums of around 50 pounds. Anything heavier will incur a fee, as will second and sometimes even first, checked bags ($25 is the norm in the U.S. as we go to press). Hotels are not likely to have scales with which you can weigh your bags before going home, so have a sense of what your bags weigh when empty and then how much weight you've accumulated through souvenirs.

If you forget something, there's not really anything that you can't buy in San Francisco. It's a major city, after all. But to save yourself hassle, bring with you the basics for rain (a compact umbrella or a poncho), for long-distance walking (good shoes with grippy soles work on the hills), and for memories (camera, film or storage cards, chargers). Above all, plan to layer your outfits. A 55°F morning can turn into a 75°F afternoon, so it's hard to be fully prepared unless you're prepared to strip off—or put on—a light jacket or sweater. That may mean that you should also pack a small daybag to tote around with you and stuff unwanted layers into on the go.

Dress to get wet. The rain comes from nowhere sometimes, and even when it doesn't rain, the air itself may grow so moist that it has the effect of a light drizzle. Remember that this might also affect your electronic equipment, so if that means you need to buy a case for your gadgets, have that ready to go, too.

SPECIAL TYPES OF TRAVELERS

San Francisco is the original outsider's city. Her citizens pride themselves on making people of every creed, every ability, and every gender (all of them, depending on how you count them) feel like they're equally a part of things. So if you do find that you have special needs as a traveler, you'll likely encounter only people who are eager to assist and to smooth the way for you. It would go against the grain of the famous San Francisco inclusiveness to do otherwise.

ADVICE FOR FAMILY TRAVELERS

San Francisco is, by and large, an extremely kid-friendly place. Many of its principal attractions, including the Golden Gate Bridge, the cable cars, the Exploratorium, and even gritty old Alcatraz, will captivate young minds. What's more, it seems like half the town is made up of young couples who are starting families of their own, so unless you head into a tony wine bar or nightclub, you'll find that restaurants are remarkably prepared with high chairs and special kids' menus—though, of course, the other side of the bargain will be that your kids will be expected to behave like they belong. In addition to the restaurants in Fisherman's Wharf and around Union Square, which by dint of their strong tourist trade are almost exclusively family-friendly, eateries along Fillmore Street, Union Street, and Hayes Street regularly host lots of kids from the area.

San Francisco is largely a civilized place, too, and one that prides itself on sophistication, so if all you've seen of the city is images on TV every June of mustachioed men prancing with feather boas down the street, then you can relax. Unless you stumble across a leather fetish parade, you'll find the residents' behavior to be nothing you'll need to shelter your kids' eyes from.

For the sanity of both kids and parents, I suggest you let the kids take an active role in planning the vacation. Believe me, they'll be more than eager to fantasize about all the things there are to do, and their excitement will only make your investment pay off. Kid-directed planning will help *you,* too—if only because sorting out the must-sees ahead of time will keep your family from quarreling later, and it will keep expectations in check.

When in San Francisco, parents should look around for the free newspaper boxes dispensing ***Parents' Press*** (www.parentspress.com), a monthly paper that rounds up events for kids and parents around town (storytelling, craft making, and the like), particularly by organizers that may only do one or two things a month and, therefore, would be hard to hear about otherwise.

Bring your own supplies to kid-proof your hotel room; San Francisco is more a business traveler's town than a family travel town, and hotels are less likely to have these things on hand. A few non-business properties, such as the Hotel del Sol (p. 44), have taken pains to secure at least a few rooms, so ask.

A few major hotels—ones too pricey for this guide—offer babysitting services to their guests for a sharp fee. There's also the fully bonded **Bay Area Child Care** (☎ 415/309-5662; http://bayarea-childcare.com); rates start at $15 per hour plus a $15 fee and a 4-hour minimum. A potentially cheaper option is the sitter-matchmaking website that operates nationwide called **Sitter City** (www.sittercity. com). However, it does not screen people offering their services—you have to do that yourself. Likewise, another good source for contacts, but one with D.I.Y. screening, is **Craigslist** (http://sfbay.craigslist.org/sfc/kid), which, on a good day, can see a dozen postings offering services. Just do your search well before you leave home while there's still time to check out your prospective nanny.

Very few museums offer family tickets, on which parents and children are admitted together for one discount price; where they exist, they're described with each attraction listing. Attractions that I deem particularly appropriate or fun for kids (and there are many) are marked with a kids.

One safety note: You'll want to keep a special eye on your kids around the cable cars and the trams because they have a harder time stopping than buses do and their tracks are open to pedestrian crossings.

ADVICE FOR TRAVELERS WITH DISABILITIES

San Francisco is ahead of the country when it comes to making life easier for guests in wheelchairs. Hotels are required by law to have at least one special room equipped for wheelchairs, and since guests with mobility issues are big business, most of them have more than one such room. True, there are still many buildings, including hotel buildings, that were grandfathered before the Americans with Disabilities Act of 1990. Many of these lack elevators and can be riddled with narrow stairways and inadequate passageways. But if the building was renovated or built recently, it will be carefully designed to be accessible to all—and locals, as residents of a liberal town, are keenly aware of accommodating those who are mobility impaired. So inquire when you book as to whether you'll have any troubles and you should get a straight answer. You might consider tackling the issue by renting a house, which provides much more room.

And what about getting around in this highly vertical city? Hill climbs can be tough on travelers with disabilities, but remember even the toughest hills are usually also scaled by Muni buses. Muni buses almost always go where you want to go, or at least a block or so away, and they're almost always equipped with a lift gate. So when in doubt about negotiating a gradient, public transport can be used as a workaround.

Another option: **Scootaround** (☎ 888/441-7575; www.scootaround.com) is a national chain with a local office. It rents electric convenience vehicles (ECVs), and it will deliver and pick up from your hotel. You probably already know that, with advance warning, the major car renters can provide you with a car that has hand controls.

For general information on both lodgings and transportation, contact **Access Northern California** (www.accessnca.com), an organization devoted to helping people find accessible lodging and arrangements throughout the area; its listings are comprehensive and frequently updated. Likewise, the city's CVB website maintains an entire section devoted to accessible travel, and you can download a multi-page guide, *Access San Francisco,* online as well (www.onlyinsanfrancisco.com/plan_your_trip/access_guide.asp). Organizations that offer assistance to travelers with disabilities include the **American Federation for the Blind** (☎ 800/232-5463; www.afb.org) and **Society for Accessible Travel & Hospitality** (☎ 212/447-7284; www.sath.org).

ADVICE FOR STUDENTS

You won't find much help. My advice boils down to: Have your ID ready to go, and always mention that you're a student, because at movie theaters and some minor attractions, it'll save you a little cash. Before leaving home, obtain some recognized ID such as the **International Student ID Card** (ISIC; www.istc.org) so that there's never a question of your eligibility.

Those under 26 who are not still in school can obtain a **Federation of International Youth Travel Organizations** (FIYTO; www.fiyto.org) card, which performs many of the same tricks as a student discount card. You can get the FIYTO from discount travel sellers and hostelling associations.

ADVICE FOR SENIORS

Just about every attraction offers a special price for seniors, and the bigger hotel chains may also offer deals though one of the following organizations.

If you're over 50, you can join **AARP (601 E Street NW, Washington, DC, 24009;** ☎ 888/687-2277; www.aarp.org), and wrangle discounts on hotels, airfare, and car rentals. The well-respected **Elderhostel** (☎ 877/426-8056; www.elderhostel.org) runs many classes and programs, both inside the city and around the Bay Area, designed to authentically delve into literature, history, the arts, and music. Packages last from a day to a week and include lodging, tours, and meals. Some are even multigenerational; bring the grandkids.

ADVICE FOR GAY & LESBIAN TRAVELERS

As you may have heard, San Francisco is one of the most gay-friendly cities anywhere on Earth. In fact, if you're hostile or ungenerous toward homosexuals, it's *you* who will be frowned upon here. It's a true integrated city. Gay folks feel welcome pretty much anywhere they go, and same-sex couples may check into any hotel without feeling self-conscious. For this reason, and for the town's proliferation of gay-oriented bars and clubs, the city is considered something of a gay paradise. Personally, I think that's going a little far—the gay folk here are increasingly of a certain generation, and there's not much of a young scene. It will also help to like leather, since several of the city's biggest bars and most popular festivals center on the fetish. Fortunately, you don't have to be into bars or sex to participate in gay culture here; there's a sizable group of people who don't get into such activities.

The ***Bay Area Reporter*** (www.ebar.com) is a publication that focuses on gay events and news, and it's available for free at most gay bars and throughout the Castro. Otherwise, the usual sources of gay travel information apply, including the mighty *Spartacus* guide, which will set the weight of your luggage to a new high. ***On*** (www.onbayarea.com) caters to upscale gay readers, while ***EDGE San***

Francisco (www.edgesanfrancisco.com) is more of a general catch-all publication about gay life in and around town, and it can be useful for finding out what's going on.

If you're still worried about possible harassment, the **International Gay and Lesbian Travel Association** (☎ 800/448-8550 or 954/776-2626; www.travelIglta.com) can connect you with gay-friendly hotels and businesses. There is a gay and lesbian community center here (p. 208), but its outreach is mostly for locals.

STAYING CONNECTED

A civic effort to provide free wireless access to the entire city fell flat, but getting online isn't hard if you bring your own laptop. Most hotels will have access— sometimes in common areas, sometimes in the room, and sometimes in both places. Strangely, it's the least expensive properties that seem to offer this service for free.

You can also find access at Starbucks (www.starbucks.com), FedEx Kinkos (www.fedex.com) and at almost any cafe. In San Francisco, where so many computer professionals work, it's a mark of a quality establishment to offer free Wi-Fi, so you'll never have to look very far before locating someplace that does.

Those without their own computers can usually find at least one computer at their hotel, sometimes for use at a nominal fee. Because of this, and the fact that relatively few tourists need to check their e-mail who haven't also brought the means to do it, there are no dedicated Internet cafes to speak of; that seems to be a '90s trend that has died.

Alternatively, locations of the **San Franciso Public Library** (http://sfpl.lib.ca.us) have terminals for public use, although you may have to sweet-talk a desk clerk to get near them. The main branch at the Civic Center is the busiest, so it might be the best place to try your luck at squeezing in.

RECOMMENDED BOOKS & FILMS

Few American cities have been as memorialized and affectionately delivered in works of literature and in movies. Many of us had our first and most romantic exposures to this exceedingly photogenic city through celluloid.

BOOKS

The *Tales of the City* series, by Armistead Maupin. This breezy, soapy, easy-to-read seven-book series about life in the city will make you wish you could have been here in the 1970s.

The Sam Spade novels, by Dashiell Hammett. The gumshoe was based in San Francisco, and these pages bring out the noir in the early 20th-century city.

A Crack at the Edge of the World, by Simon Winchester. Self-indulgent but informative examination of the Great Quake and its aftermath.

Slouching Towards Bethlehem, by Joan Didion. Her brilliant essays include a snapshot of the late-'60s hippie culture.

Howl and Other Poems, by Allen Ginsberg. The 1950s Beat generation of envelope-pushing writers took San Francisco as the center of their universe, and this is the definitive Beat generation book of verse.

McTeague: A Story of San Francisco, by Frank Norris. Grim late 19th-century tale of revenge, later filmed (in town) as the classic *Greed* (1924).

The Mayor of Castro Street, by Randy Shilts. The story of Harvey Milk: midlife transplant to activist to martyr for a nascent civil-rights cause.

The Joy Luck Club, by Amy Tan. A look at the life and traditions of modern Chinese-American women.

Roughing It, by Mark Twain. He was frank and sardonic long before it was cool, and his descriptions of the city, the mines, and the earthquakes still resonate today.

FILM & TV

You'll find no shortage of movies that were shot in and around San Francisco. In fact, your first exposure to the city was likely through the romanticized images of a silver screen. To acknowledge the city's double life as a setting for entertainment, there's even an excellent van tour offered to remind you of them (p. 127). But these are some of the most notable, or ones that were mostly shot on location and not in Hollywood soundstages.

Bullitt (1968). This Steve McQueen potboiler contains a legendary, if geographically jumbled, street chase.

Mrs. Doubtfire (1994). This feel-good family comedy was shot on location among the prettiest town houses.

Dirty Harry (1971). If you can stomach the violence, you'll get a good look at the city in this Clint Eastwood revenge pic.

Vertigo (1958). The city may not ever be shot better than it was in this Hitchcock classic with Jimmy Stewart.

Basic Instinct (1992). This is only one of a long line of popular noir movies shot around the city.

Escape from Alcatraz (1979). Clint Eastwood plots to you know what.

Foul Play (1978). This screwball thriller—a personal favorite of mine—was shot all over town, including at City Hall.

What's Up, Doc? (1971). Glimpse the skyline before the Transamerica Pyramid went up and the ugly elevated highways came down.

The ABCs of San Francisco

Area Codes The area code for the city area is 415 (if you're dialing locally, a preceding 1 is not necessary, but the 407 is), although you may encounter the 510 code, which covers the East Bay, and 650, for the Peninsula south of town. Napa and Sonoma are in 707. To dial outside of the United States or Canada, dial 011 before the telephone number. Calls to numbers that begin with an 800, 866, 877, or 888 area code are toll-free.

ATMs & Currency Exchange See "Money Matters," earlier in this chapter.

Business Hours Offices are generally open on weekdays between 9am and 5pm, while banks tend to close at 4pm. Typically, stores open between 9 and 10am and close between 6 and 7pm Monday through Saturday, except at malls, which stay open until 9pm. On Sunday, stores generally open at 11am and rarely stay open later than 7pm.

Drinking Laws The legal age for the purchase and consumption of any sort of alcohol is 21. Proof of age is often requested at liquor stores, bars, clubs, and restaurants, so be sure to carry photo

ID with you at all times. It's illegal to carry open containers of alcohol in any public area that isn't zoned for alcohol consumption (such as at a street fair), and the police can ticket you on the spot.

Electricity The United States uses 110–120 volts AC (60 cycles), compared to the 220–240 volts AC (50 cycles) that is standard in Europe, Australia, and New Zealand. If your small appliances use 220–240 volts, be sure to buy an adaptor and voltage converter before you leave home, because these are very difficult to find, even in San Francisco, which receives international visitors by the million.

Embassies & Consulates Most embassies are located in the nation's capital, Washington, D.C. Some consulates are located in San Francisco (although most of them won't perform services for their citizens), and most nations have a mission to the United Nations in New York City. If your country isn't listed below, call for directory information in Washington, D.C. (☎ 202/555-1212) or log on to **www.embassy.org/embassies.**

The embassy of **Australia** is at 1601 Massachusetts Ave. NW, Washington, DC 20036 (☎ **202/797-3000;** www.austemb. org). There are consulates in New York, Honolulu, Houston, and Los Angeles. There is a consulate at 1 Bush St.

The embassy of **Canada** is at 501 Pennsylvania Ave. NW, Washington, DC 20001 (☎ **202/682-1740;** www.canadian embassy.org). Other Canadian consulates are in Buffalo, Detroit, Los Angeles, New York, and Seattle. There is a consulate at 580 California St., 14th Floor, but it doesn't process visas.

The embassy of **Ireland** is at 2234 Massachusetts Ave. NW, Washington, DC 20008 (☎ **202/462-3939;** www.ireland emb.org). Irish consulates are in Boston, Chicago, New York, and other cities. There is a consulate at 100 Pine St., Suite 3350. See website for complete listing.

The embassy of **New Zealand** is at 37 Observatory Circle NW, Washington, DC 20008 (☎ **202/328-4800;** www.nzemb. org). New Zealand consulates are in Los Angeles, Salt Lake City, and Seattle. There is a consulate at 1 Maritime Plaza (Front and Clay sts.).

The embassy of the **United Kingdom** is at 3100 Massachusetts Ave. NW, Washington, DC 20008 (☎ **202/588-7800;** www.britainusa.com). Other British consulates are in Atlanta, Boston, Chicago, Cleveland, Houston, Los Angeles, New York, and Seattle. There is a consulate at 1 Sansome St., Suite 850.

Emergencies Call ☎ **911** for the police, to report a fire, or to get an ambulance. If you have a medical emergency that does not require an ambulance, you should be able to walk into the nearest hospital emergency room (see "Hospitals," below). For non-emergencies such as theft reports, call ☎ **415/553-0123.**

Holidays Banks close on the following holidays: January 1 (New Year's Day), the third Monday in January (Martin Luther King, Jr., Day), the third Monday in February (Presidents Day), the last Monday in May (Memorial Day), July 4 (Independence Day), the first Monday in September (Labor Day), the second Monday in October (Veterans Day), the fourth Thursday in November (Thanksgiving Day), and December 25.

Hospitals **St. Francis Memorial Hospital** (900 Hyde St., btw. Bush and Pine; ☎ **415/353-6000**) operates emergency service 24 hours a day, and it also runs a physician referral service.

Mail At press time, domestic postage rates were 27¢ for a postcard and 42¢ for a letter. For international mail, a first-class letter of up to 1 ounce costs 94¢ (72¢ to Canada and Mexico). For more information go to **www.usps.com** and click on "Calculate Postage." There's a Post Office at 180 Steuart St. (at Mission), another at 150 Sutter St. (near Kearny), and a third at 1390 Market St. (at 10th), near the Civic Center—but there are more scattered around town.

Newspapers & Magazines Although most fancy hotels distribute that shallow McNewspaper *USA Today* to use as your morning doormat, the local paper, the "Datebook" section of the *San Francisco Chronicle* (www.sfgate.com), the city's major daily, is good for finding out about local happenings. *San Francisco Magazine* (www.sanfranmag.com) is a glossy magazine that covers snooty city trends and upscale restaurants. *SF Weekly* and *The Examiner* are two free giveaway papers that usually stock more useful event information than the paid publications do.

Pharmacies Walgreens is located liberally all around town, and many of them are open until midnight, but there is one at Divisadero and Lombard (in the Marina) that is open all night.

Smoking Smoking is prohibited in all public indoor spaces, including offices, bars, restaurants, hotel lobbies, and shops. Californians simply aren't into it. In general, if you need to smoke, you'll have to go outside into the open air, and even then, often in strictly enforced designated areas. Pot smoking, though, may be another matter—still illegal, of course, but not nearly as frowned upon as tobacco.

Taxes A 7.5% sales tax is charged on all goods with the exception of most edible grocery-store items and medicines. Hotels add 14%, which stings. The United States has no value-added tax (VAT), but the custom is to not list prices with tax, so the final amount that you pay will always be slightly higher than the posted price. Some restaurants also add a surcharge marked "health"; this goes to the health insurance that they are required by local law to provide for their employees.

Telephone Generally, hotel surcharges on long-distance and local calls are astronomical, so you're better off using your **cellphone** or a **public pay telephone.** Many convenience groceries and packaging services sell **prepaid calling cards** in denominations up to $50; for international visitors these can be the least expensive way to call home. Many public phones at airports now accept American Express, MasterCard, and Visa credit cards. **Local calls** made from public pay phones in most locales cost either 35¢ or 50¢. Pay phones, when you actually find one, do not accept pennies, and few will take anything larger than a quarter. Make sure you have roaming turned on for your cellphone account, because having your own phone is definitely the cheapest way to go.

If you're a staying at a hotel and have high-speed Internet access in your room, you can save a fortune on calls by using Skype (www.skype.com), iChat, or some other Web-based calling program, since calls between members cost nothing.

Most long-distance and international calls can be dialed directly from any phone. **For calls within the United States and to Canada,** dial 1 followed by the area code and the seven-digit number. **For other international calls,** first dial 011, then the country code, and then proceed with the number, dropping any leading zeroes.

Calls to area codes **800, 888, 877,** and **866** are toll-free. However, calls to area codes **700** and **900** (chat lines, bulletin boards, "dating" services, and so on) can be very expensive—usually with a charge of 95¢ to $3 or more per minute—and they sometimes have minimum charges that can run as high as $15 or more.

For **reverse-charge or collect calls,** and for person-to-person calls, dial the number 0, and then the area code and number. An operator will come on the line, and you should specify whether you're calling collect, person-to-person, or both. If your operator-assisted call is international, ask for the overseas operator.

For **local directory assistance** ("information"), dial **411;** for long-distance information, dial 1, then the appropriate area code and 555-1212.

Time The continental United States is divided into four time zones: Eastern Standard Time (EST), Central Standard Time (CST), Mountain Standard Time (MST), and Pacific Standard Time (PST). San Francisco is on Pacific Standard Time, so when it's noon in New York, it's 11am in Chicago (CST), 10am in Denver (MST) and 9am in San Francisco, Seattle, and Los Angeles (PST). Basically you add three hours to get the East Coast time—so be careful about phoning East Coasters after 6pm. Daylight saving moves the clock 1 hour ahead of standard time. Clocks change the second Sunday in March and the first Sunday in November.

Tipping Tips are customary and should be factored into your budget. Waiters should receive 15% to 20% of the cost of the meal (depending on the quality of the service), bellhops get $1 per bag, chambermaids get $1 to $2 per day for straightening your room (although many people don't do this), and cab drivers should get 15% of the fare.

Toilets Duck into any cafe or into the lobby of any large hotel. (The St. Francis on Union Square is particularly nice.) There are no public toilets, per se, but nearly every coffeehouse has an open-door policy. Interestingly, for split-sex bathrooms, you'll notice that the California norm is to denote the men's room with a triangular sign, and the women's room with a circular sign; this makes differentiation easier for the blind.

12 The Wine Country: A Closer Look

by Jason Cochran, Erika Lenkert & John Thoreen

HOW WINE IS MADE

It sounds so simple: Harvest ripe grapes, pour some yeast in the juice, let it ferment into wine, clarify and age the result, and drink.

But making wine is much more complex than that. From arguing about the very meaning of *ripe* to controlling the ferment in order to subtly tweak flavors, the contemporary winemaker incorporates deep knowledge of fermentation, soils, and microbiology; the University of California, Davis, even offers graduate degrees in viticulture and enology. The issue of personal taste further complicates the scientific process.

On your tours of wineries, you'll hear differing stories about the "right" way to make wine, because each vintner harbors strong opinions—their way is usually presented as the right way—on wine styling. Be prepared for some inconsistencies justified by long-winded tales of tradition, and gird yourself to be overwhelmed by minutiae. If you don't prepare yourself with a little background knowledge, the wine culture runs the risk of becoming tedious. It's a major reason some laymen accuse the wine world of pretentiousness. To help you sort through the claims, and to have a greater appreciation of what you'll hear, here's a brief but broad sketch of the ABCs of making white wines, red wines, and sparkling wines.

WHITE WINES

For white wines, the winemaker wants only the juice from the grapes. (For red wines, both the juice and the skins of the grapes are essential; using the white winemaking technique, you can make a *white* wine from a *red-skinned grape*.) Grapes are picked either by hand or by machine and brought to the winery as quickly as possible. Just as a sliced apple turns brown when left on the kitchen counter, grapes oxidize—and can even start fermenting—if they aren't processed quickly. At some wineries, the clusters go through a "destemmer-crusher," which pops the berries off their stems and breaks them open (not really crushing them). The resulting mixture of juices, pulp, and seeds—called *must*—is pumped to a press. At other wineries, the whole clusters are put directly into a press (a widely used technique called, logically, *whole-cluster pressing*). When Lucy Ricardo stomped grapes in an open vat, she was using an ancient method to accomplish this post-harvest step of the process.

Most presses these days use an inflatable membrane, like a balloon, and gently use air pressure to separate the skins from the juice, which is then pumped into fermenting vessels. In the recent past, most white wines were fermented in stainless-steel tanks fitted with cooling jackets. Cool, even cold, fermentations preserve the natural fruitiness of white grapes. More recently, many Napa and Sonoma producers have begun using small wooden barrels for fermentation of white wines, especially chardonnay. This practice reverts to old-style French winemaking techniques and is believed to capture fragrances, flavors, and textures not possible in stainless steel. Barrel fermentation is labor intensive (each barrel holds only 45–50 gal. for fermentation), and the barrels are expensive ($600–$700 each for French barrels, $250–$300 for American barrels, although they're often reused for multiple harvests).

After white wines are fermented, they're clarified, aged (if appropriate), and bottled, usually before the next harvest. For the simpler white wines—chenin blanc, Riesling, and some sauvignon blancs—bottling occurs in the late winter or early spring. Most sauvignon blancs and chardonnays go into the bottle during the summer after the harvest. Very few white wines, usually chardonnays, take the slow track and enjoy 15 to 18 months of aging in small barrels with prolonged aging on the *lees*, the sediments from the primary fermentation. Those treatments are unusual, but they tend to produce chardonnays that are richly flavored, complex, and expensive.

Not all wines are created with an elite, fussy attention to detail. Charles Shaw, the brand of wine that is sold for $2 to $4 a bottle at Trader Joe's and is affectionately known as "Two Buck Chuck," blends wine from many vineyards around Northern California. It's bottled using industrial methods by the Bronco Wine Company near Napa (the plant isn't open to the public). Just as Starbucks has methods to create the same general year-to-year flavor profile no matter what each harvest tastes like, so do the mass wine producers.

RED WINES

The chief difference between white wines and red wines lies simply in the red pigment that's lodged in the skins of the wine grapes. So whereas for white wines the juice is quickly pressed away from the skins, for rosés and reds the pressing happens after the right amount of "skin contact." That can be anywhere from 6 hours—yielding a rosé or very light red—to 6 weeks, producing a red that has extracted all the pigment from the skins and additionally refined the tannin that naturally occurs in grape skins and seeds.

Almost all red wines are aged in barrels or casks for at least several months, occasionally for as long as 3 years. Most of the wooden containers—collectively called *cooperage*—are barrels made of American or French oak, and they hold roughly 60 gallons each.

The aging of red wines plays an important role in their eventual style because several aspects of the wine change while in wood. First, the wine picks up oak fragrances and flavors. (Yes, it is possible to "overoak" a wine.) Second, the wine, which comes out of the fermenter murky with suspended yeast cells and bits of skin, clarifies as the particulate material settles to the bottom of the barrel. Third, the texture of the wine changes as the puckery tannins interact and round off, making the wine more supple. Deciding just when each wine in the cellar is ready to bottle challenges the winemaker every year. To make the whole process even more challenging, every year is different depending on the harvest.

Unlike white wines, which are usually ready to drink shortly after bottling, many of the best red wines improve with aging in the bottle. Napa and Sonoma cabernet sauvignons, for example, often reach a plateau of best drinking condition that ranges from 7 to 12 years after the vintage, the year that appears on the label. However, there are no rigid rules. Some self-proclaimed cabernet freaks prefer their reds rather rough and ready. Only you can say what you like.

A few wine drinkers claim that the presence of sulfites in reds makes them feel mildly ill. There is still no evidence that proves sulfites are to blame; it's possible that for those people, feeling unwell may be triggered by tannins, yeasts, or bacteria specific to reds, or by an as-yet-unidentified interaction of them.

SPARKLING WINE & CHAMPAGNE

In Sonoma and Napa, sparkling wine plays the role of a serious specialty—serious enough to have drawn major investments from four of the best-known houses of Champagne, France, as well as two from Spain, in addition to 10 or 12 local producers.

The bubbly wine in the fancily dressed bottle may be called "sparkling wine" or "champagne," and most untrained tongues can't tell much difference. It *is* legal for wineries in America to call their product "champagne," though it galls the French, pun intended. Wineries that use the *méthode champenoise* as their production technique (it's marked on the bottles) tend to be regarded as making the best stuff. In Champagne, that method takes the form of regulations that, for the most part, codify practices. Those regulations have no force in California. Less finicky techniques include the *bulk* or *Charmat* processes.

There is no better way to understand the fascinatingly intricate "champagne method" than to see it firsthand, walking through the process with a knowledgeable guide. The harvest begins in August in Napa and Sonoma, with the picking of pinot noir, chardonnay, pinot blanc, and pinot meunier, the grape varieties of champagne. The grapes are picked a bit underripe by *still* (non-bubbly) wine standards, both to retain crispness and to avoid excessive body and flavors. The grapes are then pressed and the juice is fermented into plain—austere, in fact—still white wines. That takes two weeks. By November and December, the new wines are clear, or "bright."

Now the winemakers *really* go to work, because they need to blend the new wines in preparation for a second fermentation—this one taking place over 4 to 6 weeks right in the bottle, the very bottle that eventually comes to your table. After that, you have primitive champagne with a yeasty sediment in each bottle—a bit of a mess that must be cleaned up before sale (ask each winemaker how they do it). But for now—and perhaps for as long as 3 to 7 years—it's a benign mess. Yeast plays two virtuous roles in making sparkling wine: First, it produces the bubbles. Second, as the yeast cells decompose over time, they give sparkling wines made by *méthode champenoise* their special fragrances and flavors. Each house has its own flavor style—light or heavy—and tries to replicate it each year. That's why people say, "I'm a Mumm drinker," or "I'm a fan of Krug."

Making fine sparkling wine, and making it well, constitutes the ultimate winemaking challenge. The general belief among winemakers is that great white wines and great red wines are derived mostly from their place of origin: the right grape planted in the right soil and the right climate. Sparkling wine, though, depends more on craft and involves finesse at every step.

GROWING GRAPES

Growing grapes is farming; it's dirty manual labor, and it often involves employing disadvantaged immigrants. In contrast, winemaking, with its rarified pursuit of ideal flavors, is almost ethereal (except for rolling and stacking barrels and hosing grape skins out of the press) and has become a mostly upper-class pursuit.

Still, most winemakers spend more time in the vineyards than at the winery. Quality starts with the crop, and there's no way to compensate for bad fruit. Vineyards matter because the plant is the mother of flavor.

Everyone in the Wine Country is obsessed with the *Phylloxera vastatrix*, a soil-based plant louse that can mutate and permanently destroy entire vineyards. Vintners are learning how to head off the threat through soil science, fertilization and irrigation techniques, and careful grafting of plants with louse-resistant strands, but nothing is guaranteed. The area's growth has been derailed in the past by pests, and it could happen again.

VINES & WINES BY THE SEASON

Because you're likely to visit the Wine Country for a day or two in one particular season, you might want to know how the Wine Country looks in other seasons. Although the climate is benign, the changes from season to season still have a drama about them. In the winter, the rainy season in Mediterranean climates, the nights can be cold, dropping to 30° or 40°F (–1° or 4°C), but a sunny winter day sees highs in the 60s (high teens Celsius)—picnic weather if you're wearing a light sweater. During the same season, the dormant or dead sections of the vines are pruned through back-breaking field work.

Winter in the Wine Country also can be confused with spring elsewhere. Camellias might bloom on New Year's Day, azaleas shortly thereafter, along with the blue and yellow acacias. From December through April, the vines are dormant, stark outlines of trunks and arms, but the valley floors and hillside are lush green with common weeds and a few seeded ground covers. One of the common plants is mustard, technically a weed: You'll find great washes of bright-yellow flowers in February and March. Many vintners tolerate mustard because of its touristic value; the Napa Valley Mustard Festival occurs every spring.

The vines burst from dormancy in mid-March for the earliest varieties (chardonnay, pinot noir, gewürztraminer) and in April for the later blooming varieties (cabernet sauvignon, zinfandel). The growth is rapid—sometimes almost an inch a day. Until mid-May, there's a danger of frost. By late May and early June, the new shoots, called *canes,* have grown 3 or 4 feet in length; flower clusters start to blossom. The success of the *bloom and set,* as it's called, makes for some nervous moments: Uncontrollable elements such as hot weather and rain can compromise the crop. But, especially compared with the vagaries of weather in continental Europe, the benign Mediterranean weather in the Wine Country goes sour only occasionally.

In midsummer, usually around late July, the first signs of color show up in red grape varieties. Within a few weeks, a pretty blush becomes a deep purple, a sure sign that the grapes are ripening. White grapes change from a lime green to a golden green. They get delectably sweeter until it's time for picking.

From August through October, you'll probably see every available hand in the Wine Country harvesting the grapes. For a single vineyard it takes only a day—perhaps just a few hours—to pick the grapes, since they need to be as fresh and cool as possible. After the grapes are harvested, the vines hopefully have the chance to grow for a few more weeks, storing energy in the form of carbohydrates that will sustain them to the next spring.

After cold nights in November and December, the first winter rains knock the vibrant-colored leaves off the vines, which then go dormant until March and April, when they start the cycle again.

HOW TO TASTE WINE

Sampling the goods, otherwise known as *wine tasting,* ranks as the primary ritual in Wine Country touring. There are literally 200 or so tasting rooms, both stand-alone and within wineries, and the virtues in wine take time to notice. Most of the attendants in tasting rooms know that, generally speaking, Americans drink very little wine (10% of the population drinks more than 85% of the wine consumed), so they're used to helping people notice the flavors that their wineries are most proud of. If you encounter a staffer with attitude (unfortunately, it happens), don't buy *any* of that wine and simply move on to the next stop.

The time-honored techniques for tasting wine involve three steps: a good look, a good smell, and a good sip of each wine. You'll learn about wine most quickly if you compare samples, ideally side by side. Tasting rooms in Napa and Sonoma have their own regimens, usually offering a series of wines in what's called a *flight.* When it seems appropriate, and when the tasting room is not too busy, ask your host if you can do some comparisons.

Color can be a sign of a wine's condition, of its health, even of its age. White wines that show any browning might be going "over the hill" and have a musty, baked smell. Red wines that show a lot of rusty red might also be past their prime, and reds that show a lot of purple are probably young.

Next comes smelling. Why does the waiter in a restaurant ask the head of the table to sniff wine before pouring full glasses? Not really to see if they like it, but to make sure that bottle has fermented properly and isn't mere vinegar better suited to salad dressing. Wine can be tainted, usually by harmless contaminants in the cork or the barrels, a bit too easily. That's one reason bottles are usually stored on their side—to keep the cork moist and the seal strong.

Assuming your wine is fine, a decently shaped wineglass will direct a lot of aromas to your nose. Swirling the glass helps excite the fragrances. Comparing the "noses" of two or three wines can be very revealing, but possibly a bit frustrating, too: You "see" differences with your nose but might stumble when you try to describe them. It's not easy to describe the fragrances and flavors in wine. We're mostly reduced to similes and metaphors, to comparing wines with more familiar substances. A lot of wine writing is inadvertently humorous; some of it qualifies as bad poetry. Don't fret over the inadequacies of language to describe wine. Call us philistines or call us populists, but we think the enjoyment of wine is about *you,* and what *you* discover you like.

Despite all the ambiguity in wine descriptors, the words *aroma* and *bouquet* do possess separate meanings (though on the street we use them almost interchangeably). *Aroma* points to the characteristic smell of the various grape varieties, which can be quite distinct. When you're familiar with sauvignon blanc, it should not remind you of chardonnay. *Bouquet,* in the academy of wine, refers to fragrances that come from sources other than the grapes, such as the vanillalike fragrance of French oak. Of course, neophytes can't tell much difference.

An influential California wineman at the turn of the last century, Henry Lachman, wrote a monograph in which he described each sip of wine as having "a first taste, a second taste, and the goodbye." That's a cute way of dealing with the physiology of our mouths: In the front of the mouth, we taste for sweetness and feel the *body* of the wine; in the middle, we find acidity and the flavors of the grape; and in the back, we sense the *finish* or "goodbye," which can be long or short, supple or astringent. Imagine a tasting as having checkpoints in your mouth: front, middle, and back. Even this concept can require patience to detect. Don't simply scarf what's in the glass; let it swish around your mouth for a good while.

As you notice how a wine can be full and lush in the front of your mouth, then finally linger nicely (or fail to linger), it remains for you to decide what *shapes* you prefer in your wines. Red wines in particular show fairly clear shapes. One of the additional challenges in tasting red wines lies in recognizing that the shape changes with age. Rough, puckery, young, red wines can become supple and subtle.

Like tracking sports statistics and collecting comic books, the details can happily consume fans. It's best done by arranging a *vertical tasting:* several vintages of the same wine. (*Horizontal tastings* are several producers tasted from the same vintage.) Even three to five wines from vintages spread over, say, 10 years will give you a good idea of how much age you want to have on your red wines. Tasting rooms often have "reserve" wines or "library" wines that you can acquire for tasting. These samples are almost always more expensive.

GRAPE VARIETALS IN THE WINE COUNTRY

Which are the most prevalent grape varietals in California Wine Country? Here they are, along with their dominant flavors.

CABERNET SAUVIGNON

This has become California's most well-known varietal. The small, deep-colored, thick-skinned berry yields medium- to full-bodied red wines that are highly tannic when young and often require a long aging period to achieve their greatest potential. Cabernet, sometimes called "cab sav," is often blended with other related red varietals, such as merlot and cabernet franc (see below), into full-flavored red table wines, which are wines with relatively low alcohol content. Historically, cabernet is matched with red-meat dishes and strong cheeses, although increasingly, strict pairings are being eschewed as drinkers are encouraged to simply drink what they like.

CHARDONNAY

Chardonnay is the most widely planted grape variety in the Wine Country, and you'll find a range of it, from delicate, crisp wines to ones that are buttery and oaky—no grape benefits more from the oak aging process. They tend to have deeper golden hues as they increase in richness. This complex and aromatic grape is one of the few that doesn't require blending; it's also the principal ingredient for sparkling wine. Chardonnay is often paired with a range of dishes, from seafood to poultry, pork, veal, and pastas made with cream.

SAUVIGNON BLANC

Also labeled as fumé blanc, sauvignon blanc grapes are used to make crisp, dry whites of medium to light body that vary in flavor from slightly grassy to tart or fruity. The grape grows very well in the Wine Country and has become popular due to its distinctive character and pleasant acidity; indeed, it is now a competitor with the almighty chardonnay.

MERLOT

Traditionally used to blend out the rough edges of other grapes, merlot has gained popularity in California since the early 1970s—now wineries such as Sonoma's St. Francis are best known for producing masterful merlots that stand on their own. The merlot grape is a relative of cabernet sauvignon, but it's fruitier and softer, and usually slightly less rich. Merlots tend to be drinkable at an earlier age, though these wines, too, gain complexity with age. People tend to pair this wine with the same types of dishes as cabernets.

PINOT NOIR

It has taken California vintners decades to make relatively few great wines from pinot noir grapes, which are difficult to grow. Even in their native Burgundy, the red wines are considered excellent only a few years out of every decade. Recent attempts to grow the finicky grape in the cooler climes of the Carneros District have met with promising results. During banner harvest years, California's pinot grapes produce complex, light- to medium-bodied red wines with such low tannins and such silky textures that they're comparable to the finest reds in the world. Pinots are fuller and softer than cabernets and can be drinkable at 2 to 5 years of age, though the best improve with additional aging. Pinot noir is said to go best with lamb, duck, turkey, game birds, and fish.

ZINFANDEL

Zinfandel is often called the "mystery" grape because its origins are uncertain. Zinfandel first appeared on California labels in the late 1800s and has come to be known as California's grape. In fact, most of the world's zinfandel acreage is planted in Northern California. Zinfandel is, by far, the area's most versatile grape, popular as light and fruity blush wine (the ever-quaffable white zinfandel); as dark, spicy, and fruity red wines; and even as a port. Premium zins, such as those by Ravenswood winery in Sonoma (the Wine Country's zenith of zins), are rich and peppery, with a lush texture and nuances of raspberries, licorice, and spice. Food-wise it's a free-for-all.

CABERNET FRANC

A French black grape that's often blended with and overshadowed by the more widely planted cabernet sauvignon, cabernet franc grows best in cool, damp conditions and tends to be lighter in color and tannins than cabernet sauvignon; therefore, it matures earlier in the bottle. These wines have a deep purple color with an herbaceous aroma.

CHENIN BLANC

Planted mainly in France, chenin blanc runs the gamut from cheap, dry whites to some of the most subtle, fragrant, and complex whites in the world. In the Wine Country, the grape is mostly used to create fruity, light- to medium-bodied, and slightly sweet wines. Chenin blanc lags far behind chardonnay and sauvignon blanc in popularity in the Wine Country.

PINOT BLANC

A mutation of the pinot gris vine, the pinot blanc grape is generally grown in France's Alsace region to make dry, crisp white wines. In California, pinot blanc is used to make a fruity wine similar to the simpler versions of chardonnay. It's also blended with champagne-style sparkling wines, thanks to its acid content and clean flavor.

GEWÜRZTRAMINER

The gewürztraminer grape produces white wines with a strong floral aroma and litchi-nut-like flavor. Slightly sweet yet spicy, it's occasionally used to make late-harvest, dessert-style wine. The grape grows well in the cooler coastal regions of California. The varietal is particularly appreciated for its ability to complement Asian foods; its sweet character stands up to flavors that would diminish a drier wine's flavors and make it seem more tart.

Index

See also Accommodations and Restaurant indexes, below.

New series!
Pauline Frommer's

Discover a fresh take on budget travel with these exciting new guides from travel expert Pauline Frommer. From industry secrets on finding the best hotel rooms to great neighborhood restaurants and cool, offbeat finds only locals know about, you'll learn how to truly experience a culture *and* save money along the way.

Coming soon:

Pauline Frommer's Costa Rica
Pauline Frommer's Paris

Pauline Frommer's Las Vegas
Pauline Frommer's London

The best trips start here.
Available wherever books are sold.

Frommer's®
A Branded Imprint of ⊛WILEY
Now you know.

A Guide for Every Type of Traveler

Frommer's Complete Guides

For those who value complete coverage, candid advice, and lots of choices in all price ranges.

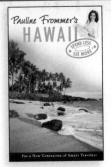

Pauline Frommer's Guides

For those who want to experience a culture, meet locals, and save money along the way.

MTV Guides

For hip, youthful travelers who want a fresh perspective on today's hottest cities and destinations.

Day by Day Guides

For leisure or business travelers who want to organize their time to get the most out of a trip.

Frommer's With Kids Guides

For families traveling with children ages 2 to 14 seeking kid-friendly hotels, restaurants, and activities.

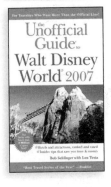

Unofficial Guides

For honeymooners, families, business travelers, and others who value no-nonsense, *Consumer Reports*–style advice.

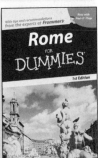

For Dummies Travel Guides

For curious, independent travelers looking for a fun and easy way to plan a trip.

Visit Frommers.com

Now you know.

Explore over 3,500 destinations.

Frommers.com makes it easy.

Find a destination. ✓ Book a trip. ✓ Get hot travel deals.
Buy a guidebook. ✓ Enter to win vacations. ✓ Listen to podcasts. ✓ Check o
the latest travel news. ✓ Share trip photos and memories. ✓ And much more

Frommers.com